Subscribing to Faith?

Histories of the Sacred and the Secular 1700–2000

This series reflects the awakened and expanding profile of the history of religion within the academy in recent years. It intends publishing exciting new and high quality work on the history of religion and belief since 1700 and will encourage the production of interdisciplinary proposals and the use of innovative methodologies. The series will also welcome book proposals on the history of Atheism, Secularism, Humanism and unbelief/secularity and encourage research agendas in this area alongside those in religious belief. The series will be happy to reflect the work of new scholars entering the field as well as the work of established scholars. The series welcomes proposals covering subjects in Britain, Europe, the United States and Oceana.

Titles include:

John Wolffe (*editor*)
IRISH RELIGIOUS CONFLICT IN COMPARATIVE PERSPECTIVE
Catholics, Protestants and Muslims

Clive D. Field
BRITAIN'S LAST RELIGIOUS REVIVAL?
Quantifying Belonging, Behaving and Believing in the Long 1950s

Jane Platt
SUBSCRIBING TO FAITH?
The Anglican Parish Magazine 1859–1929

Histories of the Sacred and the Secular 1700–2000
Series Standing Order ISBN 978–1–137–32800–7 (Hardback)
(*outside North America only*)

You can receive future titles in this series as they are published by placing a standing order. Please contact your bookseller or, in case of difficulty, write to us at the address below with your name and address, the title of the series and the ISBN quoted above.

Customer Services Department, Macmillan Distribution Ltd, Houndmills, Basingstoke, Hampshire RG21 6XS, England.

Subscribing to Faith? The Anglican Parish Magazine 1859–1929

Jane Platt
Independent Scholar

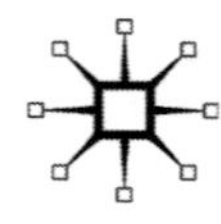

First published 2015 by
PALGRAVE MACMILLAN

Palgrave Macmillan in the UK is an imprint of Macmillan Publishers Limited, registered in England, company number 785998, of Houndmills, Basingstoke, Hampshire RG21 6XS.

Palgrave Macmillan in the US is a division of St Martin's Press LLC, 175 Fifth Avenue, New York, NY 10010.

Palgrave Macmillan is the global academic imprint of the above companies and has companies and representatives throughout the world.

Palgrave® and Macmillan® are registered trademarks in the United States, the United Kingdom, Europe and other countries.

ISBN: 978–1–137–36243–8

This book is printed on paper suitable for recycling and made from fully managed and sustained forest sources. Logging, pulping and manufacturing processes are expected to conform to the environmental regulations of the country of origin.

A catalogue record for this book is available from the British Library.

Library of Congress Cataloging-in-Publication Data

Platt, Jane, 1948–
Subscribing to Faith? The Anglican Parish Magazine 1859–1929 / Jane Platt, Independent Scholar.
pages cm
Includes bibliographical references and index.
ISBN 978–1–137–36243–8 (hardback)
1. Church of England – History. 2. Anglican communion – History. 3. Great Britain – Church history. 4. Church of England – Periodicals – History. 5. Anglican communion – Periodicals – History. I. Title.

BX5101.P59 2015
283′.4209034—dc23 2015013093

In memory of Susan (Bone) Taylor

Contents

List of Figures

Acknowledgements

Many people have contributed their expertise, guidance and help while this book has been in the making. I owe my first and greatest thanks to Dr Thomas Dixon of Queen Mary, London, and Dr James Taylor of Lancaster University, both of whom guided me through my research. I owe them more gratitude than can easily be expressed here. My thanks are also extended to Professor Arthur Burns of King's, London, and Dr Jonathan Topham of Leeds University, for their helpful advice; the committee of the Friends of Cumbria Archives, who awarded me a research grant; Canon Graham Fuller, who kindly allowed me to quote from his unfinished manuscript on Erskine Clarke; Chester Forster, who offered valuable suggestions and photographed the book's images; and Canon Dr David Weston of Carlisle Cathedral Library, whose kindly interest in the project helped propel it from an initial idea into book form. I should also like to record my gratitude to series editor Professor David Nash, of Oxford Brookes University, and Jenny McCall, commissioning editor at Palgrave Macmillan, for welcoming my project with such warmth; and the archivists who helped me in the course of my research, particularly Mark Arnold and Philippa Smith of London Metropolitan Archives and Tom Robson of Cumbria Archives, Carlisle.

There are many others whose help has been invaluable, particularly Dr June Barnes, Lynda Collin, Jade Moulds, Gordon Neil, Ghislaine O'Neill, Denis Perriam, the Venerable Dr Richard Pratt and Professor Angus Winchester. I should also thank Robert and Susan Huggard for allowing access to the private papers of Mrs Huggard's great-aunt, Austin Clare; Dan Fishman, for sharing his knowledge of the life of Queenie Scott-Hopper; and William Bullock, who offered insights into the editorship and production of *Home Words*.

I am most grateful for the support of my husband, Richard Platt, and my daughter, Professor Verity Platt, both of whom commented on the manuscript, and I would like to thank them and all my family for good-naturedly putting up with my curious obsession with the hundreds of parish magazines threatening to take over our home. Finally, I wish to record my deepest and warmest gratitude to my daughter, Belinda, without whose timely intervention, this book could not have been written.

List of Abbreviations

BL	British Library
CACB	Cumbria Archives Centre Barrow
CACC	Cumbria Archives Centre Carlisle
CACK	Cumbria Archives Centre Kendal
CACW	Cumbria Archives Centre Whitehaven
CCL	Carlisle Cathedral Library
CCR	Church Congress Report
The Church Standard	*The Church Standard and Evangelist Monthly*
CMS	Church Missionary Society
CUL	Cambridge University Library
DofD	*The Dawn of Day*
HW	*Home Words for Heart and Hearth*
LMA	London Metropolitan Archives
LSE	London School of Economics
LUL	Lancaster University Library
ODNB	*Oxford Dictionary of National Biography*
OHC	Oxfordshire History Centre
PHL	Pusey House Library (Oxford)
PM	Parish Magazine
RTS	Religious Tract Society
SDF	Social Democratic Federation
SDUK	Society for the Diffusion of Useful Knowledge
SN	Stoke Newington
SPCK	Society for Promoting Christian Knowledge
TCM	*The Church Monthly*
VPR	*Victorian Periodicals Review*

"BOOKS ARE BETTER THAN BEER, SIR."

Specially drawn for THE CHURCH MONTHLY *by* S. T. DADD.

'Books are better than Beer, Sir': *The Church Monthly* (1900) 68

Introduction

Entertaining Mrs Sloan

In a corner of Carlisle Cathedral Library, an undistinguished cardboard box is home to some dog-eared ephemera dating from 1892 to 1910. The documents illuminate the lives of members of the Sloan family, whose house at 10, Abbey Street, Carlisle, was situated in an Anglican urban parish at the heart of which was Saint Mary's church. The Census tells us that in 1901, William and Ann Sloan, both aged 47, were the parents of 11 children, the eldest of whom worked with his father in the family painting and decorating business. Despite this large family, there was no living-in servant. We might know nothing more of the Sloans had it not been that amongst the box's leaflets, text-books and pharmacy prescriptions is a collection of parish magazines, all named and addressed, some annotated.

A reading of the magazines reveals that Ann Sloan was neither one of the richer members of the congregation, nor a regular attender at the meetings of many of its societies. Her younger children were members of the church Sunday-school, William winning a prize in 1903. Another son, Herbert, was a 14-year-old chorister in 1895, the year in which all the choristers were given an apple when Mrs Sloan donated fruit to the harvest festival. In the same year Herbert saved one shilling and tuppence in his Church Missionary Society box and Mrs Sloan attended the CMS annual meeting. A neighbour's funeral is recorded in September, 1894; a daughter's baptism in August 1902; and the wedding of a son, Gerald, in July 1909, Mrs Sloan noting each occasion by writing their names at the top of the first inside page of the relevant magazine. Mr Sloan regularly promoted his business in the back of the magazine, advertising his partnership with his son in 1902, but there is no further record of his involvement in parochial life.

Saint Mary's parish magazine was typical of its time in having an outer page, or wrapper, depicting the church, several pages of local advertisements, and two pages of parish news containing the church monthly calendar, a list of baptisms, marriages and funerals, reports of church societies, and the vicar's monthly letter. The centre of each copy contained another magazine, known as an 'inset': a commercial venture, published nationwide, which parishes bought in bulk and localised by adding their own material and wrapper. Until December 1894, Saint Mary's inset was *Parish Magazine*, but, on its demise, the vicar announced a change to *The Church Monthly*. There were 32 octavo pages of illustrated reading matter in Mrs Sloan's January 1895 copy of *The Church Monthly*, including stories, sermons, recipes, gardening tips, articles on Church history and advice for lay church workers. The whole magazine, delivered monthly, cost each subscriber a minimum of two shillings and sixpence per annum; individual copies were available to purchase for 2½d per month.

That Ann kept her copies, recording key family events on their covers, and that William used the magazine to advertise the family business, reveals that at the end of the long nineteenth century Anglican parish magazines commanded a social value and relevance which made them integral to family life. As James Secord demonstrated when examining reactions to the nineteenth-century 'best-seller', *Vestiges of the Natural History of Creation*, reading offers 'important ways of defining self.'[1] By reading, preserving and advertising in parish magazines, the Sloans defined themselves as artisans, members of the reading public and Anglicans attached to their local community through their parish church. Studying both the inset and the local pages of their magazine opens a window onto their reading and suggests how it may have influenced them and thousands of others at a time of great social change. In establishing such a unique and enduring place in parish life, such magazines became not only a local phenomenon but also an exceptional publishing success, not merely confined to Britain, but read around the globe with the spread of Anglicanism. The Sloans and other readers were not necessarily subscribing to a *beau ideal* of Christian belief and practice when they paid their monthly 2½d, however, for the triumph of the parish magazine depended as much upon hard-headed business methods as upon piety. The commercialism of the age and the Church's negotiation with, and anxiety about, money, profoundly affected the parish magazine's content and publication as Anglicanism struggled to maintain its position amid manifold anxieties, as this volume will reveal.

The Anglican parish magazine: historical importance

The circulation of Anglican parish magazines like Mrs Sloan's was vast, the correspondingly high numbers deposited in British libraries and archives demonstrating their popularity.[2] Their sheer numbers demand serious scholarly attention for many important reasons. First, they illuminate the place of religion and its concerns in nineteenth- and early twentieth-century Britain. In the period covered by this book, religion still mattered to a large proportion of the population. Though the 1851 Religious Census had ascertained that only just over half the nation was attending religious worship, and of that half, only around half was attending the Established Church, scholars agree that throughout the long nineteenth century, large numbers continued to be affiliated to the Christian Churches, not only through the accepted rites of baptism, marriage and burial, but also through clubs and societies formed with the aim of drawing people into the Churches' orbit, and through education in Sunday and denominational schools, even after the formation of Board Schools supported by local rates in 1870.[3] Indeed, Callum Brown has famously argued that secularisation did not greatly affect the Churches until the 1960s.[4]

Second, regular churchgoers were not the only readers of parish magazines. As Chapter 7 will reveal, clergymen saw them as a form of outreach which travelled with them and their lay district visitors into all sorts of homes around the parish. In an age with no state provision for the very poor except through the tender ministry of the workhouse, the churches were the providers of much charity. The Church of England was by law the Established Church, its parish system until 1834 having administered the Poor Law through church vestries. Though legislation in the second half of the nineteenth century was to enforce their progressive withdrawal from secular power structures, Anglican parishes, despite problems caused by the growth of industrial towns, were largely effective, charity-dispensing communities centring on their parish churches, Church leaders building on this solid base by subdividing parishes and adding new churches in an effort to embrace every Christian in the country. As the largest religious denomination and a traditional provider of charity, the Anglican Church determinedly included the whole country in its parochial system.[5] Its parish magazines visibly demonstrated the continuing importance of Anglicanism at parish level, while also providing the Church with a comprehensive propagandist tool. Though other denominations published local magazines, Anglican parish magazines were the first denominational magazines to be localised, the Church's parish structure ensuring that the potential readership was enormous. Their study offers an opportunity to explore the reading experience of many thousands of people, their content taking us to the heart of contemporary social, political and religious concerns and anxieties, their local pages presenting the historian with a source which may be used in conjunction with other local records to illuminate parish life, both in Britain and abroad.

Third, the study of parish magazines adds to our growing knowledge and understanding of the content, production and readership of nineteenth- and early twentieth-century periodicals. Parish magazines are particularly interesting examples because they generally consisted of two types of text – local and national – juxtaposed in each number to provide parishioners with a wider reading experience than their own parish news could provide. The miscellaneous nature of magazines always generates opportunities for a fracturing of the unity of voice desired by their editors, but, while parish magazines were always determinedly didactic, their combination of local and national texts could result in a fracturing of unity neither foreseen nor desired. Obvious fractures could occur through the ubiquity of church-party rivalry, but they also occurred through fiction, illustration and advertisement, all of which allowed the commercialism of the age to permeate, and even saturate, these ostensibly religious publications.

The historiographical background

Despite their wide sales over more than a hundred years, parish magazines are the Cinderellas of the study of both religion and mass-market publishing. It will become clear from this historiographical survey that while on the one hand there has been much research on the Anglican parish and, on the other, a growing interest in nineteenth-century popular and religious magazines, in terms of parish magazine research there has been only one short volume on the Anglican inset, one scholarly examination of the significance of parish magazine local material, and minimal interest in inset localisation. Yet, in 1954, in his study of a Lancashire Victorian church, J. S. Leatherbarrow, noting the large collection of Victorian parish magazines in his vestry, hoped that, 'some time, perhaps, a full-scale book may be written which may do justice to this extremely important and influential type of popular journalism'.[6] More than half a century later, the appearance of this volume goes some way towards granting Leatherbarrow's desire.

While the growing popularity of family-history research has ensured that parish magazines have become an established resource for the amateur historian,[7] many scholars have relegated them to footnotes supporting their main themes: the disputed religiosity of the nineteenth-century poor, the secularisation debate and ritualistic controversy.[8] Owen Chadwick's magisterial, two-volume history of the Victorian Church awarded them just half a paragraph in a chapter on religious periodicals.[9] In his study of the religious press in Britain, Josef Altholz, one-time editor of the *Victorian Periodicals Review,* judged that they had nothing new to offer scholarship, referring only briefly to the first national inset, *Parish Magazine,* in a section on local magazines. Though he named two others, he failed to convey that these periodicals did not stand alone, but were localised into the magazines of hundreds of parishes.[10] The sidelining of these highly popular magazines deserves some scrutiny. Perhaps, like Altholz, scholars have underestimated the significance of the connection between the local parish magazine and its inset; perhaps the insets are thought to offer little that is new because they are seen, not only as tiresomely didactic, but also as dull pastiches of secular magazines; perhaps scholars' acceptance of secularisation in Britain has led many to dismiss Anglican printed ephemera.

Significantly, such marginalisation began quite early in the parish magazine's career. Modernists from the late-nineteenth century onward looked upon its journalism as mere amateur scribbling. Even more potently, they viewed the parish magazine as a symbol of outdated Victorian values, representing in all its awfulness the dullness and sobriety of the British middle class, as well as its hypocrisy. These judgements are encapsulated in G. K. Chesterton's trenchant comment, 'I read my parish magazine: it is an effort of local patriotism in which I believe I stand alone'; in Graham Greene's *Travels with my Aunt,* in which the local vicar's efforts to press his parish magazine upon the hero are employed to demonstrate the stultifying existence from which he longs to escape; and in *Private Eye*'s satirical 'St Albion's Parish News', published during the premiership of Tony Blair, in which the parish magazine of Saint Albion's was used as a mouthpiece for the vicar's mendacity.[11]

Modernist dismissal, combined with a scholarly tendency to prioritise high culture, caused the parish magazine to languish almost unnoticed by historians throughout the twentieth century, despite the publication of Richard Altick's groundbreaking work on the 'common reader', for even Altick expressed disappointment in the general public's preference for simple periodicals and newspapers instead of more demanding fare.[12] When Victorian periodical scholarship expanded, chiefly through the pioneering work of Michael Wolff in encouraging the creation of the *Wellesley Index to Victorian Periodicals* (1966–1989), the *Waterloo Directory of English Newspapers and Periodicals* (1997), and the *Victorian Periodicals Review,* the vast number of religious periodicals was found particularly intractable.[13] In an article in *Victorian Periodicals Review* in 1994, Altholz admitted that the *Wellesley Index* had few entries devoted to Anglican periodicals, claiming that periodicals other than high-church theology journals and those aimed at a 'high-class Sunday reading' public were of little worth.[14] It is telling that until relatively recently the only serious study of fiction in working-class religious periodicals was Margaret Dalziel's *Popular Fiction 100 Years Ago,* of 1957.[15]

The growth of Women's Studies during the 1970s and 1980s encouraged interest in periodicals for the mass-market, as scholars began to engage with women's magazines and their contributors.[16] Margaret Beetham and Kay Boardman explored the problems common to Victorian periodical scholarship: how to assess the implied readership; the advisability of constructing a methodological framework with which to analyse periodicals which are by definition multi-vocal; the exploration of the 'fractured mirror' created by multiple authorship; and the ambiguous roles of illustration and advertisement, all of which are pertinent to the study of parish magazines,[17] yet scholarship on religious periodicals still lagged behind. Jonathan Topham's study of the *Wesleyan-Methodist Magazine* is a rare example of scholarship which finally began to engage with this previously ignored area.[18] Topham's study stemmed, in part, from his interest in the history of science, a subject which, like Women's Studies, has encouraged a marked interest in Victorian religious magazines, exemplified in the work of Aileen Fyfe, and Topham's co-authors of the volume, *Science in the Nineteenth-Century Periodical: Reading the Magazine of Nature.*[19] Science apart, awareness of popular nineteenth-century religious magazines has been so low that when Chris Baggs was researching the periodicals available in Victorian ladies' reading-rooms he was 'surprised' to find so many religious periodicals, including parish magazines, in their lists, concluding that they were probably donated.[20]

Scholarly interest in the history of the English parish led to the first significant use of parish-magazine local pages as a legitimate source for the serious historian. In 2007, Rex Walford quoted extensively from them when tracing the Church's response to suburban growth in Middlesex, 1918–1945, and, in 2010, their historical importance was celebrated by Keith Snell, in an article in *Family and Community History.*[21] A historian of 'community', Snell's main concern was to celebrate the dynamism of Victorian parish life, and the 'globalised parochialism' which parish magazines helped shape as they spread throughout the world along with emigrants and missionaries.[22] But while he described the associational nature of the Anglican parish experience in some detail, he awarded only a few lines, gleaned mainly from secondary sources, to the parish magazine inset, for his aim was to describe parish life rather than to investigate the experience which a reading of both inset and local pages – the complete parish magazine – gave to its subscribers. This welcome article was merely an oasis in a desert, however, for even growing interest in parish activity relating to the Great War led to precious little investigation of what parish magazines could reveal, other than in Mark Connolly's research on the war shrines of East London, and the publication of letters from serving soldiers connected with Saint Michael's, Derby, edited by a clergyman, Michael Austin.[23] The latter publication is significant, for letters from serving personnel dominated the pages of many wartime parish magazines, yet Michael Snape's important study of religion in the British army ignored them.[24] Such dismissal of vital information at parish level cannot be explained by ignorance of the local sources alone: Robert Lee's *Rural Society and the Anglican Clergy, 1815–1914* – a spirited defence of the Norfolk agricultural worker against established religion – mined the Norfolk Record Office for parish documents, yet referred only once to a parish magazine which Lee had discovered in a secondary source.[25]

Inevitably, given the lowly status of parish-magazine publishing among scholars, it was another clergyman, Peter Croft, who undertook a short history of parish-magazine insets, sifting through them to list names and dates of publication, with brief descriptions of their history, content and approximate circulation.[26] Croft did not pretend that his was an exhaustive or particularly objective analysis. Nonetheless, he called for more study of the content, particularly the fiction, to which he alluded only briefly.[27] Fortunately, other writers have engaged with similar religious reading matter. Michael Ledger-Lomas has examined the rise and fall of denominational mass-market publishing, while Callum Brown's research material for *The Death of Christian Britain* is particularly pertinent to this study because its investigation of a large number of Scottish religious tracts, together with a small quantity of well-known nineteenth century religious and family magazines, offers interesting parallels with the themes of parish-magazine evangelicalism, popular fiction and gender-based conclusions on secularisation, discussed in this volume.[28]

Source materials

Parish magazines are to be found in national, university, cathedral and church libraries; vestries; second-hand bookshops; and the online bookshop, Amazon. Increasing document digitisation has led to their publication online.[29] Making sense of this apparent cornucopia for the purposes of study necessitated breaking it down into manageable portions. This book limits most of the source material to a 70-year period, from 1859 (the date of the publication of the first commercial parish-magazine inset) to 1929, just after the end of the Prayer Book controversy. To reduce numbers further and to focus the research, the geographical areas of study were limited to three, all in England: the Diocese of Carlisle (Cumberland, Westmorland and a small part of North Lancashire), the Diocese of Oxford (Oxfordshire and Berkshire) and the area of London served by the Metropolitan Archives (LMA).[30] LMA records have been illuminated by information collected by Charles Booth and his social investigators in Booth's *Religious Influences* survey.[31]

The sifting process eventually produced magazines from 359 parishes: 114 in Carlisle (38 per cent of those listed in the *Carlisle Diocesan Calendar* of 1910), 53 in Oxford (8 per cent of the number of Oxford parishes in 1899) and 192 in London (24 per cent of a possible 800 parishes in LMA's list).[32] There is, however, evidence in bishops' visitation returns that many more parishes had their own magazine, and Booth's investigators included 198 in their notebooks.[33] The final figure of 359 parishes represents a small fraction of the number of parishes producing magazines in the three localities early in the twentieth century.

Both James Secord and Jonathan Topham have underlined the importance, when researching the history of the book, of reflecting very different and particular local circumstances.[34] While the connectedness of Anglican parishes is confirmed in this study, advice not to ignore local differences has been heeded in the book's movement between the three geographical areas. Why choose these particular localities? London is an obvious choice because of its late-nineteenth-century status, not only as the country's capital, but also as the centre of the Empire and the world's commercial hub.[35] The contrast between its rich and poor populations, and the growth of its middle class, have been well documented through the traditions of investigation exemplified by Henry Mayhew and Charles Booth, for, as its historians maintain, 'London was a city of paradox', with the rich often living close to sheer hells of indescribable poverty.[36] The Church was highly active in inner London, as histories of its renowned 'slum priests' show, these clergymen often disobeying their bishops through their love of ritualistic innovation, the popularity of which was partly a reaction to poverty and the growth of socialism.[37] London's congregations were not necessarily parochial, however, as people often travelled from the burgeoning suburbs to hear the message they preferred.[38] Study of London's churches reveals the middle-class domination of congregations as well as the efforts of many clergy to deal with a sea of want.

Oxford, too, was a diocese of contrasts: Oxford city contained churches which were either strongly Anglo-Catholic or evangelical; and in the countryside, prosperous towns existed cheek-by-jowl with rough villages.[39] Oxford is renowned for its connection with the Tractarian movement and its role in the transformation of liturgical practice.[40] Persuaded by Tractarianism and determined to encourage Anglican liturgical reform, Alfred Mowbray, an Oxford schoolteacher, began to publish tracts and manufacture church ornament, his firm eventually becoming one of Britain's foremost religious publishers. A. R. Mowbray and Company (Mowbray's) published two well-known insets, one of which, *The Sign,* is still published, though now under the auspices of *Hymns Ancient & Modern,* a charity and publisher which also owns the *Church Times*.[41]

James Obelkevich has explored the religiosity of rural Lincolnshire; Simon Green, industrial Yorkshire; Richard Sykes, the Black Country; Diane McClatchey, the Oxfordshire clergy; religion in London's boroughs has been explored by sundry authors; but the wealth of Cumbria's church-related material has remained largely unexamined.[42] Cumbria, into which Carlisle Diocese fits almost exactly, was in many ways London's complete opposite, not only in its remoteness but also because it was a particularly evangelical diocese well into the 1870s, and, even in the early twentieth century, pockets of evangelical worship resisted ritualising trends.[43] It, too, was a diocese of contrasts, its central mountainous core bordered by industrial towns, but, most importantly for this study, it exhibited not only local particularity, but also the success of mid-nineteenth-century technological advance, which allowed, first, magazine editors to disseminate their views to the parochial peripheries, and, second, the most peripherally-based clergy to make themselves heard nationally. In 1863, Cumbria's geographical and psychological remoteness was captured by Arthur Stanley, who, in a parliamentary speech, contrasted 'the archbishop in his palace at Lambeth' with 'the humblest curate in the wilds of Cumberland'.[44] Yet, through the parish magazine inset, the humblest curate could be heard as loudly as any archbishop. The book investigates those humble voices by exploring the views of three clergymen from the Cumbrian town of Keswick, one of them utilising his inset to speak to a much greater constituency.

Though London and Cumbria were very different, they both possessed the distinction of leading the literacy league-table: the Registrar General's Marriage Signature Returns for 1839–1845 reveal that 88 per cent of marriage partners in London and 84 per cent in Cumberland could sign their names in the register.[45] In contrast, W. B. Stephens records that the result for Oxfordshire marriage partners was 60 per cent during the same period, a proportion of the population which Richard Altick comments was about the average for England as a whole.[46] The introduction of universal elementary education in 1870 resulted in an average of 90 per cent literacy in marriage signatures in England by 1885.[47] Keith Snell is convinced that the widespread reading of parish magazines must have led to an improvement in literacy, though the high literacy rates of Cumbria and London suggest that many of the poor were well equipped to read parish magazines from the start, supporting Chapter 3's evidence that localised parish magazines were an immediate publishing success.[48]

Insets 1859–1929

Peter Croft lists 37 Anglican insets published between 1859 and 1924.[49] Though not necessarily openly admitted, each inset's editorial stance was affected by the church-party debate preoccupying Anglicans during this period.[50] My analysis focusses on the earliest commercial inset, a publication known as *Parish Magazine,* which was influenced by Christian socialist ideas; *Home Words for Heart and Hearth* (known as *Home Words*), which was evangelical; a traditional high-church inset, *The Dawn of Day* (known as *Dawn of Day*); an Anglo-Catholic inset, *The Sign*; and a popular product of increased denominationalism and lay involvement, *The Church Monthly*, which advocated a mild form of ritualism.[51] All considered themselves to be leaders of the genre. Most were edited by entrepreneurial businessmen with a view to profiting themselves as well as the Church, two of them clergymen; *Dawn of Day*, however, was published by a charity, the SPCK. SPCK *Annual Reports*, the minutes of the SPCK tract committee and the minutes of Mowbray's, publishers of *The Sign*, provide the only known evidence of the business practices of the publishing firms which produced parish magazine insets.

While parish-magazine deposits from the 1870s until the period 1914–1918 are commonly found in archive collections, the comparative absence of those produced within the period 1919 to circa 1950 is striking. In the three chosen localities, only half of the parishes producing magazines during the earlier period appear to have produced them between 1919 and 1929, while in the same period only 40 per cent of parishes which had previously taken insets, continued to take them. Furthermore, within the three localities, only 18 per cent of the deposits of parish magazines dating from 1919 to 1929, form complete or substantial runs. The production difficulties experienced by all publishers during the Great War may have been a major cause of this disruption, and it is possible that extensive paper-salvage operations during both world wars effectively destroyed the evidence.[52] Moreover, from the 1920s onwards, fewer bound copies were kept in vestries.[53] Scholars have remarked on the sharp decline in religious publishing amidst dwindling church attendance after the Great War.[54]

Nonetheless, as Chapter 10 reveals, Mowbray's, publishers of *The Sign*, noted a significant rise in inset sales from the mid-1920s, following their decline in the aftermath of war, as Anglo-Catholic insets benefitted from the declining sales of less extreme examples of the genre. Yet, as Chapter 10 will explore, another kind of absence, not quantitative but qualitative, is to be found within many of the magazines themselves after 1919, their lack of vigour compared to the pre-war period betraying a state church traumatised by the war and its aftermath. Because of the disparity in archival evidence and the two periods' marked difference in tone, the major part of this book explores the history and content of Anglican parish magazines from 1859 to the end of the Great War, while a final chapter, first, traces changes in parish magazines after 1919 until the conclusion of the Prayer Book controversy in 1929, and, second, provides an overview of their reception as the twentieth century progressed.

Reflecting popular Victorian practice, parish magazine subscribers often sent their monthly numbers to a printer to be bound in board covers to make yearly volumes. Those bound for use in vestries and vicarages often kept local pages as a record of parish events while discarding the inset. Binding the insets only, to send as a gift or donate as a Sunday-school prize, effectively deleted local advertisements and news, with the result that monthly demarcations (central to an understanding of the ecclesiastical calendar) were lost.[55] For the purposes of this book, evidence from single numbers will be referenced with the month of publication, but evidence from bound copies will cite the relevant page number.

The widespread binding of parish magazines until the end of the Great War demonstrates their contemporary status, not as objects of amusement or disdain, as their later detractors would have us believe, but as items to be treasured. In 1917 Temperance Hawtin, a servant in the Oxfordshire village of Eynsham, was given 'a book of the parish magazines for 1903 to 1904 because my christening was reported in there'. Temperance found not only her name, but also 'stories and household hints as well as all the births, marriages and deaths, and all the village activities. All the local tradesmen advertised in it. Mine was a whole year's magazine made into a thick book.'[56] The signatures in the flyleaves of bound copies in record offices prove that they were often given as Sunday-School prizes or gifts, served as records of the life and death of loved ones, or were added to home libraries. Anglican parish magazines, though ignored in our time by most scholars, were an integral part of life during much of the period 1859–1929. Studying them opens that life to us anew.

Overview of the chapters

The first commercial inset emerged at the end of the 1850s, a pivotal period in publishing, termed 'revolutionary' by Altholz, when, as a result of technological innovation and the repeal of government taxes on newspapers, a cluster of family magazines appeared.[57] It was an equally pivotal period for the Anglican Church, pastoral revival paving the way for the parish magazine experiment.[58] Chapter 1 traces some of the earliest parish magazines, while the subject of Chapter 2 is the first successful Anglican inset – John Erskine Clarke's *Parish Magazine* – which, in its content, commercialism and church-party awareness, became a blueprint for the many insets which followed. Chapter 3 explores the economics of parish-magazine publishing, examining publishing records and surviving magazines in the chosen localities to determine local and national circulation and popularity. Business practices are examined through the experiences of inset and local editors whose financial uncertainties led them to adopt advertising. Chapter 4 probes the importance of church parties in determining editorial bias and magazine sales, noting the vigour of Anglo-Catholic rhetoric and evangelicalism's awareness of its diminishing influence, the inexorable march of ritualism obliging *Home Words* to modify its evangelical stance. Nonetheless, Anglo-Catholic confidence often provoked tension within the local pages of parish magazines.

Later chapters explore parish-magazine readership, investigating the nature of the reading experience, through themes of manliness, woman writers, anxiety, science and community. In Chapter 5 parish magazines' attempts to invoke manliness are seen as a means of modifying the behaviour of male parishioners, maintaining the social hierarchy, supporting imperialism and promoting the clergy through evocations of the manly vicar; but though posited as heroes, clergymen frequently became discouraged. Chapter 6 examines the contributions of female inset story writers, tracing changes in content and style over time as the rise of the professional authoress coincided with changing Christian beliefs and competition between inset publishers. The gendered nature of the material discussed in Chapters 5 and 6 leads Chapter 7 to analyse the readership, actual and implied, concluding that though men were constantly propitiated, women provided the bulk of the readership, just as they were the mainstay of the Church. The chapter also explores the readership abroad, a result of the expanding empire. Chapter 8 investigates parish magazines' deep fears for the future of Anglicanism, which they combined with strident calls for Church defence.[59] Ostensibly confident of parishioners' support, yet simultaneously despairing of their allegiance, fin-de-siècle parish magazines existed in a constant state of tension. They were much more sanguine about the repercussions of the materialistic study of science, Chapter 9 demonstrating that science was embraced as part of God's revelation of Himself until the carnage of the Great War. The chapter concludes with an examination of the Anglican approach to the conflict, when parish community spirit proved to be a greater unifier than the Church's 'National Mission of Repentance and Hope', and when diffusive spirituality was seen to impact on traditional Christianity. Many clergymen hoped for a revival of faith after the conclusion of the Great War, but it was not to be. Chapter 10 discusses parish-magazine content during the drained and weary decade after 1919, in which clerical anxiety remained though much confidence had fled, and in which passivity within the parishes allowed Anglo-Catholicism a practically free rein during the Prayer-Book controversy. It then moves on to investigate the reception of parish magazines during the rest of the twentieth century through an examination of how they were utilised in parliamentary debate.

The amount of thick description found alongside analysis throughout this book is the result of a deliberate attempt to introduce the reader to a subject that has been little studied. Despite the involvement of big publishing houses, the history of the parish magazine is a story of individuals as well as institutions. Immersion in the content helps to explain who the writers and editors were, and to contextualise their lives, influences and careers. The book's illustrations reveal that reading parish magazines was a richly visual experience, but inset illustrations were not purely decorative, for images worked with text to construct meaning. Of necessity, this short volume examines a relatively small number of parish magazines, and much research remains to be done, but through engaging with the analysis along with its connected texts and images, twenty-first-century readers will gain an understanding of parish-magazine content during the period 1859 to 1929, while experiencing for themselves the richness and complexity of this much-underrated historical source.

1
Inventing the Parish Magazine

Origins

Religious tracts

In a sense the parish magazine was born during the Reformation, when Martin Luther's emphasis on Biblicism encouraged the spread of reading.[1] In the centuries that followed, the Bible and approved religious works continued to be central to Protestantism and were utilised and adapted by British evangelicals to spread God's word to the poor and the heathen through charities such as the Religious Tract Society (RTS), the British and Foreign Bible Society and the SPCK.[2] In 1804 the RTS printed 314,000 tracts; by 1861 it published 20 million annually, together with 13 million copies of religious periodicals (which were in effect 'serial tracts').[3] As Richard Altick memorably recorded in his groundbreaking work on the history of reading and readers:

> Tracts were flung from carriage windows; they were passed out at railway stations; they turned up in jails and lodging houses and hospitals and workhouses ... they were distributed in huge quantities at Sunday and day schools ... they were a ubiquitous part of the social landscape.[4]

Hannah More's *Cheap Repository of Moral and Religious Tracts* was a collection of moral tales published in 1795, partly to maintain control of the poor because of fear of French republicanism and the popularity of the works of Thomas Paine, but More was equally concerned with a perceived lack of suitable reading material for the newly literate graduates of Sunday and charity schools.[5] Greater literacy among the poor had led to increased publication of cheap chapbooks, most of which were secular and often irreverent. More's tracts were printed to look like chapbooks so that good literature would triumph over bad in the war against what churchgoers universally termed 'pernicious' publications.[6] The parish magazine was placed squarely in the tradition of Hannah More and the tract societies in an advertisement of 1875 which claimed that each number was equal in content to 'three ordinary penny tracts'.[7] As late as 1914, an article in the inset, *Home Words*, argued that the magazine 'more than fulfils the purpose of the old-fashioned tracts', and would be read 'where they were thrown aside'.[8]

Tract distribution and the district visitor

The tract societies combined local volunteers and paid regional colporteurs to distribute religious literature. Clergymen maintained stocks in parish libraries, lending them to parishioners, as explained by this country vicar in 1858:

> A parochial library has been established ... consisting principally of books and tracts from the Tract Society and the inhabitants ... supplied gratis ... I have been in the habit for ten years of taking them two or three times in the year and some years oftener to their houses, and changing them when read. The books and tracts have been generally read.[9]

Tract distribution became a crusade. In her thesis on Victorian tract societies Sheila Haines remarks that the Church, as protector of the nation's spiritual and moral welfare, thought of the poor as lambs in continual danger from 'ravening wolves'.[10] This was a common contemporary metaphor; at the 1861 Church Congress, one speaker, noting that in some localities only two per cent of the 'mechanics or working population' attended any church, spoke of the difficulties 'in penetrating the recesses of the wilderness into which the wandering sheep have strayed'. He recommended creating a volunteer force of laity to work with the clergy, subdividing the parishes into districts and systematically visiting the people, leaving 'printed letters' which invited them to church. The Church, he said, should go out to find the people, to impress upon them its sincerity.[11]

The concept of district visiting was not new, having been introduced by the Church of Scotland minister, Thomas Chalmers, in a poor Glasgow parish in 1814. A method of reproducing the neighbourhood ties of the country parish, among widespread fears of religious decline in cities, it was widely imitated.[12] In the mid-nineteenth century, the old practice of parochial visiting by the clergy, the new practice of lay district visiting, the long-established practice of disseminating tracts and a huge growth of interest in reading periodicals were all to come together in the creation and distribution of parish magazines. The creator of the first commercial parish-magazine inset, John Erskine Clarke, vicar of Derby,[13] reminded the 1866 Church Congress that one of the best ways of attaching people to the Church was through house-to-house visiting, which would be

> not inquisitorial, not patronising, not condemnatory. Not even directly hortatory...it must be hearty, sympathising, respectful. Offering the services of a friend, not of the relieving officer; having an eye for the children, and seeking for something to commend rather than to blame; dropping a few words of good cheer over the often embittered and reckless lives of these folk.[14]

Clarke's approval of district visiting might have been an idealisation of the aims of his parish magazine, which was first published when the Anglican pastoral revival and developments in publishing were in happy alignment. Nonetheless, there were inherent tensions from the beginning, for, as Callum Brown has remarked, the 'salvation industry's' presumptuous intrusion into the home led some householders to reject district visitors.[15] The parish magazine, so eagerly proffered, was not universally accepted, let alone read, as future chapters will reveal.

Missionary and Sunday-school magazines

In the early nineteenth century, religious periodical reading was popular with all classes. Prestigious quarterlies, middle-class monthlies, violently partisan weekly newspapers and 'quality' reading for the ubiquitous day of rest all had respectable circulations.[16] One consequence of this interest was the entry into the periodical market of the official magazines of religious charitable organisations.[17] Their subscribers were often parishioners who belonged to local auxiliaries: people like Mrs Sloan, who took the Church Missionary Society *Annual Report* and who may have read its magazine, the *CMS Gleaner* (1841–1921). Printed cheaply on limp paper, missionary magazines were a familiar part of parish life by mid-century.[18] The rise of the Sunday-school movement resulted in the publication of periodicals aimed at Sunday-school scholars, primarily by the RTS. The content of *The Child's Companion or Sunday Scholar's Reward,* first published in 1824, foreshadowed that of the parish magazine inset, containing tract-like short stories, a serial story, poetry, hymns and articles on missionary work.[19] At the launch in 1878 of the SPCK's inset, *Dawn of Day,* the Tract Committee regarded it as 'just such a magazine...as clergymen and others would like to put into the hands of Sunday scholars, or to distribute among simple folk'.[20] The newest members of the reading public were thought to be childlike at best; whether seen as lost sheep or as wayward children, they were in need of guidance in all areas of life.[21]

Fear of 'pernicious' publications

Periodical publishing boomed after the reduction (1836) and repeal (1855) of the Stamp Tax, and improvements in paper-making, printing and illustration,[22] along with the increasing speed of distribution through the introduction of the Penny Post in 1840 and an expanding rail network.[23] Wilkie Collins marvelled so dramatically at the new mass audience consuming literature that Altick commented that it was 'as if [Collins] had come upon the sources of the Nile'.[24] The publications of the secular Society for the Diffusion of Useful Knowledge (1827), Charles Knight's *Penny Magazine* (1832) and *Chambers' Edinburgh Journal* (1832) instituted a craze for cheap, improving literature, both in book and periodical form.[25] Their advocates, fearful that abolition of the 'tax on knowledge' would result in an avalanche of improper publications, deliberately employed a narrative of filth and disease to indicate the contrast between 'pure' literature and the huge volume of penny publications supplanting chapbooks in the affections of the poor.[26] In 1854 Charles Knight was quoted in the *Christian Weekly News:*

> The circulation of pernicious literature is immense. In 1845 it was calculated from London alone there was a yearly circulation of...newspapers and serials of a decidedly pernicious character to the extent of 28,862,000!...The present circulation in London of immoral unstamped publications of upwards of a half-penny to three-halfpence each, must be upwards of 400,000 copies weekly.[27]

In 1861, Erskine Clarke presented a paper at the Church of England Book-Hawking Union conference. The conference covered a variety of topics, including the choice of cottage wall-prints, the importance of book-hawking in counteracting evil, and self-education for the industrial classes. Clarke's subject was 'Cheap Books and how to use them'. Concerned that too much reading of the short articles which constituted periodicals 'fritter away our minds into shreds and patches', he argued that periodicals were only 'leading strings to bring up to better things', suggesting that better reading could be had in Milton, Shakespeare, Bunyan and that famous advocate of self-help, Samuel Smiles.[28] Nonetheless, his determination to provide 'leading strings ... to better things' had already led Clarke to become a publisher of a number of periodicals and the inventor of the first commercial parish-magazine inset.

Denominational rivalry and church party division

The father of the denominational magazine was John Wesley, founder of the *Arminian* (later the *Wesleyan-Methodist Magazine*), in 1778. The concept was widely copied, provoking the disdain of Thomas Carlyle:

> [E]very little sect among us, Unitarians, Utilitarians, Anabaptists, Phrenologists, must have its Periodical, its monthly or quarterly Magazine; – hanging out, like its windmill, into the *popularis aura*, to grind meal for the society.[29]

Though Wesleyans were the first to publish a denominational magazine, there is no evidence of localisation before the 1850s, despite inter-denominational rivalry. Why was this so? The answer may lie with particular denominational priorities. During the 1850s the Roman Catholic Church in Britain was more vitally concerned with the creation and expansion of its infrastructure, including bishoprics, than the finer points of its parochialia. Cardinal Wiseman's ultramontane bid to control Britain's Roman Catholics, combined with the surge of Irish immigrants into the large towns, determined Roman Catholic centralist policymaking.[30] Roman Catholic emphasis on the sacraments rather than on the Word may also have militated against the early emergence of the Roman Catholic parish magazine. Nonconformists, whose reliance on the Word was a cornerstone of faith, were slower than Anglicans to localise their successful periodicals, but the popularity of nonconformist worship, together with its different congregational organisation, led to the creation of successful stand-alone chapel magazines.[31] Moreover, the liberal politics expressed by many local newspapers, exemplified by the *Bradford Observer* and its editor, William Byles, echoed nonconformist views, militating against any perceived need for early localisation of nonconformist magazines.[32] Peter Croft found that the localised Roman Catholic *Angelus Magazine* and Baptist *Illustrated Monthly Journal* came into existence 'a good ten years' after the first successful Anglican example in 1859.[33] Such magazines feature in Charles Booth's *Religious Influences* manuscript notebooks, published in 1902 and 1903, which contain Baptist, Wesleyan, Congregational and Roman Catholic local magazines with insets, but a far greater number of Anglican examples.[34]

The heartland of Anglicanism was the parish, but anxieties about secularisation in industrial towns resulted in what Callum Brown has termed 'the myth of the unholy city', in which the Church judged that it had failed to engage with many of its urban parishioners, the results of the 1851 Religious Census serving to underline this view.[35] Pastoral reform, which included the building of new churches in populous areas, took place after the parliamentary reforms of 1832, and no aspect of parish activity was regarded as too insignificant, as numerous nineteenth-century parish handbooks confirm.[36] John Sandford (1845) instructed the clergy on pastoral oversight, listing books for the parish library and advising on the distribution of tracts and parish visiting. Thomas Whitehead (1861) encouraged a closer relationship with parishioners through clubs and tea parties, he too recommending a parish library which clergy could supervise while getting to know the local boys.[37]

Beyond parish level, the Church had other mid-century pressing concerns which would drive it to enlist the support of even the humblest parishioner. Politically, it felt endangered when, after the passing of the Reform Act, a growing parliamentary nonconformist presence helped undermine its secular role, leading to fears of disestablishment, particularly in what Alan Gilbert has dubbed 'the period of intense Church–Chapel rivalry' in 1859, when anti-church-rate agitation was most intense.[38] It was in 1859 that the Church Defence Institution came into being and Erskine Clarke's *Parish Magazine* was published.[39] And internally all was not well. German biblical criticism provoked fears of rationalism, while Tractarian upheaval had led to the creation of three clearly defined church parties: High, some branches of which were passionately Anglo-Catholic; Low, which was often evangelical in its Biblicism and insistence on the centrality of the doctrine of Atonement; and Broad, which some called Latitudinarian because of its acceptance of new ideas. After the Tractarian leader John Henry Newman converted to Roman Catholicism in 1845, fears of what a renewed Roman Catholic Church might do in Britain intensified.[40] There may have been scant interest in these phenomena among parishioners, but to the clergy they were vital concerns demanding the mobilisation of the faithful, both in defence of the Established Church from without, and against attacks from within.[41]

When parish clergymen announced the intention of founding a parish magazine, their ostensible reasons for doing so were usually both practical and parochial: to help educate the newly literate; to form a closer bond between Church and people; to publish church accounts and notices; and to gain a place for the pulpit in every home, since many parishioners were disappointingly absent from Sunday worship.[42] But behind these reasonable justifications lay much anxiety about the Church's role. For arguably the first time since the Restoration, the opinions of the people in the pews began to matter to the Church establishment. As David Hempton has observed, religious toleration and the growth of nonconformism had shifted the balance of power 'between the producers and consumers' of Anglicanism,[43] with the result that religion, as Anthony Russell comments in his study of the clerical profession, had become 'a commodity which had to be marketed'. The parish magazine became a potentially formidable propagandist weapon by which a newly energised clergy could defend the Church nationally and locally, while also disseminating their views on the charged issue of how their parishioners should worship, as part of what Callum Brown has termed 'the greatest exercise in Christian proselytism this country has ever seen'.[44] Thus, with anxiety as its driving impulse, the Church prepared to market itself widely, its parish magazines a proactive, aggressive form of self-defence.

The first Anglican parish magazines

Some mid-nineteenth-century parish communications, such as the *Hackney Magazine and Parish Reformer* (1833–1838), appear to have been concerned with vestry matters. They were civic as well as religious, in keeping with the Established Church's earliest perceived role,[45] but perhaps the most typical early form of parish news was a single sheet hanging in the church porch, announcing service times.[46] As it became more ambitious, the developing parish magazine – commonly known as a 'leaflet' or 'parish notes' – contained church notices and accounts, with, occasionally, a printed sermon, originally given in church. A minority of parishes continued to publish such simple magazines; though usually disseminated monthly, some were quarterly or weekly publications.[47] Of the 359 parishes sampled for this study, almost one-fifth initially published a stand-alone magazine, and of these 359 parishes, around nine in ten published a commercially produced inset during the study's 70-year period.

Some committed parish clergymen produced a substantial parish magazine of their own from an early date. Of these, W. J. E. Bennett of Froome-Selwood in Somerset may be considered the progenitor of the

Anglican inset. He had no interest in the mundanities of advertising church notices to his flock; his monthly magazine, *The Old Church Porch* (which survived for eight years, from January 1854 to April 1862), contained articles written by his clerical friends 'for the use principally of the poor and unlearned', on 'holy things', including church ritual and custom, and was intended to circulate beyond Froome. Ousted from Saint Barnabas, Pimlico, because of his extreme ritualism, this renowned slum priest made parish reorganisation a central part of his ministry at Froome, the parish magazine taking its place as an educational tool alongside lay visiting, creation of clubs and charities, church and school revitalisation and ritualistic innovation.[48]

Another early example was the parish magazine of Saint John, Limehouse Fields, published monthly from 1860.[49] Printed in large script, this was a periodical specifically for poor people with developing reading skills, in which the hand-coloured illustrations had all the directness of a comic book.[50] The Limehouse magazine was particularly concerned with health, the editor urging vaccination against smallpox and the importance of clean water. An article entitled 'Murder Done Here' aimed at the prevention of 'deaths that arise from bad air, bad drainage, or overcrowded rooms'. Thrift was another major concern, the magazine advocating savings banks, living within one's income and the ultimate economic value of sending children regularly to the National School. Strikes against masters were criticised as useless in a magazine which taught obedience and duty in an economic system deemed immutable.

Like *The Old Church Porch*, the Limehouse magazine was preoccupied with church ritual. The perception that ritualism's spiritual benefits would encourage churchgoing encouraged slum clergy to practise extreme forms of it in defiance of their bishops.[51] The magazine contained explanations of Latin terms, an article on the revision of the liturgy, and illustrations of clerical attire in church, this being a contentious area of debate between high and low Churchmen.

The style and content of any parish magazine depended on the views of its incumbent. The Limehouse magazine changed when its originator, C. H. Carr, removed to a Yorkshire parish in 1870.[52] The succeeding vicar, Henry Whitehead (brother of the author of *Village Sketches*), had previously co-edited a parish paper in Clapham, the *Clapham Gazette,* which had ambitions to become more than a simple parish magazine. According to his biographer, Hardwicke Rawnsley, Whitehead was a frustrated journalist, 'always happy when he was correcting proof, or superintending the actual typesetting and printing'.[53] His literary tastes together with his broad-church sympathies encouraged contributions to the Limehouse magazine from friends like the author George MacDonald, editor of *Good Words for the Young*.[54] Though Whitehead was a renowned campaigner in moves to rid London of cholera, his magazine was not primarily concerned with health issues.[55] It was a decidedly literary magazine, and though it cost only a halfpenny and was theoretically within the economic reach of the poor, it was not designed to interest them unless they were enthusiastic autodidacts. Rawnsley claimed that Whitehead and his national school head teacher were the only persons 'above the rank of day labourer in the parish, the population chiefly consisting of dock labourers and costermongers', said by Henry Mayhew to have poor literacy, to be fond of illustrations and to ignore religious tracts.[56] Yet Whitehead refused to listen to those who urged him to 'try a tale', or 'give more for the money' or add illustrations, even when the magazine was in financial difficulties.[57] Unsurprisingly, his magazine was financially unsuccessful, his friends frequently defraying its expenses, its content clearly uncongenial to its intended readers. But the magazine encouraged other clergymen to seek advice on starting their own, which delighted Whitehead because he saw parish magazines as a means of spreading the same liberal education as the evening classes he ran for men, in the tradition of F. D. Maurice and the early Christian Socialists.[58]

Clergymen like Bennett and Whitehead may have occupied different positions in the church party debate, but their dedication to pastoral reform combined with writing ability led to the publication of their own distinctive parish magazine. Another dedicated amateur journalist, Edward Collett, vicar of Bowerchalke, Salisbury, produced his magazine from a home printing press from 1878 to 1924. It sold around 400 copies weekly, some sent to Canada, India, New Zealand, Australia, Africa and the United States, wherever his parishioners had strayed. The content typified the local pages of its contemporaries: a list of church services and saints' days; a 'vicar's letter' on a religious or moral theme; a list of baptisms, marriages and funerals; and a section containing information such as lighting-up times for bicycles, local geography, church clubs and history, local events and the vicar's firm views on anything – local, national or international – that took his fancy.[59] Meanwhile, in the vicarage of Saint John's, Upperby, Carlisle, the whole Crockett family rivalled the Brontës in their Howarth parsonage by writing, illustrating, copying and distributing the *Upperby Quarterly Messenger* from 1886 to 1888, before admitting that the undertaking had been immensely time-consuming and adding their parish to those which took the widely circulated *Carlisle Diocesan Magazine*.[60] It was generally thought difficult to produce a stand-alone magazine with enough of the improving material believed necessary for Sunday reading; it was much easier to produce parish notices, spiritual guidance and moral advice, while importing the rest.

Inset popularity

Some clergymen disliked the whole idea of parish magazines, either with insets or without, a former curate of Saint Augustine, Haggerston, expressing a common view that an 'occasional paper would supply every real need ... and would be economical'.[61] Some disliked parish magazines because they thought that reading any periodical would place readers in moral danger. In 1891, Carlisle's Archdeacon Prescott forbade the placing of periodicals in the cathedral lending library, also banning novels, even those of Charles Kingsley.[62] Clergymen often despised inset content. While he recommended his own 'letter to parishioners', the vicar of Saint Barnabas, Dulwich, thought his chosen inset undistinguished, while the vicar of Saint Barnabas, Kensington, thought the multiplication of commercial magazines 'one of the evils of the day', but declared that the local pages of the parish magazine 'are or should be of great importance to all who love their church'.[63] A substantial number saw parish magazines as two-tier publications: regular churchgoers would naturally wish to read the local pages, while the insets would only interest the poor. The vicar of Holy Trinity, Ulverston, thought his inset would make poorer parishioners 'happier and brighter than they would be otherwise'.[64] When faced with the prospect of sliding deeper into debt, the vicar of Saint John's Upperby, Carlisle, envisaged a clear choice between the inset and the local pages:

> We have been losing money. We might curtail the local matter but it seems to me the chief objects of a magazine are, one, a means of communication of church and parochial notices and events between clergy and people; two, to provide a permanent record of parochial events; and it is only incidentally that a publication with stories etcetera for Sunday reading is inserted.[65]

Yet, as the vicar of Saint Luke's, Redcliffe Square, London, admitted in 1910, the inset was 'popularly desired' by the parishioners; to the parishioners of Chiselhampton, Oxford, it was 'an old friend' giving 'words of good counsel and encouragement'; and in Holme Eden, Carlisle, the vicar wrote of his inset that 'no better pennyworth of good literature can possibly be found'.[66] Even Henry Whitehead incorporated an inset into his magazine when, towards the end of his career, he became vicar of Lanercost in Carlisle diocese.[67]

Inset success was a considerable achievement for their publishers in an era during which, on the one hand, they experienced the prejudice of those clergy who disliked the whole concept of the cheap periodical, and, on the other, competed with the hundreds of other cheap periodicals produced to satisfy the wants of Wilkie Collins's 'unknown public'; but their success could not have been possible without the speed of contemporary change. Technological, business and retail developments, Board School education, improvements in communications, the growth of periodical publishing, the spread of advertising and the very nature of language itself, which gradually shed its many local dialects and encouraged the decline of regional differences, all encouraged the spread of commercial insets, as Victorian society became ever more homogeneous.[68]

2
Erskine Clarke and *Parish Magazine*

This chapter explores the circumstances leading to the formation of the first successful inset, *Parish Magazine*, investigating its content and the motives of its editor, John Erskine Clarke, and noting the significance of Clarke's employment of the content and style of popular mid-century family magazines. *Parish Magazine*'s impact was such that it became a highly successful magazine in its own right, while forming the pattern for the many insets which followed it.

John Erskine Clarke (1828–1920)

The influences on *Parish Magazine*'s owner-editor, J. Erskine Clarke, were many. An inheritor of the evangelical spirit, he wished to save souls from hell through faith, yet, graduating from Oxford in 1850, he was influenced by high-church theology and ritual;[1] while at heart an advocate of political economy, he sought, as one influenced by F. D. Maurice's Christian Socialism, to improve earthly conditions, preaching the importance of education and sanitation; he expected Christians to read improving books, but understood the attractions of secular periodicals. To unite these competing aims he invented a magazine which, in its mature form, combined the traditional content of the evangelical tract and the appeal of the popular family magazine, while attempting to steer a via media between high and low church practices.[2]

Clarke's address to the Southern Counties Adult Education Society conference in 1860 explained that his inset had commenced in 1858 as the result of a request from his Sunday-school boys for a magazine of their own.[3] Like Henry Whitehead, Clarke embraced publishing because he enjoyed journalism, and he was obviously entrepreneurial, also publishing and editing a successful weekly magazine for children called *Chatterbox* from 1866.[4] As Altholz has observed, journalism was highly convenient for clergyman 'part-time editors'.[5] Clearly, though, there were deeper issues at stake. Clarke's biographer, Graham Fuller, regards him as a Christian Socialist in the tradition of Kingsley and F. D. Maurice, citing his series of *Plain Papers on the Social Economy of the People,* which show a similar concern for social improvement as the Limehouse magazines described in Chapter 1.[6] Not that mid-nineteenth-century Christian Socialists were socialists in the modern political sense; Kingsley and Maurice, whilst urging some social reform and cooperation between classes, did so for humanitarian reasons, rather than from any wish to change the age's standard political economy, and in many other respects they were as traditionally paternalistic as nineteenth-century Tories.[7]

Clarke was also driven to publish by his dislike of extremist Anglican views. Within its magazine format, *Parish Magazine* always quietly advocated an Anglican via media, but clearly Clarke wished to promote his theological views more loudly, for, according to Bishop Walsham How, after Clarke had overheard some of his Derby parishioners 'wrangling about ritualism and Protestantism', he determined to 'to start a paper that would be conducted on Central Church lines and show what true Church teaching was'. Thus the Anglican newspaper, *Church Bells* (1871–1895) was inaugurated after meetings between Clarke, Walsham How and other advocates of the Anglican via media during the 1867 Church Congress.[8]

Parish Magazine: an 'improving' family magazine

Erskine Clarke's concerns and interests coalesced in the invention of the first commercial parish-magazine inset, when the monthly magazine he had invented for his Sunday-school scholars in 1858, *Our Happy Home Union,* was adapted to suit their parents as well. One year later, its success encouraged him to offer it to other parishes with the name *Parish Magazine.* It offered blank outer pages for local news, to be printed locally, and a picture of each parish's church on the wrapper. Clarke's letter introducing the idea to fellow clergy indicated that he intended to follow a plan 'already applied to secular serials'.[9] He may have been referring to the practice begun around 1854 whereby London publishers sold partly printed sheets of national news, leading articles and fiction, called 'middles' or 'insides', to the publishers of provincial newspapers who added local news and advertisements to the outsides to create a product which, though it appeared to be a local newspaper, was in fact both a local and a national publication.[10]

Clarke's introductory letter listed the uses to which a local magazine could be put, such as the publication of meeting notices, club accounts and the hours and rules of parish schools. He particularly stressed the advantages of a localised national magazine which, by allowing all parishioners to hear the Church's message, would counter the attractions of 'neutral or irreligious periodicals'. Clarke assured his colleagues that the magazine's theology would be left to them; his aims were to improve social conditions and 'foster the home affections' of the people, for the inset was written to suit 'the tastes of children' and 'the handicraft-classes'. It would cost the clergy 8d per dozen of 13 with no cover, or 9d with a cover entitled *Parish Magazine*.[11] One year later, however, Clarke changed his mind over his decision to omit definite religious teaching. In some parishes the local pages of the magazine had been distributed with no overt religious teaching at all, leading nonconformists to mock *Parish Magazine* for its lack of definite theology: 'Here's the book your parson's put out; not a word of religion in it'.[12] From that point on, *Parish Magazine* contained a monthly sermon.

Erskine Clarke's address to the 1864 Church Congress criticised the 'bad literature' and lack of general knowledge in cheap secular publications. What the populace really needed was 'definiteness of religious teaching, attractive light reading [and] such wholesome fiction as was compatible with sound reason and piety'.[13] Yet the content of *Parish Magazine* was from the beginning similar to that of the *Family Herald,* established in 1842, according to Richard Altick 'for the indifferently educated reader', which, with its emphasis on the family, dominated the mid-Victorian cheap magazine market.[14] The chronicler of Oxfordshire village life, Flora Thompson, observed that the *Family Herald,* along with penny novelettes, was the favourite reading material of the women of the hamlet of Lark Rise, who raised their children on a farm labourer's weekly wage of ten shillings.[15] Each weekly issue usually contained a chapter from at least two serialised novels, a short story or two, poetry, a science column, needlework and cookery columns and a number of general facts and anecdotes. Contributors included the well-known female journalists Mary Howitt and Eliza Cook.[16] Another likely secular progenitor of *Parish Magazine* was the *Family Economist...devoted to the moral, physical, and domestic improvement of the industrious classes,* published in 1848, and in 1860 amalgamated with the *Family Friend,* another periodical containing cheap recipes, household hints, gardening, moral advice and stories.[17] *Parish Magazine* offered the 'handicraft-classes' the popular miscellany represented by these secular family magazines, shorn of what Margaret Dalziel has termed the *Family Herald's* elements of 'cautious republicanism and vague philosophical speculation'.[18] The definiteness of religious education that Clarke required was already offered by 'Sunday Reading' weeklies, such as the RTS *Leisure Hour* (1852) and *Sunday at Home* (1854), which also provided instruction and recreation through travel, natural history articles and moralising fiction.[19] Callum Brown has given all such publications the umbrella title of 'improving' magazines.[20] Clarke's ambition was to publish an Anglican 'improving' magazine so inexpensive and so widely circulated that it would be read in the homes of every Anglican parish.

'Wholesome Fiction Compatible with Sound Reason and Piety'

Influenced by 'improving' magazines and religious tracts, the first number of *Parish Magazine* consisted of 16 pages of 'sound reason and piety'.[21] Positioned within a lecture on the importance of home life was an allusion to the Holmfirth flood of 1852.[22] On damming a river to form a reservoir, Holmfirth manufacturers ignored signs of bad workmanship until eventually the dam burst, killing 100 people. *Chambers' Edinburgh Journal* blamed the mill owners who had demonstrated 'mercantile *laissez-faire* in a most disagreeable light'.[23] *Parish Magazine*, however, preferred to turn the incident into a moral tale in which a Holmfirth Sunday-scholar, having saved his pence to buy Mimpriss's *Harmony of the Gospels*, refused to meet his friends at night, instead taking 'increasing pleasure' in reading his book.[24] When the dam broke and he was swept away: 'do you think he now regrets that he spent those last three evenings of his life at home?' The treatment mirrors the evangelical tract, in which redemption through faith, description of the last hours and the 'good' death were necessary elements of a narrative rooted in seventeenth-century Puritanism.[25] In the 1850s this style was still integral to cheap religious magazines such as the RTS *Tract Magazine* and other periodicals designed for the 'cottage circle', like the *Mother's Friend* (1848–1895).[26] Here, scenes of 'gloomy and dilapidated' rooms where the 'dark-winged angel' of death hovered over 'the child's pale wasted face'[27] featured strongly, along with 'the drooping head, clasped hands, stooping figure and sad, weary look of disappointed hope'.[28]

In *Parish Magazine*, overtly evangelical tracts and stories influenced by secular models existed side by side. Though traditional deathbed scenes occurred within its poetry, illustration and short stories/tracts for more than a decade,[29] the tone of its serial fiction was more optimistic. It is possible to trace this phenomenon to broad-church and Tractarian dismissal of evangelical emphasis on the atonement, as they turned instead to a celebration of incarnation.[30] Boyd Hilton has attributed the change to distaste for Calvinism, and to the dawning perception that heaven might actually be found on earth, at a time when the possibilities of personal and business development were embraced by the middle classes.[31] Nevertheless, concern for sales was probably a major factor in the inclusion of such stories which through aping popular novels became a staple of Victorian magazine fiction.[32] As Aileen Fyfe has written of the *Leisure Hour,* religious magazine publishers were obliged to accept that 'fiction sold periodicals'.[33] Serial fiction was addictive, as one clergyman discovered as late as 1939 when his parishioners were given a free copy of the inset in January and asked to subscribe for the rest of the year, having become hooked on the serial's instalments.[34]

From the beginning, fiction filled over a third of the space in *Parish Magazine*. Clarke's aim was to publish the works of well-known authors, for in the first year he published two short stories by Mrs Gaskell. 'The Sexton's Hero', which appeared in the October number, and 'Christmas Storms and Sunshine', which appeared in December, exemplified Clarke's 'cut-and-paste' editorial technique, as they had been first published in *Howitt's Journal* in 1847 and 1848.[35] However, Clarke was clearly ambitious to publish new works, for he wrote to George Eliot requesting a story to help the clergy elevate 'notions of courtship and love', offering, as payment, one pound per page. Eliot's partner, G. H. Lewes, wrote to her publisher, John Blackwood, with her response:

> Before we left town there was an American literary agent who offered £1,200 for a story in one small volume to be published in *The Century,* a New York newspaper ... Today a letter has come from the editor of a 'Parish Magazine' – and really G. E. was almost more likely to be tempted by that audience than by the New Yorkers ... G. E. says will you please write a polite note to Erskine Clarke and say that although he sympathises very strongly with his efforts, his cooperation is impossible for want of leisure.[36]

Alas for Clarke's ambitions, *Parish Magazine*'s serial fiction was almost always contributed by minor novelists. The earliest was Matilda Anne Mackarness (1825–1881), whose writing career prefigures that of later female inset contributors, to be discussed in Chapter 6. The daughter of professional playwrights, Mackarness produced a number of novels before her marriage to a clergyman. As his death in 1868 left her with little money, she redoubled her writing efforts, producing at least one novel annually until 1881. Remembered chiefly as a children's writer, she also wrote for the *Girl's Own Paper*.[37] In her story for *Parish Magazine,* Mackarness utilised stock characters and situations of mid-Victorian popular fiction – the fallen woman, the innocent orphan, the unscrupulous male villain, the perfectionist mistress, the slatternly servant – placing them in a village where her blameless heroine could go about doing good. The story's moral tone, and what Callum Brown has described as its evangelical 'oppositional discourse', would have reassured the editor, while its romantic melodrama probably encouraged readers to obtain the next instalment of 'Cousin Bridget'.[38] Serial fiction forms a major focus of this book, for, as religious magazines mimicked secular publications in a race to compete with 'impure' literature and encourage church allegiance, the space awarded to such fiction dominated the insets that followed *Parish Magazine*. As a leaflet for the inset, *Ecclesia,* noted in 1915, 'the serial story generally decides the issue whether the parish magazine is to be taken in or not'.[39] In 1928, the inset's presence in the Saint Andrew, Earlsfield, parish magazine was explained as being 'to interest our readers in Church work and Church sentiment, and to give them a serial story to read'.[40]

'Attractive Light Reading'

Like the secular periodicals on which it was modelled, *Parish Magazine,* for all that death was never far away, increasingly provided hope for a contented life. To Erskine Clarke, the principal methods of achieving this consisted of churchgoing, temperance, deference and debt avoidance. Besides fiction, much of the magazine's 'light reading' was represented by articles on church history, natural history and missionary activity, sundry articles also demonstrating Clarke's dual interest in health and temperance. In *Parish Magazine,* the poor were always advised to remain at home, out of harm's way, far from the gambling den, the public house and other temptations of the streets.[41] The comfortable family home is a theme that runs like a thread, not only through Anglican insets, but also through secular nineteenth-century periodicals: Margaret Beetham and Kay Boardman have listed eight such magazines, in which 'home' was the title's dominant word.[42] The woodcut on the title page of the first number of *Parish Magazine* (Figure 2.1) illustrated the advice given in the article beneath. In the picture, all is middle-class domestic comfort. The paterfamilias has lowered the book he has been reading aloud to listen to a family member playing the flute, while the women busy themselves with needlework. In Clarke's article the onus to achieve this perfect home life was placed squarely on the woman reader, whose empire this was. Her failure to make the home 'cheerful and comfortable' would end in disaster, her man going, 'grumbling and cross', to the welcoming public-house. Clarke gave precise instructions to the woman reader. She was to rise early to get the washing done and the house clean; put the baby to bed by early evening; place 'a clean cloth on the table'; and have

Figure 2.1 Title Page: *Parish Magazine* (January 1859)

supper ready before her men returned. Clarke was aware that families living largely in one room found it difficult to 'get everything straightened and put to rights, so that the family can gather round the fire'. Nonetheless, it was essential, not just to their personal happiness, but to the household economy. As Bob said to Charley later in the article:

> I like best to be at home these dark winter nights; for when father comes home from the mill, and has eaten his supper, he makes baskets, and Mother sews, and I read to them out of my library books; and Mother says it is a good thing to make the most of corners of time and every little helps, for last winter she sold the baskets for more than paid the rent.[43]

Dissonance appears here in an apparent conflict between image and text. Bob and Charley clearly did not live in the middle-class home of the illustration, but in the cut-and-paste world of Clarke's periodical empire, woodcut images were often repeated inappropriately to cut costs.[44]

Parish Magazine: editorial method

Text

Clarke saw his editorial role as using 'the scissors and paste of the compiler', for *Parish Magazine*'s 'light reading' often consisted of material written by friends.[45] While rarely named, these men were sometimes identified by their initials: G. S. O., for instance, was G. S. Outram, rector of Redmill, Nottinghamshire, who in 1874 contributed a series on mammals.[46] Sermons were contributed by known via media sympathisers. Graham Fuller has analysed the devotional material in *Parish Magazine* from 1871 to 1885.[47] Revd George Venables, Clarke's partner in his newspaper venture, is represented; Henry Whitehead delivered the Christmas sermon in 1885;[48] Bishop Goodwin of Carlisle provided seven sermons.[49] Charles Kingsley's 21 sermons are worthy of comment; after his death in 1875 his widow sold all his previous unpublished writing, the large number published in *Parish Magazine* underlining the business-like quality of Clarke's approach as well as his church-party stance.[50]

Parish Magazine's fiction greatly depended on occasional contributors, usually women, the fate of whose copy 'lay entirely in the editor's hands ... no proofs were sent ... acceptance or rejection was often not notified'.[51] During the early years, elements regarded by Clarke as 'liable to misconception' were ruthlessly edited out.[52] According to F. J. Harvey Darton (editor of Clarke's magazine, *Chatterbox*, from 1901), Clarke's editing of text was

> ... masterly; nay, masterful ... The editor himself took – usurped – all responsibility of every kind, even of authorship. He *did* edit ... if a story contained a good idea with poor trimmings, [he] cut the trimmings away bodily, or re-wrote them. To make his views prevail, he added as well as took away.[53]

Illustration

Harvey Darton was contemptuous of Clarke's artists and engravers, whom he thought thorough but unimaginative. The status of engravings in *Parish Magazine* may be deduced from their usual deployment as accompaniments to short passages of text which, as Darton explained, were brought together from diverse elements as 'fill-ins' between longer articles.[54] Nonetheless, some of Clarke's artists were highly regarded during the late-Victorian era. Harrison Weir (1824–1906) produced illustrations in *Parish Magazine* over many years, his exquisite illustrations of animals appearing regularly in other contemporary periodicals, particularly those for the young.[55] As engraving was an expensive process, Weir's illustrations were recycled within Clarke's publications, those in *Parish Magazine* often appearing first in *Chatterbox*.[56]

Erskine Clarke's legacy

Progressive thinkers profoundly disliked Clarke's publications. The mid-Victorian writer, John Cordy Jeaffreson, thought his magazine fiction lacked every single good quality, and, in spite of Clarke's moderate theological stance, Jeaffreson thought his 'spiritual arrogance' calculated to rouse antagonism.[57] John Ruskin's 1870s letters to workmen, *Fors Clavigera,* criticised Clarke's Sunday-school magazine, *The Prize,* as a typically ghastly example of the cheap religious periodical which preached a specious morality encouraging working-class acceptance of a lower place in life.[58] Ruskin's opinion is borne out by a poem published in *Parish Magazine* in 1874. Entitled 'A Good Servant', its illustration of a maid quailing before the menacing figure of her mistress accompanies a text which bade her, 'never let idle vanity, tempt you your ladies' clothes to try, or in their drawers and cupboards pry', among a myriad of other injunctions (Figure 2.2).

Figure 2.2 'A Good Servant': *Parish Magazine* (March 1874)

When Clarke was interviewed by one of Charles Booth's investigators in 1900, he had become vicar of Battersea, his inset having ceased publication five years earlier.[59] It is in keeping with his pronouncements at the Oxford book-hawking conference that he made no mention either of *Parish Magazine* or the importance of a magazine to his parish work, even though Battersea supported its own parish magazine.[60] To Clarke the parish magazine was a means to an end: a method of teaching cottagers and their children what to read, and how to live appropriately; of promoting his preferred middle way between the excesses of high and low Church parties; and of aiding his fellow clergy to do the same. Nonetheless he had demonstrated the viability of the parish-magazine inset, and had stamped upon it the content and style which became standard in its successors, promoting a greater homogeneity within the Church as parishes laid down their stand-alone magazines to take nationally produced insets in large numbers. Both the iconic name and content of *Parish Magazine* were to remain the blueprint for all future endeavours. In 1858 Clarke had offered to inaugurate an inset for the SPCK. When that venerable, risk-averse body declined his proposal, he decided to go it alone with *Parish Magazine*. Twenty years later the SPCK was revitalised through copying his venture with its own inset, *Dawn of Day*.[61] *Parish Magazine* also encouraged Frederick Sherlock to reach out to the laity for clergy support through *The Church Monthly*, and inspired the creation of a highly entrepreneurial publishing dynasty, the Bullock Family, who published *Home Words*.

Later insets

When it ceased publication in 1895, *Parish Magazine* had become only one of 22 Anglican insets. Of these, *Home Words*, *Dawn of Day* and *The Church Monthly* had substantially overtaken its circulation. These insets made more use of illustration and decorative motifs, experimenting with new techniques including colour printing and photography, and, like many popular periodicals, were printed with double columns in quarto, while *Parish Magazine* had remained in octavo. Nonetheless, the content replicated *Parish Magazine*'s format of religious and moral exhortation combined with stories and 'educational' topics thought suitable for a cottage-home readership. The first page might consist of an arresting illustration from the current serial story (Figure 2.3);[62] a profile of a bishop, or an incumbent and his church might follow the monthly 'sermon' or 'talk' or 'lesson' written by a clergyman. All contained religious poetry and hymns, lectures on daily living, natural history articles, serial stories and short tract-like stories. Travel articles were common.

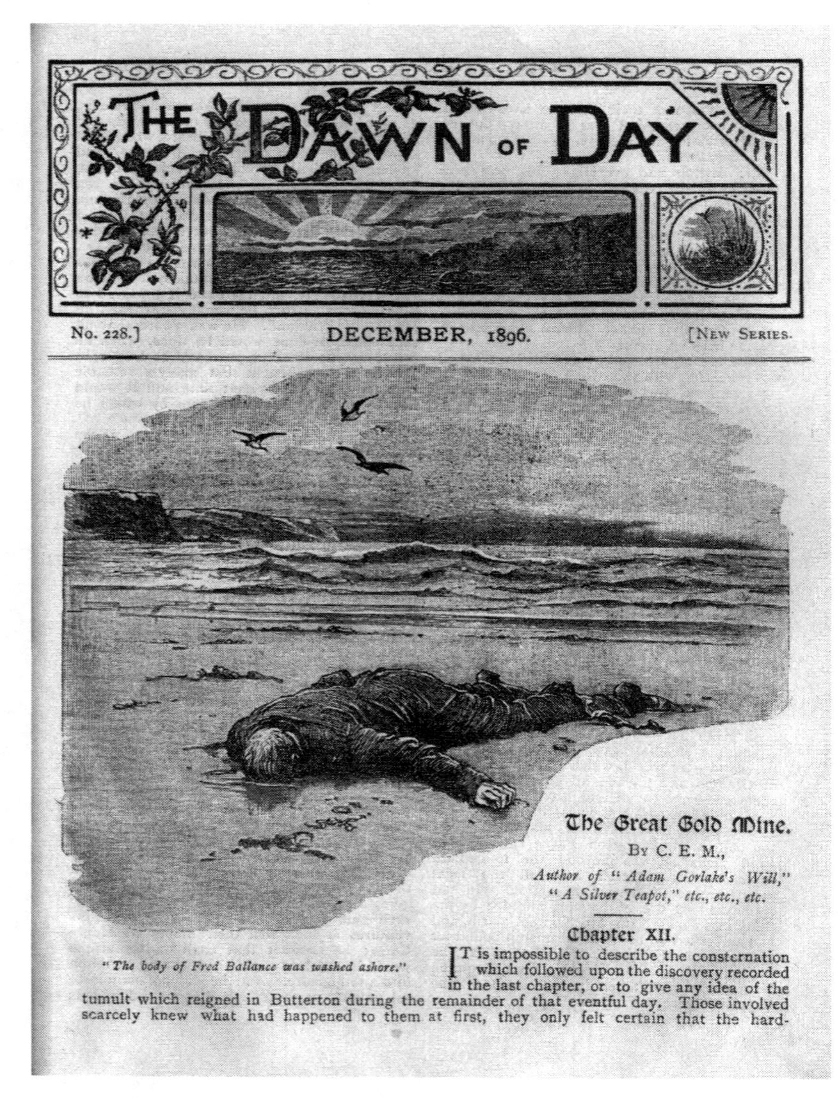

THE DAWN OF DAY

No. 228.] DECEMBER, 1896. [NEW SERIES.

"The body of Fred Ballance was washed ashore."

The Great Gold Mine.

BY C. E. M.,

Author of "Adam Gorlake's Will," "A Silver Teapot," etc., etc., etc.

Chapter XII.

IT is impossible to describe the consternation which followed upon the discovery recorded in the last chapter, or to give any idea of the tumult which reigned in Butterton during the remainder of that eventful day. Those involved scarcely knew what had happened to them at first, they only felt certain that the hard-

Figure 2.3 Title Page: *The Dawn of Day* (December 1896)

Particularly in *Home Words,* and occasionally in *The Church Monthly,* there might be a profile of a working man who had made good in the tradition of the writing of Samuel Smiles, or a description of a working-class occupation. Every magazine purported to have female cookery and needlework specialists who would also advise on marriage, health, the home and personal relationships, though the clergy wrote extensively on these subjects too. Some magazines had a gardening column, and occasionally a handicrafts section, written by men for men. There were monthly missionary, temperance and Bible-study columns, the last often on the same page as articles for the young and Sunday schools. *The Church Monthly* featured a correspondence column. From the 1880s, particularly in *Home Words,* the content was interspersed with advice, proverbs and quotations, which divided the columns into bite-sized pieces to make the pages attractive and appealing, stylistically echoing contemporary secular periodicals.

From the late 1870s, articles on Church finance and Church defence began to proliferate. 'The Church in danger', a feature of Anglican discourse since the eighteenth century which had always lain beneath the insets' apparently confident surface, became an overarching theme during the 1880s.[63] In May 1877 *Parish Magazine* contained a poem celebrating the strides made by the Church during dangerous times:

Our own dear Church of England
Has burst her banks of sloth;
Aroused are priest and people,
For dangers compass both.
For ever days of danger
Bring greater gifts of grace
And now the Church of England
Shall bless the English race.

Parish Magazine's conflation of denomination, patriotism and race, yet fear of the dangers encompassing the Church, became major inset themes, while Erskine Clarke was to influence the publication of insets in other far-reaching ways. By deliberately basing his magazine's style and content on popular periodicals he had ensured that fiction by female authors would be the insets' dominant feature, and his moderate support for his preferred church party paved the way for more extreme party views. Moreover, he had laid down the guidelines for a thoroughly commercial approach to sales, as Chapter 3 explores.

3
'Cheap as well as Good': The Economics of Publishing

The monthly circulation of *Parish Magazine* reached 15,000 in its first year when it was localised in 55 parishes.[1] Erskine Clarke acknowledged that this result was

> extremely minute when put beside the 450,000 of the *British Workman* – minute, too, when compared with the vast issues of the ... *Leisure Hour* [80,000 in 1855], and woefully minute when compared with the weekly penny numbers of the *Family Herald* and *Reynold's Miscellany* [260,000 in 1858 and 200,000 in 1855 respectively].[2]

Two years later, the circulation of *Parish Magazine* had reached 17,000,[3] and, in 1872, advertisements announcing the popularity of the magazine both in Britain and the colonies threatened publishers with litigation if they adopted its name, thereby usurping its copyright status.[4] By 1885, when a speaker at the Church Congress described the taking of localised parish magazines as 'almost universal', the combined monthly circulation of the 15 insets on the market was half a million; by 1893, it was said to have reached a million and a half: Clarke had tapped a rich vein.[5] This chapter explores the important economic dimension of publishing, distributing and selling these popular magazines, noting through descriptions of the careers of their major editors and proprietors that inset publishing was as competitive as any secular alternative. Individual localities had pronounced inset preferences, which may be traced to their clergy's adherence to church parties, a preference eagerly served by inset editors. Despite their popularity, however, parish magazines often sold at a loss, leading inset and local editors alike to turn to commercial advertising, as a means of remaining solvent.

Survey of inset popularity

A survey of parish-magazine insets deposited in the London Metropolitan Archives and the archive centres and libraries of the dioceses of Carlisle and Oxford was carried out to gain an understanding of their geographical spread and determine their popularity over time. As discussed in the Introduction, there are obvious drawbacks to this research method; it would be foolish to argue that what we see is the total number of parish magazines when so few were discovered compared to the total number of parishes, and even within the magazine deposits of individual parishes there are many gaps. Nonetheless, the results of the survey, seen in Figure 3.1, shed a certain objective light on inset publishers' partisan data.

Allowing for gaps in the archival record, the trajectories in each locality are similar: a slow start which plateaus around 1870–1880, rises to a peak in the first decade of the twentieth century and drops before the Great War. This corroborates Callum Brown's estimate of 1904 as the year of peak growth of Anglican Church membership as a proportion of population.[6] To an extent, the trajectory also agrees with Simon Eliot's analysis of the publication of periodicals of all types during the same period. Through examining published trade information, Eliot demonstrated growth in the 1850s, acceleration in the 1870s, even more rapid growth in the 1880s, and a further rise in the 1890s, with a falling off in the early

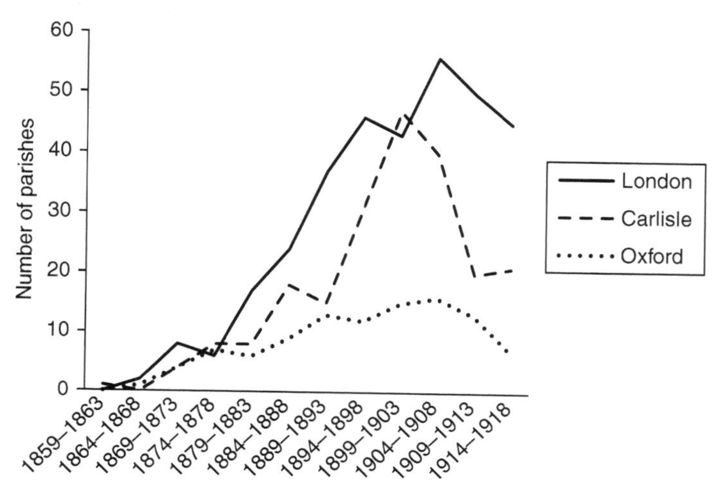

Figure 3.1 Anglican Insets in London (Metropolitan Archives) and Carlisle and Oxford Dioceses (1859–1918)

1900s.[7] When comparing religious and secular publishing, however, Eliot found that religious magazines remained almost static, at a third of all titles, through the 1860s and 1870s; though their number grew modestly in the 1880s, growth in the number of secular titles was much greater, so that by around 1900 religion's share of the magazine market had been cut by half.[8] The 1890s saw the number of new insets, which had previously risen at a similar rate to secular periodicals, begin to fall (Figure 3.2).[9]

Eliot blames religion's apparent failure in the magazine market on 'relentless secularisation'.[10] Those who have debated this phenomenon have differed over when it occurred: Jeffrey Cox and Hugh McLeod appear to agree that Anglicanism reached a peak in the 1880s; Simon Green placed it in the 1920s, but Callum Brown discovered only 'relatively moderate' decline in overall church membership between 1900 and 1955: church attendance appeared to decline only because people were attending less frequently.[11] Whatever the truth of these claims, it is undeniable that fears for the future of Anglicanism suffused parish magazines from the 1880s, a phenomenon which forms a major focus of this book. Michael Ledger-Lomas argues that such anxieties worked in the short term to prop up the religious magazine trade by encouraging the development of strong denominational and sectarian identities through which the clergy courted lay support.[12] This is exemplified by the arrival of *The Church Monthly* in 1888 – the editor a dedicated supporter of clergy and lay parish partnership – and the publication of a number of high-church magazines in the early years of the twentieth century. Espousing various degrees of ritualism, high-church insets competed in their own niche market.[13]

Editors trumpeted the growth of their circulation figures as a means of advertising the product or impressing society members. The SPCK's

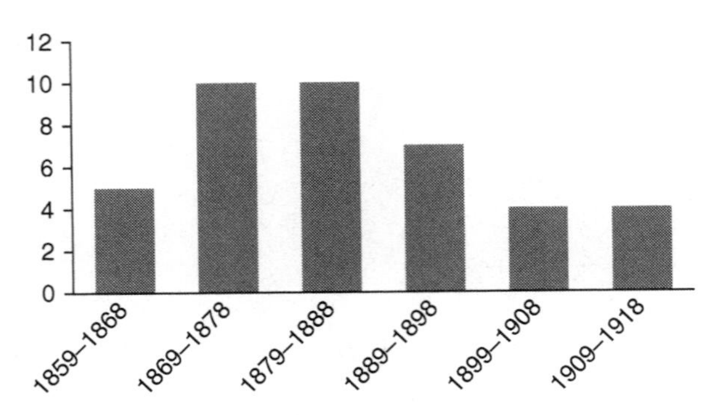

Figure 3.2 Known Anglican Inset titles (1859–1918)

tract committee, which oversaw *Dawn of Day*, occasionally presented the inset's monthly circulation figures in SPCK annual reports.[14] Ten separate years' data, from 1878 to 1908, are presented in Figure 3.3, the circulation reaching a peak of 650,000 in 1904. The archive of Mowbray's, publishers of *The Sign*, includes a rather impressionistic chart of monthly circulation figures dating from 1905 to 1957 (reproduced here as Figure 3.4), demonstrating a higher circulation than *Dawn of Day* by about 1911.[15] By 1913 *The Sign*'s monthly circulation was said to be 700,000.[16]

These figures compare favourably with sales of late-nineteenth-century secular periodicals. According to Richard Altick, in 1886 the circulation of *Lloyd's Weekly Newspaper* was 750,000; in the Easter week of 1897, *Tit-Bits* reached a high circulation of 671,000; in 1899 the circulation of the *Daily Mail* was 543,000.[17] Of the popular religious monthlies, *Good Words'* circulation was between 80,000 and 130,000 in the 1870s.[18] Comparisons between the circulations of *The Sign*, *Dawn of Day* and the *Church Times* – which claimed it was the only Anglican periodical to achieve a mass circulation, with the 'largest sale of any Church paper in the kingdom' – are particularly illuminating: in 1900, circulation of the *Church Times* was 45,000, less than a tenth of the circulation of *Dawn of Day*, while at the end of its first year *The Sign* had achieved a circulation of 100,000.[19] This evidence suggests that the impressive sales of parish magazines should lead to a revision of scholarship in which parish-magazine circulation is taken seriously into account.

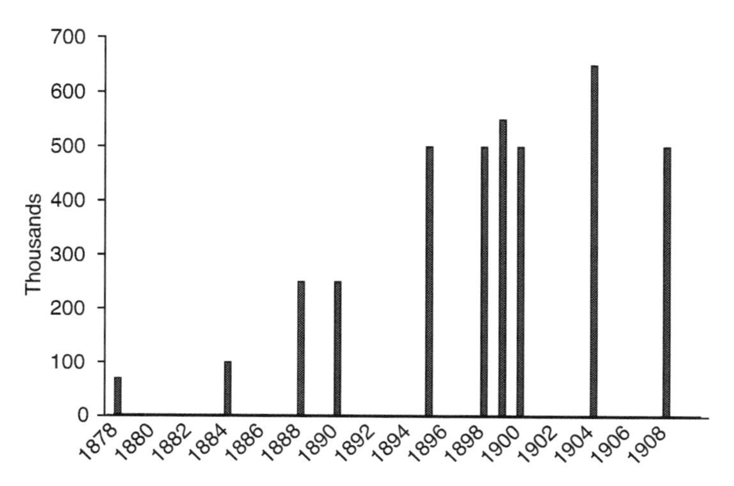

Figure 3.3 *Dawn of Day* Monthly Circulation Figures taken from 10 SPCK annual reports (1878–1908)

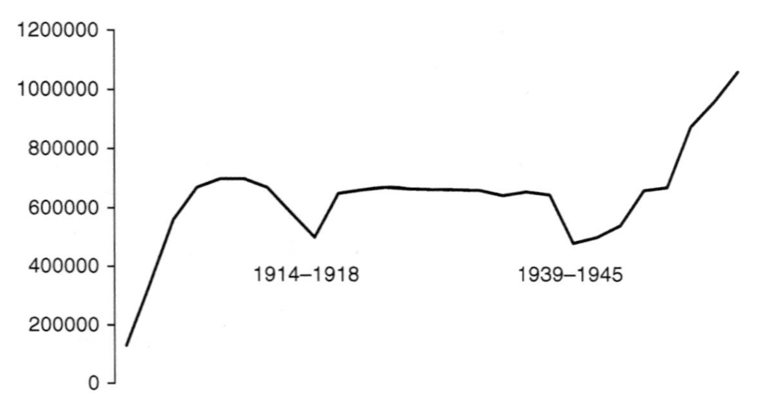

Figure 3.4 *The Sign* Monthly Circulation Figures (1905–1960) by permission of the Principal and Chapter of Pusey House, Oxford

Charles Bullock and *Home Words*

In its bid to gain readers, inset publishing was as competitive as any secular alternative. Revd Charles Bullock, proprietor and editor of *Home Words,* constantly advertised in a number of publications, wooing the clergy with the possibility of 'reaching the entire population, many of whom may never enter the church', through half-price grants.[20] Described as a 'little man with tireless energy', Bullock published five different religious periodicals. In 1872, after one year, the monthly circulation of *Home Words* was 90,000; in 1876 it reached 250,000 (a feat which *Dawn of Day* only achieved after ten years).[21] One of the most enduring of Anglican insets until its amalgamation with *The Sign* in January, 2009, *Home Words'* monthly circulation was 1,100,000 in 1964.[22]

Home Words' editorials regularly recommended Bullock's Sunday-reading magazine, *The Day of Days,* his penny newspaper, *The Fireside News,* his weekly penny journal, *Hand and Heart,* his books on royalty, Sunday-school prize books, religious novels and localised annuals. '*Home Words* and *The Day of Days* are twin magazines, alike in size and price (1d) each. We want our readers to take both; and then each reader to gain another', Bullock wrote in *Home Words* in December 1885. Advertisements, styled as 'chats' with the editor, extolled the virtues of his latest books, and offered reductions:

> Special Offer: When 25 copies are ordered *direct* from the Publisher, *Home Words Office,* they will be supplied ... at 10d each.[23]

Placed beneath and between devotional articles, hymns and biblical references, Bullock's advertisements were intrinsic to the text, a ploy typically employed by advertisers in late-nineteenth-century family magazines.[24] Even the high-minded SPCK allowed the firm of Seigel to advertise its medicinal syrup through 'short stories' sharing space with devotional literature.[25] The reason Bullock gave for his aggressive advertising was always the same: to further the great work of the Gospel, never to increase his burgeoning publishing empire, which enabled him to resign his parish three years after founding *Home Words* and, with the help of his sons, to build a family business which was highly successful until the mid-1960s, when the circulation of *Home Words* began to fall.[26]

At its advent, *Home Words*, like *Parish Magazine*, consisted of 24 pages. Like *Parish Magazine*, its illustrations had often appeared previously, either in Bullock's other publications or in secular magazines such as the *Illustrated London News*.[27] Until the 1890s, Bullock also saved costs by printing his serial stories without illustration. Nevertheless, the magazine's attractive double-column layout, liberal use of decorative capitals, numerous full- and half-page illustrations of non-fiction subjects, and the issue of bound copies covered in blue and gold, ensured that *Home Words* was a visual delight.[28] From the 1890s, populist marketing techniques included serial story illustration, the use of the colour red within the text, photographic reproduction, and a free coloured print in every January issue.

Always aware of new journalistic developments, Bullock adapted the 'celebrity interview', presenting Church dignitaries as if they were bona fide interviewees by reporting elements from their published speeches and sermons as if given personally to the magazine.[29] Popularised through the New Journalism's 'human interest' stories of the 1880s, the celebrity interview employed both adulatory biography and reported speech to create a 'star system', which became, as Margaret Beetham has observed, 'the prototype of the media personality'.[30] This could be adapted to show the Church in the best possible light. 'Interviews' with bishops appeared alongside articles on well-known missionaries, sportsmen and industrialists, so that a panoply of famous individuals seemed to be applauding Anglicanism, and, naturally, *Home Words*. After 1902, when Charles Bullock's layman son, Herbert Somerset Bullock, became editor,[31] genuine celebrity interviews in which the interviewer took a lively part would have rivalled those in any secular periodical.[32]

Like many of his contemporaries, Bullock saved production costs by writing much of the copy himself,[33] his name appearing beneath an average 30 per cent of the text during the 1870s and 1880s, though many unattributed articles were probably his. Within many of these articles, Bullock exploited the country's admiration for Queen Victoria. While he would have admired Victoria's moderate evangelicalism, for she disliked Ritualists and supported attempts to control their influence,[34] Bullock was also exhibiting business shrewdness, for books about royalty were popular as a result of the growth of popular affection for the monarchy, buoyed by imperial success.[35] Bullock's books on Queen Victoria – *The Royal Year* and *The Queen's Resolve: I Will Be Good* (1887) – were heavily advertised in *Home Words*, with inducements for bulk purchase by the parishes.[36] A new edition of *The Queen's Resolve*, published during the Jubilee of 1897, claimed to have sold 175,000 copies since its first appearance ten years before.[37]

As in cheap secular periodicals,[38] and as already noted in Erskine Clarke's magazines, material in Bullock's publications was conveniently recycled. During the Jubilee year of 1887, Flora Thompson was given a bound copy of a magazine 'because it contained extracts from a book written by the Queen'. She read it many times: 'everything was re-read in that home of few books'.[39] In later years she could never remember the title: was it *Good Words* or *Home Words?* It was quite probably Bullock's *Home Words* of 1887, which contained instalments from Victoria's book, *Leaves from the Journal of our Life in the Highlands*, which Bullock had taken from *Home Words* of 1884.[40]

While Bullock's patriotic works were clearly central to his commercial venture, cannily making links between royalty, patriotism and evangelicalism, they also firmly supported working-class book ownership. To Bullock, 'the printing press is the Church's lever – what is read in the home is second only to what is heard in the pulpit', and he always maintained that the Church could introduce 'good reading' into 'every home in the land'.[41] In a lifetime of reading, a whole library of his books could be obtained for very little outlay, all bound in his trademark blue-and gold-board covers. In his will, he left a publishing empire and £52,560 to his family, directing that copies of his books should be given to London street missionaries, his old parishioners and their children.[42]

Assessing inset popularity

When W. T. Stead opined in 1886 that the best editors should have the qualities of 'a real man, who has convictions, and capacity to give them utterance in conversation as well as in print', he might well have been referring, not only to the highly successful Charles Bullock, but also to Frederick Sherlock, editor and proprietor of *The Church Monthly*. Both men displayed a combination of religious commitment, writing skill, commercial hard-headedness and careful product placement, while also possessing the ability to address the Church Congress with aplomb.[43] Sherlock had learned his trade as a writer of temperance articles and as editor of Bullock's *Hand and Heart* before publishing his own rival magazine in 1888.[44] Though both editors defended Church Establishment and Anglican schools to the hilt, Bullock's major cause was evangelicalism, while Sherlock supported moderate church ritual while also campaigning to improve clergy finances and the status of the laity, these last concerns probably accounting for the meteoric rise of his inset during the 1890s.

Only three years after the publication of the first number of *The Church Monthly*, Sherlock took substantial advertising space in a variety of periodicals, secular and religious, to announce the results of a survey, carried out by the *London Diocesan Magazine*, showing that in London his inset had outstripped its rivals.[45] But Sherlock was not alone in trumpeting his editorial success: at different times, *Dawn of Day, Home Words* and *The Sign* each announced that they were the most popular inset. When the incidence of major inset titles in the three studied localities is aggregated in five-year periods from 1871 to 1919 (Figure 3.5), it becomes clear that Bullock and Sherlock were accurate in considering their magazines to be market leaders; *Dawn of Day* was an obvious third choice, while *Parish Magazine*, which ceased production in 1895, and *The Sign*, which was a late starter in 1905, featured less often in the records. But when the incidence of the most popular insets is charted over time, the speedy rise of *The Church Monthly* from 1888 is mirrored by its equally swift fall from grace from about 1904, along with *Home Words* and *Dawn of Day*, though sales of *Home Words* began to recover after the Great War (Figure 3.6). Early in 1911, Sherlock's offer to sell *The Church Monthly* to

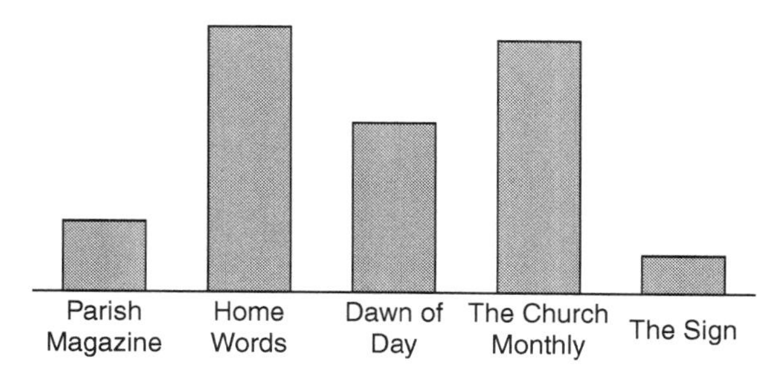

Figure 3.5 Popular Anglican Insets aggregated over five-year periods, from total number of Insets in Carlisle, Oxford and the Metropolitan Archives (1859–1919)

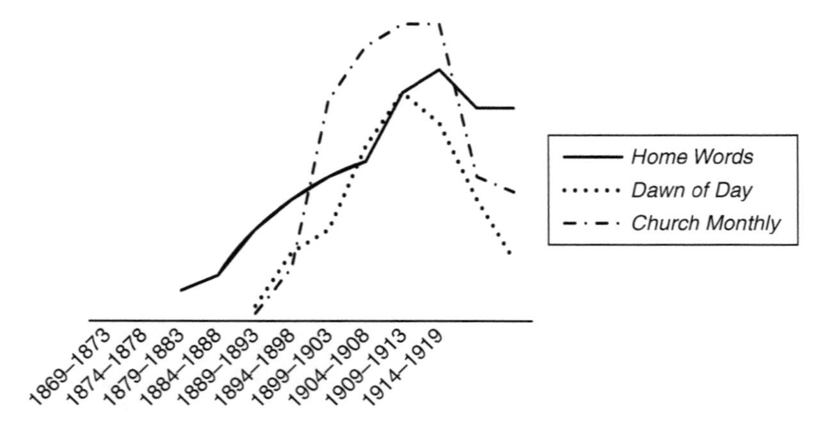

Figure 3.6 The three major Anglican Inset titles in all three localities (1869–1919)

Mowbray's was rejected, investigation having revealed that *The Church Monthly* had incurred substantial losses.[46] Months later, Sherlock was sued by his paper supplier over unpaid bills.[47] Sherlock died in 1914, his magazine having been taken over by the Churchman Publishing Company circa 1912.[48] *The Church Monthly* eventually merged with *Home Words* in 1947.[49]

During the period 1859–1919, individual localities had pronounced inset preferences which may be traced to their clergy's adherence to church parties. Oxford's Tractarian background is well known. Being home to Mowbray's might infer its clergy's preference for this publisher's first inset, *The Gospeller* or (after 1905) *The Sign*, but the diocese's popular choice of the 'high and dry' *Dawn of Day* reveals that during the period 1869–1919, high-church Anglicans were not necessarily Anglo-Catholics (Figure 3.7). According to its apologist, Arthur Downer, evangelicalism persisted strongly in seven Oxford city churches.[50] The four with deposits in the Oxford History Centre all took *Home Words*; the rector of a fifth, St Aldate's, was counted a subscriber by Charles Bullock.

Carlisle had been one of the first Anglican dioceses to accept an evangelical dean, Isaac Milner, in 1792.[51] Evangelical influence intensified under Bishop Samuel Waldegrave (1860–1869)[52] and was reinforced by the notorious Francis Close (dean of Carlisle 1856–1881), who once said of Cardinal Newman that he would not trust him with his purse.[53] As the prevalence of Bullock insets in Figure 3.8 illustrates, evangelicalism pervaded the diocese. Analysis of the inset choice of 64 parishes in

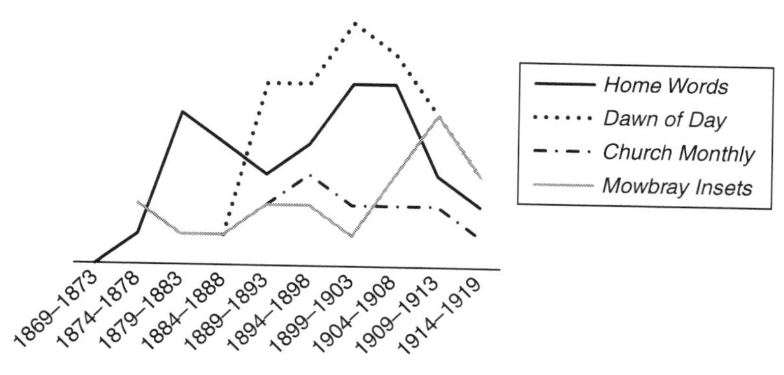

Figure 3.7 Popular Anglican Insets in Oxford Diocese (1869–1919)

Carlisle diocese reveals that lay patrons of livings had no effect on inset choice, but where the liberal-minded, moderate Ritualist, Bishop Harvey Goodwin (bishop 1869–1891) was patron, 90 per cent took *The Church Monthly* after 1888, suggesting his influence and that of his successor, John Wareing Bardsley, who, though at heart a moderate evangelical, was determined not to be linked to a particular church party.[54]

Ritualists and evangelicals continued to oppose each other in Carlisle diocese until well after the Great War. *The Sign* and its doctrinal opposite, *The Church Standard* (published alongside *Home Words* by the Bullock family), appear in local records around 1910, at the end of a troubled decade in which John Kensit, leader of the Protestant Truth Society, led Protestant marches in cities around the country, including Carlisle.[55] Anti-Catholic passions ran high during Kensit's crusades, and he was killed in Liverpool when a boy threw an iron bar that struck his head.[56] As revealed in Figure 3.8, while many parishes took the officially backed *Church Monthly*, there were strong evangelical influences at work in Carlisle diocese.[57]

The combined strength of Anglo-Catholic insets *Goodwill, the Gospeller, The Sign* and *Ecclesia* in London (Figure 3.9) is indicative of the popularity of Anglo-Catholicism in the capital. The presence of *Goodwill* (1894–1910) is symptomatic of the determination of many Ritualist clergy to engage with social problems. Brainchild of clergyman James Adderley, it supported politically active Christian Socialism in the 1880s and 1890s, spearheaded by the Guild of St Matthew, led by Stewart Headlam.[58] As in Carlisle, however, *The Church Monthly* appears to have triumphed in London for about 20 years after its advent in 1888, before falling away.

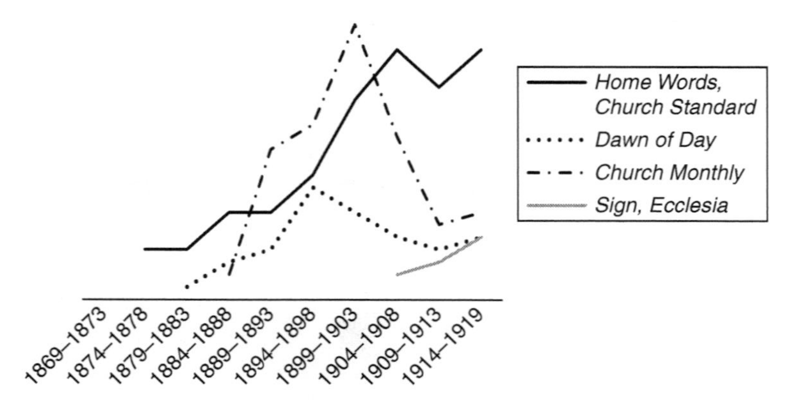

Figure 3.8 Popular Anglican Insets in Carlisle Diocese (1869–1919)

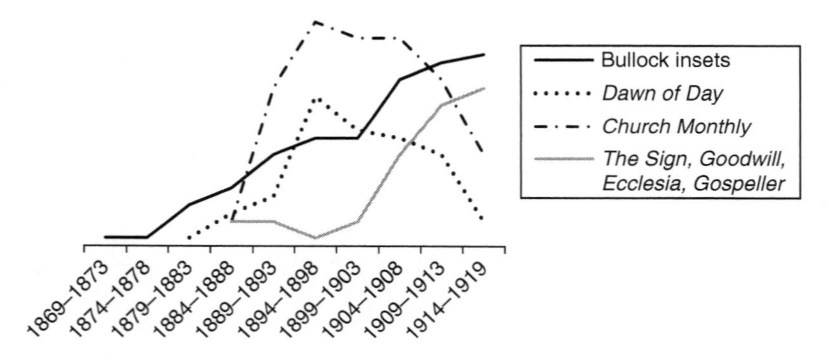

Figure 3.9 Popular Anglican Insets in the Metropolitan Archives (1869–1919)

The Church Monthly's editorial insistence on lay support for a beleaguered clergy was fed by the spectre of disestablishment,[59] but the solid popularity of evangelical and high-church insets in the three localities up to 1919 demonstrates the overriding significance of church party allegiance and a concomitant attraction to, or fear of, Catholic practices as partial determinants of the insets' success. At the end of the Great War, insets traditionally representing diametrically opposed church-party views, *Home Words* and *The Sign,* survived neck and neck into a new era. In 2009 they became one, but only one title was to endure: *The Sign.*

Having taken note of inset popularity, many dioceses began to publish their own diocesan and ruridecanal magazines. *Carlisle Diocesan Magazine* began publication in 1890, its aim to bring 'perfect unity' by drawing the Church closer to the far-flung inhabitants of the diocese.[60] Priced at a penny, it provided an alternative to the commercial insets. Listings in Mitchell's *Press Guide* reveal that 75 per cent of English dioceses published their own diocesan magazine by 1922.[61] Those parishes which could not afford their own magazine often joined with others, as evidenced by the growth of the ruridecanal magazine which often maintained the practice of including a commercial inset. In Oxfordshire, Abingdon ruridecanal magazine served 17 parishes by 1914, while, by 1924, four rural deaneries in Carlisle diocese had gradually combined to publish a magazine serving 47 parishes, many of them tiny.[62] The small village of Raughton Head near Carlisle sold about 110 localised magazines monthly in 1903, but this number was thought too low, and the work involved too wearisome. The incumbent's final letter introducing the new ruridecanal magazine presages the parochial changes of the twentieth century:

> With this number we complete the second year of our Parochial Magazine... But, as in most country places, the circulation is too limited to defray the expenses of it, and so I have welcomed a proposal which has lately been made... Several Vicars in the two rural deaneries of N. and S. Carlisle are combining to bring out a magazine with a page or so of local matter for each parish, and I am joining with them. This will have the double advantage of enabling us to halve the price of the magazine (which will be 1d monthly) and of getting news of our neighbours for nothing! It will be a new illustration of the old saying, 'Union is strength'.[63]

'Can anyone tell us how to make a magazine pay?'

Clearly it was difficult to make parish magazines pay their way. Though Keith Snell suggests that 'money-making seems to have been secondary' to the religious and social purposes of inset publishers, the practices of Charles Bullock and Frederick Sherlock demonstrate that insets were thoroughly commercial undertakings whose publishers, while promoting their particular vision of Anglicanism, were also in business to make a profit.[64] But even though financial inducements, such as a month's free trial, extra copies with the first order or a half-price grant, were regularly offered to parish clergy,[65] the majority of parishes made a loss on localised parish magazines. Until the 1880s the retail price was usually a penny, as religious magazines sought to match the price of cheap 'pernicious' alternatives.[66] As late as the mid-twentieth century, writers of parish magazine manuals claimed that the problems of magazine finance heaped anxiety upon parish incumbents, for it was the clergy who bore the brunt of first finding purchasers and then encouraging them to pay their pennies, this aspect of the parish magazine business having been adroitly delegated to the parishes by the publishers.[67] The only means by which the Lakeland village of Witherslack could afford its own inset was through the patronage of the local estate owner. 'The winter of my discontent has been turned into glorious summer', wrote the vicar in 1907, 'since a promise has been given me by our generous parishioner and friend, Lady Derby, that the financial deficit on the magazine shall be met and wiped off.'[68]

The parish magazine became a useful medium in which to publish the accounts of parish societies. Keith Snell admires the 'community-enhancing' nature of the collection of these small sums of money, though 'magazine committee' accounts often make dismal reading.[69] The Gosforth, Cumbria, 'Magazine and Almanack Account' of 1897 was in a happier state than most because it had a made a small profit the year before, had given away its parish almanacks free, and most subscribers had paid.[70] Carriage costs were considerable, but a parishioner had donated £1 so that the eventual loss to the rector was 14/11d. This would be paid out of his Easter offering or his stipend at a time when the incomes of parish clergy were widely dissimilar and could be comparatively low. One of the rector's Lake District colleagues existed on an income of just £110 a year, this low stipend not unusual and known generally as a 'starvation' living.[71] The Saint Andrew's, Headington, Oxford, parish magazine accounts for 1880 (Figure 3.10) show a similar picture to Gosforth's. There was no advertising to offset costs, and, despite a profit in 1879, there was no balance to carry forward to the following year. The rector stood the shortfall of 10 per cent of the total outlay. As in Gosforth, the almanack was free. Even priced at the high price of 2d, the magazine could not always pay its way.[72] By the 1880s, larger parishes had introduced advertising, and it was then possible to make the profit desired by so many incumbents to augment parish charities.[73]

Parish magazine local pages were often printed by local publishers, but some inset publishers printed the local pages at additional cost.[74] Publishers' inset and localising prices are necessary to the understanding of rates charged, but there are very few extant records.[75] The SPCK provides the best available information on inset finance, through tract committee minutes and the society's annual report.[76] While *Home Words*, with its coloured headlines and copious illustration, was considered an expensive option,[77] *Dawn of Day*, with its unrivalled access to the SPCK's

Received			
Parish Magazine Account	£	s	d
Balance in hand from 1879		13	8
Magazines sold through District Visitors	11	1	0
Annual subs of 2s each	6	9	0
Magazines sold at the post office		12	4
Sale of old magazines		1	6
From Rev C. P. Longland	2	17	6
Due to the treasurer		2	2
	21	18	0
Expended			
Parish Magazine account	£	s	d
To W.R. Bowden for 216 monthly copies	20	8	0
250 copies of parish almanack	1	10	0
	21	18	0

Figure 3.10 Saint Andrew, Headington, Parish Magazine Accounts (1880)

back catalogue, was proud to claim that it was one of the cheapest insets, *The Sign*'s directors regarding it as their main competitor in terms of price.[78] *Dawn of Day*'s wholesale price structure, then, represents one of the lowest available.

In its first year, the wholesale cost of one copy of *Dawn of Day* without localisation was ½d, post-free, but localisation by the SPCK added significantly to the cost: for 250 copies, the charge was 12/6 extra; for 500 copies, an extra 15/-. In 1884, postage costs were added, and a sliding scale of prices for bulk-buying, dependent on the number of pages localised – two, three or four – was introduced. Smaller parishes clearly found it difficult to sell large numbers of copies: in 1888 the lowest number of localised copies permitted was reduced to 50. Figure 3.11 reproduces the unit cost for buying the inset containing two pages of local news from 1878 to 1888. The SPCK discontinued printing localised material in 1889, the unembellished *Dawn of Day* sent to the parishes at the cost of 2/9d per 100 (three per penny). Parishes unwilling to print their own pages could employ the Beverley firm of Wright and Hoggard (The Minster Press), specialists in the printing of localised content.[79]

The SPCK's sliding scale undoubtedly helped large parishes which for 1,000 magazines paid just over ½d per magazine. Saint Anne's,

Dawn of Day Unit Prices (d.)	1878	1886	1888
Unit price 100 no localising	0.5	0.33	0.33
Combined inset and localising 50, title only			0.9
Combined inset and localising 100, 2 pages		1.98	1.98
Combined inset and localising 250, 2 pages	0.7	1.01	1.01
Combined inset and localising 500, 2 pages	0.86	0.79	0.79
Combined inset and localising 1,000, 2 pages		0.65	0.65

Figure 3.11 *Dawn of Day* Unit Prices (1878, 1886, 1888)

Wandsworth, sold 1,000 copies per month in 1918,[80] but this must have been unusual before 1900, for in 1883 Charles Bullock made space in *Home Words* to announce that 900 copies per month were sold in Leyton, East London.[81] Large villages like Headington might have ordered 250 copies at just over 1d each (Figure 3.10 shows that the parish sold 216 copies per month in 1880), but small villages, which might sell fewer than 100 copies per month, were charged almost 2d each. If the magazines were to be sold at 1d, then all but the largest urban parishes would have lost money without some kind of aid package in the form of fundraising, advertising or generous subscription. From 1889, the relatively modest cost of 2/9d per 100 from the SPCK would have been considerably increased by the cost of localisation elsewhere.

In 1910, under pressure from his parishioners, the rector of the Cumbrian parish of Caldbeck reluctantly agreed to publish a magazine. Though the religious oversight of the population of Caldbeck's 180 inhabited dwellings was shared by his church, a Quaker meeting and two Methodist chapels, the rector took 100 insets, raising the number to 170 in 1912.[82] He fretted annually over how to make his magazine pay its way, but it prospered, partly because, as will be explored in Chapter 9, he encouraged local people to take ownership of it through contributing articles, advertising within its pages and organising its distribution. In 1914, *Home Words* explicitly recommended that lay helpers should run their parish magazine because only those with 'a good head for business' would have the necessary time and expertise to make it a financial success. The writer advised on advertisement charges: '£2.10s to £12 a year according to the class of parish'. The editors were to show the magazine to local traders, reminding them that for a circulation of 500:

> For £1 a year the advertiser gets 6,000 advertisements. This impresses him; and then you point out that a Church Magazine does not (like a newspaper) get cast aside next day, but lies on the table and is turned to and consulted for a whole month.

In this way 'drapers, grocers, clothiers and cycle makers... printers and music-sellers' would become the parish magazine's 'best customers' and enable it to 'make a profit of up to £40' a year.[83]

Advertising

The necessary commercial exchange which occurred as editors of insets and local pages turned to advertising to avoid financial loss turned parish magazine readers into potential consumers of commercially produced goods. As George Kitson Clark observed in 1950, English religion 'has always had a tendency to be practical', and it was this practicality which opened the door to materialism.[84] Illustrated advertisements, beginning with Bibles and religious books and then patent remedies, were included in *Dawn of Day* from 1888, when the placing of advertisements in religious magazines such as the *British Weekly* had become commonplace.[85] The same period saw the rise of the advertising agency, which enabled the business of advertising to be assigned to experts who would deliver results.[86] Inset advertising was as competitive as any other. In 1907, two years after the launch of *The Sign*, disappointed in its advertising revenue, Mowbray's dismissed its advertising manager and engaged Walter Freeman, owner of an advertising agency in Fleet Street, to improve performance, on commission of 17½ per cent of cash received for all advertising orders.[87]

According to Lori Anne Loeb's study of Victorian advertising, patent medicine advertisers targeted the religious press particularly. In 1890, for example, such remedies comprised 39 per cent of the advertisements in *Christian Age*, but only 5 per cent in *The Lady*.[88] By 1896, almost half of *Dawn of Day's* advertising was for health-promoting products such as cocoa, invalid food and medicines, religious publications comprising most of the rest.[89] Loeb speculates that, to the advertiser, the very process of 'deliverance' from disease through use of these products exhibited a pleasing parallel with evangelical theology to help boost sales.[90] This conjecture is completely borne out in inset advertising, the otherwise highly serious *Sign* in 1906, for example, containing a 'martyr' to constipation who was cured by taking Seigal's Syrup, and 'a direct act of Providence' which allowed a doctor to save his own life by eating Grape-Nuts.[91]

In common with secular magazines, advertising in parish-magazine local pages often focussed on women's bodies, so that images of the wasp-waists of willowy girls riding bicycles, and of woollen underwear leaving little to the imagination (Figure 3.12), jostled for space with the vicar's 'letter' and articles tendering moral advice.[92] The contradictions involved in comparing the clergy's constant recommendation of 'self-sacrifice' with the hedonism of advertisements such as those for ladies' corsets in the parish magazine of Saint John Upper Holloway, which assured their wearers of 'a new pleasure in life', may have been confusing.[93] Similarly, in 1901, Teddington parishioners were advised on one page of their magazine to keep their minds 'detached from the power of the world', while on the next page they were reminded of the financial benefits of local advertising.[94]

Local advertisers in Penrith adopted a self-consciously religious narrative. Those who bought bicycles were 'the chosen people'; buyers of shoes were offered 'a word of advice'; mineral water offered 'extreme purity'; and a house containing a hot-water boiler was 'paradise assured'.[95] Such advertising suggests, on the one hand, as David Nash has argued, that religious discourse was intrinsic to the way ordinary people expressed themselves,[96] their common religious and educational heritage making strong connections with their parish church. But, on the other hand, it suggests that parish magazine readers were already seasoned religious consumers. Inheritors of 'an age of divided opinion', their intellectual lives were 'as competitive as that of business', their viewing of religious text adjacent to or combined with advertisements for underwear, bicycles or hot-water boilers reinforcing the perception that Anglican religious affiliation was just one option in a world of expanding choice.[97] Sarah Flew has advanced a similar argument, remarking of the Church's fundraising schemes that the 'economic exchange of goods' involved in bazaars and entertainments 'made the Church simply one product amongst many'.[98] Yet, as Keith Snell remarks, such local community activity may have bound Anglicans 'in a common sense of purpose' which helped tie the geographical parish to the Anglican church at its centre, thus reducing the dangers to the Church engendered by both nonconformism and apathy.[99]

Parish clergy who were hostile to magazine advertisement found themselves at a disadvantage, especially in poor urban parishes, such difficulties revealing themselves particularly clearly in the magazine history of Saint Augustine's, Haggerston. Saint Augustine's was an Anglo-Catholic 'slum' parish, memorably described by Charles Booth as part of a 'crescendo of ritualistic and Romish practices'.[100] In January

Figure 3.12 'The Fashion in Woollens': *Penrith Deanery Magazine* (August 1910)

1887, the vicar wrote that he had decided to take *Dawn of Day* because of its 'sound Church teaching', but also 'to confess the truth, because it is cheap as well as good'. He looked forward to this with both hope and fear: 'Parish magazines are not as a rule a financial success, but they may be and often are carried on without serious loss.' His anonymous magazine editor was more sanguine, expecting the circulation to be 'splendid'. The cost to parishioners was to be 1½d a month, rather more, in 1887, than the usual 1d, a possibly unwise move in such a poor parish. In January, 500 copies of *Dawn of Day* were ordered. In April the editor complained that many of the February and March numbers

Saint Augustine, Haggerston	Sales to nearest £	Loss to nearest £
1888	8	3
1891	7	5
1893	6	6
1894	5	8
1896	4	9
1897	4	11
1900	3	10
1904	2	10

Figure 3.13 Saint Augustine Haggerston Magazine Sales (1888–1904)
Source: London Metropolitan Archives, P91/AUG/25-6

had not been sold. The extracts from the annual magazine accounts for 1888 to 1904 seen in Figure 3.13 tell their own story. The editor had been so keen to make the magazine a success. 'Can anyone tell us how to make a parish magazine pay?' he asked. The answer would have been obvious in Penrith and Kennington, but the editor was totally opposed to advertising: the magazine was not a 'tram car or an omnibus' to have advertisements plastered all over it.[101] The magazine closed in 1905. Anglo-Catholic clergy may have brought colour and ceremony to the East End, but many of their poorer parishioners, as Sarah Williams and Jeffrey Cox have argued, did not necessarily wish to attend Church or, it seems, to belong to Saint Augustine's wider community by paying for a parish magazine.[102]

Conclusion

Despite their failure in some poor urban parishes, parish magazines, together with their insets, grew in popularity during the second half of the nineteenth century along with religious publications generally, reaching their peak circulation around 1904, even though religion's share in the periodicals market had by then been cut by half. Parish clergy generally chose their inset on the basis of its church party allegiance. The popularity of Anglican ritualism led to a proliferation of high-church insets, but competition between them allowed the evangelical *Home Words* to emerge as market leader of the genre. The urge to encourage lay support of the clergy led to the temporary popularity of *The Church Monthly,* but its moderate stance eventually failed to make its mark, leaving the field to its more extreme rivals. Entrepreneurship was a key factor in any parish magazine's success, Charles Bullock demonstrating a thoroughly commercial flair, both for advertising and for publishing populist illustrated articles in an attractive format. Competition among inset editors was rife, and methods to overcome rivals were aggressive.

4
Editors, Writers and Church Parties, 1871–1918

This chapter contrasts religious content in *Home Words* and *The Sign* to explore these magazines' depth of allegiance to church parties. Despite their partisan nature, most insets aimed to allow few ripples of controversy (the stock-in-trade of Church newspapers like the *Record*) to disturb the calm pool of their Anglican vision for cottage folk. Consequently, the casual reader, glancing through his inset's conventional content of stories, sermons and advice, would imagine that its particular brand of Anglicanism was universally adopted. *Home Words*, conscious of its position as market leader, was careful to tread this path, its formerly overt evangelicalism fading away over time as Anglo-Catholicism became more popular. Such popularity enabled *The Sign* to be open in its pronouncements. Its masthead avowed that it was 'not ashamed to confess the faith of Christ crucified', and it did so stridently, according to its particular party view. Meanwhile, in parish-magazine local pages, the church-party debate could provoke openly expressed strife.

Evangelicalism in *Home Words*, 1871–1918

Charles Bullock's writing always expounded the conversionism, activism, biblicism and crucicentrism central to evangelicalism.[1] Bullock provided a platform for the Church Missionary Society, promoted the views of temperance reformers, encouraged charitable giving and lionised well-known evangelicals such as J. C. Ryle, E. H. Bickersteth and Lord Shaftesbury throughout his editorial career. Contributors who expounded evangelical theology in such series as 'Lessons from the Book' were supported by fiction writers in stories which brought sinners to God through repentance.[2] During the 1870s, the popular poet and hymn writer, Frances Ridley Havergal, was a typical contributor.[3] Bullock had been her father's curate, their warm relationship resulting in the inclusion of her poems and prose articles from *Home Words'* first year (1871) until long after her death in 1879.[4] Havergal's verse proclaimed the evangelical conversionism and crucicentrism at the heart of their shared faith:

> 'Forgiven until now!' For Jesus died
> To take our sins away;
> His blood *was* shed, and still the infinite tide
> Flows full and deep today.[5]

Home Words' link with the evangelical tract is exemplified in an article of 1876 which described Queen Victoria's visit to the grave of Legh Richmond's *Dairyman's Daughter.*[6] The dairyman's daughter's evangelical 'good' death was paralleled by Havergal's own, as described by Charles Bullock in August, 1879.[7] Her final words, 'Thou hast died for sinners, therefore Lord for me... It is all over – blessed rest', were recounted to demonstrate not only the presence of her Saviour but also the rightness of the evangelical theology which had been the bedrock of her life: 'The Atonement was the sole ground and the constant ground of her confidence'.[8]

Born in 1829, one of the six children of a grocer, Charles Bullock entered the Church through school-teaching and St Bees Anglican theological college.[9] St Bees, on the Cumberland coast, was founded for those who could not afford to gain Oxbridge degrees at a time when church and clergy numbers were expanding.[10] The diary of one of its alumni, Joseph Brunskill, is tinged with the shame of being obliged to attend such a low establishment, graced in the 1840s by the sons of farmers and tradesmen.[11] It is therefore unsurprising that some of Bullock's regular contributors were men with similar backgrounds and views, such as George Everard (1828–1901), one of his closest friends and a contributor to *Home Words* from 1872 to 1893.[12] Like Bullock, Everard combined evangelical commitment with a passion for writing, producing hundreds of tracts over the course of a long life.[13] According to the evangelical discourse of his daughter, he was 'saved' as the result of a Damascus-Road experience in the streets of Manchester. Praying for God's forgiveness, he dedicated himself to His service by training for the Anglican ministry.[14] As Kenneth Hylson-Smith has suggested, evangelicals were not sophisticated theologians; biblical revelation and personal access to God for His atoning forgiveness and salvation were simple tenets which translated well into parochial preaching, tracts and magazine articles.[15] Everard set forth the evangelical position in simple terms he thought Bullock's readers could understand, using homely analogies to explain evangelical teaching on the infallibility of the Bible, justification by faith and the work of the Holy Spirit.[16] Moreover, having lost four children himself, he knew how to offer comforting words to those who grieved.[17]

While Everard was a professional writer, it was the parish clergyman who dabbled in authorship who provided much of *Home Words'* religious copy; men such as William Odom (1846–1933). Like Bullock, his background was undistinguished: son of a cooper, he initially worked as a bank clerk.[18] Like Bullock, he attended St Bees, returning as curate to the evangelical Sheffield church which had nurtured him. A correspondent for the (evangelical) *Record* for nearly half a century, he entered into contentious correspondence in a variety of newspapers, wrote historical biographies and theological works, contributed to *Home Words* and other Bullock publications, and took *Home Words* in his Sheffield parishes for 40 years.[19] In his *Fifty Years of Sheffield Church Life, 1866–1916,* he recalled extended visits to Charles Bullock's Eastbourne home, where his 'revered and much-valued friend' introduced him to other *Home Words* contributors.[20] He was featured (Figure 4.1, bottom left) in Bullock's monthly 'Portrait Gallery' of evangelical clergymen in 1884, and his books were recommended 'as the best antidote to the mass of unhealthy and poisonous publications now issuing from the press' in *Home Words'* Christmas supplement in 1893.[21] Odom regarded himself as a complete amateur as an author, but he was proud of his achievements, manifested in a row of volumes on his study shelves. When asked how he was able to combine writing with running a busy parish he replied that he had done it 'by using up odd minutes'. His pen had been his recreation and his hobby and he had honed his skill by writing his own parish magazine.[22]

Home Words occasionally contained contributions from evangelical luminaries such as Edward Hoare (1812–1894), vicar of Tunbridge Wells.[23] Nephew of Elizabeth Fry and associated with the Clapham Sect, he had preached at the funeral of the architect of Anglican evangelicalism, Charles Simeon, and had fought for the cause at the Church Congress. At the time of his death, however, he was widely regarded as one of the last links with an earlier age,[24] for, by then, evangelicals were losing their rearguard action against the popularity of ritualism. Kenneth Hylson-Smith refers to the 'dispirited' years of the fin-de-siècle, in which the once-important players had become old, few young men of calibre replacing them.[25] Thus, at the turn of the century, a younger family

Figure 4.1 Reverend Odom: *Home Words* (1884) 231

member, Edward Newenham Hoare, was a frequent contributor of fiction and prose articles to *The Church Monthly* and *Dawn of Day*, a course of action unthinkable in Hoare senior.[26] Similarly, Bullock's reporter at the 1893 Church Congress mused that though Canon Wilkinson, the aged rector of Birmingham, was 'a true son of the Reformation; a faithful representative of the Scriptural Church of England', and thus an icon of everything *Home Words* held dear, his principles were no longer pleasing to everyone. His age was passing: 'take him for all in all, we shall not look upon his like again'.[27]

As James Whisenant's research has demonstrated, the evangelical party was in disarray from the mid-1870s, as moderate evangelicals moved to accommodate popular ritualistic innovation.[28] Bullock's editorial stance appears to have been rather less than moderate, observed in advertisements for anti-Ritualist literature and a series of attacks on ritualism contributed by J. C. Ryle, provoked by events surrounding the Public Worship Regulation Act in 1874.[29] Even when evangelical bishops moved in a moderate direction, Bullock continued to refer to them in wholly evangelical terms. In 1880, on becoming bishop of Liverpool, Ryle openly espoused moderate evangelicalism, but *Home Words*' response was to continue to praise him fulsomely as a fine follower of the early evangelicals.[30] Bullock's conservative evangelicalism was driven by fear of Anglo-Catholicism's Romeward movement, his anti-Catholic sentiment appearing within articles purporting to teach Church history. A typical narrative involved the character assassination of 'the Romanising' Saint Wilfred, who 'trampled underfoot' all his enemies, one of his dying commands to request 'the sheet in which his dying body was clothed, still moist with his last sweat, to be sent to the abbess, Cyndreda: 'his devoted friend'.

> Such was the man who mainly aided in this rapidly corrupting age in the introduction of the absurd claim of Rome to that ecclesiastical supremacy in England which has ever been so disastrous in its consequence, and so utterly subversive of civil and religious liberty.[31]

Such allusions disappeared after Bullock's retirement in 1902. By then evangelical contributions had become far more restrained. Not only were they intellectually undemanding but they were also theologically anodyne, supporting Adrian Hastings's judgement that turn-of-the-century Protestantism had become 'moribund'.[32] As Anglo-Catholic worship grew ever more fashionable among the laity as well as the clergy, *Home Words* developed into a moderate, low-church magazine, intended to appeal to all types of reader without provoking offence. It remained the best-selling inset well into the twentieth century, not only because it was so bland, but perhaps also because it was the only inset which, to quote Hastings, 'an abandoned majority' of Protestant Anglicans could wistfully regard as their own.[33]

'A Sweet, Saintly, Christian Business'? A. R. Mowbray and *The Sign*

Home Words' increasingly moderate church-party position would have been unacceptable at *The Sign*. Anglo-Catholic insets were far more strident in their party allegiance, the growing confidence of Ritualists nationally allowing such insets to exhibit party spirit openly and, on occasion, aggressively. John Shelton Reed's analysis of the growth of ritualism, *Glorious Battle*, accentuates the belligerence with which some Anglo-Catholics approached Christian practice, his chapter on London's Ritualist slum priests, 'Ritualism Rampant', describing their adoption of a 'fighting' faith from the mid-1860s.[34] Though, as noted in Chapter 3, *The Sign*'s directors demonstrated a similar commercialism to that of Charles Bullock in their determination to out-sell *Dawn of Day*, *The Sign*'s publisher, Mowbray's, is chiefly remembered for its high-church piety, its Oxford shop the probable model for Sue Brideshead's workplace in Thomas Hardy's *Jude the Obscure*:

> It contained Anglican books, stationery, texts, and fancy goods: little plaster angels on brackets, Gothic-framed pictures of saints, ebony crosses that were almost crucifixes, prayer-books that were almost missals. He felt very shy of looking at the girl in the desk... Before her lay a piece of zinc, cut to the shape of a scroll three or four feet long, and coated with dead-surface paint on one side. Hereon she was designing or illuminating, in characters of Church text, the single word, A L L E L U J A. 'A sweet, saintly, Christian business, hers!' thought he.[35]

This 'sweet, saintly Christian business' was the product of Tractarianism, as evinced in Alfred Mowbray's book of illustrations, *The Deformation and the Reformation,* published in 1868, which sought both to denigrate low-church evangelicalism and to encourage church ornament and ritual. An article in *The Stationer, Printer and Fancy Trades Register* in November 1896 attributed Mowbray's success to the fact that all employees were 'ardent church workers'. The eminent Anglo-Catholic, Percy Dearmer, was employed as the firm's literary adviser from 1909.[36] One of the leaders of the English Catholic or 'English-Prayer-Book' movement, as distinct from ultramontane alternatives, he popularised the notion that the English Church had from earliest times enjoyed its own style of worship.[37] His influential *Parson's Handbook,* which aimed to guide clergy through the ritualising minefield, was first published in 1899; Mowbray's published his *Is Ritualism Right?* in 1903.[38] It was Mowbray's women, however, who arguably contributed most to *The Sign*'s success. After Alfred Mowbray died in 1875, his widow and daughters continued to run the business, which included Mowbray's first inset, *The Gospeller*. Encouraged by the growth of the market they decided to publish a new 'first-class' inset, edited by a professional journalist, Edwin Judges, who was appointed from the *Surrey Comet* in 1903 to combine inset editorship with chairmanship of the firm. He was soon approached by Gertrude Blackburne (born c. 1862), a London writer and journalist, who was appointed *The Sign*'s deputy-editor, a position she held for 46 years.[39] Blackburne's name did not appear within the magazine, though she may have been 'Heartsease', who advised on Bible reading,[40] and it is possible that hers were the opinions expressed in the answers given to correspondents, a contemporary phenomenon in which, as Margaret Beetham discovered, 'a game of hide and seek' was frequently played around gendered editorship of periodicals.[41]

Blackburne gave *The Sign* its name, having attended a ceremony in Milan during Holy Week when the unveiling of the Cross had been greeted with repeated cries of 'Il Signo!'[42] An inset's ideology was generally expressed through its title: while *Home Words* emphasised biblical preaching (*words*), and *The Church Monthly*'s articles were characterised by an emphasis on clerical and lay involvement in parish affairs (*church*), worship and ritual were stressed by *The Sign*, the references both visual and textual. *The Sign*'s pseudo-medieval printing (Figure 4.2), and the contents of its articles, while unequivocally Anglo-Catholic, were so in Percy Dearmer's very specific sense. In June 1906, for instance, Saint Paul's, Knightsbridge, was described as an 'English Prayer-Book Church'. Written after the Royal Commission on Ecclesiastical Discipline had poured oil on troubled waters by allowing bishops discretion in settling ritualistic disputes,[43] the article on Saint Paul's appeared to accept the Commission's rulings but made sure its readers understood that Saint Paul's ritualistic elements – altar-lights, vestments, incense – were 'sanctioned by the bishop ... after the Old English use ... we must obey the commandments of the Catholic Church'. This was an unambiguous signal that theirs was not only an ancient usage but also an English one, and therefore more legitimate.[44]

Figure 4.2 *The Sign*: Masthead (1905)

Paralleling the custom of secular magazines, *The Sign* published a correspondence page: 'The Why and the Wherefore', in which anonymous questions 'on the Church's services and customs, the furniture and ornaments of churches and kindred topics' could be put to the editor.[45] Some were general queries on churchgoing etiquette, but others were more pointed: 'Will you teach me where the Church of England teaches that our Lord is really present in the elements after consecration?' was asked in 1906, the same month that the pronouncements by the Royal Commission on Ecclesiastical Discipline had expressed the difficulties of interpreting the Real Presence:

> As to the mode of this Presence [the Church] affirms nothing, except that the Body of Christ is given, taken, and eaten in the Supper only after an heavenly and spiritual manner, and that the means whereby the Body of Christ is received and eaten is faith. Any Presence which is not to the soul of the faithful receiver the Church does not by her Articles and Formularies affirm, or require her ministers to accept.[46]

The final paragraph of *The Sign*'s reply was characteristically direct. 'When our Lord first gave the Holy Communion to His disciples, He said, "Take, eat; this is my Body..." It is needless to say that he meant what He said.'[47]

The Sign's approach to its correspondence may be contrasted with that of *The Church Monthly*, in which readers were requested to write to Frederick Sherlock with questions 'which are of interest to the majority of our readers'. The magazine's emphasis on the partnership between laity and clergy in church affairs allowed questions to be answered on churchwarden-ship, hymn tunes, parochial church councils, church property law and the Lay-Helpers' Association; questions of general interest included poetry, emigration, typewriting and pianos.[48] While readers of *The Sign* were expected to be Anglo-Catholic devotees, the editorial choice of their questions in *The Church Monthly* suggests that Sherlock was determined to encourage lay parochial involvement while recognising the secular world beyond the church gate.

Localities, church parties and inset choice

Whether the views of inset editors were read or not largely depended on the parish clergy who had the ultimate power of choice. This was consistently on church-party lines. Evangelical parishes tended to remain with *Home Words* for long periods. Saint Saviour's, Wandsworth, for instance, took the inset from 1871 to 1938,[49] and the parish of Lanercost, Cumbria, which first took *Home Words* in 1886, appears to have persisted with it until its merger with *The Sign* in 2009.[50] After 1878 there was a greater choice of high-church inset, from the conservative *Dawn of Day* to the ultramontane *Ecclesia,* though many folded quickly. The febrile nature of Anglo-Catholicism in London allowed almost half the sampled London parishes to change from one high-church inset to another. Over a period of 45 years Saint Columba, Haggerston, successively took *The Banner, New and Old for Seedtime and Harvest, The Gospeller, Goodwill, The Sign, Dawn of Day* and *Ecclesia*.[51] Though far more muted, the trend for constant change of inset among high-church parishes occurred in Oxford and Carlisle dioceses, particularly in Oxford city, where, from 1891 to 1918, Saint John, Cowley, became progressively more 'high' as it changed from *Dawn of Day* to *The Sign,* and then to *Ecclesia.* The Cowley priests quarrelled with *Dawn of Day* over advice given on the desirability of fasting before early morning communion. The inset's judgement was that it was lawful to eat a little breakfast, but the Cowley priests, appalled at this laxity, demanded an apology (which they did not receive) and adopted *The Sign* from its first month of publication.[52] Apparently, even *The Sign* was capable of theological error. In January 1914, Cowley's parish magazine announced that, because some of *The Sign*'s published answers to correspondents had been theologically unacceptable, there would be a change to *Ecclesia*.[53]

As Chapter 3 explored, insets might also be changed because of prohibitive costs, or change could be forced on a parish through the folding of a particular favourite: Mrs Sloan was obliged to read *The Church Monthly* after 1895, on the demise of *Parish Magazine*. Change might also occur after the arrival of a new incumbent with a church-party allegiance different from that of his predecessor. Frequently the change was to a high-church inset, an experience which occurred in the parish of Saint John, Keswick.

'Undiluted Popery' at Saint John's Church, Keswick

Morley Headlam became the incumbent of the evangelical parish of Saint John, Keswick, in 1906, remaining until the end of the Great War.[54] A keen Ritualist, Headlam first expelled women from Saint John's mixed 'cock and hen' choir, replacing them with surpliced male choristers.[55] Then he set about 'beautifying' the chancel and sanctuary and providing 'proper furnishing of the House of God'.[56] As church embellishment had become popular, it was not confined solely to Anglo-Catholics, but Keswick's evangelicals found the changes disquieting. Vicar and parishioners clashed at Headlam's first Easter Vestry. Some cavilled at the 'undiluted popery' of carrying palm leaves in the Palm Sunday procession; some were concerned at the vicar's wearing of vestments; yet others disliked his employment of 'false and unscriptural doctrines'. When Headlam's response was reported negatively in the local press, he deliberately kept back the parish magazine to take more time to answer his detractors.[57] Accordingly, its next three numbers emphasised the Church's catholicity.[58] Many readers were unimpressed, for there were dissentient voices when Headlam changed the church hymn-book from the evangelical *Hymnal Companion* to one preferred by Ritualists: *Hymns Ancient and Modern*.[59]

In accordance with the evangelical views of earlier incumbents, Saint John's choice of parish-magazine inset was *Home Words*.[60] After Headlam's arrival, the magazine was consistently delivered late, Headlam blaming first the railway system and then the Keswick Convention, the product of the evangelical holiness movement, held annually in Keswick, which, predictably, he disliked.[61] In 1909, while encountering his greatest problems with parishioners and local journalists, he carried out a coup. Announcing an examination of parish-magazine finances, 'on careful enquiry' he had discovered that the wholesale cost of *Home Words* was such that the Keswick printer of the local pages had been supporting the parish from his own pocket. The printer had suggested choosing a cheaper publication which, though it was only five years old, already had a circulation of 540,000 copies a month. It was called *The Sign* and had been recommended by the (Ritualist) *Guardian* church newspaper. 'So I propose to adopt his suggestions, and look forward with interest to the January number'.[62] While *The Sign*'s cost price was only ½d, *Home Words* cost at least twice as much, thus providing the ammunition needed to change to the inset of the vicar's choice.[63] The change was made with no further discussion, the parishioners of Saint John's encountering a very different magazine from that to which they were accustomed.

'Under New Management' at Saint Matthias, Stoke Newington

Incumbents did not necessarily edit the local pages of their parish magazines. Sometimes they remained as figureheads, while the editing was done by laymen supplying the requisite 'good head for business', symptomatic of growing encouragement of parishioners' involvement in the running of local church affairs.[64] A busy incumbent might encourage his curate to subedit the magazine with lay help. While this frequently resulted in what the rector of Caldbeck called 'a feeble catalogue of services and classes',[65] it could unwittingly reveal tensions in parish affairs which incumbents had ignored in order to maintain a pleasing fiction of unity. Though invocation of agreeable and pleasant community could clearly be advantageous, this desired unity of voice was capable of being breached, as in the case of the subeditor of Saint Matthias, Stoke Newington.

Saint Matthias was a Ritualist church, judged by Charles Booth's investigator to be 'useful and active', its population 'entirely working class' 'tending to squalor in many streets'.[66] According to the investigator's notes, the rector was pious, but feeble and lacking in influence, but the style of the anonymous editors of the magazine was more robust, as may be judged from their declaration in 1892 that 'the editors have consecrated their pens to the cause. What interest would their names have? They are ready to say with George Whitfield, "Let our names perish, if Christ's may but endure and be exalted"'. Though we cannot be sure, it is possible that the editors may have included one or more of the church's three curates, though a layman was also involved, the rector having formed an association of parish workers, divided into sub-committees, including a magazine committee.[67] The unnamed 'subeditor' appears to have been responsible for the correspondence pages. Correspondence was encouraged, much of it on ritualistic matters, as in *The Sign*, Saint Matthias having been one of the first Anglo-Catholic churches in London, the scene of anti-Tractarian rioting in the 1850s – a memory greatly celebrated by correspondents.[68]

A determinedly jolly tone permeated the magazine throughout 1892 and 1893, with much boyish teasing over parish sports-fixture results.[69] An editorial of August 1892 published letters from its admirers, one of whom remarked that while many parish magazines ultimately degenerated into notice-sheets, Saint Matthias's magazine's 'spirit of enthusiasm' was very refreshing. By July 1893 the magazine's circulation had reached a thousand and it had received a dazzling review in the *Guardian* newspaper.[70] Controversy appeared from mid-1894, when Frederick Verinder responded negatively to an article on 'the model parish' contributed by the rector.[71] Secretary of the Guild of St Matthew and author of at least 16 books on socialism,[72] Verinder personified the late-nineteenth-century alliance between socialism and Anglo-Catholicism.[73] Believing that cooperation in the parish and equality at the altar were insufficient, he asserted that the model parish would only become a reality when complete social equality had been achieved. Correspondence in the magazine became heated as controversy also arose over Welsh disestablishment, the more traditional members of the congregation supporting the majority of Church leaders who opposed it, while Anglo-Catholics urged disestablishment as a means of restoring the Church to its apostolic roots.[74]

Matters came to a head in April 1895 through acrimonious correspondence between socialist sympathisers and their opponents on the opinions expressed in Robert Blatchford's socialist polemic, *Merrie England*, published that year in a cheap edition.[75] Thomas Dixon contends that Blatchford was Britain's 'most widely read socialist propagandist', quoting the Labour politician, Manny Shinwell, who recollected that Blatchford's writings did more than any others of his generation to encourage socialism among the working class.[76] Though some East-End church activists became increasingly sympathetic to socialist ideas, in the 1890s they were still in the minority.[77] To air socialist opinions in such a conservative organ as the parish magazine was to wave a red rag at a bullish opposition, exciting much anger. The timing of the hostility was significant: Stewart Headlam publicly supported Oscar Wilde during his trial that spring, losing the Guild of St Matthew much support.[78] The subeditor was called to a meeting of the magazine committee, accused of 'grossly abusing his trust' and removed from his post. It was also announced that 'due to a severe indisposition', Frederick Verinder had been unable to contribute his promised paper on 'Church Reform', and that the following month the magazine would appear 'under new management'.[79]

Later numbers of the magazine were bland, their few printed letters no longer airing opinions likely to inflame readers. Like the majority of London parish magazines, contributions were confined to such unifying issues as the Church calendar and history, club reports, the hiring of domestic servants, and bazaars. Openly expressed controversy clearly upset the congregation, but to those outside its ranks it may have underlined why they disliked Anglicanism, adding to the underlying anti-clericalism in London's slum areas which led one of Charles Booth's investigators, Arthur Baxter, to remark in his notebook:

> Has not the average man who stands outside the churches some reason for thinking that the intemperance, the impurity, and the gambling against which ministers of religion are always thundering are no worse than the fighting, the lying, and the uncharitableness which fill so large a place in the daily lives of so many of these good people [inculcating the feeling that] 'we don't want nothing to do with no bloody parsons?'[80]

The tensions and anxieties played out at Saint Matthias during 1892–1895 were a product of religious commitment and social responsibility intensified by the experience of ministry in a London slum parish and exacerbated by a pronounced party spirit brought about by growing Anglo-Catholic confidence. Such strains produced an openly multi-vocal magazine which became a site of conflict and contradiction. As revealed in Keswick, other local magazine editors were unafraid to exhibit their church party allegiance with all its attendant difficulties, their contributions blatantly revealing the schism within Anglicanism. This behaviour excited a loss of respect among some of the laity and was determinedly avoided by Frederick Sherlock, who aimed to create a *beau ideal* of churchmanship, and Charles Bullock, who, though always informed by party spirit, attempted to increase sales by encouraging a wider readership than the dwindling number of evangelical devotees. But as ritualism became increasingly popular, and as inset choice was usually made by the clergy along church-party lines, Anglo-Catholic editors of insets and local parish pages appeared justified in their boundless confidence.

5
Manly Men and Chivalrous Heroes

Though Gertrude Blackburne was an important figure at Mowbray's until the early 1950s, she initially earned less than half the editor's salary.[1] She was also a completely anonymous figure within the pages of *The Sign*. Men and their concerns dominated Anglicanism during the long nineteenth century; women such as Blackburne were confined to a supportive role. This chapter investigates the Church's attitude to men and the attitude of men to the Church through the lens of local and inset parish-magazine contributions. It begins by establishing the number of male contributors to three of the major late-nineteenth-century insets, and then moves to investigate clergymen's efforts to encourage male church attendance, their concept of the manly man, and the enduring legacy of Charles Kingsley's Muscular Christianity. Clergymen's attempts to invoke manliness – both as a means of modifying the behaviour of male parishioners and of understanding their own conduct – are investigated through contrasting the insets' fictional clergymen with their real-life compatriots, the latter often positioning themselves as heroes or victims struggling in the face of adversity. The chapter finally describes how parish magazines supported the cause of British imperialism by invoking the chivalrous hero in religious, racial and personal-heroic narrative.

Male contributors

While male clergymen obviously dominated their magazines' local pages, most inset contributors were also male. During 1896, when the parish magazine's popularity was nearing its height, the number of named male contributors to *Home Words, Dawn of Day* and *The Church Monthly* averaged 83 per cent, similar to the results of Richard Altick's survey of British writers from 1800 to 1935, which discovered that 80 per cent were men.[2] Predictably, in 1896, three out of five named male inset contributors were clergymen, the same proportion continuing into the twentieth century in *The Church Monthly*, which always aimed to support the clergy's concerns.[3] But, just as Altick's survey noted a fall in clerical contribution to all periodicals, particularly after 1900, by 1907 only half the named male contributors to the populist *Home Words* were clergymen; their place was taken by laymen at a time when lay participation in Church affairs was growing, amid recognition that Anglicanism was slowly becoming a partnership of equals.[4] The participation of women inset writers also grew, as will be discussed in Chapter 6.

Males and churchgoing

In 1897, on arriving at Preston Patrick, Westmorland, the new vicar lost no time in equating manly behaviour with Christianity by informing his male parishioners that his aim was to change their nominal churchgoing by making them 'real manly followers of Jesus Christ'.[5] The expression of manliness through chivalrous behaviour was constantly urged by those in authority.[6] Mark Girouard has described chivalry as a code of gentlemanly conduct attempting to glue together all kinds of men in an unstable social world,[7] for, as Callum Brown has commented, the industrial revolution's rapid urbanisation process caused the social elites to judge rough male behaviour as a problem needing to be solved.[8]

Working-class males were the parish clergy's greatest problem: it was hard to entice them into church. Charles Booth made a characteristic assessment, on watching working-class Londoners on a Sunday:

> The river Lea on a fine Sunday morning is very animated. The river is crowded with boats, and the towing paths...are alive with people... public houses do a good trade. The Salvationists are there, unheeded; man and pipe and dog form a purely working-class picture.[9]

Callum Brown has concluded that where women attended church more, men usually attended more too, and, in a study of Yorkshire parish records, John Wolffe discovered clergymen who maintained that their work with men was as successful as with women.[10] The local pages of parish magazines support Wolffe's research by demonstrating that the clergy went to great lengths to attract men. Male bell-ringers were particularly encouraged,[11] and most parishes maintained a working-men's reading room or club, the Church attempting to ally itself with the ubiquitous male practice of smoking by instituting smoking concerts and socials. It was hoped that the 'clouds of smoke and hearty choruses' would encourage male involvement, though, as Jeffrey Cox has averred, the churches were 'at a ludicrous disadvantage' when competing with secular clubs, which sold beer.[12]

Young working-class boys were often sent to Sunday school, and those who could sing could be enticed to join the newly surpliced, male, church choirs by the fact that Anglican choristers were usually paid.[13] When their voices broke, however, they could be lost forever, as noted in this recollection of a northern childhood:

> My mother used to go [to church] regularly. She used to go to sewing classes and did a tremendous amount of work for them. My father never went. He used to be in the choir there and then when his voice broke of course they didn't want him and that finished him. He never went any more. He moved his connection altogether with the church.[14]

As with working-class men, working-class boys were often considered problematical. The 'naughty boy' problem arose frequently, the clergy at their wits' end over what to do.[15] 'Drat the boys!' screamed a headline in the magazine of Saint Matthias, Stoke Newington, after some undisclosed offence at the Boys' Club.[16] Over several decades the parish magazine of Headington Quarry, Oxford, agonised over boys' behaviour. They stole from the offertory box, damaged gravestones and terrorised the staff at the church school; the windows were broken so regularly that they were permanently boarded up.[17] Boyish violence could be appropriated by the Church for its own purposes, however, church-party antagonism resulting in boys taking a major part in demonstrations for and against ritualism.[18] Saint Augustine's, Haggerston, encountered the problem in 1895, correspondence to the parish magazine deploring the behaviour of ultra-Protestant youths who accosted the congregation after evensong, handing out pamphlets which they stated would provide a 'cure' for 'popery'.[19] When a 'gang of roughs' attacked the congregation of Saint Columba, Haggerston, some who had hitherto stood on the sidelines joined the Ritualist cause to defend the underdogs.[20] Oxford undergraduates were capable of unruly behaviour in defence of Anglo-Catholic practices, several young men waving their church flag while trespassing in the city's gardens in what one remembered as the 'happy days' of 1910.[21]

Yet, as Wolffe finally concurs, despite all that was done to involve them, there were fewer men than women in the pews: by 1911, Anglican women outnumbered Anglican men by more than 40,000.[22] Incumbents remarked upon the disparity regularly and forcibly in their monthly 'letter'.[23] In October 1903, the vicar of Witherslack was delighted when a visitor expressed pleased surprise at the number of male churchgoers,[24] but he had attended the harvest festival, a key event in the village's cultural calendar, which the local farmers, possibly from atavistic causes, attended en masse.[25] Booth discovered that even in London more people attended harvest festivals than any other service: at some churches it was 'a struggle to get in'.[26] Church services at Witherslack were usually dominated by females, the vicar remarking that men usually distinguished themselves by their non-attendance.[27] In 1907 he was perturbed enough to insert into his magazine a poem which began

> An angel stood within the church and sighed,
> For looking down the lofty aisles he cried:
> 'Are none but women here?' On life's hard way
> Have men no need of help? No need to pray?'[28]

Picturing the religious male

As Callum Brown has argued, the rise of evangelicalism caused men to be cast as potential sinners, while women became their saviours.[29] Inset articles addressed the inexorable results of male error: drunkenness, poverty and the break-up of the home, presenting cosy scenes of domestic happiness as the desired alternative (Figure 5.1). Such polarities had a long history in tract publishing, but men may have found them fundamentally objectionable, for, as Brown suggests, when expected to conform to behaviour pleasing to the 'angel of the house', men refused to surrender their innate masculinity, resulting in their search for more obviously male pursuits.[30] We may conjecture, then, that appeals to male parishioners to become manly by following Jesus Christ fell on deaf ears, particularly if they had ever glanced at images of the Saviour in *Home Words* (Figure 5.2).

The insets always contained more images of nubile women, heroic clergy, cute children, loyal dogs and English royalty than Christ; a phenomenon of other Protestant religious periodicals, and a possible consequence both of their positioning as family magazines and their fear of the Romanising effects of the crucifix.[31] The few images of Jesus, therefore, stand out. They were influenced by William Holman Hunt's

Figure 5.1 'The First Home Words': *Home Words* (1906) 146

Figure 5.2 'Jesus, the Door': *Home Words* (1907) Frontispiece

The Light of the World.[32] Holman Hunt's Jesus emerged as a result of the painter's desire to create a historically 'real' portrait of Christ following the publication of David Friedrich Strauss's *Das Leben Jesu.*[33] However, as Gillian Beer has contended, Holman Hunt's reality was always an imaginative synthesis of 'smoky' images from the past, so the Christ who emerged resembled the hero of an ancient romance.[34] Moreover, the models used for the figure of Jesus were two females: Christina Rossetti and Elizabeth Siddal.[35] Famously, *The Light of the World* was ridiculed as make-believe by Thomas Carlyle, and, despite its popularity, this androgynous Christ, an artistic combination of what Sean Gill has termed 'masculine strength and feminine weakness', knocked at a door which only those inside could open, rendering him ultimately impotent.[36]

Inset images of a decidedly non-muscular Jesus feminised Him still further. In some, He interacted with children, deliberately glorifying the home angel's child-care role, so that He became in essence, 'a woman with a beard'.[37] To bereaved parents, the painting of 'Jesus, the Door' welcoming children to heaven, reproduced in Figure 5.2, may have been deeply consoling, the vicar of Saint Lawrence, Appleby, recalling that when *Home Words* had displayed the original during the Barrow Church Congress, a grieving couple had wept and begged to buy it, but, as Callum Brown argues, most men were unimpressed by the Redeemer in such a tender materialisation.[38]

How could men be encouraged to follow 'a woman with a beard', or, to quote Sean Gill, accept Christ as 'the hypostatic union of gendered opposites'?[39] And how could Christ's representatives on earth hope to influence men toughened by the experience of 'real life'? One response was to promote the Anglican clergyman as a fictional role model. Clergymen were rarely the heroes of popular fiction during the early days of family periodicals, even in religious magazines, and in the mid-century high-church works of Charlotte Yonge, they were too retiring and cerebral to be obviously heroic, but the approach most attractive to broad-church adherents was to make the clergyman into a man's man by turning him into an action hero.[40] According to Edmund Gosse, Victorian enthusiasm allied to romanticism turned hero-worship from a virtue into a religion at a time of national anxiety and religious doubt.[41] Heroic clergymen, then, could demonstrate that the Church was the legitimate home of manly men.

Muscular Christianity

A clergyman who had boxed at Oxford; who felled an attacker with 'a heavy left-hander over the eye, which laid him prostrate in the dust';

who foiled the attempts of a gang of local farmers to bully church-goers; who stopped a titled seducer of village girls in his tracks; who, first, rescued passengers from a rail crash, and then workmen from a landslide; who visited the sick, no matter how poor; who succeeded in endearing himself to parishioners, even his former enemies; and who both adored and protected his beautiful, young, pregnant wife: such a clergyman was a hero indeed, considering that these deeds were accomplished during the first year of his first curacy (Figure 5.3).[42] This was the plot of Henry C. Adams's novel, *Fighting his Way: Leslie Rice's First Curacy,* which, in 1889, entitled 'Leslie Rice's First Curacy' was an early *Church Monthly* serial story. Adams (1817–1899) was both a parish clergyman and a prolific professional author in many genres, including schoolboy adventures.[43] Crucially, the hero of 'Leslie Rice's First Curacy', set nearly 30 years previously in 1860, embodied the ideals of Charles Kingsley whose mid-century Muscular Christianity encouraged the clergyman to become, as David Newsome has put it: 'a man amongst men… setting the standard of paternal care, domestic piety, manly vigour and unselfish loyalty which he expected his neighbours to emulate'.[44] Such a man was Leslie Rice.

While the Christian Socialism of Kingsley and F. D. Maurice was fading by 1860, their vision of public service remained, and was combined with the public school reforms of Dr Arnold of Rugby to support the vision of Christian manhood which Kingsley had thought necessary to confute what he saw as the feminising tendencies of Anglo-Catholicism.[45] Arnold's Rugby was not the first school to encourage *esprit de corps* among boys.

Winchester, too, experienced a rebirth during the first half of the nineteenth century, and it was here that the author of *Fighting His Way* was educated, and to which he returned as a master, departing in 1851 to become a parish curate.[46] In 1857, Thomas Hughes's phenomenally successful *Tom Brown's Schooldays* was published as a tribute to Arnold, but, as Mark Girouard has argued, Hughes's novel went beyond Arnold's desire to make boys morally good, by making them not only good, but good at games and fisticuffs as well, the last provided that the cause was just.[47] Leslie Rice owed his characteristics to public-school reform and the writings of Kingsley and Hughes. That Adams's story appeared in *The Church Monthly* in 1889, so soon after the inset's advent, is indicative, not only of the continuing power of the idea of Muscular Christianity, but also of the unsettled nature of Victorian codifications of gender identity, a concern often associated with ritualism's closeness to 'effeminate' Roman Catholicism.[48] Leslie Rice's ebullient maleness, then, suggests endemic anxiety about clerical masculinity.

Figure 5.3 'He was evidently excited.' H. C. Adams, 'Leslie Rice's First Curacy': *The Church Monthly* (December 1889)

Leslie Rice's exploits also demonstrate the popularity of the boys' adventure story. Such stories were common in the insets during the 1890s and resemble those in the *Boy's Own Paper*, first published in 1879, the aim of which was, to quote Kimberley Reynolds, to bring boys to Christ, while avoiding 'sordid subjects and sensational styles'.[49] The publishing firm of Routledge marked H. C. Adams and two other male inset contributors – R. M. Ballantyne and George Manville Fenn – as its rising stars.[50] When Edward Salmon commented on 'What Boys Read' in the *Fortnightly Review* in 1886, he referred to the talent, not only of Adams and Ballantyne, but also of the Revd T. S. Millington, another regular inset contributor.[51] Their names, he contended, guaranteed not only moral worth but also a strong story.[52] Ballantyne's writing career spanned nearly 50 years. His *oeuvre* represents a gentler type of boys' story akin to evangelical tracts, where physical strength was made to give way to bodily weakness in self-sacrificial trials which curbed their heroes' ebullient masculinity.[53] Jeff Benson, the coastguard hero of Ballantyne's serial story in *Home Words*, published in 1888, gloried in his physical strength, but the debilitating paralysis he endured after saving the crew of a sinking ship taught him that suffering – God's refining fire – creates real men.[54] George Manville Fenn produced similar stories for *Dawn of Day*, as the SPCK also attempted to attract male readers through utilising its extensive stable of children's school-prize writers.[55] His novel, *Gil the Gunner,* was thought the ideal gift for boys at St Catherine's Church, Hatcham, the two most promising choirboys of 1892 being presented with the book by the parishioners, bought with the proceeds of the choir fund.[56]

Leslie Rice's adventures took Ballantyne's evangelical understanding of Christian manliness to greater extremes, for Adams's Muscular Christian approach relied on a sense of malevolent violence. Children were attacked by others on the way to Sunday school, and the villagers existed fractiously in an atmosphere of drunken ignorance and belief in witchcraft, while the price of bread rose and farmers threatened their tenants with eviction, leading to an armed uprising, all of which the brave vicar foiled in the cause of bringing his flock back to the old rural order based on faith and *noblesse oblige*. As Jose Harris argues, and as discussed in Chapter 8, fear of what the newly enfranchised and unionised working man might do during a time of ideological uncertainty caused anxiety from the 1880s.[57] Manly fiction – disguised as a parochial history portraying the clergyman in uncompromising terms as a strong leader bringing his parish to a returned sense of wholeness – might assuage men's anxiety about their diminishing sense of superiority to women, encourage readers to respect and admire the clergy, and help maintain Anglican allegiance in an age of religious plurality.[58]

Women were peripheral to such stories, being kept from danger, confined to their own separate sphere.[59] Rice's wife, Lucy, was awarded the lesser role of confidante, her pregnancy usefully underlining his virility. However, in a narrative twist, Adams devoted a whole chapter of the book version of *Fighting His Way* to Lucy's discovery of the uprising, when her single-handed confrontation of the perpetrators led to her dramatic premature labour.[60] Omission of this from the inset suggests that Sherlock saw no need for a fearless female in a man's world.

The heroic clergyman: fighting and cycling his way

Anglican obsession with chivalry is exemplified by the career of the Revd Samuel John Stone and his narrative poem, *The Knight of Intercession,* first published in 1872.[61] Stone, a frequent contributor to both *Home Words* and *The Church Monthly,* combined dedication to his East-End parish with professional authorship, his biographer averring that he exhibited 'the vigour of a Muscular Christian… the oratory of a preacher, the challenge of a campaigner, and the sensitivity of a poet'.[62] The hero of *The Knight of Intercession* travelled incognito 'doing true *devoir* as a noble knight' by rescuing maidens, redressing the wrongs of widows and the poor, and blessing those who had wronged him.[63] Similarly, 'Return to Town' – a poem in *The Church Monthly* by the incumbent of St Bartholomew's, Gray's Inn Road, London – portrayed the clergyman as a questing knight:

> ... Back to the earnest warfare,
> Back to the help of man,
> Back with growing endeavour
> To work with a will while I can
> Work among the teeming masses
> Of Adam's fallen race,
> To reach out a hand in mercy
> Some evil to efface.[64]

Nineteenth-century clergy were generally treated deferentially; some were well liked.[65] Parish magazines capitalised on such popularity by portraying the real-life clergyman as a hero. *Home Words* ran an essay competition with the title 'The Heroism of the Clergy', and 'manly' clerical portraits appeared monthly in most insets.[66] Handsome young curates were often fêted in local pages.[67] Of great interest to their parishioners, as shown so clearly in the English novel, young curates were the Sir Galahads of the parishes, carrying out their lonely quests through the barren wastes of slums, faceless suburbs and villages that industrialisation had left behind.[68] These knights were regularly presented with steeds so they could go about doing good: not on horses but on bicycles, the popularity of cycling at the turn of the century linking the Church with modernity by allowing the curate to do more home visits and mission-church services. One of many was the curate of Saint John's, Keswick, who received a 'Singer Model B, fitted with all the most recent improvements, including Dunlop's '96 tyres, patent steering lock, and full tangent spokes', in 1896.[69]

Despite such public esteem, many clergymen considered themselves economic and social victims,[70] regularly recording in their monthly 'letter' that they were obliged to be out in all weathers on home visits where rampant infection exposed them to disease, and, having become ill or old, possessed no savings on which to retire.[71] The vicar of Holy Trinity, Hoxton, took more than a year off to recover from pneumonia.[72] Writing in the third person, the incumbent of Merton, Oxford, complained in the winter of 1892:

> Continued strain has prostrated the vicar. Being obliged to take services when very weak, several funerals have thrown him back. For more than twelve months he has had no holiday and frequently on Sundays has had six services entirely to himself after a week filled up with classes and meetings every evening![73]

Even the vicar of Wordsworth's romantic haven, Grasmere, was 'strongly recommended to recover energy and nerve power by another winter's change to a bracing place'.[74]

The regularity with which the clergy went on recuperative holidays led Robert Tressell's socialist polemic *The Ragged Trousered Philanthropists,* to ridicule the Revd John Belcher, whose health was so poor that his congregation regularly paid to send him to the South of France.[75] Hugh McLeod contends that such negativity formed a persistent background to late-Victorian life, 'these fellows in black coats' being regularly derided.[76] The insets constantly expressed concern over anticlericalism. In 1884, *Parish Magazine* published a story in which a Manchester curate invited a bricklayer who had taunted him with having 'nought to do but walk about in a long black coat and get a lot of brass', to accompany his home visits. When confronted first with a case of smallpox, second with a man in his coffin who had died of scarlet fever and, finally, a house where there was typhus, the bricklayer agreed not to say any more 'agin you parsons'.[77]

Frequent infections, unmet hopes for preferment, the psychological frustration of dealing with others yet feeling very much alone, and the creeping Victorian crisis of faith, must have sapped many clergymen, even the most devout, the last exemplified by Richard Jefferies's 'Modern Country Curate', and famously described in fiction by Mrs Humphry Ward.[78] Even the country clergyman, who was far less exposed to wholesale poverty and disease, was capable of discontent. Though he continued to carry out an important function in terms of his religious cure of souls, there was a sense, encouraged by the loss of older parochial responsibilities such as school-teaching and law enforcement, that his role was contracting, and that he was increasingly becoming an administrator: a role more suited to a busy town parish.[79] Owen Chadwick has noted that as country clergy suffered from 'melancholy', with little to do amid 'slow-moving minds', the fashionable place to be by the 1890s was the urban parish, with all its duties and responsibilities.[80]

Hudson Shaw, vicar of the Lake District parish of Thornthwaite, typified such clergymen. Born to an impoverished family in Leeds, his consuming interest was the urban poverty he had observed in the 'overcrowded streets and courts' of northern cities, his 1890s parish magazine oozing with dissatisfaction at his rural location.[81] Though an experienced university extension lecturer, he could not motivate his apathetic parishioners:

> We have been obliged to close the evening Continuation Classes as the average for the month has only been five, three short of the number required by the County Council. It is a pity that lounging should be more attractive than knowledge ... in the struggle for work the least educated will 'go to the wall'.

As his Darwinian final paragraph reveals, Shaw saw his parishioners' lack of enthusiasm for education as demonstrating their backwardness, and he told them so, accusing them of indulging in superstition and witchcraft, in which Christian rites of passage were used like protective charms.[82] Shaw's deepest complaints about Thornthwaite, however, centred on the unbearable weather and his financial difficulties, as in this description of the drive to boost parish funds:

> We scarcely had breathing time to recover a large loss on a concert got up to aid our finances – a loss caused by a great snowstorm on the night of the entertainment – when part of our ceiling fell in.

With this came his final announcement:

> This January number will be the last one. The magazine has been run at a considerable loss ... the living of Thornthwaite has decreased considerably during the last year, and it is now below £120 per annum ... and the vicarage is large and requires a good deal of keeping up.

Carlisle Diocese already had the fourth-lowest-paid clergy in England, but Shaw's financial difficulties were worsened by an agricultural slump which had depressed clerical incomes.[83] As Anthony Russell has argued, the clergyman became a professional in the late-nineteenth century, but, deprived of the necessary career or income structure to give him parity with the law or medicine, and threatened by a state intent on taking over his traditional charitable concerns, he was still expected to organise his work around them, and then to make up any shortfall in parish finances.[84] The latter was possible given a private income, but Shaw's assets were meagre, and without a professional infrastructure, he was, for a time, obliged to remain marooned in his Lakeland fastness. The story ends happily however. By 1915, Shaw had achieved his ambition; he had become rector of St Botolph's, Bishopsgate, his residence in Spital Square surrounded by all the poverty he could have desired, his crusading spirit given new life as he advocated the preaching of women through his association with the early Anglican feminist, Maud Royden: a very modern lady in distress.[85]

Sporting heroes

The ideal Christian hero, as the inset stories intimated, combined faith, bravery, self-sacrifice and sporting prowess. In 1898, *Home Words* published a photograph of three who personified all that the insets attempted to convey. The Studd brothers, having been converted through their father's association with the American Evangelist Dwight D. Moody, gave up worldly aspirations to work for God. The brothers, all Cambridge scholars, were world-class cricketers.[86] In 1898 the brothers were famous enough for their photograph to be printed in *Home Words* with no explanatory article.

Responding to the popularisation of commercialised leisure, parish clergymen used the fame of such manly Christians as the Studd brothers to encourage participation in team games. Dominic Erdozain has argued that religious organisations are in danger when their 'pragmatic use of leisure' to gain supporters turns into dependence. When 'action displaced worship' in the late-nineteenth-century Church, he contends, there was a consequent sapping of spirituality.[87] This judgement would have cut no ice with clergy facing the problem of what to do with boys who were too old for the church choir and Sunday school, such clergymen viewing sport as a perfectly legitimate means of maintaining allegiance to the church while encouraging morally acceptable behaviour. London clergymen interviewed by Charles Booth's researchers were consciously proud of the open spaces they provided for sporting events.[88] Cricket, with its public-school ethos, was considered ideal to introduce to boys' clubs.[89] Eighty per cent of the cricket pitches in Hackney's Victoria Park were named after the Apostles, a sure sign of the number of church clubs playing the game.[90] Articles about W. G. Grace appeared in *Home Words* in 1893 and 1898,[91] and Grace contributed his own article, 'Cricket as a Pastime for the Working Classes', to *The Church Monthly* in 1896. Directed primarily at those who organised church cricket clubs but occasionally addressing working-class males as well, Grace contended that it was the game's moral benefits which truly counted. Not only was it a 'healthy manly exercise' but it was played with 'a strict observance of rules' with no gambling. He advised players to play the game honestly: 'what is worth doing at all is worth doing well.'[92] His advice would have been equally valid on the playing fields of Eton or within the pages of the *Boy's Own Paper*.

Football divided the clergy into those who thought the sport encouraged the sins of betting and drinking, and those who regarded it as a spur to male church attendance.[93] It was clearly not the sport of gentlemen: Dean Francis Close was appalled at the thought of a clergyman player being kicked by the 'hob-nail' shoes of a working man.[94] From the 1880s, however, football flooded local pages, every parish match reported, every win celebrated. In 1902, the parish magazine of Saint James, Barrow, included advertisements for football boots 'worn by the leading players', as professional football became increasingly popular in the industrial north.[95] Saint Matthias, Stoke Newington, published seasonal 'cricket gossip' and 'football gossip' columns, but it was the captains of the football teams, two young men, Reginald Rodick and Walter Smith, whom the 1891 census names as clerks, who were regarded as parish heroes.[96] Smith's photograph appeared after the team had won seven consecutive matches, and Rodick was the subject of a poem which ends:

> But oh, he wears a laurel crown,
> His pedestal's near heaven;
> They stamp and shout when he comes out;
> He's pride of men, and pet of ten
> The king of his eleven.[97]

At the beginning of the Great War, a number of clergymen expressed their dislike of professional football; some viewed it as a national sin which had led to war, while others censured working-class football supporters who did not immediately volunteer for the forces.[98] Nevertheless, the Church as a whole attempted to embrace the professional game. In February 1910, the Bullock family's *Church Standard* announced that a footballer had been ordained. That October the inset reported that the bishop of Lincoln had preached the sermon in Lincoln on 'Football Sunday', when a procession of several thousand followers had marched to church for a special afternoon service.[99] Clergymen who had declined to join in games with the great unwashed were superseded by others eager to identify with working men.

Constructing imperialism: Hardwicke Rawnsley

The career of Hardwicke Rawnsley, contemporary and neighbour of both Hudson Shaw and Morley Headlam, encapsulates much that has been written about manliness in this chapter, while demonstrating its links with Anglican imperialism. Closely related to Tennyson, raised on family readings of *The Idylls of the King*, Rawnsley was inducted early into the ideals of chivalry. Educated at Uppingham by his godfather, Edward Thring, whose reforms were based on Dr Arnold's godliness and Kingsley's sportsmanship, he could not fail to have been a Muscular Christian. As an Oxford undergraduate, he became a friend and admirer of John Ruskin, a relationship which lasted until Ruskin's death.[100] For most of his professional life Rawnsley ministered in the Lake District, close to the homes of Ruskin and his poetic hero, Wordsworth. Today he is celebrated as a founder of the National Trust, but his parish magazine, his contributions to *The Church Monthly* and his many books, poems and printed sermons reveal much about the construction of Anglicanism's imperialist narrative.[101]

God is not absent from Rawnsley's Crosthwaite parish magazine, but sometimes He is elusive. Rawnsley referred to his county and country more than to the Almighty, and 'history' almost as much, references to 'God' often appearing in a historical rather than a spiritual context, such as the finding of an ancient scroll in the Libyan desert, or in patriotic mode when eulogising young men who had given 'their lives for God, Queen and Country'.[102] Word-groups appearing frequently are 'man/manliness', and those that may be regarded as patriotic and imperialist: 'England/country/empire'. Rawnsley was not unique in this. He represents a type common to the insets exemplified by Frank Bullen (1857–1915).[103] As famous in his day as Conrad, Bullen wrote sea-stories combining the excitement and righteousness of imperial adventure with the conventional evangelical notion of self-sacrifice.[104] Patrick Dunae begins his article on boys' literature and the British Empire with a quotation from Bullen, who declared that a boy 'would be knocked down' if he dared breathe a word against imperialism at school.[105]

Rawnsley was addicted to versifying. Odes flowed from his pen, much to the amusement of the journalists at *Punch*, where his style was affectionately satirised.[106] Poems appeared in his parish magazine almost every month, some previously published in secular periodicals such as the *Pall Mall Gazette* and the *Cornhill Magazine,* and in religious publications like *Good Words,* though some, such as obituaries and accounts of local happenings, of purely local interest.[107] Rawnsley's poems and monthly letters exhibit the patriotism and imperialism of the age, with its summons to selfless bravery, as in this offering on the death of Cecil Rhodes:

> ... For this man saw beyond the common ken,
> Adventurer not for self or sordid lust –
> He felt the Imperial mission in his blood;
> And sharer of siege-famine, drouth and dust,
> Or bold within the Matabele den,
> He ruled by right of Saxon hardihood.[108]

Rawnsley expressed a commonly held notion that because of divinely ordained racial hierarchy those 'of Saxon hardihood' were superior to other races, while African peoples were the most inferior: 'the white man's burden', to be evangelised through Church missionary activity. The theme was endemic in parish magazines, as Figure 5.4 suggests.

Missionaries were frequently eulogised in church pulpits, reports of those whom their home-congregations supported often appearing in local pages.[109] In the early 1880s, the congregation of Saint Philip and Saint James, Oxford, followed the progress of Mr Janson, their missionary in Central Africa, through correspondence which appeared monthly in the parish magazine. Like the era's popular schoolboy yarns, Janson's manly exploits appeared by turns exciting, dangerous and funny, but within two years he had died 'in uninterrupted agony' from cholera. The magazine printed his last Oxford sermon, given before his departure for Africa and the way of life which ultimately killed him:

> I am going to try and fight for God in a far distant land, where, I humbly believe, He has called me. He only knows whether I shall stand here again – and that does not much matter! In God's name... I give you first the challenge, 'Art thou with us or our adversaries?' And then the words of peace... be strong and of good courage; be not afraid... for the Lord thy God is with thee.[110]

In a poem composed by a member of the congregation in his memory, Janson was honoured for 'bearing the Master's cross to heathen land... and laying down his life'.[111] Janson was a Christian hero, a good

"BLESSED ARE THE PEACEMAKERS." (See Page 215.)
Specially drawn by F. W. BURTON.

Figure 5.4 'Blessed are the Peacemakers': *The Church Monthly* (1906) 205

knight who died for a great cause, his 'manly' rhetoric fusing *Boy's Own* derring-do with both religious and imperialist fervour.

Rawnsley, too, merged missionary and imperialist agendas to regard any who died in the country's service as Christ-like, as in this ode to soldiers killed by the Matabele tribe:

> We keep Christ's Day in Cumberland,
> But you are in your graves –
> You who for Britain bravely stood
> To save a world from sin, and blood
> Of sacrifice and slaves.[112]

This rhetoric echoes the country's response to the fate of General Gordon, the 'solitary hero' who in the face of certain death held out against 'the alien hordes': these words taken from contemporary press reports.[113] Bullock's *Home Words* eulogy emphasised Gordon's Christian 'spirit of humility and self-sacrifice',[114] while *Parish Magazine* combined knightly deeds with gamesmanship by describing him as 'the burning and shining light of chivalry': Britain was the only land that could have borne him, the British character having been hardened by the 'mimic warfare of rough games for the bare sake of the sport, bent on winning, yet not beaten though the day be lost'.[115] In parish magazines and in journalism generally, the notion of noble service was laced with sports and military rhetoric to allow empire building and Christian expansionism to become synonymous.

By the beginning of the twentieth century this rhetoric had become ubiquitous, exemplified in *Home Words'* front covers, emblazoned with coats of arms which appeared military while representing the Anglican dioceses, and *Home Words'* 1906 Frontispiece (Figure 5.5), the figure of 'Christ's faithful soldier' favoured over the feminised Jesus as the symbol of masculine Christianity.[116] Ruskin's utopian ideas were incorporated into the ideals of his Guild of St George.[117] Thus, Rawnsley's sonnet on Ruskin's death ends:

> And all the men whose helmets ever wore
> The wild red-rose St George for sign has given,
> Stand round, and bow the head and feel their swords,
> And swear by him who taught them deeds not words,
> To fight for Love.[118]

Rawnsley was at the forefront of the Keswick celebrations of Queen Victoria's two Jubilees. According to Mark Looker, it was the Jubilees which most intensified imperialistic rhetoric in the religious press, the Churches, keen to bolster their own position, contributing substantially to imperialism through their celebration.[119] Rawnsley – an expert on bonfire-building – took charge of the bonfire which was lit on Skiddaw on each occasion. At the coronation of Edward VII he organised a national chain of bonfires, about which he wrote for *Home Words*.[120] Rawnsley's bonfires were inspired by Macaulay's poem on the Armada, in which the warning 'red glare on Skiddaw' had 'roused the burghers of Carlisle', indicative of a contemporary preoccupation with England's important place in history; but his bonfire-building activities also resonate with the philosophy of another dedicated imperialist, Robert Baden-Powell, hero of Mafeking and author of *Scouting for Boys*.[121] The scouting movement

Figure 5.5 Frontispiece: *Home Words* (1906)

swept the country after the second Boer War, on a tide of patriotism and a general desire to improve the mental and physical strength of boys.[122] 'We want Boy Scouts', announced an article in the parish magazine of Saint Augustine, Highbury during the Great War:

> If we are to make the glorious British Empire the greatest blessing to the whole of mankind history has ever known, then we boys must buck up and do our bit, and see that every British boy is taught to be a true citizen, worthy of... the flag we are so justly proud of.[123]

Though Rawnsley would never have ended a sentence with a preposition, the sentiment would unquestionably have given him deep satisfaction. His belief in chivalry, romanticism, patriotism, Christian idealism and manly heroism all contributed to his embrace of British imperialism. In the thick of the Great War, after great loss of life, his rhetoric remained the same:

> Honour – for this you go
> On a dishonoured foe ...
> True knight and gentleman fight to the end.
> Whether you stand or fall,
> Hark! To the empire's call.[124]

This verse encapsulates the chivalrous values that Rawnsley expounded to his Crosthwaite flock for 30 years. They were the values employed by the scouting movement; by the authors of books for boys and men; and by politicians who wished to influence men to do their bidding. They were used to encourage working men to emulate ideals derived from the public schools, through the espousal of Muscular Christianity with its encouragement of team sports. They were also intrinsic to the Church's projection of itself as the Church of the nation; its attempts to encourage male church attendance; and to the self-image of its clergy. But though inset editors portrayed clergymen as heroic, the local pages' often frank admissions of clerical difficulties succeeded only in showing them to be as human as the most ordinary of their parishioners: not 'manly men' but ordinary men; not 'muscular' but fragile. Besides, the rhetoric of the manly man, as put forward by men, could be revealed to be a chimera through the serial stories of women writers; a subject to be explored in the next chapter.

6
'Scribbling Women': Female Authorship of Inset Fiction

As discussed in Chapter 5, towards the end of the nineteenth century there were a great many more male inset contributors than there were females. Needlework, cookery and children's columns, and short poems used as fillers between longer articles, were typically the preserve of women, such contributions occupying a modicum of space, appearing and disappearing over the years, apparently at an editor's whim. But women dominated the authorship of fictional narratives, which afforded them a much more significant presence. In 1896, for instance, they contributed 88 per cent of the total fiction in *Home Words, The Church Monthly* and *Dawn of Day*. From the inset's earliest period, the ubiquitous serial story, frequently contributed by a woman, occupied about a third of available inset space. While there were few female contributors, their input was highly significant.

Callum Brown has engaged extensively with the binary oppositions of evangelical narratives – godliness and ungodliness, pious woman and sinful man – in which women are agents of men's redemption. Brown considers that, as such evangelical codes had become the bedrock of virtually all popular fiction by the nineteenth century, it is 'almost inappropriate' to distinguish between the fiction of secular and religious magazines.[1] This chapter seeks to add to the discussion by arguing that while much early inset fiction written by women expressed genuine piety, the female writers of later narratives cynically utilised evangelical codes to suit their own secular purposes. Meanwhile, inset editors, keen to increase their magazines' circulation in a competitive market, capitalised on the popularity of the popular novel while exploiting the transient fame of some female authors and the desperation of others. The chapter argues that though commercialism and religious conviction are not mutually exclusive, the extent to which female contributors pursued profit and self-advancement undermined both the spirituality of earlier female contributions and the religiosity of Anglican inset fiction as a whole.[2] Outlining the careers and texts of representative female contributors of inset fiction and poetry from 1871 to 1914, the chapter begins with Charles Bullock's early evangelical female contributors, moving on to the high -church sentiments of female contributors to early numbers of *Dawn of Day*. Change accelerated in the 1880s, around the advent of *The Church Monthly*. Contributions from early twentieth-century female authors in *The Church Monthly* and other insets are examined towards the end of the chapter.

Home Words: evangelical fiction

The evangelical novelist Charlotte Maria Tucker (1821–1893) was one of Bullock's earliest serial story contributors.[3] Known by her pseudonym, ALOE (a Lady of England), this wealthy daughter of a chairman of the East India Company was a prodigious writer of over 150 of what Kimberley Reynolds has termed 'strenuously' didactic novels, the proceeds of which aided missionary work. In late middle-age she became a missionary in India.[4] As noted in Chapter 4, the evangelical poet Frances Ridley Havergal contributed to *Home Words* because of her friendship with its editor, but Tucker probably contributed out of a sense of duty to the evangelical cause.

While equally evangelical, most of Bullock's early female contributors were comparative unknowns, some contributing to his publications for decades. Like some of Bullock's clergyman contributors, they regarded didactic writing as a fortunate synergy of faith and writing ability, and the source of a moderate remuneration. Bullock's attitude to female writers may be gleaned from his memoir of Harriet Beecher Stowe. Considering her influential life, Bullock's strongest impression of the author was not her powerful novel, *Uncle Tom's Cabin,* but, first, her evangelical conversion, and second, her ability to write while bringing up six children, his article dwelling on a scene in her kitchen which involved her simultaneously feeding a baby, entertaining two toddlers, instructing an inexperienced servant, baking cakes and writing an article designed to keep the family solvent.[5] True to the evangelical notion of women's role, Bullock praised her writing but admired her domesticity even more.

Home Words: Emma Marshall and Agnes Giberne

In 1863 the evangelical RTS gave its tract writers advice on the 'essential rules of healthful fiction'. First, stories were to be moral, with no sense that 'vice' was being invested with interest. Second, they were to be 'natural' – true to nature and to fact, and free from 'false representations of life and exaggerations of character'. Lastly, they were to be 'unexciting – leaving the spirit calm and the passions not unduly moved'. Writers were asked to base their stories on life, and to choose subjects with some intrinsic interest.[6] The serial stories of Emma Marshall and Agnes Giberne, analysed below, illustrate how this was put into practice in the service of *Home Words*.

Emma Marshall (1828–1899), an evangelical married to a grandson of the famous tract writer Revd Legh Richmond, contributed 11 serial stories to *Home Words* between 1873 and 1894.[7] Most of her fiction could have been published by the RTS. 'The Lost Jewel' (1879) was an allegory on Luke 12:34: 'For where your treasure is, there your heart will be also', in which a retired lady's maid discovered that her family was of greater worth than an emerald bequeathed by her old mistress, but then stolen. After the loss, the rector's wife helped the victim to use her remaining inheritance to do God's work by setting up a coffee house as an antidote to male drunkenness. Biblical allegories, temperance stories and examples of male error are obvious staples of the religious tract, but the plot of another Marshall serial story, 'Only Once' (1877), reveals the influence of contemporary secular fiction. Though it dealt with the stock tract theme of a village girl courted secretly by a village squire who, just in time, realised the error of her ways, there were other influences at work, for the story was exciting: would she or would she not succumb? The story recalled the mid-nineteenth-century realist novel, exemplified by George Eliot's *Adam Bede* and *The Mill on the Floss,* though Marshall's treatment of a maiden's ruin was different from Eliot's, for Marshall's female protagonist remembered her Church teaching, thus realising her mistake without losing her virginity, and was permitted a happy ending through being allowed to return and to marry, though only within her social class. While forgiven, her sin was not to go unpunished, however. Fleeing to the safety of home through a rainstorm, she developed rheumatic fever and was crippled for life.

A review in the high-church *Monthly Packet* thought Marshall's stories just right to be read aloud to members of the Girls' Friendly Society, while in her study of Sunday-school prizes, D. M. Entwhistle discovered that they were equally admired by nonconformists.[8] The stories' romantic content no doubt ensured their popularity, such negotiation with the secular crucial in ensuring that they were read, while their didacticism assured clergymen of all denominations that they were ideal for working-class women: sinfulness was punished, right conduct rewarded and romantic relationships did not cross class boundaries.[9]

Another evangelical, Agnes Giberne (1845–1939), contributed at least 18 serial stories and much else to *Home Words*, her connection with the inset lasting nearly 50 years to 1920. Though her stories recorded changes in daily living, such as the progression from horseback to bicycle, their didactic content remained the same, for, alongside her obvious evangelicalism, preoccupation with class boundaries dominated Giberne's fiction. One of her earliest serial stories, 'The Witherings', followed the misfortunes of an unemployed gardener, saved from penury by his consumptive daughter's love of hymn singing. The girl's Christian virtue was rewarded by a wealthy lady who employed the father, but, after neighbourhood gossip over the theft of some money, he was dismissed as a thief. After months of hunger and distress, all was resolved and the father absolved of the crime, but he was not bitter, for he had trusted in God's justice; his family had been humbled, having learned, in true tract manner, the bitterness of sin and the purifying powers of suffering.[10]

Such overt moralising, which nevertheless absolved the upper classes of sin while penalising their servants, was heartily disliked in some quarters. In her article for the *Westminster Review*, 'Silly Novels by Lady Novelists', George Eliot remarked on the 'mental mediocrity' of females who wrote 'drivelling', 'feeble', pious, 'twaddle'.[11] Giberne's intention was clearly to encourage cottage folk to trust in God and be grateful for small mercies, while remaining in the station to which they had been appointed. Though the end of the nineteenth century brought changes in government social policy and consequently in attitudes to poverty, Giberne continued to press working-class acceptance of their betters as the providers of charity and judges of right conduct. A typical tale in 1898 praised the gratitude of a godly, impoverished woman who was rewarded with a few coppers for returning a lost purse instead of appropriating its five guineas for her pressing rent arrears.[12]

Charles Bullock considered 'Tim Teddington's Dream, or Liberty, Equality and Fraternity' to be Giberne's greatest contribution to *Home Words*, publishing it in 1873 and reproducing it, for 'our working-class friends', in a penny edition in 1885.[13] 'Never did author succeed more thoroughly in blending amusement with instruction.... Tim's experience in the South Sea Islands will enable [British workmen] to answer the few noisy agitators who would plausibly persuade us to hand old England over to the tender mercies of a Republic', he claimed in his introduction, which went on to ridicule the radicalism of the nonconformist MP, John Bright.

Tim Teddington, having joined the village radicals to stop 'the rich trampling on the poor', and having drunk too much at a public-house meeting debating universal suffrage, went home, quarrelled with his 'sensible' wife over social revolution, sat down in his chair and fell asleep. He dreamed that he and his fellow radicals were equal citizens of a South Sea Island, holding everything in common, but, while some men worked hard, others wasted their opportunities by doing nothing. Meanwhile, the women decided that, as they were equal to men, they would do no housework; they wanted liberty, and with Tim's wife as their leader, they intended to take it by force. Tim awoke in terror, convinced that radicalism could not work. He took his problems to the village rector, who, through quoting Scripture, convinced him of the foolishness of attempting to overturn traditional society: some men were called to high positions, others to have humble lives, but all partook of God's care, and those who meddled with God's laws would certainly be damned. So Tim departed a wiser man, happy to know his place.

This narrative was a common one, echoing Hannah More's *Cheap Repository Tracts* of the 1790s. In 1864 Erskine Clarke utilised it in a poem which followed the fortunes of Matthew Hart, a labourer who despaired of his social and economic position until returned to happiness by experiencing in a dream the 'difficult' lives of gentry-folk.[14] The anxiety over social and political change which had led More to write her tracts was to return in the 1880s, when, amid much unease over the 'condition of England', 'the masses and the classes' were encouraged to pit themselves against one another in a party-political struggle which paternalists found alarming.[15] In her Sunday-school prize study, D. M. Entwhistle discovered that religious texts for the young and poor changed in emphasis during the last quarter of the nineteenth century, from evangelical stories of sin and repentance to tales presenting prescriptive lifestyles, 'blue-prints for respectability', as a means of sustaining the status quo.[16] Giberne's story belonged to this conservative desire to stem the tide of democracy. Reviewing the book and its sequel in 1892, the magazine *Hearth and Home* admitted that the content was trivial, but confirmed prevailing attitudes by remarking that 'the people who read these pleasant little volumes are not critics, and are not given to reasoning'.[17] Some of Giberne's readers, however, may have understood only too well Tim Teddington's terror at the thought of his wife being raised to an equal footing with him. As Anna Clark has argued, artisans feared female competition in the workplace, their anxieties highjacked by employers in the paternalist cause.[18] Clearly Giberne and her editor were at one with those men who aimed to keep women within the home: their proper sphere.

Woman's mission

The average nineteenth-century clergymen held a resolutely conservative view of women's role, exemplified in a popular poem, *The Rights of Women.* Andrea Ebel Brozyna's research on Ulster female piety discovered that it had appeared in the *Irish Presbyterian* of January 1855.[19] It also appeared in an 1865 anthology, *The Wild Garland,* where it was attributed to a 'Mrs Little'.[20] It was clearly seen as an important text by Charles Bullock, because it appeared, unattributed, in *Home Words* during the inset's first year of publication.[21] In 1889 it was quoted with approbation by the Revd E. J. Hardy, a frequent *Home Words* contributor who wrote influential books on marital relationships,[22] and it was repeated in parish-magazine local pages; the vicar of Cliburn, Westmorland, for instance, quoted it in full while fulminating over the women's suffrage campaign in January, 1907, over half a century after its appearance in Ireland:[23]

> The rights of women, what are they?
> The right to labour, love and pray;
> The right to weep with those that weep;
> The right to wake when others sleep.
> The right to dry the falling tear,
> The right to quell the rising fear;
> The right to smooth the brow of care,
> And whisper comfort in despair.

The poem continued in similar vein for six further verses, ending:

> Are these thy rights? Then murmur not
> That woman's mission is thy lot;
> Improve the talents God has given;
> Life's duties done – thy rest in heaven.

'Woman's Mission', the phrase made famous by such early-Victorian evangelicals as John Angell James and Charlotte Elizabeth Tonna, was woman's recompense for Eve's wicked temptation of Adam, allowing her to make amends through piety and self-abnegation.[24] In early inset illustration, her meek downward gaze before men was universal; if she ever looked upward, it was to her heavenly Lord in prayer and supplication.[25] But – as Frank Prochaska has argued – the concept of woman's nature and mission was in flux during the nineteenth century, a gap widening between conventional religious teaching and what industrial, social and political change had unlocked in terms of employment possibilities, married relationships and women's perceptions.[26] Nevertheless, nineteenth-century editions of *Home Words* denied any possibility of change.

Towards the end of the Great War, a series about women 'by one of them', in the local pages of the Saint Anne, Wandsworth, parish magazine, criticised men who treated women as 'playthings' or 'slaves', the writer suggesting that woman's 'mission' was now to win greater equality through gaining 'respect' for her sex.[27] Around the same period, inset fiction also began to suggest that relationships between devout men and women were more equal.[28] As perceptions changed, illustrations of the female characters who demonstrated this equality were also transformed. The meek downward gaze virtually disappeared, while images of women, even those in prayer, began to appear sexually charged, even in Agnes Giberne's pious fiction.[29] Illustrations which sexually objectified women were quite unexceptionable to their creators – jobbing artists who were influenced by changing trends within the secular magazine market – but they inserted yet more contradiction and ambiguity into an already conflicted arena. Contradiction is equally apparent in Agnes Giberne's own life experience: while much of her fiction counselled meekness before men, she was an independent author, earning her own living, a phenomenon which this chapter will revisit.

Dawn of Day: The SPCK and High Church piety

The SPCK was a determinedly high-church society, but its opinions on wholesome fiction for the poor were very similar to those of the evangelical RTS. As the doyenne of the Tractarian novel, Charlotte Yonge, explained in an article, 'What books to lend and what to give', stories should reflect 'quiet domesticity', domestic training and a protest against 'penny-dreadful' romance.[30] Thus the SPCK tract committee reported in 1882 that Crona Temple's *Out of the Shadows* was 'a story of village life in which a practical lesson is drawn from the observation of the Rogation Days', while the same author's *'With Swallow's Wings* was 'a tale of humble life, inculcating cheerfulness and self reliance.'[31] 'Crona Temple' was the pen name of Clara Lavinia Corfield (1846–1916), a vicar's daughter who wrote at least 30 novels.[32] *With Swallows Wings* was serialised in *Dawn of Day* in 1882, its mixture of simple liturgical and moral teaching typifying that inset's early fiction.

Christina Rossetti (1830–1894) was an early contributor to *Dawn of Day*, though not of the poetry for which she is now admired, but of 'street Arab' stories featuring East-End waifs whose goodness redeemed their cruel parents, these stories attaining popularity from the 1860s.[33] In Rossetti's work, however, as befitted a friend of Charlotte Yonge, the devotion of Anglo-Catholic women church-workers and members of sisterhoods was emphasised.[34] Though often in poor health, Rossetti did occasional voluntary work with the inmates of the Saint Mary Magdalene Penitentiary, Highgate, a religious foundation dedicated to the improvement of 'fallen women', which was probably the source of her material. 'Aunt Christina's piety, her grimness and rectitude' were well known to her brother's children, her biographer remarking that in her last 20 years of life her writing was chiefly devotional; including daily collects, scriptural commentaries and improving tales for children, much of it was donated to the SPCK.[35]

Dawn of Day: Maria Louisa Molesworth (1839–1921) and the school-prize market

At its birth in 1878, *Dawn of Day* was classed as a magazine for both 'simple folk' and Sunday-schools.[36] In a manner reminiscent of George Newnes's editing of *Tit-Bits,* the editor, Revd Edmund McClure, created the cheapest of all parish magazine insets by utilising copy from SPCK's vast back-catalogue, for which payment had already been made, with the result that McClure's form of 'cut-and-paste' journalism containing fiction for all the family became one of the market leaders of the genre.[37]

J. S. Bratton's research into children's fiction has found that after the formation of School Boards in 1870 scope for the publication of children's prize books widened, bringing with it a more pragmatic attitude to religious publishing, in which didacticism was tempered by the Boards' insistence on literary merit. By definition School Boards were secular and, as a result, they could also be radical, the London School Board being particularly choosy about which books to give as prizes.[38] The SPCK rose to the School-Board challenge, its success in this area probably accounting for the inclusion of Maria Louisa Molesworth's *The Little Old Portrait* as a serial story in *Dawn of Day* during 1884. Molesworth was well regarded as a children's writer, Edward Salmon contending in 1887 that she was 'the best story-teller for children England has yet known'.[39] *The Little Old Portrait* was no moralising tract in the Giberne or Rossetti style, but attempted to explain the French Revolution through exploring the emotions and motivations of children, the story's morals embedded within the action rather than openly didactic. According to Bratton, it was for these reasons that Mrs Molesworth was one of the London School Board's favourite authors. Gifted writers like Molesworth were rarely published in the insets, even in *Dawn of Day*, which could call on a long list of established authors, but her more secular style was to be duplicated by a host of writers with far less talent and originality.

Dawn of Day: 'plunderers and sharks' and lady authors

Dawn of Day's female story writers have been largely forgotten: the SPCK paid them a small fee for their copyright and subsequently ignored them. As advertised in the SPCK tract committee report of 1878, 'MSS are submitted to the committees, with whom rests the responsibility of accepting or declining them ... If an MS. is accepted, payment is received for the copyright; if it is declined, it is returned post free.'[40] According to SPCK's biographer, the five to ten pounds paid for tracts and prize books earlier in the century had been greatly reduced by the 1870s, yet in 1890 the profit from the book sales of this supposedly charitable body amounted to £7,660.[41] The anomaly caused Walter Besant of the Society of Authors to question his members on just how much they had earned from writing for SPCK, afterwards depicting the society's committee members as 'shady' 'knaves and sweaters', who defrauded authors 'under the guise of a religious society in the sacred name of Christ'.[42] The society's defence: that the tract committee was inundated by manuscripts from lady authors of Sunday-school literature, 'anxious to earn pocket-money', was conspicuous in its denial of women's need or desire to earn a living wage.[43]

In the mid-1850s, Nathaniel Hawthorne's memorable sentence, 'America is now wholly given over to a damned mob of scribbling women, and I should have no chance of success while the public taste is occupied with their trash – and should be ashamed of myself if I did',[44] was mirrored by George Eliot's suggestion that most women were motivated to write by boredom and vanity,[45] yet Emma Marshall wrote 'at white heat' after her husband had lost his position in a bank, and, towards the end of her writing career, Agnes Giberne's heart condition and failing eyesight propelled her into applying to the Royal Literary Fund because she was almost destitute.[46] Yet the motives of female writers were almost always more nuanced than simple poverty or even the egotism that Eliot's satire suggests. Margaret Beetham has shown that women's demand for satisfying paid work had become a dominant theme in women's magazines by the 1880s, not only for money, but also for self-belief and independence.[47] In her analysis of Victorian serial fiction, Laurie Langbauer argues that many women writers, marginalised by male canonical authors, postured as breadwinners to hide their professional ambition, concentrating on professionalism rather than artistry, thus flooding the periodicals market with their offerings. If the second half of the Victorian period is considered a minor period for the novel, with no major novelists after the death of George Eliot, she contends, then it is because 'minor' players accepted their lower status as chroniclers of the banalities of domestic life in order to be published.[48]

Austin Clare (1845–1932)

Typical of Langbauer's 'minor players' was the novelist Austin Clare whose publisher, SPCK, utilised some of her novels as *Dawn of Day* serial stories between 1879 and 1905. Born Wilhelmina Martha James, the eldest of nine children of a wealthy clergyman, she lived in a small village near Alston, Cumberland, where she visited parishioners and taught in the parish school when not travelling widely with her family.[49] When otherwise unoccupied, Clare found time to write stories in a summer house in the grounds. Not that the family was impressed by her penmanship: the only allusion to her writing in her mother's extensive diaries is the laconic, 'Mon 5: M.A. returned. "Carved Cartoon" came. Patty James's book written as "Austin Clare"'.[50]

Based on an imagined episode in the life of the woodcarver Grinling Gibbons, *The Carved Cartoon*, published by SPCK in 1874, established Austin Clare as a historical novelist, and was well reviewed in such high-church periodicals as the *Monthly Packet*.[51] It was undoubtedly loved by some of its readers, as evinced by this correspondence in an American magazine:

> The author's pen holds the reader entranced ... the noble character and brilliant talents of the young hero shine star-like through the surrounding darkness of greed, avarice, and poverty.[52]

The Carved Cartoon was undeniably a children's story: SPCK advertised it in *Dawn of Day* in 1878, when the inset was described as a Sunday-school magazine, and Bratton has bracketed it with Mrs Molesworth's books as examples of improved literary quality on the SPCK's list.[53] In 1885, paralleling *The Church Monthly*'s aim to encourage lay support, SPCK's tract committee determined to widen its inset's scope to include adults, so that it would be 'more suitable to enlighten the mass of the people upon the position and claims of the Church of England'.[54] The understanding of the working-class adult, particularly the working-class woman, however, was not considered much greater than a child's. Moreover, it was essential to guard her purity, for the influence of periodical reading on women was widely feared.[55] As Edward Salmon declared in his article for the *Nineteenth Century*, 'What Girls Read':

> Girls' literature ... enables girls to read something above mere baby tales, and yet keeps them from the influence of novels of a sort which should be read only by persons capable of forming a discreet judgment. It is a long jump from Aesop to Ouida and to place Miss Sarah Doudney ... between Aesop and Ouida may at least prevent a disastrous moral fall.[56]

Sarah Doudney (1841–1926), an evangelical novelist and niece of the editor of the Anglican inset *Old Jonathan,* was a frequent *Home Words* contributor.[57] Though Salmon had been writing about girls generally, it was plain that girls' stories were thought eminently suitable for the female working-class readers of cheap religious magazines. Thus, Austin Clare's oeuvre was ideal for *Dawn of Day*'s purposes, combining the sexual innocence of the girls' story, the traditional moral-didacticism of the tract and the requisite high-church theology.

Clare continued in similar vein throughout her association with *Dawn of Day*. A short story of 1896, 'The Red Geranium', had a tract-like theme extolling the 'gratitude' and 'patience' of a crippled charwoman's daughter with a drunken father, though the influence of Trollope and Margaret Oliphant probably ensured that the liveliness of the story lay in its description of the cathedral close which lay under the girl's window, and the pretty dean's daughter who visited her.[58] 'The Shadow of a Cloud', serialised in 1905, defended the Anglican Church against tithe-hating Cornish Methodists, its heroes a brave young tithe collector and his Methodist girlfriend who disobeyed her community to defend him and later joined the Anglicans.[59]

'The Change in Robert Holt, Narrated by Himself', serialised by *Dawn of Day* in 1898, witnessed developing aspects of Clare's content and style. Combining Church defence with the excitement of the crime novel, it defended both Church and country in a cautionary tale about the danger posed by London anarchists. After political radicalisation in London, a young man joined an anarchist cell bent on the murder of an MP living in his childhood village. Finding employment on a farm there, he fell in love with the farmer's daughter, realised the error of his ways and eventually foiled the anarchist plot through his love for both the girl and the Church. The village curate – a former slum-priest – befriended and redeemed him, the clergy regarded as playing a unique role in negotiating between rich and poor.

As early as 1878 the tract committee had reported that Clare could write a 'vigorous story for rough lads and others: 'The author has a large experience in the education of boys, and can thoroughly enter into their struggles and temptations.'[60] Presumably the reference was to Clare's assistance at the school on Alston Moor, but her experience of anarchists was purely literary. Anarchists were in the news throughout the 1880s and 1890s, after the bomb assassination of Tsar Alexander of Russia in 1881. Conrad wrote a novel based on a failed bomb attack at the Greenwich Observatory in 1894.[61] In 1897, the James family diary notes that while on holiday, Austin Clare and her mother read Mrs Baillie Reynolds's popular anarchist novel, *To Set Her Free*.[62] Henry James wrote a novel on the same theme. First published as a serial in *The Atlantic Monthly* in 1885–1886, *The Princess Casamassima* explored anarchists' violent initiation into their secret societies, the terror they engendered, and their members' inability ever to escape.[63] When Clare attempted this scenario, she too projected a decided atmosphere of menace, but her background and choice of publisher determined that her anarchist recruit would be saved through faith and the redemptive quality of the rural Anglican parish.[64]

While Austin Clare taught that the Church could conquer evil, the danger and outright violence embedded in her tale, like that in 'Leslie Rice's First Curacy' (see Chapter 5), is striking. Like Adams, Clare expressed contemporary anxieties about Anglicanism while representing a transitional stage in fiction for cheap religious magazines, balanced between carrying out the instructions of the RTS of some 20 years before, and writing under the influence of secular fiction such as sensation, invasion and crime novels, all of which grew in popularity from the 1860s through the *fin-de-siècle*.[65] That female inset contributors chose to demonstrate their embrace of modernism through the medium of religious fiction is made even clearer in the sections that follow.

The Church Monthly and L. T. Meade: 'an empty game'?

Richard Altick's survey of British writers from 1800 to 1935 discovered that the proportion of female writers who in census returns described themselves as professional rather than amateur rose from 8 per cent of the total in 1881 to 16.6 per cent in 1931.[66] To the emancipated woman, fiction authorship was not only fashionable and respectable, but also potentially lucrative, the large number of religious journals providing a ready outlet for those who aimed to support themselves by their pen. Hence, the mid-nineteenth-century torrent of unsolicited manuscripts to editors, witnessed by George Eliot, continued.[67] Two quotations from *The Church Monthly* give a flavour of the hope and determination of fledgling writers at the turn of the century: 'We have mislaid the address of the author of the above verses, and shall be glad to receive it in order to forward an honorarium as promised'; and, in a short story: 'it is [a letter] from the editor of one ... of the magazines telling me that he likes the article I have sent him so much that he will always be ready to give me work.'[68] Work was now the thing: the aim, to be a consummate professional. L. T. Meade provides an example of how this worked in practice.

Meade (1844–1914) arrived alone in London aged 21 from her father's vicarage in Ireland. Determined to become a commercially successful journalist and author, she supported herself entirely from the beginning. As her style matured she completed up to 14 books a year, also contributing to magazines for adults such as *The Strand* and *Shafts*, and to girls' publications like *Girls' Realm* and *Atalanta*, which she co-edited from 1887 to 1893. Most famous as a writer of girls' stories, she is reputed to have earned from £600 to £1,000 annually.[69] Critics, both then and now, have been divided over her merits. Edward Salmon thought her as good as most writers for boys, while the *New York Times* found her plots, 'weird, thin and unconvincing'.[70] Kimberley Reynolds and Sally Mitchell have condemned her stereotypical and reactionary ideas cloaked in the garb of the 'new woman', but Helen Bittel regards the inconsistencies of her fiction as part of her deliberate encouragement of girl readers to consider their own position in an era of conflicting views of women's behaviour.[71]

The Church Monthly serialised Meade's *Betty of the Rectory* during 1907, the year before its publication by Cassell, confirming its high status in an advertisement in the November 1906 number.[72] Positioned to encourage the introduction of *The Church Monthly* into new parishes, the advertisement placed Meade's name at the head of its list of 1907 contributors, drawing the reader's attention to the story's 'specially drawn' signed illustrations by Paul Hardy, a well-known illustrator of articles in *The Strand* and *The English Illustrated Magazine*, and of books as various as George Manville Fenn's boys' story, *To Win or to Die*, and Macaulay's *Lays of Ancient Rome*.[73] Though the trend was towards a growing number of lavish illustrations in each inset number, paralleling the development of illustrated newspapers, Hardy's illustrations for *Betty of the Rectory* were more sumptuous than most because Meade's story was preoccupied with appearance and behaviour in fashionable society, as befitted Betty's status as the daughter-in-law of a titled lady.

The social activist, Helen Bosanquet, commented disapprovingly on the necessity for the heroes of cheap secular periodicals to be aristocratic, with long, thin torsos, pointy feet and lofty eyebrows, whereas the women were to be 'fashion plates with a great wardrobe at their disposal' (Figure 6.1).[74] Although Meade informed her readers that, as a good clerical wife, Betty eschewed such frivolity, the text (and consequently the illustration) belied this in its minute description of drawing-room furniture, candle-lit dinners, orders to servants and changes of dress. Clearly the insets' earlier stern insistence on thrift for poor cottagers had disappeared, in what was in reality a woman's magazine wish-fulfilment story with 'churchy' overtones in an opulent upper-class setting. For this story not only to be published but also to have merited the expense of lavish illustration illuminates *The Church Monthly*'s editorial policy in 1907.

The story's central drama was the secret drug habit of the rector which, as Betty was to discover, was based on fear of inheriting his

Figure 6.1 'Betty of the Rectory', *The Church Monthly* (1907) 5

father's insanity. There are obvious similarities to the sensation novel here, as the rector was not his supposed father's son, and the source of the mystery was his mother, the haughty Lady Pevensey. Lady Pevensey was not quite Lady Audley, but she, too, was deceitful, and the theme of madness was central to both Meade's and M. E. Braddon's narratives.[75] Allusions to insanity hint at British fears of degeneration after the second Boer War, while a fictional narrative based on drug addiction might suggest Meade's awareness of neurosis among the urban middle-class.[76] If Meade, who had lodged with a doctor's family on first coming to London, aimed to initiate a dialogue on these themes this would have been perfectly acceptable: she had valid points to make, couched in more modern, medicalised language than that of earlier didactic fiction.[77] But, while illustrating Meade's dexterity in using known literary conventions, the themes in 'Betty of the Rectory' remained resolutely superficial. J. S. Bratton finds her stories inimical, not only for their use of well-worn formulae but also for the emptiness in the telling and the moral 'meaningless' to Meade herself, who, according to Bratton, carelessly turned the respected genre of the religious novel, which for over a century had been able to 'provoke compassion and difficult self examination', into 'an empty game'.[78]

Betty of the Rectory illustrates contradictory elements in *The Church Monthly*'s approach to fiction. The illustrations diluted the rector's weakness by portraying him as conventionally tall, handsome and heroic throughout his troubles – even in the act of feeding his addiction he was awarded a halo (Figure 6.2) – while the text portrayed him as thoroughly weak in his lack of self-control, his feeble attempts at a cure contrasting with the good sense of the doctors who attempted unsuccessfully to help him, the difference between his assurance in the pulpit and his pathetic behaviour when alone clearly made. As Callum Brown has noted, the overarching evangelical narrative from which nineteenth-century novels sprang demanded a discourse of female piety in opposition to male weakness.[79] Meade appeared to submit to this formula; her central message was that, whatever disasters befell, a woman should honour her wedding vows and sacrifice self for duty. As Bosanquet remarked of the heroines of secular magazines, 'their role is to be injured and misunderstood, loving and faithful through all affliction ... any outbreak of originality would be very disturbing'.[80] But while appearing to support the Church's conservative views on women, Meade's elevation of the heroine at the expense of her husband undermined Sherlock's editorial mission. Over almost 30 years, Sherlock had encouraged an unquestioning admiration of the parish clergy, but

Figure 6.2 'Geoffrey Returned the Bottle to its Place': *The Church Monthly* (1907) 128

Meade's narrative suggested that clergymen were weaker than women, that they were less wise than other professional men, and that, far from being heroes, they had feet of clay: propositions which could be deemed thoroughly anticlerical.[81]

Visually, there were few differences between Meade's rector and Henry Adams's manly Leslie Rice. The two stories also coincide in their evangelical understanding of female moral strength and determination: while Betty supported her husband despite discovering his secret, Adams's heroine foiled a working-class plot. Yet the female feistiness of the original novels disappeared after their adaptation by *The Church Monthly*. In Meade's novel, Betty was called away to her sick sister's bedside. Returning unexpectedly, she found her husband comatose in his study after succumbing to temptation. Gazing upon his unlovely appearance, the scales fell from her eyes. This was a grim scene, skilfully written, but, like Adams's wife's confrontation with the angry workers, was removed from the inset version. Moreover, sub-plots germane to the narratives of both novels were also removed, leaving them one-dimensional, a phenomenon not unusual in secular magazines, where compression of serialised novels had been problematical since the days of Charles Dickens.[82] Inset serial stories were edited to last no longer than one year; some lasted for six months or less, *The Church Monthly* cutting its serial stories more than any of the sampled insets. Ironically, Frederick Sherlock's new year editorial for 1907 promised 'to keep up a high standard of editing', but the strains which caused him to attempt to sell *The Church Monthly* to Mowbray's in 1911 (noted in Chapter 3) may already have been apparent.[83] We cannot know for sure, as there are no extant business records, but if the bravery of the two heroines was cut merely to fit the available space, and Meade's fiction published merely to boost sales, then we may conclude that *The Church Monthly* was as commercial in its attitude as Meade herself. Well might the SPCK fulminate against

> many publishers and authors [who] are not now so much restrained by ethical considerations as were their predecessors. Indeed, to judge by means of the fiction annually poured forth, it would seem that the easiest access to notoriety and to commercial success is an appeal in literature to the lowest motives in human nature ... significant of the great change which has come over writers of fiction in our own day.[84]

Indeed, the 'great change' had occurred within their own sphere.

Other goddesses of the pen

As Chapter 1 noted, the serial story could be a deciding factor in whether a parish magazine was taken in. A star writer, L. T. Meade would have attracted female non-churchgoers. *The Sign*'s 1907 serial was written by Mrs Baillie Reynolds (Gertrude Minnie Robins, c.1875–1939), already noted as the author of an anarchist novel read by Austin Clare's family in 1895. In 1928 she was bracketed with contemporary literary stars Ethel M. Dell and Baroness Orczy, in Patrick Braybrooke's wry look at women's fiction, *Some Goddesses of the Pen*.[85] Braybrooke's definition of a writing goddess was one who had become thoroughly popular through allowing the reader to be 'amused, thrilled and led ... away from everyday realities', one of Baillie Reynolds's virtues being her ability to write exciting thrillers whose villains 'are so attractive ... so clever, so human, so much like ourselves', a talent which allowed her work to translate well to the cinema between 1918 and

1925.[86] It was difficult to engage fiction contributors at a price which publishers were prepared to pay.[87] Mowbray's offered Baillie Reynolds 50 guineas for her novel's serial rights, but had to raise their offer to 60 guineas, evidence both of the increasing negotiating power of successful female writers and of their protection of their copyright, with which Baillie Reynolds, who went on to chair both the Women Writers' Club and the Society of Women Journalists, would have been familiar.[88]

That female inset contributors wrote to fit particular commercial markets is by now obvious. May Wynne contributed to *Home Words, The Church Standard, The Church Monthly and The Sign* (together representing a broad spectrum of mainstream Anglican theology) between 1907 and 1929. *Home Words* published stories by the Irish novelist M. E. Francis (1859–1930) in 1907 and 1908. They reveal nothing other than a moralist bent and a diffused Christianity, yet Francis has been described as the Catholic Mrs Gaskell;[89] her portrayal of her husband's Lancashire estate, *A North Country Village*, published in 1893, described parochial priests, masses and rosaries as if the Reformation had never occurred.[90] Matilda Betham Edwards (1836–1919) was a Francophile who wished to be remembered for her travel writing. A feminist and friend of Barbara Bodichon and Sarah Grand, she was a religious sceptic, yet her children's hymns appeared in *Home Words*.[91] Most of Austin Clare's later fiction comprised realist novels featuring the countryside around Alston.[92] In *The Conscience of Dr. Holt*, published in 1908, she used the name of her redeemed anarchist, but on this occasion made him a doctor with an ethical dilemma, religion playing no part in resolving it.[93] Mary and Elizabeth Kirby, a sisterly duo who wrote evangelical novels and stories for religious periodicals such as the *Quiver*, contributed a story on sabbatarianism for Charles Bullock in 1873, but were, first and foremost, botanists, responding to a long-standing tradition which allowed women access to science through the 'ladylike' study of plants.[94] Even Agnes Giberne had another career entirely as a successful science writer.[95]

As Nicola Thompson argues in her study of the motivation of non-canonical Victorian female novelists, both their lives and their fictions were 'fundamentally conflicted'. She cites Charlotte Yonge, who held highly conservative views on women yet sympathised with the limitations society placed on them.[96] This may also be said of Christina Rossetti, in her support of sisterhoods operating in the East End, for sisterhoods were, as the first shoots of high-church feminism, thought subversive of clerical authority.[97] Thus, women's motivations for writing, their chosen genres and their opinions often appear contradictory. So, when Gillian Avery points an accusing finger at May Wynne for 'flogging her imagination to invent madder and madder schoolgirl scrapes', she may have overlooked Wynne's 1910 serial story in *The Church Standard* in which the heroine sacrifices herself in a chivalrous attempt to save others, this written during a period when feminists had begun to claim that chivalry was not a male preserve.[98] Moreover, when Laurie Langbauer calls Charlotte Yonge a 'priggish hypocrite' for opining that women had brought their inferiority upon themselves, and when we ourselves perceive dissembling in the lives and writings of some of the writers discussed in this chapter, we should beware knee-jerk accusations of insincerity, and consider the difficulties under which they worked.[99]

And yet, despite understanding the impositions placed upon female writers, we appear to have travelled far from the evangelicals with whom this chapter began, particularly when we consider that L. T. Meade's pious posturing was acceptable to the editor of a magazine which purported to be religious and didactic, while the secular London School Board disliked it, refusing over many years to place Meade's novels on its prize list.[100] What has become clear is that inset editors were keen to publish the work of those who had found even the slightest degree of fame, in their competition for readers.

Lady Bell's literacy survey of the poor in northeast England discovered that people who read penny literature expected a strong love interest and 'a mild dose of religious sentiment'.[101] Readers of fiction written by Meade et al. in their parish magazine would have discovered that while love interest predominated, religious sentiment was very mild indeed, particularly if they were old enough to remember the earliest numbers of *Dawn of Day* or *Home Words*. Eventually there was little substantive difference between inset stories and those in such secular magazines as *Horner's Penny Stories*, which, echoing Lady Bell, Dora Bucknell, born in 1882, recalled as 'sentimental, sort of love stories, and a bit of religion in them as well…I used to skip the religion and the romantic bits, and get on with the story'.[102] The vague, diffused Christianity of the *fin-de-siècle* became intrinsic to inset fictional material as written by women, its premises at variance with the religiosity of clerical contributions coexisting within the same wrapper. That parish clergyman recognised this, but did not care, is undeniable. In 1915, the vicar of Saint Augustine, Highbury, referred witheringly to the insets' 'nice stories and love tales', yet he was prepared to take an inset if parishioners were willing to pay for it, hoping that his local pages would be read by a greater constituency.[103]

Queenie Scott-Hopper (1881–1924): reaching 'rock-bottom'

Despite the insets' employment of literary 'stars', the career of Queenie Scott-Hopper[104] attests that editors continued to use minor authors to their own advantage by paying them small sums to produce stories and pious verse, and that women colluded in this by continuing to send unsolicited manuscripts. Scott-Hopper contributed to *Dawn of Day* between 1911 and 1921. Like Meade and May Wynne, she also contributed to other insets: *Home Words* (1914–1919), *The Sign* (1915), *Banner of Faith* (1916) and *Ecclesia* (1918). Louis James has contended that as faith came under pressure, belief in traditional religion transmogrified into interest in fantasy, ghost stories and the occult, the last turned into profitable novels by Marie Corelli.[105] Around 1900, the pages of the insets began to be adorned by female angels, often bearing a resemblance to the pretty, lispingly innocent children found in popular American books for children, and who seem to embody the period's fuzzy spirituality.[106] Scott-Hopper's vaguely mystical verse containing angels and visions was probably acceptable to editors across the church-party divide because it reflected popular taste. It was also thought suitable for children. In the introduction to an American anthology to which she contributed, her verse was described as 'romantic ... simple ... entirely undisturbing'.[107] That its subject was fairies is unsurprising.

Scott-Hopper was ambitious to succeed as a writer, the contents of her personal papers, and the lists of her publications in the British Library Catalogue and online demonstrating her determined use of her talent as poet, short-story writer, novelist and librettist.[108] Of her numerous publishers, some – like Mowbray's and The Faith Press – were religious; some – such as Wells Gardner Darton and W. T. Stead – were overtly moralistic;[109] but Scott-Hopper also wrote song lyrics published by Boosey and Novello, secular novels and poetry for Nelson and Harrap, and contributed to popular children's anthologies, such as Blackie's *Children's Annual*.[110] Her address books illustrate her continual search for work, one of the pages suggesting that she may have approached Ella King-Hall, P. G. Wodehouse's literary agent, to represent her.[111] Walter Besant praised the literary agent's role as the middleman between the 'rapacious' publisher and the inexperienced writer, particularly in the latter's relations with periodicals. 'It is next to impossible to be going round to editors offering things for acceptance, hat in hand. The businessman does it for me.'[112] But through the intervention of the 'businessman', the relationship between female contributor and editor, exemplified in the friendship between Charles

Bullock and Frances Ridley Havergal, noted in Chapter 4, was greatly weakened.

Of the religious publishing firms listed in Scott-Hopper's address book, the *Christian Herald* is quoted as asking for 'bright, crisp, complete stories, 2,000–5,000 words…suitable for a religious journal'. Secular publications, such as the *Daily Graphic* and *Daily Mail,* appear in greater numbers, an annotation above the latter stating that it 'pays more than any other paper! Is courteous to [occasional contributors] whose MSS are not returned'. Names include the new (the BBC) and the traditional (*Home Chat*), often noting their terms of payment. *St George's Magazine* paid 42/- per 1,000 for short stories; *John O'London's Weekly* and *The London Magazine* paid three guineas for 2,000–3,000 words; and *Little Folks,* a guinea per 1,000 words. The insets' terms of payment were not given, but elsewhere the average payment appears to have been in the region of a guinea per thousand words.[113]

Scott-Hopper's determination to earn her own living may be explained by the fact that her solicitor father was bankrupted twice, suggesting that she was obliged to be careful in managing her budget.[114] Her life story is implied in her novel, *Rock Bottom,* in which the eldest sister copes with an unsatisfactory father's financial disasters by using her writing talent, first by penning verse for her local newspaper, then by approaching established publishers.[115] But writing as a professional career produces its own anxieties. In 1924, after appearing to suffer from writer's block, Scott-Hopper committed suicide by cutting her throat with a razor, her local newspaper reporting:

> She was rather highly strung, was nervous and had sleepless nights. She was a writer, but had not been getting ideas as quickly as she wished. Her mind seemed a blank, and she did not write as she would have liked.[116]

Tellingly, she had visited her bank that morning.

In a story for *Dawn of Day*, published in 1911, Scott-Hopper described a district visitor's dismayed reaction to the 'cheerless, joyless life' of a young sufferer of chronic illness. Later, through an angel's visitation, the district visitor understood the 'mysteries of God's providence' which allowed the girl to suffer.[117] In her own distress, Scott-Hopper was clearly unable to find the consolation she had hoped to give to others.

Kate Flint has observed that, by the close of the nineteenth century, writing had become an acceptable occupation for a middle-class woman, allowing her to make a living while remaining womanly, many women fantasising about the possibilities of success.[118] But, as Flint concludes, it was harder for women than for men.[119] Scott-Hopper, like many female writers before her, fused her religiosity and writing talent to some effect in religious periodicals, but financial and practical considerations, coupled with her determination to succeed professionally, encouraged her to write for any and every outlet which would accept her work. The 50-year span between two religious poets, Frances Ridley Havergal and Queenie Scott-Hopper, comes to an unhappy end here, in commercialism, diffused religiosity, and, for Scott-Hopper, despair.

Conclusion

Religion clearly became compartmentalised during the *fin-de-siècle*. Faith and its effects were central to earlier religious fiction, but, later, religion became only one element rather than the driver of such narratives. The earliest evangelicals had published stories to save souls while teaching people to lead moral and useful lives in the place they thought God had assigned to them. Towards the end of the nineteenth century, keen to retain readers and profits, inset editors introduced conflicts and contradictions through publishing stories by best-selling female authors whose skills and proclivities lay more in entertainment than in didacticism, however much they masked their secular plots. That these female authors trivialised religious expression during a period when women increasingly dominated not only inset fiction authorship but also Anglican congregations and charitable work, is both a fact and a great irony.[120]

7
Parish Magazine Readers

If Anglican parish magazines feature in autobiographies, it is inadvertently, as trivia, yet Chapter 3 confirmed their high circulation. Who read them? This chapter considers whether they were read by 'women', 'ladies' or both; whether they were read by men; and whether children read them. It attempts to determine the occupations of the heads of the households into which they came, asking whether these people were always Anglican, and where they stood in the social hierarchy. Named bound copies in archive collections suggest that they found their way into disparate households, including those of clergymen, farmers, labourers and skilled workers, but, as some were given as gifts or prizes, how can we know whether they were read?

Assessing the readership of periodicals has traditionally been problematical, when little information is to be had. Some scholars have turned to the texts themselves to discover how readers were represented, while others have attempted to discover readers empirically, through autobiographies.[1] In *Gender and the Victorian Periodical,* Hilary Fraser et al. combined these approaches, producing empirical evidence to demonstrate real reader response while divining a periodical's 'implied' readers through the texts themselves.[2] This approach will be used here, beginning with the implied readership of insets and local pages, before turning to competition results, correspondence, church records and the few memoirs available to uncover the parish magazine's 'actual' readers.

Inset readership: the implied reader

On the face of it, the insets' implied readers were the working classes. In 1859 Erskine Clarke's *Parish Magazine* was designed to be read by 'the handicraft classes', 'cottagers' and the 'uninstructed'; in 1896 a sermon in *Home Words* addressed to 'working men' was written in the understanding that they formed a substantial part of the readership.[3] Margaret Beetham has commented that magazines are generally only available to those with the optimum levels of 'literacy, income, leisure and space' for reading,[4] yet parish magazines may have been very widely read, for clergymen and district visitors pressed them on the very poor, and those who bought them were expected to pass them on, in the manner of the evangelical tract.[5] As Charles Bullock remarked in 1873:

> Our working friends have abundantly proved their readiness to purchase good reading rather than bad, when it is offered in a cheap and attractive form... Assuming that each copy obtains five readers before it is destroyed, *Home Words* now reaches monthly about half a million readers![6]

With their roots in the family magazines of the 1840s and 1850s, insets contained articles for everyone in the family unit,[7] though, as Callum Brown has observed and Chapter 5 confirmed, magazines that 'affirmed piety within a family setting' were less likely to attract men than secular magazines.[8] At the end of the nineteenth century, *The Church Monthly* and *Home Words* harnessed the sentimental genre-style illustration of the age to depict an idealised reader (Figures 7.1 and 7.2). While both illustrations delivered moral messages concerning the importance of reading the right material, the prelapsarian quality of rural life, the dignity of labour, the importance of thrift and the blessings of home, they also emphasised a key gender difference: men were allowed to relax with their magazine after work, while women were expected to combine reading with household tasks. 'Reading', remarked a vicar's daughter, born in 1865, 'was a recreation, not an occupation; we were often asked if we had no sewing to do when we were seen with a book.'[9] Nonetheless, *Home Words*' depiction of female silent reading demonstrates a decided change of emphasis from *Parish Magazine*'s mid-century portrayal of the female listener, as seen in Figure 2.1.

The implied female reader: not quite a lady

When Lady Florence Bell investigated the reading habits of early-twentieth-century women in the industrial north-east, she found that, because they had no definite time to set aside for leisure, women inevitably read less than their men-folk; while many women could read, they read little, some reading magazines only on Sundays, some of the opinion that time was better spent on needlework.[10] Because magazines for women

Figure 7.1 Frontispiece: *The Church Monthly* (1900)

assumed that articles on home management were essential reading,[11] the insets made this into a major feature, numerous articles on budget cookery, plain sewing, vegetable gardening, fowl keeping and cottage cleanliness targeting the working-class woman specifically.

Figure 7. 2 Frontispiece: *Home Words* (1883)

Until the eve of the Great War, the insets contained no articles on fancywork or embroidery, though the beautification of churches through women's needlework was a constant theme within local pages.[12] Neither was attention given to charity bazaars. Almost entirely organised by females, the charity bazaar, which could encompass all classes, was frequently and vigorously reported locally. When All Saints, South Lambeth, promoted a bazaar opened by Princess Louise in August 1885, several pages of its magazine were devoted to reporting minute details of the proceedings.[13] When a poor Carlisle parish organised a bazaar to pay off its church debt in 1900, it was opened by the countess of Lonsdale, with the bishop of Carlisle taking the chair. The bazaar programme's brazen advice to 'buy, buy, and when you've no more money, bye-bye', is unsurprising, given our understanding of parish-magazine business methods.[14]

Frank Prochaska's chapter on bazaars in *Women and Philanthropy in Nineteenth-Century England* marvels at their popularity, in which 'the lady of the manor might be found selling antimacassars next to a labourer's wife selling flowers',[15] yet this bringing together of the 'two nations' through charitable commercial endeavour was ignored by inset editors, Charles Bullock remaining silent on its merits. Perhaps Bullock disliked bazaar raffles, which some churchmen regarded as a form of gambling.[16] Perhaps he was one of many Churchmen who preferred to encourage congregations to exercise Christian stewardship through systematic giving, rather than funding Church work through commercialised schemes, even though, as seen in Chapter 3, commercial advertising in parish magazines was almost ubiquitous by the late-nineteenth century.[17] But though Church leaders like William Boyd Carpenter, Bishop of Ripon, spoke out against bazaars as 'unfortunate necessities... an indictment against the liberality of Churchmen',[18] they formed, for woman churchgoers, a highly popular means of combining their organisational and artistic skills with social interaction and charity work.

Margaret Beetham's analysis of the *Family Herald* distinguished between the 'women' whom that magazine was addressing, and the 'ladies' whom it was not.[19] Insets usually addressed females as 'women', 'mothers' or 'persons', rarely as 'ladies', their place squarely in the working-class cottage. The distinction was made particularly clear in fiction. Ruth Lamb, in 'Poor Lil's baby', serialised in *The Church Monthly* in 1900, demonstrated the semantic as well as the social difference between her family of 'ladies', and 'poor Lil': the 'woman' who collapsed outside their door.[20] Fraser et al. point out that the word 'woman' had derogatory associations (not quite a lady) until the advent of the 'new woman' late in the nineteenth century,[21] but even in 1910 the magazine of the industrial parish of Holy Trinity, Carlisle, referred to the females who arranged the annual garden fete as 'ladies', and those who attended evening classes at the old ragged school as 'women'.[22]

If one were to believe some inset articles, the 'woman' reader left her cottage only to attend Mothers' Meetings, during which she employed her plain-sewing skills to make simple clothes for her family or the missionary effort, but parish-magazine advertisements reveal that females were greatly valued for their purchasing power. Increasing prosperity brought greater consumer participation in the last quarter of the nineteenth century, resulting in a redefinition of the role of the Victorian home, which, as Lori Ann Loeb has pointed out, became as much a 'centre of consumption' as a 'temple of virtue', even for the working classes.[23] If the working-class woman possessed the power of choice then she was a dangerous phenomenon, like Eve before her, particularly when young. To this effect, insets regularly called upon older women to dispense both household and moral advice in a role similar to the traditional woman's magazine 'agony aunt', though they and the editors decided on the agonies involved, as no such letters were requested from readers. Margaret Pelham Burn, widow of a Norwich vicar, who was both an inset reader and contributor, having won second prize in *Home Words'* essay competition in 1907,[24] became the all-wise elder figure in 'When the Day's Work is Done: a monthly talk with mothers and others', which appeared in *The Church Standard* throughout 1910.[25] In 1907, another clergyman's widow, Lina Orman Cooper, posed in *Home Words* as 'Aunt Marjorie', advising Phoebe, newly engaged and ignorant of household tasks, how to black-lead grates, wash cutlery, choose furniture, maintain her complexion to make herself attractive to her husband and, above all, live frugally on a clerk's salary.[26]

By the early 1900s, the wives of clerks and 'respectable' artisans appeared to be *Home Words'* implied female readers. The rise of the literate worker in clerical or technical occupations, a result of urbanisation, has been well documented, the number of men in clerical occupations rising from 2,000 in 1861 to 157,000 in 1901.[27] The popular insets mirrored social change: no longer purely educative magazines of the poor, they became, in part, materialist magazines for upwardly mobile folk with time and money to spare. The frequency with which they printed four-part-harmony hymns was matched by local-page advertisements for that contemporary status symbol, the piano, as music making became an important part of family life.[28] On advising the newly married on their furniture, inset contributor, Revd E. J. Hardy, remarked in 1885 that the popularity of the home piano was 'inevitable'; he supposed that those who could not buy would hire.[29] In 1914, *Home Words* offered its female readers sewing patterns to make themselves fashionable Sunday outfits to wear to church.[30] This was in marked contrast to 1870s attitudes when, for instance, a *Parish Magazine* article urged readers not to follow contemporary fashion which it considered 'ugliness invented by vice itself', or when Henry Whitehead addressed his Limehouse congregation on the sinfulness of fine clothing.[31] Wearing her smart new clothes, the implied female reader of 1914 sold luxury homemade goods such as sweets for church funds in bazaars, as the bazaar made its appearance in the insets at last.[32] Thus, at the outbreak of war, the implied female inset reader was perceived to be a civilised, smartly dressed woman – even if she were not quite a lady.

Mistress, maid and district visitor

Inset articles for church-workers, particularly female district visitors, multiplied from the 1880s. By 1910, the Anglican Church could muster 74,009 district visitors, over 90 per cent of them female.[33] Research in Crosthwaite (Keswick) and Headington (Oxford) parish records supports evidence in the pages of the insets themselves that district visitors were predominantly middle class. At Crosthwaite, 17 of the 19 named district visitors in 1880 were females living on unearned income;[34] Headington district visitors in 1880 were either living on unearned income or were the female relatives of bankers and solicitors; one was titled.[35]

District visitors were not universally beloved and could approach their duties with dread. 'Perplexity', for instance, wrote to the *Monthly Packet* in 1895, seeking help for the indifference she encountered when dealing with her allotted 16 households in a London slum, while Louise Creighton, wife of the future bishop of London, admitted in the 1870s that 'it was a great effort' to visit her allotted street in Oxford: 'I do not remember anything interesting about the people.'[36] Insets attempted to address visitor and visited within the same wrapper. Placed between texts aimed at working-class readers, a *Church Monthly* article of 1897 openly criticised thoughtless young girls and bossy women who, though they gained entry to the homes of the poor through the delivery of parish magazines, were unable to understand their everyday problems.[37] Other inset articles attempted to address the different social classes together by treading a fine line between commending the value of district visiting to poor 'women' and engaging with the 'lady' visitor. In 1886, *Dawn of Day* featured a conversation between a young wife and her husband, a railway porter, in which she explained that she had been visited by a 'nice lady': a district visitor, who had left her a parish magazine. The article also contained a plea for more district visitors, for, 'there is hardly any work which is more important, and like every other "deed of mercy" it brings with it a double blessing: it blesses both those who do it and those for whom it is done'.[38]

A unifying element of this approach was the insets' insistence on the importance of the home to mistress and maid, visitor and visited, but, arguably, the glue that bound them was the era's general acceptance of hierarchical deference. In April 1882, *Dawn of Day* printed Felicia Hemans's poem, 'The Stately Homes of England', the mansions of the rich, among their 'tall ancestral trees', contrasted with

> The Cottage Homes of England!
> By thousands on her plains,
> They are smiling o'er the silvery brooks,
> And round the hamlet-fanes.
> Thro' glowing orchards forth they peep,
> Each from its nook of leaves,
> And fearless there the lowly sleep,
> As the bird beneath the eaves.[39]

At the beginning of the twentieth century, one of Hemans's 'lowly' ones – maid-of-all-work Susan Bone – enjoyed observing the young ladies from the local landed estate as they made their way into church. The attraction lay in their beautiful clothes, particularly their white summer dresses, for, as a result of her poverty, Susan was constrained to wear a dark skirt all summer long.[40] Susan's acceptance of social difference is mirrored in a serial story by Agnes Giberne, published in *Home Words* in 1892, in which the vicar's wife refers to her poor neighbour as her friend: 'And why not? Though we occupy different positions in life, that need be no bar to friendship'. Despite this, however, her 'friend' took her tea in the servants' quarters.[41] David Cannadine has argued that until the 1950s hierarchical deference was endemic, the Church's insistence on 'rank, station, duty and decorum' underlining the preordained nature of the poor person's station in life.[42] Mistress and maid could be addressed together but were separated by an ocean of difference, whether in church, in poetry, or in the parish magazine.

The implied inset male reader: 'the man who thinks'

The implied male reader's distinguishing feature was his inferiority. In 1900, Dean Farrar, lecturing the working man on his reading choices, offered him in patronising tones a conservative canon which, apart from its enthusiasm for the works of Alfred Wallace, was substantially the same as that offered by Charles Knight's *Penny Magazine* and the SDUK

70 years before. Farrar's attitude was mirrored in the article's illustration which forms the frontispiece to this book.[43] Inset articles explaining church history and traditions betrayed a similar condescension, exemplified in a pointed contrast in content and tone between Revd P. H. Ditchfield's book on the parish clerk, published in 1907, and his article on the same subject, published in *The Church Monthly* in 1909: the one, serious and scholarly; the other, simplistic and anecdotal.[44]

As noted in articles for 'ladies' and 'women', masters and men could be addressed separately within the same article. In 1902, for instance, a certain Farmer Simpson – 'a man of method' – was praised for his business acumen, and his 'lad' bidden to be grateful that his employer took so much interest in the farm.[45] In 1896, W. G. Grace attempted to address both masters and men in an article on cricket in *The Church Monthly*, but his article was in reality a lecture to the providers of manly recreation, offering advice on how to save working men from sin.[46] Over time, however, it became apparent that the working classes could be useful to the Church. When, in 1896, evidence came to light that only 5 per cent of Anglicans were willing to volunteer for church work, it was clear that lay helpers of all kinds were greatly needed.[47] By virtue of their sex, men, unlike women, began to be addressed as prospective partners in parish leadership, and the inset developed into a site where practical details of male church membership could be explored through articles on church finance, parish work and the uneasy relationship between Church and State. Male readers were encouraged to become churchwardens, magazine editors, club treasurers and Sunday-school teachers.[48] In 1910, *The Church Standard* published a series for such men entitled 'An open letter to the man who thinks',[49] but who exactly was being addressed?

Margaret Stacey's study of 1950s Banbury demonstrated that virtually all those in the highest occupational status groups attended an Anglican church. In this prosperous town, the local squire sat next to the altar in the chancel, the gentry sat in the front pews, the middle classes behind them and the working classes at the back. According to Stacey's research, the middle and upper classes assumed a duty to lead in the church's lay organisations: 'assumptions with which both leaders and led concur'.[50] Charles Booth's London investigations discovered, however, that 'artisans and the sons of working men employed as clerks' assumed lay responsibility in poorer parishes,[51] and it was these who figured most prominently in the insets' attempts to encourage male church workers, though occasionally the 'deserving poor' could also be addressed. While Keith Snell has noted that parish magazines frequently referred to working-class males as 'gentlemen',[52] the sobriquet should not be taken at face value. Poor men who attempted to help their church could be regarded as 'the other' by inset writers who treated them as rare prize exhibits. When, in 1907, the Revd William Burnet described his railway-station mission services to *Home Words* readers, he produced a photograph of his (unnamed) flat-capped churchwarden to prove that the Church was not 'dying of dignity' (Figure 7.3), yet his mode of address, typified by the sentence: 'occasionally an invitation is given to some earnest converted young man to offer a few words of "testimony" for the encouragement of his "mates"', betrayed the clergy's generally patronising attitude to the working-class male.[53]

Over the second half of the nineteenth century the insets clearly changed their ideas on who the implied reader actually was. From being posited as a poorly educated 'cottager' in 1859, by the outbreak of the

Figure 7.3 'My Churchwarden': *Home Words* (1907) 276

Great War the implied reader had become many things: sometimes a working-class woman situated as the home-angel in need of advice; sometimes a committed woman church-worker of indeterminate class, though probably not a 'lady'; sometimes a 'lady' district visitor; sometimes a working-class man whose habits needed to be strictly controlled; and sometimes one of the clerk or artisan class who could interest himself in church work while patronising those beneath him. It is clear, however, through an examination of this patchwork of disparity, that the Church gradually began to value all of its adherents to a degree, and to encourage them to work for it, whoever they were: a revolutionary change compared to its opinions of half a century before. 'Truly the wind from Heaven has breathed upon the dry bones', commented *Dawn of Day* in 1900, praising this new 'army of lay helpers in which artisans vie with their leisured brethren in voluntary work for the household of God'.[54]

Local-page readership: the implied reader

The number of parish-magazine bound copies found in archives suggests not only their contemporary popularity but also the clergy's awareness of the significance of parish magazines as historical documents. According to the vicar of Holy Trinity, Carlisle, the implied readers of his magazine were not yet born:

> It will form a record, which will be of value in the future as history. Many happenings in the past would be of great help to us now, if they had been thus recorded for our information.[55]

Such clergymen betrayed the self-consciousness of the late Victorians, who, according to Miles Taylor and Michael Wolff, 'historicised everything', including their own age.[56] It was the era of the antiquarian, when the founding of such projects as the *Victoria County History* (from 1899) placed late Victorians in the role of guardians of the past. When bound, as a *Church Monthly* editorial remarked in 1896, the parish magazine 'becomes of permanent interest as a record of Church work'.[57]

Clergymen everywhere were apt to think that a parish magazine's audience would be wide, its influence pervasive. Their parish magazines aimed to bind congregations together, even in fashionable parts of London where, because much revenue was traditionally raised by pew rents, the upper and middle classes customarily travelled from other parts of the city to experience their preferred brand of Anglicanism.[58] When the vicar of the village of Westward, Cumberland, introduced his parish magazine in 1893, he appealed to the whole parish: 'all who are trying to serve the one Master in the same locality'.[59] When All Saints, South Lambeth, parish magazine appeared in January 1884, the vicar remarked that it was to be a record of all that was interesting to local Christians. Churchmen and dissenters would 'often' find something to interest them, but church workers 'always' would. The magazine would be for all classes, and 'as frequently as we can', there would be a corner 'for the working men', even those who worked on the railways.[60]

Those clergymen who claimed that their magazine belonged to everyone may have unwittingly expressed a wider truth, for, as Callum Brown has suggested, what some historians have termed 'secularisation' was actually the determination of many to 'associate with a church without worshipping in it'.[61] Just as some parishioners only attended baptismal, wedding and funeral services, yet felt themselves fully affiliated to the Church, the parish magazine was well placed to become a signifier of belonging to such 'occasional' Anglicans, forming, for them, an almost painless means of association without attendance or even belief: not, 'believing without belonging' – a memorable phrase coined by Grace Davie – but, 'belonging without (necessarily) believing'.[62] Such nominal involvement could go some way towards reassuring parish clergy that the Church was still at the centre of community life.

The parish almanack

Unless destitute or ill, Anglicans usually had to part with money to access a parish magazine, but, as a cheap means of publicising religious services, parish almanacks could be distributed gratis, giving them guaranteed entry into the homes of the poor.[63] The religious almanack was devised in 1829 by the SDUK to combat astrological publications.[64] In 1858 an almanack published by Bemrose and Sons even made provision for the addition of parish news, predating Erskine Clarke's inset by a year.[65] At the 1885 Church Congress, Charles Bullock counselled district visitors to take their own tacks, thus ensuring that the almanack was 'fixed for the year on cottage walls', the middle classes clearly possessing no qualms about what we might now see as gross abuse of private space.[66] A similar condescension may be observed in Revd G. W. White's 'Straight Tips for Working Men' in *Dawn of Day* in 1886:

> Get a Church almanack with the daily lessons marked on it. Perhaps one of your little ones can read ... let him or her find the place and put

> a daily marker ready for father... You can then read the chapter, say the collect for the week and the Lord 's Prayer all together.[67]

A story in *The Church Monthly* in 1905, which described a 'cheerful little parlour... the gay prints and parish almanack on white-washed walls, the children's brightly-bound Sunday-school prize books on the table', illustrates the insets' continuing notion of the ideal cottage home.[68]

The actual reader

The inset reader

From the late 1880s, inset correspondence and competition pages published readers' names.[69] *The Church Monthly* occasionally ran correspondence columns, while *Home Words* offered an essay-writing prize for adults and, from 1910, encouraged its readers to contribute parochial news. This section assesses the actual readership of *The Church Monthly* and *Home Words* during the period when parish-magazine reading was at its height.

Children were always expected to read insets; usually they were awarded their own page adjacent to Bible knowledge quizzes and competitions.[70] Because the entries required clerical validation and contained entries from Sunday-schools and schools, they cannot accurately represent the readership, but the names of child prize-winners published in *The Church Monthly* during the 1890s show, in association with the 1891 census, that three-quarters were girls. While the majority of winners had an artisanal background, one-third came from middle-class homes. There were very few labourers' children. In 1907, *Home Words'* essay competition resulted in 92 prize-winners, three-quarters of whom were female, mirroring the gender balance of *The Church Monthly*'s child-competition winners.[71] Most winners were under 30, suggesting that the magazine was read in the home of their parents or within a church youth organisation. Of the 92 winners, only 15 could be located through the 1901 census; full details were not divulged and several winners had used obvious pseudonyms, for, as Fraser et al. make clear, not all given names in correspondence columns were genuine.[72] Of the 15 known winners, two became professional writers and two were related to clergymen;[73] one-third lived in a household headed by a professional; a further third lived in a household headed by a clerk; only two came from families headed by a skilled manual worker. There were no unskilled labouring families in the sample.

Throughout 1914, *Home Words*' 'Red-Letter Church News' printed letters from 156 readers. Nearly half the named contributors were women, one-third were laymen, and the rest were clergymen. Two thirds of the women were unmarried. Most correspondents to *The Church Monthly* during the periods 1888–1889 and 1907 used pseudonyms.[74] Their original letters were not published, but the content may be deduced from *The Church Monthly*'s responses:

> Aggrieved: Your vicar is quite in the right, and so far from condemning him, you should...loyally support him in his endeavour to consider the wishes of the parishioners as a whole.[75]

Advice was given to the treasurer of a mutual improvement society, a bell-ringer, a 'young Churchman' and a 'good Churchman', among others, most of whom seemed to have experienced problems with their clergyman. All were sternly admonished. 'H. Jeevons' and 'a mistress' received advice on good but moderately priced schools, and a 'servant' was advised to put her money in the Post-Office Savings Bank.[76] 'Perplexed' was urged to consult the head librarian at the British Museum, and 'K. A.' received information on children's books on 'Church defence'. Party politics and controversial theology were discouraged:

> F. Dunkerton: The present parliament was elected in July 1886. Your second question, 'how long will it last?' is too difficult for us to answer.
>
> A Friend: Our magazine is intended for *Church* folk and besides our space is too limited for the discussion of so debatable a topic.[77]

These readers were indeed 'Church folk'. Not poor, but not rich; educated to some degree; interested in debating Church topics; disappointed in their vicar; worried about their children's education and reading material, they seem disconcertingly familiar, not least in the dissatisfaction they reveal. Sherlock's determination to promote lay support in the parishes by acting as a conduit clearly opened his magazine to unanticipated expressions of negativity.

Taken altogether, competition results and correspondence show that at least two-thirds of correspondents were female, often unmarried, some of them with literary ambition, probably using essay competitions to hone their skill. Most correspondents tended to be middle or upper working-class, often church workers, but clergymen and their families were correspondents too, the clergy's involvement as readers exemplified not only by competition results but also by a small number of inset articles directed specifically at them.[78] Predictably, the evidence points to the 'in-house' nature of inset readership, the correspondence offering no proof that insets were influencing non-churchgoers, evidence with which Michael Ledger-Lomas agrees, his study of the spectrum of religious publishing during the last quarter of the nineteenth century demonstrating that religious publications appealed to a large niche market in the churches rather than the 'indifferent' world outside.[79] Those contributing to insets formed a highly specific subset, however. To find other readers we must seek elsewhere.

The international reader

By the end of the nineteenth century there were 10,000 British missionaries serving within the British Empire.[80] As seen in Chapter 5, parishes supported their own missionaries, frequently corresponding with them and printing their letters in parish-magazine local pages. Keith Snell has referred to the 'global outreach' displayed by even the smallest parishes in their dealings with missionaries and missionary work.[81] Missionary reports and letters were monthly fixtures in the insets. One missionary stationed in India wrote that he greatly prized his copy of *The Church Monthly* as a reminder of home:

> It was a poem in your magazine which first led me to turn my thoughts to the mission field.... I have been at this remote Indian station for 3 years. With so little to read... your pleasant pages are greatly prized by me as a monthly reminder of the homeland.[82]

Much space in both insets and local pages was devoted to urging skilled workers to emigrate to British possessions overseas. In 1911, when 455,000 people left Britain, almost half went to Canada, 18 per cent to Australia and 7 per cent to South Africa.[83] Where emigrants went, Anglicanism and its parish magazines followed.[84] Mowbray's *Gospeller* – never the most popular inset – claimed in November 1881 that '150 parishes, some as distant as New Zealand, Ceylon and Newfoundland, have chosen this medium for making known the machinery of their parishes'. The national libraries of Australia and Canada contain localised copies of *Home Words* from 1880 to 1896.[85] In 1900, *The Church Monthly* claimed that it regularly appeared in New Zealand, recording its deep gratitude 'to countless friends in all parts of the world'. It reminded its readers that emigrants 'are always glad to receive a copy of the Magazine monthly and thus be kept in touch with their native place', urging those at home to 'send those across the sea a magazine every month', for the sum of one shilling and sixpence.[86]

Emigrants' letters were frequently published in local pages; Keith Snell notes that they were even read from the pulpit.[87] As Jonathan Rose has commented, they tended to make emigration attractive.[88] In November 1891, businessman Henry Spiers wrote from Port Elizabeth, South Africa, to the vicar of Camden Church, Camberwell, thanking him for the parish magazine he received each month, and thanking God that life in Port Elizabeth was 'much the same as in England'. His 'cottage' was opposite the church, the congregation had raised £1,000 in three days in a bazaar, and he was expecting the English cricketers to visit soon.[89] Joseph Milburn wrote to the parishioners of Saint John's, Keswick, about the roughness of his journey to Johannesburg by mule wagon. 'I never took off my clothes except to change them the whole time.' Two other Keswick men had joined him, their wages £7.10s a week for eight hours' work a day, which they considered a small fortune.[90] Other emigrants, however, were not so fortunate. The congregations of the two churches in Keswick gave financial support to a family migrating to America. When both parents died, the eldest son requested help to support his siblings. In the early 1890s, his letters charting his progress appeared in both parish magazines.[91]

Some emigrants fondly recalled their parish activities back home, a farmer's wife in America remembering the Mothers' Meeting at Saint Andrew's Church, Penrith:

> There is not a Wednesday passes but I am thinking about you all at the Mothers' Meeting, and wondering what Miss Tyson and Miss Harvey are reading to the mothers ... My mother sent us the Parish Magazines for the last year, and we were very proud of them. Remember me kindly to all the ladies and all the mothers.[92]

The emigrant readers of parish magazines were similar to those at home: professional churchmen, middle-class business people, skilled artisans and the 'deserving' poor. Their home church and their Englishness were inextricably linked, the parish magazine performing an important function by connecting them to those left at home, while its traditions spread, alongside Anglicanism, around the globe.[93] As Keith Snell argues, the parish magazine did not merely look inwards. As it reached out to readers far away it encouraged its readers at home to regard themselves as part of a larger family, all within the safe arms of the National Church and the British Empire.[94]

The local-page reader

The individual's absorption in family and community life may account, at least in part, for the popularity of local parish magazines. Not only did Mrs Sloan appear as a donor in her parish magazine, she also annotated the numbers containing the names of her family and friends, for while church workers were frequently listed, the magazines also recorded the names of those, like Temperance Hawtin of Eynsham – first encountered in the Introduction – who had been baptised, married or buried at church. By recording such rites of passage, parish magazines encouraged those who rarely entered church to read about their family's activity, whatever their socio-economic status. The death of a faithful worshipper would often result in a published obituary, used by Anglican clergy as a form of democratic memorial to parishioners, rich and poor.[95] In November 1897, Hardwicke Rawnsley recorded the deaths of the wife of a local squire and two young children, one a farmer's daughter, the other the daughter of a gardener; all recalled with equal warmth.[96] In the winter of 1901 he typically recalled in verse the life of a local butcher's wife:

> For this kind heart, tho' nursed in humble state,
> Took all the parish to its tender keeping,
> Cared for the children at the Sabbath school,
> Succoured the poor and helped the desolate,
> Did what she could to spread Christ's golden rule,
> And so we gave God thanks and left her sleeping.[97]

Did people of other denominations read Anglican parish magazines if, as already noted, clergymen considered them suitable for everyone in the parish? The Carlisle diocesan visitation returns of 1900 provide several clues. Some clergymen, particularly in country districts, visited every house themselves, or made sure that their female relatives did so, one of their means of effecting entry, delivery of the parish magazine.[98] Though some made it clear that only their 'own people' were visited, others stated that they or their lay helpers visited everyone in the parish, regardless of denomination. 'The Parish Magazines are taken round each month by either myself or Mrs Hale...I make no difference between church and chapel people when visiting', wrote Revd Hale of the city church of Saint John's, Carlisle. 'I take the ruridecanal magazine round myself. It gets me into almost every house every month. And I like to draw attention to particular articles in it and talk about them', wrote the vicar of the tiny village of Newton-Reigny.[99]

Such visits may well have been unwelcome, for tensions between Anglicans and nonconformists often emerge in the local pages of parish magazines. During 1903 a rancorous correspondence published in the Aspatria, Cumberland, parish magazine, emerged as a result of the vicar's invitation to other denominations to join the Anglicans at church on Christmas day. Sensing that their chapels were being slighted, Aspatria's Primitive Methodists and Congregationalists refused to attend, whereupon the vicar (a Ritualist) published a series of articles to 'oppose error' and demonstrate the 'vulgarity of [nonconformist] sensational preaching'.[100] Nonetheless, his antipathy to local nonconformists did not deter him from contributing a Christmas article to *The Church Monthly*, the subject of which was the 'jolly' reunited family. That his final paragraph unwittingly quoted George Wither – a Parliamentarian poet and friend of Oliver Cromwell – underlines the irony.[101] As Keith Snell has remarked, local strains such as this may have militated against parish-magazine reading by nonconformists.[102] Nonetheless, while the determinedly 'in-house' nature of the insets may have been off-putting, the community nature of local parish magazines could be particularly appealing to nonconformists in rural areas, as will be explored in Chapter 10.

Other means of engaging non-churchgoers involved subscribers lending their magazines to friends and neighbours, the vicar of Dalston, Cumberland, complaining in 1896 that if those who read the magazine for free would actually buy their own copy, the circulation would double.[103] Some parish magazines were deposited at local libraries.[104] Many were sold through local newsagents; St Peter-Le-Bailey parish magazine could be obtained from four Oxford newsagents as well as through district visitors.[105] Urban parishes, such as Camden Church, Camberwell, and Saint John's, Keswick, usually sold their magazines through the local printer-cum-newsagent who printed their local pages, but Holy Trinity, Hoxton, sold its magazines through a pharmacy as well.[106] In some villages, parish magazines were positioned at the hub of community life by being sold in post offices. At Headington Quarry, Oxford, the postmistress, Katie Cooper, served the community for 63 years from the 1890s.[107] Mrs Cooper not only sold the parish magazine, she also bought her own copies and had them bound, donating one to the church in 1949.[108]

Headington district-visiting notebooks record the names of the 'poor', many of them laundresses and widows, who were offered the parish magazine by their district visitor.[109] 'Perplexity' – noted earlier as the district visitor who wrote to the *Monthly Packet* in 1895 – claimed that, though virtually none of the poor women in her allotted street attended church, a good half of them bought the parish magazine when she proffered it.[110] Edward Salmon opined in 1886 that the working classes only read their Sunday newspapers because they were delivered to the door.[111] Personal delivery, then, was crucial: parish clergy often complained about a type of lady district visitor who tended to accuse her 'people' of not wanting to take the parish magazine, when in reality she had forgotten about them or delivered them too late.[112]

When parish magazines did eventually reach people's doors, were they actually read? Elizabeth Roberts's Barrow-in-Furness oral-history project hints at some possible answers:

> Mr B1B (born 1897), his mother, a cook-in-service before her marriage:
>
> 'After Sunday dinner Mother used to get these little books like *Home Chat* and she'd read those and Saint Mark's Church magazine.'
>
> Mr W1B and Mrs W1B (born 1900), her mother, a fancy-box maker before her marriage:
>
> Mr: 'She got the church parish magazine.'
>
> Mrs: 'No, I don't think she did. I think she read *Thomson's Weekly* and part of *John Bull* and I loved *Thomson's Weekly*. M' Dad took *Empire News* and *News of the World* on Sundays.'[113]

Mr B1B clearly saw the parish magazine as Sunday-reading for older women. *Home Chat* (1895–1958) was a typical late-nineteenth-century cheap magazine for women, which Richard Hoggart conflated with Sunday-school prize literature, the authors of which, as seen in Chapters 5 and 6, were frequent contributors to the insets.[114] As three of the Barrow churches took *Home Words*, the townspeople were as likely to have read *Home Words* as *Home Chat*, and it is possible that, in attempting to remember his mother's reading material, Mr B1B had mistaken its title, just as Flora Thompson probably did, as noted in Chapter 3. Mrs W1B, giving evidence in the late 1970s, had loved the secular periodicals of her girlhood, and was dismissive of her mother ever having read such a poor alternative as the parish magazine.[115] According to

Hoggart, *Thomson's Weekly News*'s portrayal of the minutiae of domestic life represented all that was working-class in the late-nineteenth-century press.[116] Its ample coverage of sports and trade-unions may explain its popularity in industrial Barrow.[117]

'Hidden lives'

Lists of baptisms, weddings and funerals, obituaries, names of church workers and magazine subscribers, district visitor records and Roberts' oral histories bring us close to the people who bought parish magazines. Evidence from a small number of family histories proves that they were used, even if not necessarily 'read'. The poet Norman Nicholson (1914–1987), son of a gentleman's outfitter in the Cumbrian mining town of Millom, recalled being taught to read by his grandmother and aunt during the Great War:

> They had no alphabet books or cards or blocks, but made do, instead, with the illuminated capital letters at the head of each paragraph in 'Home Notes', the monthly inset in St George's parish magazine.[118]

Home Notes was a secular woman's magazine and therefore not localised in any Anglican parish.[119] Like Flora Thompson's hazy memory of *Good Words/Home Words,* Nicholson's recall of his parish magazine's name was probably inaccurate, but *Home Words,* which was taken in a neighbouring parish, used a gothic typeface for its headlines during the Great War.[120] Norman Nicholson and Flora Thompson both read parish magazines for reasons important to them but unlike those imagined by the clergy. Thompson wished to read about Queen Victoria, but lived in a house with few books; the capital letters of an inset were utilised by Nicholson's relatives when paper was scarce. Similarly, in the Cumbrian mining town of Distington, a child called May Dalton used the flyleaf of a 1901 bound copy of *Home Words* to practise her 'tens and units'.[121] Parish magazines were ephemeral texts, capable of being passed on, thrown away or used for any variety of household tasks, including the most perfunctory. Unless saved and signed, their readers' names and lives are lost to us.

When, in her book *Hidden Lives,* Margaret Forster set out to document the experiences of her mother, grandmother and great-grandmother, she was searching for a secret involving illegitimacy in a proud working-class family.[122] She did not find it, but, in attempting to lay bare the ordinary lives of four generations of women, she inadvertently revealed some real parish-magazine readers. Her great-grandmother, Margaret Ann, abandoned an illegitimate baby around 1893, before entering service as a housemaid to William Stephenson, a painter and decorator living near Saint Mary's church, Carlisle. Like William Sloan, whom we met in the Introduction, Stephenson advertised his business in Saint Mary's parish magazine. Margaret Ann's name does not appear there, but the Stephenson name appears repeatedly in reports on Sunday-school and church charities; one of the sons was a Sunday-school superintendent.[123] It is tempting to think that Margaret Ann attended Saint Mary's 70-strong branch of The Girls' Friendly Society, the Church organisation for working-class girls, though in that 'pure' organisation she would never have dared reveal her secret.

To gain her position with the Stephensons, Margaret Ann may have used the servant registry advertised in Saint Mary's parish magazine.[124] Still to be found in *The Lady*, advertising of this type was common to middle-class women's periodicals.[125] Though the registry promoted in Saint Mary's magazine was a private commercial endeavour, free servant registries were a feature of many parish magazines, from the tiny Cumbrian village of Thornthwaite to the largest London parishes. Here, readers seeking domestic help could be put in touch with prospective servants who had been personally vetted by the vicar's family or other upstanding members of the congregation.[126] Like advertisements for pew rents, which were often printed on the front of urban parish magazines,[127] such registries demonstrate the rigid class boundaries existing among the readership, highlighting the class-ridden nature of Anglicanism, but they also reveal the parish magazine's versatile nature. Like Flora Thompson and Norman Nicholson, servants and mistresses put parish magazines to their own private uses, and, echoing the advertisements for household goods which crowded the local pages, the magazine could become a medium for the commercial exchange of human labour, scanned eagerly when in need by both sides.

Margaret Ann's daughter was a regular churchgoer, so when her own daughter (the novelist Margaret Forster), aged four, sought to prove that she could read and should be sent to school, she 'picked up a copy of the parish magazine [and] duly read aloud the bishop's Easter message, stumbling over only a few words'.[128] Throughout the family saga, the parish magazine would have been evident. Perhaps lying casually on a table, it would be used to check the times of church services or to find the addresses of advertisers; baptism, marriage and funeral lists would be scanned each month, the vicar's letter casually or dutifully read, the contents of the magazine tying this working-class family to its Anglican roots well into the middle of the twentieth century.

Conclusion

The Anglican parish magazine was useful to its readers in many ways, not all of them quantifiable and not all religious. It could be read as spiritual text, in-house 'club' communication, or trades directory; it could be cherished or defaced with equal ease. It attracted readers of all ages and of both sexes, in places as far apart as New Zealand and Newfoundland. Beginning as a means of communication between the Church and the poor, it expanded its remit when education and the benefits of industrialisation created a more sophisticated readership which, though still often viewed as working-class, began to be seen as essential to the Church's maintenance of its national position. Parish-magazine local pages assumed a particular importance, regardless of class or church attendance. They were a means of noting baptisms, marriages and funerals; advertising businesses; finding domestic goods and suppliers; communicating with families overseas; seeking work; engaging servants; and much else. Twentieth-century commentators expressed their modernism by finding parish-magazine reading inexplicable, but the magazines' wide geographical readership and longevity demonstrate that they played a significant role, nationally and internationally, even in lives not closely connected with the life of the Church. Yet most readers' names discovered through research were female; almost all district visitors were female; most advertisements were aimed at female homemakers; and there were more female competition winners than male. Moreover, the dominance of the inset romantic serial story points to a female readership. Women were the major parish-magazine readers, but while much of the material was aimed solely at them, editors constantly tried to encourage a male readership.[129] Conscious of attack on many fronts, parish magazines devoted increasing space to Church defence, their need for support great, their discourse one of deep anxiety, as Chapter 8 will explore.

8

Stormy Waters: 'How Can the Waves the Bark O'erwhelm, With Christ the Pilot at the Helm?'

Anxiety is a particularly distinctive feature of the nineteenth-century Anglican parish magazine. To some extent this is unsurprising, for anxiety has long been identified as fundamental to Victorian culture: Walter Houghton explored it over half a century ago in *The Victorian Frame of Mind*.[1] The parish magazine's combination of family periodical and denominational publication, however, ensured that the anxiety was both secular and spiritual, in effect inflicting a double dose of unease upon its readers. In its pages may be found not only all the 'fear and worry' which Houghton associated with a society in transition,[2] but also a narrative of hopelessness about the future of Anglicanism.

Callum Brown dates increasing Anglican anxiety to the late-eighteenth century when, as a result of industrialisation, 'the Church in danger' – a slogan which had been used to encourage the faithful for centuries – was deliberately developed into an overarching thesis of 'religion in decline'.[3] David Nash has noted the 'persistent, disappointed and waspish tone' in which the Church discussed its failures after 1850, while Sarah Flew has drawn attention to the Church's apprehensive response to diminishing lay financial support, particularly from the 1880s.[4] The continuing rhetoric of anxiety often overwhelmed parish magazines' traditional Christian teaching, despite their role as propagandist publications which aimed to attract the unaffiliated and encourage the faithful. Why did their contributors potentially damage the Church's reputation by airing their anxieties so loudly and openly, when the Christian message proclaims that perfect love casts out fear? Nash has suggested that such tactics were a means of 'rallying and galvanising' support for the state church in dangerous times,[5] a possibly counterproductive ploy, for, as this chapter reveals, such negativity repeatedly drowned out optimism for Anglicanism's future. The metaphor 'drowned' has been carefully selected, for the anxiety endemic to nineteenth-century Anglican parish magazines often expressed itself through the iconography of the sea voyage and the shipwreck. This chapter examines such sea iconology, first, through the figures of the sailor and Jesus in their roles as pilots, and, second, through changing discourse on the shipwreck. It goes on to discuss two major anxieties which suffused parish magazines – obsession with money and fear of socialism – and ends with a discussion of evasive and contradictory attitudes towards the Anglican 'family' through an examination of the 'voyage home'.

The sea voyage

Visual and textual references to the sea suffuse nineteenth-century insets. In 1896, *Home Words* allotted over a third of its space to them, its references to shipwrecks averaging two per month, admittedly an extreme example because of the publication that year of a serial story based on fishing, but other insets, too, employed similar references, particularly in their clichéd romantic serial stories, and within articles on science and technology which demonstrated the Church's approval of material progress and patriotism.[6]

Scholars commonly agree that, particularly during the fin de siècle, sea narratives and iconology were everywhere employed to underline Britain's self-image as a mighty maritime political and commercial power, and to promote the superior nature of British manhood in the person of the clean and honourable British seaman.[7] Cynthia Behrman contends that the sea was one of Britain's great organising myths – the island home, the sailor's heroism, the navy's importance as a symbol of empire and the Pax Britannica creating a particular British romance.[8] In Western culture the sea could also function as a spiritual metaphor. The instrument of death by drowning, it could become the believer's means of spiritual rebirth. In the voyage of life, the one true guide was Jesus, the heavenly pilot, and heaven was the one true port, but the sea could also cast sinners onto the rocks in the inevitable shipwreck of the godless life. George Landow has contended that Victorian fears over loss of faith led the shipwreck narrative to become one of the post-Enlightenment's most dominant images.[9]

Figure 8.1 'Life's Sunrise: Christ at the Helm', Free Gift with Bound Copy: *Home Words* (1914)

Christ at the helm

The few inset images of the Christ figure tend to depict him in his relationship to the sea rather than as the more traditional good shepherd. Frequently he was a pilot, as evidenced in Figure 8.1, 'Christ at the Helm', in which a young man guides his boat with Jesus's help. In Victorian culture the sailor was the ultimate hero, braving the sea to protect his island home, proud symbol of the sea-faring northern Europeans who were regularly portrayed as the originators of the British race, *Home Words* eulogising Princess Alexandra by quoting Tennyson's lines on her betrothal: 'Sea-king's daughter from over the sea... Saxon and Norman and Dane are we'.[10] In the insets, the sailor's life took on mystical proportions as writers fused his heroism with the Christian life-journey. In youth he was often rash, as demonstrated by Chapter 5's coastguard, Jeff Benson, struck down with sickness before achieving faith through humility. Mature sailors could be portrayed as sinful, achieving peace and the hope of heaven only through self-sacrifice during terrible storms,[11] while the elderly seaman became a wise, all-knowing patriarch.[12] Clergymen – those heroes of the parishes – could thus regard themselves as sailors, piloting their boats in choppy seas, as suggested in Figure 8.2 and in this advice to ordinands in 1857:

> You are now like a sailor standing at the water's edge and surveying that vast ocean on which your lot is soon to be cast ... count well the cost. Hesitate ere you launch irrevocably on the eventful voyage ... Once set apart for the work of the ministry, there is no receding from it.[13]

Fictional shipwreck

Storm and shipwreck in early parish magazines were typically predicated on evangelical teaching on sin and forgiveness. In 1859, *Parish Magazine* published a short story by Mrs Gaskell in which the waters which engulfed her hero on the sands of Morecambe Bay were the punishment intended for the sins of his enemies, for whom he willingly became the atoning sacrifice.[14] In Oxford, in 1872, the evangelical vicar of St Peter-Le-Bailey equated local flooding with the experiences of Noah, pleading with his flock to repent by attending church, the Ark that would save them from sin and hell.[15] In the evangelical *Home Words*, shipwreck was frequently used as a metaphor for the fragility of human life and the necessity for the soul's daily preparation for death, exemplified in Agnes Giberne's serial story for 1896, 'Nobody's Business', where, in the first chapter, the heroine was saved only just in time:

> In the booming rush of billows and the blinding dash of spray a vision had come to her eyes of a distant hill and a cross thereupon, and ONE whom she knew hanging patiently on the Cross; and her whole soul leapt up in a passionate prayer for pardon, because she had doubted His love. 'I shall never doubt Him again. He will now take me HOME', she thought.[16]

Nonetheless, while the beginning of Giberne's story was traditionally evangelical, the central narrative concerned a coastal community's practical need for a lifeboat, so, after dealing quickly with shipwreck as a portal to the heavenly home, Giberne then used the conventions of romantic fiction to reach her happy ending: the gift of a lifeboat and the marriage of her rescued heroine. After the first chapter, the Christian faith of the main characters merely added religious tone to the predominantly secular narrative, for though the story was peppered with wrecks which decanted dead bodies onto the beach of a Cornish village, Giberne ignored the spiritual state of those who had died in favour of the secular

Figure 8.2 'Pilots and Guides': *The Church Monthly* (1905) 242

experiences of the living. This approach was frequently adopted by female fiction writers, as seen in Chapter 6, but some clergyman writers used the same technique. Of eight fictional sea narratives sampled from the most popular insets, 1877 to 1916, danger at sea served as a means of teaching moral lessons whilst providing the requisite exciting backdrop to predominantly secular activities.[17]

Many of inset fiction's plots involved bankruptcy. As Landow has remarked, bankruptcy was the 'bourgeois' version of working-class destitution.[18] Richard Altick finds it one of the most pervasive themes in Victorian fiction.[19] It loomed so largely in Dickens, Thackeray, Trollope and sundry lesser novelists that Barbara Weiss named her study of the subject *The Hell of the English*.[20] To be a Victorian bankrupt was to undergo shipwreck in its post-enlightenment sense. Dickens used the metaphor in *Little Dorrit* when describing the collapse of Merdle's Bank.[21] It was also used at the climax of 'The Great Gold Mine', a *Dawn of Day* serial story in 1896, when the fraudulent mine-owner died in a shipwreck while escaping his investors (Figure 2.3).[22] During an escalation of company fraud in the 1890s, newspaper stories about such con men abounded.[23] In 'The Great Gold Mine', the peace of a country village was destroyed by the return of a ne'er-do-well son, Fred Ballance. Producing gold nuggets, legal documents and a prospectus, he invited the inhabitants to buy shares in his Californian mine, guaranteed to yield more interest than the banks.[24] The complete village hierarchy, from railwaymen to the squire himself, invested in the mine.[25] When the scam was uncovered, it was found that the gold was false, the address of the firm's head -office was false, there was no gold mine and Fred had never set foot in America. Only the vicar saw through the young man's veneer. 'With a man like Fred Ballance to steer the ship, he'll think that it is the best policy to save his own pickings and throw the rest overboard,' was his judgement. The seafaring metaphors grew as the story reached its climax. The stationmaster described 'all that could, crowded in ... poor folk, rich folk'; a farmer responded, 'I was as near being in this here boat as well could be'; and another remarked that alas he 'was in the same boat with his neighbours'. Towards the end, they all knew that 'a calamity...must soon break upon them in full force', and eventually, 'the hard-earned savings of their toilsome lives had all been swept away'. Fred fell from a ferryboat after a collision in fog, his spiritual state and that of his innocent fellow shipmates unrecorded, for one of the principal points of the narrative was not Fred's spiritual life-journey but his defiance of hard work and honest commerce. Fred was the very anti-Christ of parish magazines' gospel of work and thrift, his character-type frequently appearing in contemporary novels.[26]

The other main thrust of the narrative of 'The Great Gold Mine' was abuse of trust. The success of Victorian commerce depended on a generally accepted morality which, as James Taylor has argued, was fuelled by evangelicalism, but limited-liability investment caused grave disquiet because it did not necessarily obey the rules.[27] Fred's reappearance began a train of events leading not only to the abject poverty of some of the smaller investors, but also to the squire's financial embarrassment, his heir's subsequent inability to maintain the estate, and the potential collapse of the hierarchical system based on land-ownership which, according to the author, had previously worked so well. Fear of change from an old order to a new dominated the narrative: the shipwreck involved not only the squire and his villagers, but also a whole way of life.

The shipwrecked Church

True to the family-magazine origin of the insets, their most common sea images were naval and commercial vessels, sailors, fisher-folk, life-boat-men, coastal scenery and seascapes. Holidaying children abounded as the seaside became the focus of both the middle-class holiday and the working man's day-trip.[28] Yet regularly, among all these propagandist signifiers of a prosperous nation at peace with itself, its God and its national church, images of storms and wrecks were the means of uttering loss and loneliness in a world where Christ the pilot could no longer automatically be assumed to hold the tiller – images which had become a common metaphor for spiritual loneliness as part of the Victorian crisis of faith in the prose works of Carlyle, and in the poetry of Coleridge, Tennyson, Clough and others.[29] But while such canonical writers used the drifting, rudderless ship to describe their own loss of faith and sense of cosmic loneliness, inset authors used it to illustrate a faithless future in which the Church was doomed. In March 1886, a poem in *Parish Magazine* entitled 'The Church Threatened', began:

> My Mother Church! I scarcely knew
> How dear thou wert till full in view
> Thy foes pressed on, assailing still,
> With taunt and scorn, men of ill-will,
> Who fain would rend thy garments fair,
> And cast thee to the cold, bleak air:
> Such hate have they (as wolves to sheep),
> And thou dost veil thine eyes and weep.

It continued:

> My Mother Church! O Mother mine!
> Why should we fear for thee and thine?
> How can the waves the bark o'erwhelm
> With Christ the Pilot at the helm?
> Does He not hear the bitter cry,
> 'Master we perish utterly!'
> To storms of passion and ill-will
> Can He not whisper, 'Peace, be still?

The question was left hanging, because as previous chapters have suggested, the Church felt threatened on all sides during the 1880s, the anonymous poet here doubting the heavenly pilot's ability to save Anglicanism's frail ship in the face of such storms.[30]

Fear of the future and a call for Church defence seemed a justifiable Anglican reaction to the election of the atheist Charles Bradlaugh to the House of Commons in 1880. Owen Chadwick quotes a bishop who, in 1888, complained that atheism was everywhere, even in the club or in the conversation of young ladies at dinner.[31] Secularisation was a constant anxiety. Church schools competed with local board schools after 1870, with a resultant loss of specifically denominational teaching, and as more men were enfranchised, and trades unions and the Labour movement grew, the Church began to fear socialism and its associated possibilities of atheism and violence.[32] To Jose Harris, events in the 1880s created a 'great chasm' in the structure of society, as far-reaching as the 1960s; far more so than the two world wars.[33] While clergy feared socialism and atheism, they were even more concerned at the possibility that the enfranchisement of more nonconformists after the 1884 Reform Act would lead to disestablishment. Thus, while each stanza of 'The Church Threatened' returned to the metaphor of the Church as a protective mother, there was no help to be had, for the cast-out Mother Church could only weep. To the Victorians, the term 'wreck' could denote loss of female virginity and respectability.[34] Thus, the foes rending the 'garments fair' of a sexually objectified 'Mother Church' combine with the image of a storm-tossed ship to invoke a profound sense of unease.

Another *Parish Magazine* poem of 1886 was still more pessimistic. Written by a clergyman's daughter and dated 'Christmas 1935', it imagined the effect on Anglicanism, 50 years on, of disestablishment, through a woman looking back to the time when her radicalised husband had become a secularist:[35]

> He told me that the parsons were a greedy set of fellows,
> And doing nothing for us but pocketing our cash;
> That the churches were a nuisance only cumbering the ground up,
> And the service in the Prayer Book was just a lot of trash.
> Down with the pews and pulpits! We've the green fields all around us!
> What are pulpits after all, but the work of mortal hand?
> We'll worship in 'the open' with God's blue sky above us,
> And nobody a-telling us to sit, or kneel, or stand.
> No tithes and Easter Offerings, no collections in the land!

The churches were closed and turned to other uses:

> Many a Sunday, just from habit, I have taken up my prayer-book,
> And walked towards the dear old church where I used to pray.
> Twas all shut up, and dreary, and a notice on the door-post
> Said 'Art and Science Classes are held here once a day.'

The disappearance of the churches made the situation worse:

> Like a ship without a rudder, a crew without a captain,
> We drifted aimlessly about, with no one to command!
> There were the severed bodies, but the heads of all were wanting,
> And 'Give us back the Parsons!' was the cry on every hand.

Here the drifting, pilotless ship was the symbol of all that would be lost if churchgoers failed to protect not only the Church but also the nation. In a poem in *Home Words,* containing the verse,

> The good old Church of England!
> A faithful guide be thou,
> Amid the dangers and the doubts
> That crowd around us now

the facing page's photograph of needle-sharp rocks above an angry sea, graphically illustrated just how dangerous the Anglican's journey had become.[36]

'Church defence' to protect Anglicanism's established position, buildings and endowments, and to disprove the 'wild assertions' of nonconformists and secularists, rose to a crescendo in parish magazines at the turn of the century.[37] With Irish disestablishment (1871) had come disendowment and its simultaneous financial loss, encouraging nonconformists to hope for disestablishment in England. While Irish disestablishment had divided some Anglo-Catholics from the rest of the Church, the campaign for Welsh disestablishment (1894–1895, 1909, 1912) and the battle for ownership of, and denominational teaching in, elementary schools (1886–1902) tended to unite the church-parties, all sampled insets and many parishes campaigning vociferously on behalf of the Church.[38] As ever, Hardwicke Rawnsley attempted to sum up the situation in a sonnet, 'Church and State', which castigated those who

> Would with their illiberal sword illiberally
> Hew Church from throne and state, and would untie
> Those Holy bonds of wedlock God decreed.[39]

The sonnet appeared in Crosthwaite parish magazine in December 1885. One month later Rawnsley referred to yet another of his concerns: money, in particular, his own.[40] Like most clergymen, he feared moves towards disestablishment, but he was also typical of his colleagues in exhibiting anxiety over being put 'out-of-pocket' through increased parochial costs, for clerical anxiety about personal finance dominated even that of Church defence.

Money matters

Parochial giving

It is indubitable that during the period covered by this book, the Church of England was deeply anxious about its diminishing finances. In her study of Church funding, 1856 to 1914, Sarah Flew notes a pronounced decline in formal giving by upper and middle-class Anglicans. Their weakened perception of the importance of Christian stewardship, she argues, led to their reluctance to take responsibility for Church finances, while Church leaders firmly held that religion should be paid for by their congregations in much the same way that they paid for medical and legal services. As also noted in Chapter 7's discussion of church bazaars, Flew's research reveals that parishes increasingly grew to depend on commercial endeavours to raise funds no longer available through individual philanthropy, government agencies, church rates or pew rents. The commodification of religion at all levels of the Church, Flew contends, caused consumers to believe that Anglicanism was 'just one more leisure product on the market', so accelerating its decline.[41]

The parish magazine – ironically, itself, 'just one more leisure product on the market' – became the organ through which congregations could be addressed on the need for Christian stewardship. Readers were reminded that, because the Church was not bankrolled by the government, but existed on its endowments, individual financial contributions would make the difference between Anglicanism's success and failure.[42] In 1900, W. M. Sinclair, archdeacon of London, reminded *Dawn of Day* readers that if they were to allow the clergy to sink into poverty, religion would become universally despised, commenting that this could only be avoided if shillings from the poor as well as guineas from the rich were forthcoming.[43] Lay churchmen were also urged to engage with the local press to give the Church a wider platform on which to plead its case. Advice to parishioners was militant: 'Cling to, and if need be, fight for the retention of our parish churches, and hand them down inviolate to future generations as past generations have handed them down to you'.[44]

Some parishes, however, appeared unable to give larger sums; parish magazine local pages record that many were too poor, while others were engaged in raising finance for new churches, or in settling debts caused through church building or refurbishment.[45] Offertory money, which might have sustained the parish clergyman, was said to be generally given to support parish charities such as the poor and schools, but even here there were difficulties in raising sufficient funds, local pages frequently printing disparaging comments when the offertory fell below expected amounts.[46] The Easter offertory had traditionally been offered to parish clergy, and though the practice had largely died out, it was resurrected during the last quarter of the nineteenth century.[47] Each year Frederick Sherlock placed Easter Offering advertisements close to devotional material in *The Church Monthly*, reminding churchwardens that the scheme was a means of increasing slender stipends, and inviting them to introduce it into their parishes.[48] At the same time, his inset's illustrations depicted widows and children contributing their pennies to the collection plate, in a mute appeal for more.[49]

Commercialism

Samuel Smiles's pronouncement, 'Economy may be styled the daughter of Prudence, the sister of Temperance, and the mother of Liberty', encapsulates the economic advice given to inset readers throughout the long nineteenth century.[50] Similar extracts on thrift and self-help from Smiles's published books, as well as dozens of articles on such entrepreneurial projects as bee and poultry-keeping, appeared so often that we may be forgiven for regarding Smiles as the insets' patron saint. Countless articles equated money with righteousness, exemplified in

Charles Bullock's allusion to the Bible in 1898 as 'a wonderful collection of divine cheques...with God's own signature at the foot... which are always cashed...at the Bank of Faith'.[51] The working man was implored to dedicate himself to a combination of hard work, temperance and thrifty living which, together with cleanliness and Godliness, would lead to a life of financial independence and the holy grail of respectability: providing he kept his money safely in the national Post-Office Savings Bank. In Figure 8.3, a Gravesend coal carter is observed opening 'an account with Her Majesty', *Home Words* here representing the post-office account as the home of the patriot as well as the thrifty. In 1898, Canon Frank Langbridge's poem 'I Know a Bank' contrasted the hell of the public house with the heaven of the post-office savings bank, in a typical conflation of the sacred with the commercial.[52]

Saving with the Post Office clearly took the saver to a peculiarly English heaven, but investing elsewhere was depicted as having dire consequences. Working men traditionally saved through local friendly societies and benefit clubs, but these were heartily disliked by clergymen, as funds could be embezzled and members often met in pubs.[53] In 'John Harker's Bond', a *Church Monthly* serial story of 1893, most of a village's working men paid into a burial club which met at the pub, but the licensee absconded with their money. To compound the misery, the local bank crashed, taking with it the savings of the rest. Naturally the Church, in the person of the vicar, was on hand to offer advice, encouraging everyone to invest in the Post-Office Savings Bank, while driving home the moral that speculation and gambling were close cousins.[54]

Panic over bank crashes, added to general anxiety over Victorian commercial practices, occasioned frequent fictional narratives of financial ruin.[55] In 'The Forge of Life', a *Parish Magazine* story of 1865, the owner of a prosperous village shop lost his money when the skulduggery of his bank's partners led to suspense of payment, prompting his wife's unusually subversive criticism of the middle classes in their role as bankers:

> Heaven help us all ... and all the hundreds of poor honest folks that are going to be ruined by the villainy of those rich bankers ... Every farthing that the managers take into a bank, knowing that they can never repay it, is stolen.[56]

Her husband defended the bankers as men who suffered too, the anonymous writer, like the Church generally, clearly torn between giving blame where blame was due and supporting the commercial status quo.

"OPEN AN ACCOUNT WITH HER MAJESTY!" [See Page 37.

38

Figure 8.3 'Open an Account with Her Majesty': *Home Words* (1885) 38

A similarly contradictory message was embedded in Revd A. R. Buckland's 'The Patience of Two', published by *The Church Monthly* in 1893, in which a respectable young couple – a clerk and a teacher – had their marriage hopes dashed when the clerk's 'wicked' brother involved them in a newspaper swindle, a common phenomenon, as demonstrated by an article in the *Girl's Own Paper* in 1886 which warned readers not to enter into advertised schemes which required sending money in advance.[57] In 'The Patience of Two', the brother financed a quack-remedy sales business he had seen advertised in the press, by using the family home as collateral.[58] The family eventually faced homelessness when the business failed and bailiffs were sent to possess the house. In the manner of romantic fiction, however, the arrival of a letter from a long-lost uncle who had made his fortune in a South-African gold mine put all to rights, this narrative ploy being the deus ex machina which could bring both fortune and ruin in nineteenth-century fiction. Though written by a clergyman, the tale's message, apart from that of avoiding newspaper swindles, was a contradictory one: while speculation was wrong, it could deliver financial security.[59]

Clergymen in the insets' financial-ruin stories were often portrayed as above temptation. Representing God and morality, they stood firm in financial storms. L. T. Meade, however, deliberately subverted the ideal of clergy moral superiority by depicting her clergyman as weak. She was not alone. In 1894, Mrs C. W. Hawksley's serial story in *The Church Monthly* dealt with a clergyman's thoughtlessness with money which led to accusations of embezzlement. He was saved from imprisonment by the quick thinking of his brother-in-law, a doctor, who discovered the evidence necessary to acquit him, the narrative, like Meade's, praising the secular professional while denigrating the clergyman.[60] As we have seen, women writers, with their own agenda and preoccupations, were capable of undermining the Church within its own citadel through their exploration of contemporary themes.

Socialism

During the rise of socialism, the Church echoed widespread conservative fears that social unrest might lead to revolution.[61] Over time, however, the insets inched closer to a realisation that 'the working man' should be propitiated, shown in sundry articles which discussed or attempted to engage him (Figure 8.4), fuelled by debates at the Church Congress which in 1906 was addressed on unemployment by Independent Labour Party member George Lansbury.[62] Debate was also informed by press and parliamentary reports, and by social surveys carried out on working-class living conditions from the 1880s through to the outbreak of war in 1914.[63] Despite this, the sampled insets would not countenance socialism, fearing the secularism of the unions, which left 'the

Figure 8.4 'My Hobby is Working Men': *Home Words* (1907) 185

unanchored life without chart, compass or steersman at the mercy of every impetuous current and perilous squalls', even while recognising that social problems had left the country 'surging' with anxiety.[64] 'Labour has become a secular denomination with its creed, its faith and hopes and its semi-worship,' opined Revd G. S. Reaney in *The Church Monthly* in 1900.[65]

Parish-magazine local pages have left us with a wider assessment of the debate. In early parish magazines, differences between rich and poor were regarded as part of God's plan. As the Saint John, Limehouse, magazine declared in 1861:

> God made some rich and some poor on purpose. That the rich might feel that they had some to take care of and that the poor might feel that somebody cared for them. He meant them to have these kind feelings for one another.[66]

Even at the end of the long nineteenth century it was common for clergymen of parishes removed from industrial areas to agree with the insets that strikes were disastrous, and to go even further by declaring that strikers were 'the enemy'.[67] At Crosthwaite, Rawnsley ensured that his published opinions did not offend the mine owners with whom he was on intimate terms: after a particularly harrowing local accident which left 109 children fatherless, he was certain that no blame could be attributed to the mine's management.[68]

In large cities, where poverty was endemic, socialism was a source of clerical anxiety, not least because it led to the invasion of churches by marching socialist activists. The year 1887, which culminated in Bloody Sunday when demonstrators clashed with police in central London, had seen a build-up of protest marches.[69] In January the Social Democratic Federation – 'in military array' – invaded Saint James's Paddington during Morning Service, causing consternation, particularly when the demonstrators began to hiss during the intonation of 'O Lord save the Queen', and at the end of the Eighth Commandment (thou shalt not steal). The vicar considered that the devil himself had been present that day, but admitted to 'unusual' stillness and solemnity during the whole of the service, while the sermon was listened to with 'perfect attention'. He attributed this to the power of prayer rather than to self-control on the part of the SDF.[70] The problems which erupted at Saint Matthias, Stoke Newington, during the 1890s, when socialist sympathisers gained temporary control of the magazine, were documented in Chapter 4. The subeditor's belief in social equality ensured that he lost his position, the congregation's opinion of his stance encapsulated in correspondence sarcastically proposing Jack Cade as the church's new patron saint.[71] Some East-End clergymen sat on the fence, the vicar of Saint Columba, Haggerston, having compassion for workmen unless they drove wages too high.[72] Sympathetic clergy, however, allowed their congregations to put the issue of socialism to open debate. In June 1888, Saint John's, Keswick – an urban parish much more independently minded than Rawnsley's rural Keswick parish until the advent of Morley Headlam – invited Brooke Lambert, vicar of Greenwich, to preach on 'The Church's Practical Work in Relation to Socialism', and in the following month, members of Saint John's Literary and Scientific Institute debated Thomas More's *Utopia*.[73] In 1896, 'socialism' was the subject of a debate in the men's society of the West London parish of Acton, encouraging the largest attendance of the year, those who approved of socialism winning the debate despite the impassioned speeches of its detractors and the vicar's call for moderate views to prevail.[74]

The parish of Acton took *Home Words* which, in the same month as the socialism debate, published an article on 'Social Problems', condemning 'state-interference' in favour of 'self-help', a philosophy embraced by insets from Erskine Clarke's *Parish Magazine* onwards over half a century. Later in the same year, an article by H. Somerset Bullock suggested that future working men would cease to work if awarded government hand-outs.[75] Like *Home Words, The Church Monthly* had no truck with socialism. In November 1889, its report of a clergyman's visit to a working-man's club exemplified the average Anglican clergyman's attitude towards the working man, despite the very public efforts of contemporaries such as Brooke Lambert and Bishop Westcott of Durham to bring the two nations together.[76] In the club, the clergyman chanced to meet with a socialist he recognised: 'an enemy'; 'the atheist and scoffer of his flock'. After trying to evade him, the clergyman remembered his duty. 'Was it a call from the Master to this poor wanderer? He would do his best to make it so to this ignorant, unbelieving brother.' At last, in the vicarage garden, through a shared love of flowers, the socialist's 'poor deluded mind' was opened to see the truth in 'his selfish nature', as the mysteries of God's creation were opened to him.[77]

Some clergymen attempted to meet the working man halfway. One of these was Edward Newenham Hoare, the Liverpool vicar introduced in Chapter 4. His *Church Monthly* serial story of 1903 involved a builder who frequently quarrelled with his socialist nephew over politics, the duty of care to employees, and shoddy building techniques.[78] The local landowner, aided by the vicar, sympathising with the young idealist but determined to show him the error of his socialist ways, encouraged him to help build a garden-city suburb which would be managed by the landowner, the Church and a committee. Like the anti-socialist clergyman introduced earlier, Hoare's vicar hoped that contemplation of a garden would lead the errant working classes back to God, but he also admitted that much could be learned from socialism, revealing the influence of early-twentieth-century Christian socialist ideas which, as Callum Brown has noted, regarded social problems as 'economic, political, moral and educational', rather than predominantly religious.[79] Hoare was clearly influenced by the erection of Lord Leverhulme's garden-suburb, Port Sunlight, in 1888. In 1901, Port Sunlight was the venue of a garden-city conference attended by social reformers and pastoral idealists such as Ebenezer Howard, founder of the garden-city movement. Letchworth Garden-Village was inaugurated in the year Hoare's story was published.[80]

Many inset plots drew on a similar nostalgia for rural life and community.[81] Of 80 sampled inset stories published between 1877 and 1916, more than half were set in the countryside or on the coast, with only one in ten set entirely in the city, while the majority of the insets' illustrations were of rural pursuits or settings in which farming was seen as the model for the ideal life, despite a crisis in British farming: a result of foreign imports during the last quarter of the nineteenth century.[82] Keith Snell notes the sense of community and 'local pride' radiating from parish-magazine local pages, often centred on the goodwill created by the charity of local patrons.[83] There are many examples of such largesse. During the summer of 1902, Abingdon parish magazine reported on the celebrations at the end of the second Boer War, when – after tea and cakes at the rectory, and skipping, egg-and-spoon races and tugs of war in the school field – a barrow loaded with twelve dozen oranges for the schoolchildren was wheeled down from the big house, resulting in the singing of the National Anthem and 'For he's a jolly good fellow'. In December 1903, the ladies of the manor descended on the school at Kingston Bagpuize and 'transformed it into a scene of beauty' by erecting a Christmas tree 'covered with candles and gewgaws almost touching the ceiling'.[84] These happy scenes demonstrate the parochial community that Snell observed. He does not comment, however, on the late date at which they became numerous. In the 1860s and 1870s, local-page contributions, apart from the vicar's letter, were terse, usually confining themselves to comments on parish charities and finances.[85] As Snell has noted, they dealt more expansively with parish schools, particularly after a government or diocesan inspection, for many schools were then managed entirely by the Church.[86] From the 1880s, the emphasis increasingly shifted to voluntary parish clubs, treats and societies, the reports, sometimes contributed by the laity, growing longer and more elaborate. The sense of community they inculcated in both urban and country parishes helped tie readers to their spiritual home, the Church, but they also offered a sentimental narrative which suggested the virtue of remaining contented with one's lot, however unequal the opportunities, at a time of simmering social resentment and political unease.

Home and the Anglican family

Financial ruin caused the family in 'The Patience of Two' and the farmers in 'The Great Goldmine' to fear the loss of their home, and caused the guiltless family in 'The Forge of Life' to lose both their home and their business. Clearly, contemplating the loss of the family home when the alternative for many was the workhouse, was the cause of much Victorian anxiety. Parallel to this was increasing unease about the security of Britain, the island home, following political and economic growth in Germany, particularly the expansion of its navy, post-1900 inset fiction sometimes casting the German as a villainous spy in disguise.[87] Undoubtedly, the very word 'home' was loaded with meaning.

'Home' figured largely in this chapter's earlier discussion of the spiritual shipwreck, for the Christian was taught that his main aim in life was to reach his heavenly home. The symbolism of the full title of *Home Words for Heart and Hearth,* with its motto, 'the heart has many a dwelling place but only once a home', would have been immediately understood. As scholars have observed, Victorian domestic and religious ideology were presented as identical, 'Mother Church' and the 'angel in the house' both sanctuaries in a dangerous world.[88] The Christian's earthly and heavenly homes were securely elided, as in an illustrated poem in *Home Words* in 1877, 'Waiting for "a footstep that we know"', in which mother and child await both the earthly and the heavenly 'master', the mother meditating on the death of her last baby and the coming of the heavenly master to take them all to live together 'by-and-by'.[89] While few images of the Holy Family were seen in *Home Words* and *The Church Monthly*, Marian worship being highly undesirable to many Protestants, Madonna and Child were suggested by the perfect mothers and children who peopled inset iconology. In the poem's illustration, not only was the fire 'burning brightly' and the house 'clean and neat' but the mother was pretty and the child winsome, because the metaphor of the perfect home could be used to advertise a variety of moral and social messages.[90] The Church promoted itself as the Mother, while the clergyman and the head of the household were representatives on earth of God the Father. The parish church was every Anglican's home, not only taking all its adherents into itself, but also allowing women church workers to remain in their role as angels of the house while out and about on Church business.

The importance of the family was buttressed by the Church's promotion of the family life of the royal family, aided by what John Wolffe has judged its canny self-presentation as an 'ordinary' family with ordinary joys and woes.[91] Parish magazines formed a perfect vehicle for such advertisement, the significance of home-life bolstering both Church and monarchy.[92] Predictably, the death of Queen Victoria was greeted with sorrow in both insets and parishes.[93] Fascination with her offspring continued unabated during the Edwardian period, Edward VII's penchant for sexual intrigues and actresses overlooked in favour of his respectable home life, his imperfections patriotically ignored.[94]

Similarly, the bullying tactics of white missionaries in Africa during the Crowther affair were scrupulously hidden from parish-magazine readers.

The prevalence of racism in Britain predictably ensured that praise for the first Anglican black bishop, Samuel Crowther, occurred alongside frequent denigrating references to 'niggers' and 'savages' on local pages and in inset fiction.[95] Nonetheless, in 1864 *Parish Magazine* heralded Crowther's journey from slave to West-African bishop with much pomp.[96] His subsequent career was celebrated with a heroic portrait in a congratulatory two-page spread in *Home Words* in 1890, the year in which, despite leading what his biographer has termed 'a blameless life', he was ousted by evangelical 'white zealots'.[97] *Home Words* dodged the real reason for Crowther's resignation, just as it evaded other potentially embarrassing episodes concerning the Anglican Church 'family'.[98] In 1899, 'clerical lawlessness' over ritualism became a cause célèbre when a Ritualist curate's 'abduction' of an evangelical vicar's son was widely discussed in the secular press,[99] but there was virtual silence in the insets other than an anodyne remark in *Dawn of Day* that clergymen in Winchester diocese always obeyed their bishop's authority.[100]

When analysing the hypocrisy and self-deception at the heart of the 'Victorian frame of mind', Walter Houghton pointed to the evasion tactics employed by Victorians to enable them to maintain impossibly high standards of thought and behaviour. By 'deliberately ignoring what was unpleasant' and pretending that their version of events was the 'whole truth', they indulged in 'decorative lies'.[101] Charles Bullock put this rather more opaquely in 1889. Introducing his newspaper, *Fireside News*, to *Home Words* readers, he explained that it would not deal with 'ecclesiastical' topics; as it was a newspaper for 'the homes of the people', its distinct mission was to teach 'the secret of national, social and domestic happiness and prosperity'.[102] Like children, inset readers always received a bowdlerised version of events for their own good. They were never really trusted. Though they were increasingly expected to help the clergy, they were frequently regarded as disappointing 'lay hinderers'. Frederick Sherlock, who made his name by advancing the cause of lay partnership, labelled some of his readers 'miserable, intriguing' wire-pullers, indulging in petty name-calling at parish-meetings.[103] They were accused of being 'spiritual vagrants', 'wandering about from one place of worship to another, not settling down in any church as their religious home', complaining of dull services and quarrelling with other members of the congregation and the clergy.[104] If, as David Nash has suggested, this disparagement was intended to promote better expressions of churchmanship, it contradicted traditional Christian messages of mercy and love which existed in parallel with it, often on the same page.[105]

Conclusion

Parish magazines used the themes of the voyage and the journey home to teach Anglicans how to live the Christian life in the Church's motherly care, but through their repeated consternation at Anglicanism's own impending shipwreck, their criticism of churchgoers, and their embrace of the commercialism, evasion and hypocrisy of the age, they unwittingly exhibited many of Anglicanism's contradictions. An article published in *The Church Standard* in the summer of 1910 highlights the problems engendered by the Church when dealing with its own 'family' in an indifferent, commercialised world.[106] A report on the 'Seaside Mission for Children', which travelled around resorts advertising its presence each day by building an elaborate 'church-castle' in the sand, was dominated by anxiety made all the more poignant by its seaside setting. After reporting complaints that had been made about its young missioners, whose zeal had apparently outrun their indiscretion, the article turned to the animosity that the mission's presence had provoked among local businessmen. Bathing-machine owners had attempted to chase off the missioners by deliberately placing machines too close to the seated children, while some town-councillors had attempted to ban the mission, regarding the missioners as 'gloomy Jeremiahs' intent on spoiling the children's pleasure. The article reported that the missioners found it difficult to be heard over the sound of the sea: a telling metaphor, we may think, for Anglicanism in a new century.

After examining texts like this we may judge with Matthew Arnold that the sea of faith was retreating, the secular world either ignoring the Church or pressing its concerns more and more upon it, controlling it in ways perhaps more than it knew. There is little wonder that the Church exhibited contradictory aims: on the one hand longing to return to the safety of village, squire and country church, but, on the other, recognising its responsibilities in negotiating with new political and economic ideas and assimilating social change. Parish magazines attempted to allay anxiety and encourage denominational allegiance through the evasion of awkward truths and the expression of a deeply felt conservatism, but while their many voices expressed paradoxical views, they achieved unity in their all-encompassing fear for Anglicanism's future and an attendant need for Church defence.

9

The Challenges of Modernity: Scientific Advances and the Great War

This chapter takes the parish magazine forward to the Great War, first, by examining the evidence it provides for the Church's attitude to science. For some, scientific understanding undermined the basis of religious belief and was ultimately the Church's most formidable opponent, but the way in which science was presented to its reading audience permitted no cleavage between them, the Church always adapting its stance to suit new discoveries. During the carnage of the Great War, however, the Church denounced science as intrinsic to German barbarism, the result of Germany's espousal of godless modernism. After the Allied victory, the Church returned to its original position, science then being seen to aid the British war effort. The chapter examines some of the Church's difficulties during the Great War by contrasting Archbishop Davidson's National Mission of Repentance and Hope with events in local parishes. Here, a heroism narrative, when combined with community solidarity and clerical sensitivity, was able to support parishioners where the rhetoric of guilt and repentance did not. The chapter moves on to discuss changes in common religious belief which allowed the Angel of Mons to become a central figure at the war's lowest point, a phenomenon in which the parish magazine played an important part.

Science

Constantly urging congregations to return home to God, fearful that secularism was driving the Anglican ship towards the rocks, parish-magazine rhetoric was at times hectoring, at others self-pitying. At the beginning of a new century, the rector of Killarney tried

> ... to pierce the misty future. It seems now to us to be a descending slope. Most of us feel as if we had reached a highest point. But who can tell? ...The mist hides all. There will be needed fresh efforts to make the poor and needy happier, to sweep away the reproach of intemperance, gambling, impurity, selfishness, the love of money.[1]

More than to Anglicanism's traditional foes, the future, had the rector but known it, belonged to science, but, unlike its generally negative response to socialism, the Church's pre-war reaction to scientific discovery involved a willingness to accommodate itself to new thought. This is unsurprising since, after the Enlightenment, the practice of science as a cultured activity had attracted many clergymen.[2] Moreover, the invention of new technologies guaranteed the British Empire's supremacy. To the editor of *Dawn of Day*, however, the Church's embrace of science was essential because the spread of scientific knowledge through education and the secular press had encouraged congregations to become more 'rational and questioning'.[3] As Michael Ledger-Lomas has remarked, developments in publishing allowed the reading public to access texts which the Church 'would have preferred to suppress or ignore'.[4] Until 1914, the Church, as demonstrated in countless tracts and religious family magazines, usually attempted to take science into itself, to make captive, and so tame, new developments, so that what might have been regarded as threatening was accepted as part of God's revelation of Himself.[5]

From 1871 to 1914, articles on science and technology occupied around 10 per cent of inset space, mirroring that found by Peter Broks when researching the science content of a group of contemporary magazines.[6] It also reflected the proportion of science talks compared to other subjects in parish men's clubs and the number of science books compared to others in contemporary parish libraries.[7] If Katie Cooper had used her parish library at Headington Quarry in 1889, for instance, she would have had a choice of 305 books, almost all non-fiction, of which, according to the catalogue, 33 were on science.[8] Should Austin Clare have attended the parish library at Alston, her choice of science books in the non-fiction section would have been 16 out of 128.[9] Occasionally inset science articles extended, like serial stories, over many months, but most filled short paragraphs, while others were 'tit-bits', filling in space around longer articles on faith and its practice. During the 1890s, such snippets, entitled 'Science Gossip', were gathered together each month in *Dawn of Day*, illustrating the reader appeal which popular science was judged to have.[10]

Of 698 named contributors to the four best-selling insets between 1871 and 1914, only 39 wrote on science and technology. Most of them were male, a third of them, clergymen. Only two of the seven female science writers contributed articles before 1900, perhaps reflecting cultural mores which promoted the arts as more suitable for the female brain.[11] Nevertheless, the count of one female science writer to six males supports Peter Broks's conclusions based on his own magazine selection, for though he found that the proportion of female science writers to males was one in eight, he also discovered that the 'proselytising' magazines in his group provided female science writers with greater opportunities.[12] This phenomenon is replicated within the insets, where evangelical novelists like Agnes Giberne were trusted to contribute theologically sound science for poorly educated adult readers whose understanding was often considered little better than that of children.

Progress

True to their family-magazine inheritance, insets regularly featured articles on technology, such as the description of the invention of the 'Spinning Jenny' in *Home Words'* first number, and Edison's invention of the phonograph in 1888.[13] Contributors considered inventions like steam-power, electricity, photography and telegraphy as God-given 'secret forces' which they contended would lead to a greater understanding of the ways of the Holy Spirit.[14] As noted in previous chapters, the Church thoroughly endorsed Britain's imperial power, so new armaments technology was greatly admired, as seen in Figure 9.1, an illustration from a *Church Monthly* article eulogising Lord Armstrong, the Tyneside industrialist, in 1905.

Until the beginning of the Great War, much science writing acclaimed human progress. Articles on how to improve health were a staple of insets and local pages from the beginning. *Parish Magazine* and *Dawn of Day*, for instance, included articles on clean water and air,[15] while, as noted in Chapter 1, the magazine of Saint John, Limehouse Fields, advised parishioners on how to avoid disease spread by faulty drainage and infected water. During the 1890s, Rawnsley's Crosthwaite magazine described safe butter-making and milk sterilisation in an attempt to combat tuberculosis.[16] As developments in bacteriology and antisepsis resulted in increasing trust of the medical profession's handling of disease, inset articles presented medical science as a benevolent force, improving readers' lives. The doctor was given an increasingly prominent role, not only in articles and illustrations but also in fictional narratives.[17] This resulted in a very visible separation of the spiritual

Figure 9.1 'Armaments on Tyneside': *The Church Monthly* (1905) 140

from the physical, a *Church Monthly* poem noting in 1906 that the doctor and the clergyman entered the sickroom as equal partners with entirely separate roles:

> One stands beside the bed of pain,
> Finds help and cheer when all seems vain
> And brings back hope and health again.
> One by the shadowy valley waits
> To aid the soul in desperate straits,
> Or point towards Heaven's opening gates.[18]

The widening division between the spiritual and physical realms became a cause of clerical concern, one contributor to *The Church Monthly* doubting the necessity of his presence at the deathbed when faced with increasing numbers of the dying who saw no need for the presence of a priest to assist their journey out of life.[19] However, such negativity over the advance of scientific knowledge only occurred when the clergyman's status was visibly affected. At all other times inset writers embraced science as part of God's creation.[20]

Charles Darwin

References to Charles Darwin and the theory of evolution may be used to assess the manner in which acceptance of scientific discovery was relayed to parish-magazine readers. As *Home Words* typically evaded controversy, articles on evolution were completely absent from its pages, Charles Bullock remarking that, 'as a general rule it [is] best to let poisonous literature alone'.[21] Before his advent as an editor, however, Bullock had publicly mocked both Darwin and the author of *Vestiges of the Natural History of Creation*, concluding, 'the Bible by virtue of its divine origin is the basis of all true scientific discovery... scientific discovery can never contradict it'.[22] Many evangelicals disliked Darwin's theory, as did individuals within other Church parties, partly because Darwin was championed by socialists,[23] but, though they did not enter into the debate, parish magazines signalled the eventual acceptance of evolutionary theory, though the acceptance was nuanced.

Explaining the physiological reasons for 'Tears and Laughter' to *Dawn of Day* readers in 1901, John Polkinghorn commented on Darwin's experiments on his baby son, and an experience related by Mrs Gaskell, as examples of facial-expression recognition. By then, Darwin and Gaskell were regarded as instantly recognisable names, but the problematical implications either of Christian denomination or of scientific discovery were ignored, the eminent scientist and the wife of the Unitarian minister enfolded into the Church's wide embrace as surely as when Darwin was interred in Westminster Abbey.[24] It had not always been so. In 1874 the SPCK tract committee argued over whether to include T. G. Bonney's *Manual of Geology* in its list, Bonney being an outspoken supporter of Darwin.[25] Nonetheless the language of evolution had become so intrinsic to clerical discourse by the 1890s that, while discussing the housing of the poor in *The Church Monthly*, the bishop of Guiana felt able to describe social class in evolutionary terms: the poorest were born without backbone; they belonged to the 'invertebrate order of men', and would always form society's underclass.[26] In 1896, the year that Frederick Temple – progressive Churchman and supporter of evolutionary theory – was consecrated as archbishop of Canterbury, *Home Words* capitulated by publishing an article by a clergyman about the great apes, entitled 'Distant Cousins', referring approvingly two years later to 'that man of science, Charles Darwin'.[27] Meanwhile, 'Science Gossip' on pollination in *Dawn of Day* commented unself-consciously on the 'fierce competition' going on between plants which would lead to the 'extermination' of the weakest,[28] and inset fiction exhibited a populist understanding of the inheritance of acquired characteristics, many stories proffering the notion that good breeding would ensure successful behaviour characteristics and maintain class hierarchies.[29] Though born in poor circumstances, heroes and heroines possessing superior looks and taste frequently found that they were the offspring of high-born folk, and it was their fine breeding, along with their faith, which allowed them to cope with adversity.[30]

The insets clearly absorbed scientific naturalism into Anglican theology. In 1900, Dean Farrar, who had preached at Darwin's funeral in 1882, suggested in *The Church Monthly* that working-men should read works by Alfred Wallace along with the Bible, Dante and Milton, while Canon T. P. Garnier demonstrated the Church's acceptance of evolution in *Dawn of Day*.[31] Garnier acknowledged that only 'within its own province' was the Bible 'inspired of God'. The Bible was not a work of science or even of historical accuracy. Its account of the Creation was 'telescoped and conveyed in a pictorial form' to describe 'a progressive work of creation ... under the control and direction of the Divine Mind'. Although anything was possible for God, He had probably ordered the creation of the world through the 'law of evolution, which after all, is the law of progress'.

Garnier insisted that God did not work by blind 'natural laws'. He had entered the creation process at some point to create man, taking a lower organism and 'into this lower organism he, so to speak, "breathed" the capacity for the beginning of a higher life', Garnier here adopting Darwin's own words from the closing passages of *Origin of Species*:

> There is grandeur in this view of life, with its several powers, having been originally breathed by the Creator into a few forms or into one; and that, whilst this planet has gone cycling on according to the fixed law of gravity, from so simple a beginning endless forms most beautiful and most wonderful have been, and are being, evolved.[32]

Darwin inserted the words *'by the Creator'* in the second and later editions.[33] Christians like Garnier, who could not accept that evolution was a haphazard process, could then consider Darwin's theory as a form of Christian evolution.[34] In 1915, Camden Church, Camberwell, parish magazine reported a sermon by Archdeacon Basil Wilberforce of Westminster Abbey entitled 'Why does God not stop the War?'[35] Explaining God's apparent indifference, Wilberforce invoked 'the immutable law of evolution ...To suspend this war even once by omnipotent interference would be to obliterate it wholly and turn man into an automaton,' but he dismissed the theory of random natural selection in favour of the 'divine germ', which worked within the emerging consciousness of created things to create the ultimate perfection, with Christ as its perfect specimen: the ultimate evolved man whom all humans would eventually resemble.[36] Wilberforce was the youngest son of Samuel Wilberforce, bishop of Oxford, whose confrontation with Thomas Huxley, in Oxford in June 1860, is well known.[37] Here, in Soapy Sam's son, we see an earnest attempt to distil the views of both these mid-Victorian antagonists, as the Church negotiated its path through new philosophies.

Natural history narratives

As Aileen Fyfe discovered when investigating RTS mid-nineteenth-century publications, popular science could be deliberately imbued with 'Christian tone', RTS writers ensuring that biblical quotations and references were placed in otherwise secular texts, usually at the beginning or end.[38] This technique, which became well established and remained popular with the public, may be observed in inset natural-history articles.[39] 'All things are the work of God and whatever His hand has fashioned must surely be worth man's notice and study', declared William Houghton (1828–1895), in *Parish Magazine*, while conducting a walk round a pond in 1859, though his article made no further reference to religion.[40]

Natural history was the subject of over 60 per cent of science articles in the four best-selling insets from 1871 to 1914.[41] Natural history writing was informed by a well-established understanding of the two Christian books: the book of nature, and the book of revelation.[42] Some writers approached the problem of the Bible's account of the creation by encouraging readers to read the two books together: God had created the world, and his 'work' was 'nature'; studying one book would help the Christian understand both.[43] Agnes Giberne, whom we have already met variously employed as evangelical, romantic novelist and writer of anti-socialist polemic, was the author of numerous books on astronomy and geology, contributing a series on the former to *The Church Monthly* in 1893.[44] Though her narrative was almost completely secular, she adopted religious tone in her initial reference to the Creator of the book of nature:

> Suppose a father gave his children a beautiful book full of exquisite pictures and curious writing; and suppose the children were so busy with their cakes and toys that they tossed the book aside and never gave it another thought?...This is exactly how thousands behave towards the splendid book of nature, which our Father in Heaven has given to us. We know little as yet about the book, though that little is extraordinarily more than our forefathers ever managed to make out; and our readings are very often mistaken. Still, if once we begin to use our eyes, trying to spell out even one sentence of it, we are sure to be drawn on by the fascination of what we find.[45]

Parish-magazine references to William Paley's natural theology are rare. As Jonathan Topham discovered when examining reviews of the Bridgewater Treatises, nineteenth-century Churchmen felt uncomfortable with Paley's theory because it did not admit emotion: the language of the heart.[46] The traditional clergyman naturalist promulgated a kinder theology of nature.[47] Arguably the best known in his day was J. G. Wood. By writing anecdotally – a typical convention of natural history writing for the masses – Wood captured the language of the heart by dwelling on the morality of animals, of use to inset editors as it encouraged similar moral behaviour in humans.[48] Another such writer was Frances Orpen Morris. By appearing to grant animals souls, his 'Natural History Anecdotes', published in *Home Words*, supported the Church's view that religion and science were in harmony.[49] Similarly, a poem on fossils by the bishop of Durham, published in *Home Words* in 1902, attempted to harmonise science and religion by relating fossils' slow creation and imagining their resurrection at the Day of Judgement:

> God shall create new heavens and new earth,
> And will He give these trees of stone new birth?
> Unfolding from the rocks at His command.
> Green boughs to wave and shade a sinless land?[50]

The many publications of popularisers like Wood ensured that the theology of nature reached a wide audience.[51] It may be discerned in parish magazines well into the twentieth century.[52] Over time, however, some inset natural history writing changed its emphasis, as exemplified by his contributions over 20 years to *The Church Monthly* of Theodore Wood. Though Richard Noakes's analysis of scientific articles in the *Boy's Own Paper* discovered that when the young Theodore Wood collaborated with his father, J. G. Wood, he still worked within a theology of nature; his mature natural history articles in *The Church Monthly* were objective in content and tone.[53] Scholars have pointed out that it was as a result of observing the activities of such creatures as the ichneumon wasp that Darwin was led to question the love of an all-powerful Creator.[54] Famously, this particular insect lays its eggs inside a caterpillar, its progeny then hatching and eating the caterpillar alive. Theodore Wood included this information in an article on garden pests in 1893.[55] Having dealt with the ant, he turned to a 'yellow hard and horny' empty skin, created when a 'deadly little enemy' laid its eggs in 'the hapless insect'. The 'hungry little grub' thus produced 'devoured all its limbs and skin'. Wood then moved on to the ladybird and its meal of aphids without further comment. This was indeed Tennyson's 'nature red in tooth and claw': a world away from Wood Senior's anecdotes about the dog's loyalty to man and the cat's devotion to her kittens. Its emphasis on the fight for life was pure Darwinism, Wood having become the 'devil's chaplain' whom Darwin had envisaged recording the 'horridly cruel works of nature'.[56] Another Darwinist, Edward Step, contributed to *The Church Monthly* during the same period.[57] A professional naturalist, Step used his entries on plants in the first edition of Arthur Mee's *Children's Encyclopaedia* (1908) to demonstrate natural selection.[58]

Parish science

Inset science articles seldom differed from the views expressed in local parish magazines. The female reader of Oxford's Dorchester Abbey parish magazine, after accepting some aspect of evolutionary theory in her inset, might, on turning to her 'vicar's letter', have confronted the literal meaning of Genesis through his warning that because of her sin, 'the grand and beautiful work of God's creation was spoilt', but such potential conflict was rare.[59] On the contrary, local pages frequently referred approvingly to science, in particular to science lectures run in conjunction with parish men's clubs.[60] In 1889, science books in Headington Quarry library included T. S. Ackland's *Creation as told by Theology and Science,* published by the SPCK in 1874, and other titles, such as *Nature's Wonders,* and *A Chapter on Science: Six Lectures to Working Men.*[61] In 1893, Saint John's Keswick literary and scientific institute contained a well-rounded collection including Samuel Laing's *Human Origins,* which taught evolutionary theory; Benjamin Kidd's *Social Evolution,* which supported a religious approach to the new science of sociology; and A. M. Fairbairn's *Christ in Modern Theology,* which attempted to mediate between science and religion.[62] Neither of these libraries, however, contained works by Darwin.

Of earlier parish libraries, that of St John, Limehouse Fields, in 1871 contained only seven books which might be loosely attributed to science, four of which were on Christian apologetics, including William Paley's *Natural Theology* and *Evidences of Christianity,* and Butler's *Analogy*.[63] Clearly, readers in Limehouse wishing to understand the relationship between science and religion with recourse only to the parish library would have had to base their views on natural theology. All the more interesting, then, is a letter that appeared in the Limehouse parish magazine in 1872, the year of the publication of Darwin's *Expression of the Emotions in Man and Animals,* and the year after the publication of

The Descent of Man. The letter is unusual, not only because it appeared at all when letters to parish magazines were rarely printed in full, but also that it was, first, amusing, and, second, said to have been penned by a woman, referred to by her initials, H. A. S. Writing to complain about the vicar's recent sermon denouncing the showiness of fine clothes, H. A. S. expressed the belief that the love of dress elevated humans over animals, building a picture of the ascent of man from the level of the savage through love of ornamentation, reaching a peak of civilization in the well-dressed woman. She admitted that taste depended to some extent on a person's 'phrenological development', but nevertheless fine dress was proof 'that they have got beyond the animals and have taken the first step on the ladder of ascension'. She went on to question Saint Paul's judgement in the matter of women's dress and ended by determining to ornament her bonnet, whatever the vicar's view on the matter.[64] Almost certainly H. A. S. had been affected by Darwin's theories, her reference to phrenology suggesting she was also interested in natural law. James Secord has shown that new scientific ideas spread widely as a result of the publication of cheap editions.[65] Living in London, H. A. S. could have come across reviews of Darwin's newest book as well as cheap editions of *The Origin of Species* and books on phrenology. She seems to have determined on an independent view, however, given that Darwin's research focused on the ornamentation of some male creatures in order to attract females, and she certainly did not appear to conform to the stereotypical embarrassed lady blushing at Darwin's theory of emotions envisaged by *Fun* magazine in a cartoon of 1872.[66] Moreover, her censure of Saint Paul demonstrated an acquaintance with biblical criticism that could not have been gleaned from the parish library. As discussed in Chapter 1, Saint John's, Limehouse Fields, was a poor parish, but by 1870 it had attracted churchgoers from outside through its literary vicar, Henry Whitehead. Like Whitehead's friend, the writer George MacDonald, H. A. S. was probably different in social class, education and attitude from many others in the parish who may have been entirely indifferent to the problems of science and religion.[67]

The Great War

As previously described, parish magazines usually claimed scientific discoveries as evidence of God's unfolding revelation to man. Indeed, as George Landow has argued, the Church has responded to every advance in secularisation by adapting or abandoning its religious forms and doctrines as a means of demonstrating that it is capable of achieving a purer faith. Thus, the Church brought science into its fold, by, as Landow terms it, making a necessary retreat in order to advance.[68] However, as scholars have argued, lack of conflict between science and religion is not always regarded as morally acceptable. In some circumstances religions feel the need to resist scientific advances.[69] The accommodation between the two was called into question at the beginning of the Great War.

Commenting on the earliest battles of the war, Morley Headlam's Keswick parish magazine demonstrated a sea change in Anglican thinking by criticising science, which had enabled Germany 'to prostitute itself to the devil through its advanced weaponry'.[70] One month later, a contributor to the *Church Quarterly Review* criticised German liberal theology which, influenced by evolution theory, had sullied German morality, leading to acceptance of the materialism of anti-Christian philosophers such as Nietzsche. Disastrously for Europe, the Germans had valued science over faith. The author argued that the period from 1850 to 1890 in Britain had been too optimistic in its 'boundless confidence' in the influence of science to do good.[71]

The Church was in a difficult position in 1914. The traditional preacher of Christ's gospel of peace, it nevertheless knew that the only way it could demonstrate its national relevance was by approving the use of force.[72] One means of doing so was by vilifying the German national character, depicting the Germans as a debased and evil race. By allying Germany to immoral scientific advance, the Church could demonstrate its patriotism while also encouraging traditional religious belief. That this attitude to science and technology conflicted with the British build-up of armaments was excused because of German brutality. Morley Headlam embraced this view: German barbarism had to be opposed because it was in utter opposition to the British sense of honour.[73]

The home front

Numerous parish magazines furnish evidence for the conduct of the war at home,[74] but while most magazines underline the fervour with which the call to arms was received in 1914, some continued to allow anxiety about money, church attendance and ritualism to dominate other issues. In October 1914, for example, the vicar of Abingdon mused that the war was the one subject which 'dominates our thoughts now', but by November he had reverted to fussing over the wearing of black stoles and kneeling during the celebration of Holy Communion,[75] and throughout the war, the vicar of Holme Eden, Carlisle, castigated his flock for indulging in 'worldly pleasures' instead of attending church.[76]

Nonetheless, many parish magazines recorded in some detail the determined war work of their congregations.[77]

The bedrock of the government's wartime recruitment drive was its appeal to patriotism. In this it was thoroughly supported by parish clergymen, functioning as the mouthpiece of the national church. As already noted, Keswick's Morley Headlam was an enthusiastic advocate of the war, as was his contemporary, Hardwicke Rawnsley, vicar of Crosthwaite. As Chapter 5 revealed, Rawnsley's torrent of odes based on chivalry, patriotism and imperialism continued after 1914, despite enormous Allied casualties.[78] Rawnsley's near neighbour, Canon William Simpson, rector of Caldbeck, also ensured that his local boys heard the Empire's call. The outbreak of war had shocked the parish, he wrote in September 1914, but parishioners should know that, because their army was fighting for freedom and justice, they could pray for victory with a clear conscience.[79] That October, he organised the local Lonsdale Battalion recruitment drive at Caldbeck; as Callum Brown has remarked, parish clergymen often functioned as unofficial recruiting sergeants.[80]

As the official recruiting officers visited each town and village, local clergymen published names of recruits. The following poem appeared in the Caldbeck parish magazine early in 1915. Written by the local fish merchant, it purported to express the thanks of the war office for Caldbeck's positive response to the recruiting drive:

> My dear old friends at Caldbeck,
> Accept my warmest thanks
> For the nice young lads you've sent
> To join Lord Kitchener's ranks.
> I marvel at their smartness,
> Which would credit any town,
> I never thought that Caldbeck
> Could send a 'Bertie Brown'.
> As time goes on dear comrades
> I'll want the ranks to swell,
> But you've done your bit at Caldbeck
> With Joe and Willie Bell.
> The Germans say our army
> Is nothing but a myth,
> But they'll alter their opinion
> When we send our Private Smith.
> We'll drive them into Berlin

Like coneys in a net,
For we've a splendid army now,
Including Ted Primett.
There's Gwordie Mark, a good old pal,
Who left his work at school,
And as he came I heard him say,
'Remember Hartlepool!'
And then there's Georgie Richardson,
A lad known far and near;
He'll keep the Allies to the front
And Germans in the rear.
They've robbed and burned and plundered,
Done everything that's bad,
But they've not begun to reckon yet
With Johnnie Thoburn's lad.
We shall wage this war to a finish,
We mean to see it through,
And could you send a few more lads
Like Edgar Ashbridge's two?
If they should join the Lonsdales,
Their lot with them to throw,
They'll mate with Gwordie Dobson
Who comes from Ratten Row.
Urge them to join the army
Before it be too late.
If they can't come with Winder lads,
Then come with Isaac Gate.
And when the war is over
Caldbeck will laud her sons
Who sacrificed 'Home Comforts'
And went to fight the Huns.[81]

These names were published again in the parish magazine over the war years: Bertie Brown was killed; several were injured. Throughout the war, updated prose versions of the roll of honour appeared regularly – along with war news, casualty lists, obituaries and letters from Caldbeck combatants. This was a frequent occurrence in parish-magazine local pages elsewhere, the printing of such letters echoing the practice of provincial newspapers, but more intimately.[82]

At the beginning of the war, letters to local parish magazines often evoked boys' adventure stories. Terms such as 'heroic bravery' were applied to the actions of soldiers who wrote that they were 'ducking and dodging' and 'having a lively time of it with bombs'.[83] Soldiers at training camps wrote that it was 'a perfect picnic'.[84] The Camden Church Camberwell parish magazine printed similar cheerful messages, usually from ex-choristers. A stream of letters from a young corporal named Ernest Terraneau came to an end in July 1916 when he was killed in action at Gommecourt, prompting his parents to praise his chivalrous heroism by altering a verse from one of the popular war-time poems of John Oxenham to read, when published in the magazine:

> Heedless and careless still the world goes on
> And leaves us broken. Oh! Our son! Our son!
> ... He died as few men get the chance to die,
> Fighting to save a world's morality;
> He died the noblest death a man may die,
> Fighting for God, and Right, and Liberty;
> And such a death is immortality.[85]

As Michael Finn discovered when exploring Liverpudlian reactions to the war, a community-focussed discourse of heroism made the conflict appear intelligible, and bereavement bearable, to those at home.[86] To that end London streets witnessed the mushrooming of wayside crucifixes, and war shrines containing the names of those who had gone to fight, foreshadowing the later ubiquity of war memorials.[87] Though encouraged by Anglo-Catholic Churchmen who hoped it would lead to greater Christian commitment, the phenomenon was usually community-based, even in the poorest streets, where people donated shrines or gave their labour free, to provide a focus for expressions of anxiety and grief.[88]

As the war intensified, Caldbeck magazine's lists of missing, wounded and killed lengthened, and its mood grew sombre. For some time the censor was unable to prevent news about the realities of war reaching even the smallest community through soldiers' letters, and in Caldbeck details of conditions at the Front seeped out in understated remarks such as 'it was awful, it was something awful, you begin to feel it' (from the Dardanelles); 'up to the knees in mud...get this terrible job over'; 'waist-deep, very dirty, in mud' (from the Front in France).[89] Homesick country boys described the farmland they found abroad, comparing it unfavourably with the fields at home.[90] In the summer of 1916, Joe Harper wrote to the rector, remembering evenings playing tennis on the Caldbeck rectory lawn: 'My thoughts are often centred on the ... Cumbrian mountains'.[91] Letters to families from superior officers detailing the deaths of husbands and sons found their way to the rector, and thence the magazine.[92] In March 1916, Corporal Yeomans, a father of five, was the eighth Caldbeck man to die, but the 'killed in action' list grew longer. By January 1917, it had grown to eleven.

Caldbeck rectory became the headquarters for community war work, receiving knitwear, clothing, Red Cross parcels for soldiers and eggs collected by schoolchildren for the National Egg Collection Fund for the wounded. In towns and cities the Church's role could be purely parochial. In London, the vicar of St Philip's, Arlington Square, and his female congregation continued to carry out church charity work despite the departure of most of the men – clergy, choristers, lay helpers – to the Front.[93] Camden Church Camberwell encouraged (though it did not organise) local elementary schools to collect eggs, jam and cigarettes for the wounded, responded wholeheartedly to a letter from Queen Mary requesting Christmas presents for soldiers abroad and, like many parishes, supported a government initiative to house Belgian refugees.[94] As Simon Fowler has demonstrated, few war charities were Anglican. Though some were run by individuals, denominations or small groups, a growing number emanated from town and county councils, a demonstration of the diminution in the Church's formal role in society.[95] Nonetheless, in wartime Caldbeck, as in many rural areas, the church was at the very centre of the war effort, and the rector, in the roles of both local official and religious leader, the man to whom many turned.

Anglican chaplains

During the course of the war the number of serving Anglican chaplains rose from 89 to 1,985. By late 1915 they were being encouraged to minister close to the front lines.[96] This led to fatalities: 98 died as a result of their wartime activity.[97] Many London curates enlisted as chaplains, as noted in the parish scrapbook of Saint James-the-Great, Bethnal Green, which contains pages from its parish magazines. Though earlier pages were devoted to the church's continuing love affair with ritualism and its notorious sympathy for socialism, from 1914 the scrapbook concentrated on the deeds of its fighting men, particularly its three curate chaplains: one 'somewhere in France', another on board HMS *Orion*. Described in the parish magazine as 'one of the family', the latter became lightweight boxing champion of the British fleet. This popular 'fighting parson' went on to become vicar of his old parish in 1922, exemplifying the enduring strength of Muscular Christianity.[98] The notice of the death of the third curate praised his bravery for remaining with his men during heavy shelling, his death 'the death of honour'.[99]

When the vicar of Flookburgh, Lancashire, became an army chaplain, he left his parish-magazine readers in no doubt of war's 'terror and muck and blood', 'mud and dust and flies and stinks', in his monthly letter from France.[100] Though wounded, he returned to the front, but was gassed in 1918. Just before his eventual return to Flookburgh, the clergyman who had come out of retirement to deputise for him collapsed in the pulpit.[101] Such local clergymen, and chaplains who were decorated for bravery or who died in action, were celebrated, not only by their congregations, but also by their wider communities, the small, undistinguished-looking but much-decorated Cumbrian vicar, Theodore Hardy, for instance, still remembered in his native county, his memorial in Carlisle Cathedral a tribute to his heroism on the Western Front.[102] Just before Theodore Hardy was killed, he was offered the rectory of Caldbeck, Canon Simpson having died in 1918. Caldbeck parishioners were devastated to lose two 'heroes' at once, for the devoted war work of both men was greatly admired.[103]

The national mission of repentance and hope

The Flookburgh war letters attempted to balance the horror of war with the vicar's conviction that the 'great sacrifice' of a just cause was leading soldiers back to God and a national religious revival on their repatriation.[104] The letters frequently claimed, however, that men were innately sinful creatures, a traditional Christian belief which formed the basis of an expression of national guilt known as the 'National Mission for Repentance and Hope', inaugurated by Archbishop Randall Davidson in 1915. As Shannon Bontrager contends in his study of Great War nationalistic mythology, having assured the British that God was on their side, the Church faced criticism, religious doubt and outright secularism during the heavy losses of 1915. A traditionally Christian means of expiating a country's sin, the National Mission switched the focus of attention from German atrocities to the godlessness of the British people as the cause of God's wrath and British military failure.[105]

Keswick's Morley Headlam, a local organiser and mouthpiece of the Mission, expounded its meaning in his parish magazine. All had a share in the national sin; the country, having become debased through materialism, had only just been 'saved' by the outbreak of war. Parishioners were exhorted to obey the call to 'days of contrition, intercessions, prayers ... abstinence, self-examination and profound humiliation for past negligence'.[106] Meanwhile *The Sign* insisted that 'All have done wrong. We are all in it – the Church and all.'[107] Anglo-Catholics had raised the question of national sin very early in the war, the Mission appealing to them because they anticipated that it would encourage a greater reliance on ritual in worship.[108] Thus, while organising the Mission, Headlam secured a side-altar as an aid to prayer – a ritualistic development which his congregation had previously blocked.[109] As Callum Brown has noted, such Churchmen hoped to exact 'a religious dividend' from the war.[110]

Some clergymen were sanguine about the Mission's success: 'The historian of the future will record how in 1916 the Church of England ... began to awake to the responsibility of applying the teaching of Jesus Christ to all the complex relations of human life', wrote the vicar of Saint Mark, Plumstead Common.[111] But, as William Sachs's history of twentieth-century Anglicanism demonstrates, the people who responded to the Mission were those who were already keen churchgoers.[112] Most others, after some initial interest, stayed at home, for, as Bontrager contends, many may have cavilled at being stigmatised while their loved ones were fighting and dying for their country.[113] At Caldbeck, the rector's response to the Mission was more equivocal than his involvement in local recruitment might have suggested, perhaps because his son, a hospital chaplain, had openly professed 'despair' at the Church's approach to the war.[114] 'It is thought' that British wrongdoing has caused the war; 'it is thought' that God has sent war as a punishment', began the rector's first letter on the subject. Though in the summer of 1916 he set about organising Mission events, he apologised in the autumn for deferring reports on these activities, until eventually reference to the Mission disappeared altogether, as he said himself, 'crowded out by other things': principally local news and mounting reports of dead, injured and missing Caldbeck soldiers.

Even Morley Headlam was moved to acknowledge that, locally, the National Mission had been unpopular. The response was the same nationally. The prominent socialist vicar Conrad Noel called it the mission of 'funk and despair'; the outspoken bishop of Durham, Hensley Henson, regarded it as 'a grave practical blunder'; and even Sachs, an Anglican apologist, deemed it an unmitigated disaster.[115] Recommending repentance for individual and national sin was clearly unpopular. How could it have been otherwise, when Headlam listed all of his parishioners: 'lawyers, brewers, politicians, landlords, agents, commercial travellers, shop-keepers, shop-assistants, shareholders in companies, trade unionists, clergymen, lodging-house keepers, domestic servants, masters, mistresses – employers, employed', as sinners?[116]

Insets 1914–1918

As seen in Chapter 3, demand for insets diminished after about 1910, but the Great War was to lower sales further, at least six insets ceasing production between 1916 and 1920.[117] SPCK and Mowbray's wartime annual reports are characterised by contraction. As the cost of raw material was prohibitive, paper supplies were restricted, so the number of pages was reduced and copies available to parishes limited. In 1917 the two publishers came to a mutual understanding, as a result of which inset cost price rose by 10 per cent, arousing protest from hard-pressed parish clergy.[118] In the parishes the struggle to pay for insets often became too much. Some clergymen relinquished them in favour of a single sheet of local news; Morley Headlam, who had been insistent on changing to *The Sign,* gave it up altogether in 1917.[119]

Though the insets reduced their numbers of pages, paper quality was poorer and prices doubled, their wartime content remained much the same as before, albeit laced with a martial flavour. Having initially responded with enthusiastic articles urging male readers to fight for 'Motherland and King',[120] they continued to provide the same monthly diet of sermons, serial stories, recipes, prayers, poems, clothes patterns, Bible-teaching and church news as before. The stories' heroes were now chaplains, soldiers and sailors, while their heroines had been released from the home to become war workers, businesswomen and nurses.[121] Recipe pages helped housewives with food shortages; prayers and poetry centred on the suffering of the armed forces abroad and their loved ones at home; women's clothes patterns included a 'military jacket' and 'Sunday-Dress Economies'; Bible-teaching highlighted biblical soldiers; and the church news section applauded women as both homemakers and war workers, while approvingly noting clergymen's attempts at non-combative war work on farms, in mines and in munitions factories.[122] In short, the most popular insets adapted their material and survived the war intact.

The Angel of Mons

While *Home Words* supported the National Mission, it sought to represent it as a medieval crusade, promoting it through its back catalogue of heroic chivalry illustrations, which had been previously used to encourage manliness.[123] In selecting this iconography *Home Words* astutely echoed the secular press which had adopted the same rhetoric to help its readers cope with the gruesome battle scenes it unflinchingly reported.[124] In this time of national anxiety, however, a growing diffusive Christianity needed a more effective outlet than the 'romantic glamour' of medievalism.[125] Spiritualism found a ready audience, but though the Church condemned spiritualism, it opened the way to compromise through emphasising the intervention of angels.[126] As previously noted, the popularity of Anglo-Catholic iconography and a growing diffusive Christianity during the years leading up to the war led to increasing numbers of images of cherubs and angels on inset pages. After mounting British losses, these became more numerous, in parallel with depictions of angels on the battlefield, frequently seen in newspapers and on postcards.[127] Parish magazines were highly involved in the dissemination of a narrative concerning the appearance of the Angel of Mons, as told below, based on research by David Clarke.[128]

During the retreat from Mons in late August 1914, half a million men died. Moved by the carnage, a *London Evening News* journalist, Arthur Machen, wrote a story, 'The Bowmen', in which a retreating soldier invoked the aid of Saint George, whereupon a company of ghostly Agincourt bowmen enabled his group to escape. In 1915, when trench warfare was decimating the English army, Machen's story was republished by a spiritualist magazine, *The Occult Review,* and a Catholic newspaper, but, when it appeared in the Anglican parish magazine of All Saints, Bristol, the bowmen had mysteriously changed into female angels. Apparently a certain Miss Marrable had heard about the angels from a friend of a friend, and had written about them to a clergyman who then published her account as truth in his parish magazine, the story then spreading virally from pulpit to pulpit; magazine to magazine. It was believed by thousands. According to Clarke, the story was allowed free rein by the government because it helped the war effort. Its support for the concept of miracles and repudiation of atheism clearly pleased the Church. Despite noting that it could not be authenticated, *The Sign* published the story on its cover in September 1915, along with a suitably emotive poem by Queenie Scott-Hopper.[129] Clergymen referred to it for years as a historical fact.[130] After the war, *Home Words* sent Agnes Giberne to interview soldiers who had encountered angels. She could find no eyewitnesses, but her interviewees appeared to believe that such visions had occurred to others, leading Giberne to find 'no difficulty whatever in believing that ... the Heavenly Visitants were there'.[131] Their transcendent qualities plainly filled a vacuum created by the horrors of the war and a growing retreat from traditional worship.

Conclusion

The Church's response to scientific advance and the Great War may be seen as a complex tale of failure, change and success, exemplifying the grave difficulties under which it laboured at the end of the long nineteenth century. The people and the Church needed one another's support during the war. Wayside shrines, a discourse of heroism and the Angel of Mons story appealed to the people's mood, the last demonstrating the parish magazine's significance in acting as a conduit. In 1920 the vicar of St Michael and All Angels, Paddington, writing in his parish magazine, recalled the Angel of Mons when reporting that members of his congregation were conscious of 'a Something in church on Michaelmas Day. Some heard, some "saw", and to some of those present a door was opened in heaven, an Apocalypse was vouchsafed. *Seraphim stabant super illud: et clamabant alter ad alterum.*' (Angels were in attendance above him... one called to another).[132] Yet the thrust of the vicar's remarks did not build on the spiritual gift of the congregation's epiphany, but reverted immediately to the Church's pre-war hierarchical and financial narratives: praise for a local bishop, and anxiety about the size of the offertory which, the vicar hoped, would contain the pennies of the poor as well as the 'paper and silver' of the rich. In conflating God and Mammon, the Church, as this study has stressed repeatedly, continued to prioritise status and money. A bastion of social inequality, it nevertheless demanded funds from all, rich or poor, for its national survival. The parish magazine, the pulpit and the appearance of angels were exploited to further this aim.

Despite the best efforts of the insets to report it in a positive light, the National Mission exposed the weakness of Church leadership during the war. The Mission did not reflect either the national mood, which was intent on celebrating individual and collective heroism, or changes in theology, which had moved on from an emphasis on national sin to a celebration of the individual life. Perhaps Church leaders deserved the post-war censure of Bishop Charles Gore: 'You youngish ones must start off the Church of England again,' he wrote to a naval chaplain. 'We old ones have made a mess of it.'[133] Yet the Church's reaction to nineteenth-century scientific advance had shown that it could accept change, the insets demonstrating how, over many decades, science was largely integrated into a godly narrative of progress and the Divine purpose. Having signalled its disapproval of Germany's scientific advance during hostilities, once victory was assured, the Church resumed its approval of science, Morley Headlam thanking

God in 1918 for 'work of mind and hand which has made us ...strong in munitions of war'.[134] But the war had effectively destroyed such optimism, its strains too immense for the National Mission or even the discourse of heroism to reassure the people that the Church was in control. Instead they looked to be saved by female angels, symbols of a new age of diffusive Christianity.

Nonetheless, Anglicanism proved through its wartime activity at grass-roots level that its parochial structure continued to be of both national and local importance. For the duration of the war many parish churches acted as local centres for the war effort, enabling clergymen to provide leadership of both spiritual and secular community activities, their parish magazine local pages playing an important part in supporting them and their parishioners at a time of great anxiety.

10
Anglican Parish Magazines 1919–1929 and Beyond

While rejoicing at Allied successes during the last year of the Great War, Morley Headlam ruminated on becoming an army chaplain, explaining to his parishioners that, as he was over 45, he was thought too old: this despite the fact that his close contemporary, Theodore Hardy, had enlisted in his fifties and had been decorated three times.[1] Now that victory was assured, Headlam ignored the National Mission's condemnation of the British people, instead praising their faith and patriotism: 'For all the ancient faith of our race which makes the nation's spirit unconquerable, we thank God.' That year he left Keswick for the leafy parish of Horsham in Sussex: 'a definite preferment...the work of the Holy Spirit'.[2]

'Parish Magazines are under a cloud – they've had a bad run'

For those who questioned attitudes such as Headlam's, the twentieth-century parish magazine was seen as a symbol of Anglicanism's failings; its public profile duly suffered. In 1930, the *Strand* published 'The Parish Magazine', a short story by Arthur Conan Doyle which echoed a story published in *Punch* in 1897.[3] As a trick upon their suburban Anglican community, a group of self-consciously 'modern' young things inveigled a printer into adding a supplement to their parish magazine, which ridiculed their elders' hypocrisy, social snobbery, pretension, fraudulent business practice, sexual deviancy, malicious gossip and secret vice. In Conan Doyle's narrative the supplement remained undelivered, but in *Punch* it reached the congregation, the magazine's circulation growing enormously as those sitting next to each other in the pews greatly enjoyed their neighbours' discomfiture.

Mary Cholmondeley's novel, *Red Pottage*, published in 1899, poured deliberate scorn on parish-magazine insets. To Cholmondeley, herself the product of a country rectory, their clerical contributors, lacking talent, experience and objectivity, made the parish magazine risible. *Red Pottage* featured a rector who imagined that, because he was editor of his parish magazine, he was ipso facto a man of letters; on reading the publisher's proofs of his sister's novel, and recognising its unsympathetic portrayal of a clergyman as himself, he burned the manuscript as unworthy and pernicious literature.[4] George Orwell and Barbara Pym also linked the parish magazine to disagreeable clergymen. In Orwell's *The Clergyman's Daughter*, Charles Hare's monstrous behaviour caused his daughter to deliver the magazine in a state of nervous collapse, while Pym's parish-magazine references in *Some Tame Gazelle* served to underline both the hypocrisy of the archdeacon and the moral weakness of his curate.[5] Almost wholly contemptuous and mocking, modernist novelists used such references to suggest that the modern world had no time for the mores of the immediate past.

This was also true of clerical luminaries such as Dick Sheppard.[6] His popular book criticising Anglican institutionalism, *The Human Parson*, published in 1924, disdained parish magazines: 'Parish magazines are under a cloud – they've had a bad run'.[7] He regarded the insets with particular loathing: 'I abominate those inside pages of the magazine'. To Sheppard, the parish magazine's mission was to present 'a monthly challenge to high living and high thinking' through book reviews and articles on general themes written with Christian tone, by 'friends who can write'.[8] Many parish clergymen echoed Sheppard's views: parish magazines were 'an uninteresting evil'; 'nearly always dull'; 'the vicar's monthly purgatory'.[9] Some sought to help their colleagues by writing instruction manuals. That of J. B. Goodliffe judged the usual parish magazine 'puerile'. Goodliffe was particularly scathing of inset serial stories, which he thought suitable only for 'the working class…the sentimental novel about the vicar's daughter suits their mentality…but it is quite ignored and sometimes ridiculed by the educated'.[10] The manual of J. M. Swift, vicar of Garston, Liverpool, considered the parish magazine's religious propaganda 'woefully ineffective', but Swift's remedy – the inclusion of 'imaginary dialogues for instruction', written by the parish incumbent – merely repeated an age-old staple of the evangelical tract; such dialogues had featured in Erskine Clarke's defunct *Parish Magazine*.[11] We may consider Dick Sheppard's appeal for a distinctly intellectual parish magazine similarly off-kilter, when we recall the fate of Henry Whitehead's high-minded offering at Limehouse, described in Chapter 1.[12] Goodliffe's disdain for inset serial stories may have been equally misled. In 1926, for instance, the women who dominated Mungrisdale Parochial Church Council in Cumberland successfully lobbied their vicar for the inclusion of *Home Words* in their local magazine, yet these landowners' wives and daughters could hardly be labelled working-class sentimentalists.[13] As Adrian Hastings has remarked, those, like Sheppard, who, 'with despair in their hearts' sought to guide the Church after the Great War, were 'desperately battling...with hearts aflame but often pretty little sense of what they themselves hoped for'.[14] Whether the war caused a tsunami of change after 1918 or merely helped unleash it, is immaterial in this context, for Anglican clergy observed it, and their reactions ensured that the anxiety persistently documented in this book continued to dominate parish magazine content.

Circulation 1919–1929

As discussed in the Introduction, archive deposits of parish magazines of the 1920s and 1930s are too meagre to make sweeping conclusions about their circulation. Nevertheless, *The Sign*'s monthly circulation figure, reproduced in Chapter 3, indicates that parish magazines continued to be sold in large numbers. Having reached a high point of 700,000 in 1913, *The Sign*'s circulation fell to 500,000 during the Great War, but by 1925 it had risen to 662,000. It fell to below 500,000 between 1939 and 1945, but rose to well over a million during the 1950s.[15] *Home Words*' monthly circulation was 1,100,000 in 1964.[16] These high circulations were not to last. In 2009, *Home Words* was incorporated into *The Sign* under the auspices of *Hymns Ancient & Modern*, a charity and publisher which also owns the *Church Times*.[17] In 2014, *The Sign*'s circulation had fallen to 35,000.[18] Nevertheless, the strength of inset sales during the period 1925 to 1960 supports Callum Brown's argument that church membership in early-twentieth-century Britain witnessed 'no great haemorrhage'.[19] Only the strongest insets survived, however. Sales of *Dawn of Day* never returned to their turn-of-the-century levels, the annual reports and minutes of SPCK revealing a crisis in post-war religious book publishing which led the society to allow the failing *Dawn of Day* to drift, while the serious Anglo-Catholic journal, *Theology*, and more popular publications, such as the journal of the Mothers' Union, were prioritised.[20]

Chapter 3 suggested that, up to 1919, competition between insets was on predominantly church-party lines, though the market leader, *Home Words*, was always a determinedly populist magazine. The few parish-magazine deposits dating from 1919 to 1929 reveal that *Home Words* continued to be the most popular inset overall, while *Dawn of Day* and *The Church Monthly* faded, allowing *The Sign* to become *Home Words'* major challenger (Figure 10.1). When *The Sign*'s circulation is added to that of the high-church *Dawn of Day*, the moderate Ritualist *Church Monthly*, and ultra–Anglo-Catholic magazines like *The Fiery Cross*, *The Symbol*, *The Sentinel* and *Ecclesia*, however, it becomes obvious that, by 1929, Anglo-Catholicism, particularly the English rite as presented in *The Sign*, had become England's dominant form of worship (Figure 10.2). The same pattern is found in the individual localities, and is particularly remarkable in Carlisle diocese, for while *Home Words* (along with Bullock's *Church Standard*) continued to be the most popular inset, *The Sign* conquered all

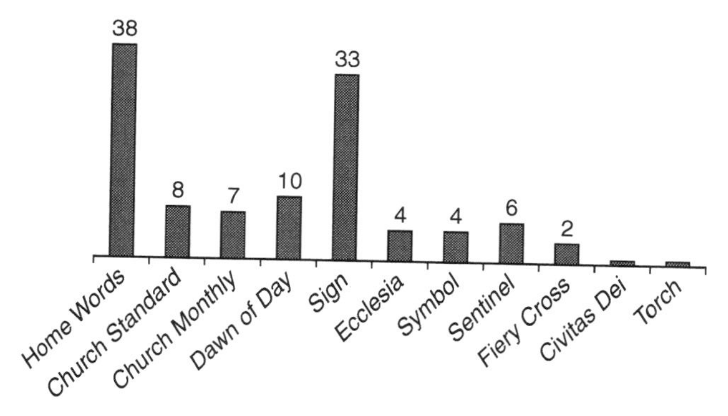

Figure 10.1 Anglican Insets in Carlisle, London and Oxford (1919–1929)
Source: Cumbria Archives, London Metropolitan Archives, Oxford History Centre

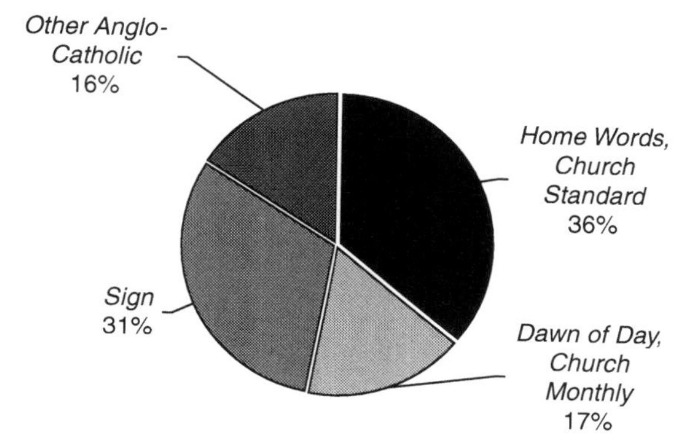

Figure 10.2 Popular Anglican Insets in Carlisle, London and Oxford (1919–1929)
Source: Cumbria Archives, London Metropolitan Archives, Oxford History Centre

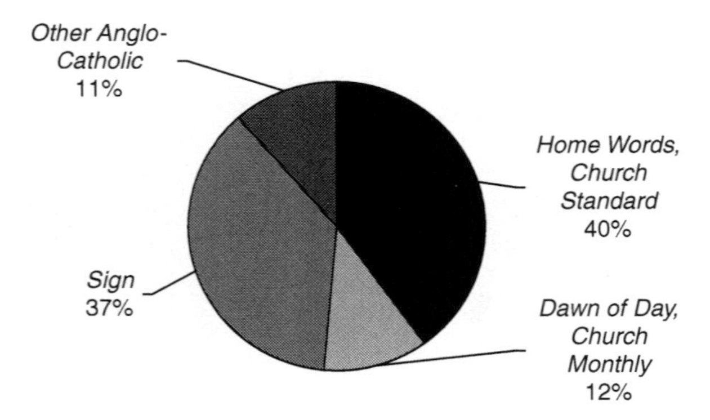

Figure 10.3 Popular Anglican Insets in Carlisle Diocese (1919–1929)
Source: Cumbria Archives

others to become *Home Words'* major rival, as this previously low-church diocese embraced Anglo-Catholicism (Figure 10.3).[21]

Addressing new realities

In 1919 the SPCK religious literature committee was asked to consider the publication of a new magazine 'which would appeal to a class different from that aimed at in *The Dawn of Day*; suitable to localise in parishes which could charge 2d a number'.[22] Plainly *Dawn of* Day's original audience of uneducated working-class adults and Sunday-school scholars had been abandoned in favour of those possessing a modicum of education and economic security, a phenomenon observed in *Home Words* before the Great War, as noted in Chapter 7. *Dawn of Day* was relaunched as *The New Day* in a shortened form in 1929.[23]

In 1909, *Home Words'* editor, Herbert Somerset Bullock (1871–1963), founded *The Church Standard*.[24] Though much of this inset's material was very similar to that of *Home Words*, some of its articles were slanted towards the politicised urban working man and his family, as the Bullock dynasty attempted to address new social and political realities.[25] Both insets featured evangelical clergymen, but over time, as the number of conservative evangelical bishops diminished, H. S. Bullock favoured moderate bishops from old evangelical families, such as Cyril Bardsley of Peterborough, or those, like Bertram Pollock of Norwich, who, while claiming no party allegiance, were sympathetic to Protestant causes.[26]

In 1920, members of the magazine committee of Saint Gabriel's, Bounds Green, London, insisted on changing to *Home Words* from *The*

Sign. In advertising the change, the vicar did not attempt to compare the magazines' religious content. Instead, he acknowledged that a parish magazine should be 'of general interest to all', not just to church members.[27] After the Great War, *Home Words*' 'general interest' articles were routinely contributed by experienced professional journalists like George Wade and Sarah Tooley, while the prolific popular novelist, May Wynne, replaced Agnes Giberne as the inset's preferred serial-story writer.[28] Tooley and Wynne were guaranteed crowd pleasers. H. S. Bullock resembled his father in understanding the economic wisdom of providing the public with a 'good read', though the son's eminently readable magazine betrayed little of its evangelical descent.

Anglo-Catholicism: flowing 'with unbroken force'

On the front page of its first number in 1905, *The Sign* welcomed 'the tide of spiritual progress' which had begun with Tractarianism and now 'flowed with unbroken force'. By the 1920s, the unstoppable energy of Anglo-Catholicism had largely taken over Anglican worship, *The Sign* confidently outlining how far the movement had come.[29] Its monthly gossip page, 'Church Life Today', traced the careers of popular Anglo-Catholic clergy and their bishops; numerous articles relayed liturgical instruction; crucifixes and old-master prints of Christ and the Virgin Mary illustrated pietistic poetry; and each month 'Our Query Corner' continued to deal with lay enquiries on issues such as confession and minute points of the etiquette of Anglo-Catholic worship.

The Sign's readers were encouraged to believe that they belonged to an elite group of 'loyal church people'.[30] Though they were members of the catholic (universal) Church, their allegiance was to the English rite,[31] while other Anglicans constituted an outer circle.[32] Evangelicals and nonconformists were cast out even further, for *Sign* readers were taught that the term 'Protestant' was illegitimate because it did not appear in the Bible. In the parishes, the differences between English-rite Anglo-Catholicism and its ultramontane alternative, Western Catholicism, could be starkly presented.[33] Holy Trinity, Sloane Street, espoused the English rite, its parish magazine devoted to explanations of its belief and practice, protestations of loyalty to the Church of England and opposition to ultramontane developments:

> The only way to check the development in the Roman or ultramontane direction is to see to it that a definite English ceremonial is adopted ... to maintain the tradition and to show people that the

> English use really exists and can be exhibited as the natural setting for the Prayer Book service.[34]

Those who wrote to the magazine to express their disapproval of Anglo-Catholic practices, such as the wearing of vestments, received short shrift, the editor remarking that if they desired simplicity they should look to their own garments.[35]

Elsewhere in London, ultramontane churches such as Saint Cyprian's, Clarence Gate, immersed their congregations in masses for the dead, adoration of the Blessed Virgin Mary and other features of the Western rite.[36] Saint Cyprian's was designed by Ninian Comper in the medieval manner to underline the Church of England's continuity with Catholicism.[37] The tone of its parish magazine is enshrined in the following extract:

> Through the misty early morning air we hastened to Mass on Candlemas Day, and through the early twilight of a February afternoon St. Cyprian's windows gleamed with the flickering light of the tapering candles on the pillars within, as we returned joyfully to continue the Festival of Our Lady's Purification ... Softly sweet music breathed as the choir ascended to the Rood Loft for Evensong, and some who were present were fain to imagine that Our Lady herself might be joining in her own song, *Magnificat* ... [After] 'Arise, shine, for thy Light is come,' came the Blessing of the Candles, according to ancient rite, ere we knelt to receive them from the hands of our Vicar, seated in the Sanctuary entrance, with his faithful acolytes around.[38]

Conservative Evangelicals: defending 'old paths of spiritual truths'

Parishioners in the parish of Farlam in northern Cumberland were the recipients of a very different message. As noted in the Introduction, Carlisle diocese had been deeply evangelical, retaining pockets of evangelicalism well into the twentieth century. At Farlam the vicar, Thomas Smith, railed at both liberal theology and Anglo-Catholic liturgical change, while continuing to preach a highly traditional evangelical message.[39] The evangelical party having split into factions as a result of the perceived Anglo-Catholic threat, Smith placed himself firmly in the traditionalist camp: 'the Bible is the secret of England's greatness ... if an Englishman really loves his Bible, he will never allow his beer to get the upper hand', he pronounced in 1924.[40] When, in 1922, the evangelical Church Missionary Society split into two as a result of arguments over liberal biblical criticism, Smith supported the newly created Bible Churchmen's Missionary Society which operated on conservative evangelical lines.[41] Though he knew he was 'a small popgun', Smith used his magazine to fight for 'old paths of spiritual truths and primitive rites'. Taking sideswipes at bishops and archbishops, he criticised the 'mass in masquerade' which was supplanting older forms: 'Spectacular performances, eye-pleasing colours, ear-pleasing music and nose-pleasing incense', constituted a 'devil's service' which offered the English people a stone instead of the bread of life.[42]

'We are all Ritualists'

The highly coloured parish magazines of the Western Catholic and conservative evangelical traditions tend to be memorable, but they do not represent the majority. As John Maiden has observed, the rise of Anglo-Catholicism resulted in a gradual toleration of 'milder' Anglo-Catholic practices, resulting in a 'centre-high' position, which adopted much Anglo-Catholic ritual while remaining loyal to episcopal rulings.[43] In 1912, a London vicar's declaration, 'we are all Ritualists' – though written to persuade a reluctant congregation of the legitimacy of making the sign of the cross – was nonetheless emblematic of centre-high adjustment.[44] The parish of Burneside was typical of many in Carlisle diocese. Having been traditionally evangelical, it was required to change its practices when, in 1921, a new incumbent introduced altar lights, plainsong, frequent Holy Communion and confession.[45] Nonetheless – reflecting the practice at Saint Gabriel's, Bounds Green – the new vicar changed the parish inset to *Home Words*, regarding it as 'the best ... that we can get'.[46] As previously noted, nineteenth-century ritualist incumbents had generally changed the parish inset to one which echoed their church-party allegiance, but by the 1920s the uncontroversial blandness of *Home Words* was clearly seen by some as perfectly acceptable reading material for centre-high Anglicans.

Women

Until her death in 1920, Mrs Rogers, a member of the congregation at Saint Michael and All Angels, Paddington, edited the parish magazine, led the Mothers' Union, organised the district visitors, and washed the church surplices and altar linen.[47] As noted in earlier chapters, women like Mrs Rogers dominated congregations and were the backbone of parish work. Many were attracted to high-church worship, as evidenced in the nineteenth century by the rapid growth of sisterhoods.[48] Women's fondness for needlework allowed incumbents to encourage female church workers to move in a centre-high direction; the vicar of Burneside, for instance, involved female parishioners in beautifying objects used in the communion rite.[49] Women's involvement in church decoration – particularly for the great festivals – and their provision of altar hangings, banners, kneelers and so on, chimed with the aesthetics of Anglo-Catholicism to such an extent that Ritualists could count on their help in effecting liturgical change, despite the replacement of lady members of 'cock and hen' choirs with surpliced boys, noted in Chapter 4.

During the early twentieth century, the Mothers' Union took its place alongside mothers' meetings to become a significant part of parish life, but the movement was still a traditional one, supporting the notion of separate spheres of influence.[50] After 1919, the Enabling Act gave women parity with men by allowing them both to vote for and to serve on the Parochial Church Councils which replaced parish vestries.[51] The Act altered the gendered face of lay church management. In 1927, for instance, women took 19 of the available 30 seats on the Saint Andrew and Saint Michael, Enfield, PCC; women also began to exert a strong presence as parochial representatives at diocesan conferences.[52] At the same time, inset articles demonstrated a greater emphasis on training female church workers,[53] while the untrained district visitor, who had used parish-magazine distribution as a means of entry to the houses of the needy, was gradually sidelined, much of her work having been taken over by Church professionals and government agencies.[54] Volunteer 'distributors' now often delivered parish magazines in a purely religious capacity.[55]

Nevertheless, whether she was a PCC member, 'lady' delegate, volunteer distributor or trained church worker, the Anglican woman of the 1920s continued to fill the same self-effacingly supportive role as Paddington's Mrs Rogers. While inset fiction featured working girls leading independent lives, their 'happy endings' always included marriage and a retreat into domesticity, while intelligent young women were urged to renounce their dreams of education if needed at home.[56] Meanwhile, *Home Words* devoted a monthly double-page spread to household hints in 'Our Weekday Pages for Women with Homes', while remaining characteristically silent on such divisive subjects as the unorthodox preaching activities of the Anglican feminist Maude Royden.[57]

Church attendance

As noted in Chapter 9, the Great War led many clergymen to anticipate that the country's sacrifice would lead to religious revival.[58] Optimism continued into the 1920s, bolstered by the Church's official involvement in remembrance ceremonies and the erection of war memorials, though delays and discrepancies could lead to tension between clergymen and their parishioners.[59] It was found particularly gratifying that men came to church in large numbers for memorial services, the vicar of Holy Trinity, Sloane Street, arguing that this proved that the English were 'incurably religious' at heart, but, as Callum Brown has argued, the religious services in which men played a major role were essentially part of civic religion, characterised by the activities of the British Legion.[60] The expected religious revival did not take place, despite the clergy's efforts. As Simon Green has suggested, this disappointment may have led clergymen to underestimate church attendance.[61] In parish magazines throughout Cumbria, London and Oxford, clergymen lamented absent congregations. In inner London, cathedrals were blamed for seeking to justify their existence by 'touting' for custom with 'popular services' which enticed people from their local churches, while wartime bombing raids were held responsible for breaking up congregations which were then 'scattered abroad'.[62] At Aston Tirrold, Oxfordshire, few children were said to attend church.[63] In Westmorland, the vicar of Burneside compared his empty church with the crowded bus to town, as his congregation sought new amusements, while in Cumberland, the vicar of Lanercost lamented the erosion of Sunday and 'a loss of taste for spiritual things'.[64]

As previous chapters have demonstrated, such complaints, particularly about the non-attendance of males, were not new, and though bombing raids emptied some London churches, the long-established practice of pew-renting had always encouraged the peripatetic nature of city-church congregations. Moreover, Rex Walford's description of interwar church building in the suburbs of north and west London shows that the Church continued to stimulate pockets of 'optimism, vitality and growth' during the 1920s.[65] However, when the vicar of Farlam commented in 1924 that most of his flock attended church only on alternate Sundays, he was probably observing a general trend, for, as Callum Brown has also noted, while people still went to church after the Great War, they appear to have done so less frequently.[66] Nonetheless, as Brown also declares, such casual churchgoers continued to maintain links with their local church, Farlam's vicar tacitly acknowledging this by continuing to address his absent parishioners through his magazine. This was particularly true of country parishes. In Cumberland, Great Salkeld parish magazine was delivered to 79 per cent of the inhabited houses in 1921; in 1925, Mungrisdale parish magazine was taken 'by nearly every house'.[67] It could also be true of the suburbs: Rex Walford discovered that in North Harrow the parish magazine of the new church of St Alban was delivered to over half the area's houses in 1930.[68]

Missionaries

One means of reducing clerical gloom at home was to emphasise the success of missionary work abroad, parish magazines devoting much of their available space to news of the missionaries whom they supported.[69] As a self-congratulatory article in the Saint Andrew and Saint Michael, Enfield, parish magazine pointed out, the nineteenth-century 'great revival' had resulted in 130 overseas dioceses created by missionary 'zeal'.[70] During the 1920s, missionary work was still seen as a 'glorious adventure' in which 'forgotten corners of the empire' could be explored by intrepid heroes.[71] Underlining this point, *Home Words* printed a monthly missionary page, 'The Church at the Front', consciously allying missionary work with recent military victory.[72] Having diluted its evangelicalism, the magazine's preoccupation was now the reporting of overseas evangelism.

In the parishes, pre-war imperial confidence was to persist in optimistic articles from missionaries abroad.[73] Some clergymen, influenced by W. W. Cash's book, *The Muslim World in Revolution*, published by SPCK in 1925, claimed that Christianity was on the point of conquering Islam:

> Everywhere the East is changing; and the creed of Mohammed is rapidly dissolving. The missionaries are exultant, for it is a great hour; and Mohammedans themselves are pressing round them in eager curiosity about that other faith ... of which their own is but a feeble caricature.[74]

Yet anxiety about civil strife and secularism at home led to prescient fears that Christianity 'must find a great rival, if it does not find a friend' in the Muslim's sense of brotherhood, 'which knows no distinctions of race or colour'.[75]

Anxiety

After 1918, local reports of parochial activities such as city-church bazaars, village-church fêtes, football and cricket matches, lantern lectures, whist drives and Mothers' Union meetings – sandwiched between mounting pages of local advertisements – signified a determination to return to pre-war normality. At the same time, parish magazines continued to exude all of their previous anxiety.[76] While some fear was based on the country's perceived secularism, much was based, as previously, on the clergy's financial needs, in particular, clerical stipends and pensions, dilapidation schemes and freewill offerings, while ritualising clergy regularly demanded new church furnishings.[77] Saint Anne's, Shoreditch, parish magazine contained a monthly column entitled, 'Our Wants', which, during 1921 included:

> Money as usual and a lot of it
> Money as usual
> £7 to finish off those old debts ... but that is only the beginning
> Subscriptions by envelope ... coke for the winter ... our Bazaar
> Urgent! Still the same still unsatisfied. The fault, dear people, is not mine but yours for professing to be Christians.[78]

There were many other worries. Some centred on the shortage of candidates for the ministry, which led to justified fears that parishes would be amalgamated, particularly in country areas.[79] Others centred on politics, but, while Bolshevism was universally condemned for its atheism and violence, few clergymen used their parish magazine to speak out against the Labour Party or industrial unrest.[80] The strikes of the 1920s were often portrayed as distant annoyances which delayed the annual Sunday-school outing or the printing of the magazine, while attitudes to Welsh mining families receiving charitable aid echoed the condescension of those who had organised parish clothing and coal funds during the nineteenth century.[81] In most country and suburban parishes, poverty and industrial unrest seemed far away, and were of little interest.[82]

The industrial parish of Saint James, Barrow, which suffered much post-war distress, took as its inset *The Torch*, a magazine published by the slightly leftist, Industrial Christian Fellowship. During the General Strike, both inset and vicar counselled restraint. G. A. Studdert Kennedy, the famous wartime chaplain popularly known as 'Woodbine Willie', wrote in *The Torch* that workers had never before enjoyed such luxurious lives, while Saint James's vicar asked for mutual trust.[83] These articles were mild, yet the *National Review* regarded the typical *Torch* reader as a 'tigerish Bolshevik'.[84] The vicar of Burneside would have agreed with the *National Review*. One of a minority of clergymen who roundly condemned the General Strike, he even censured the bishops who had attempted to negotiate between the strikers and the government, his aim, perhaps, to appease a leading member of his congregation, the owner of the local paper mill.[85] Meanwhile, the essential conservatism of the major insets was expressed in a story in *The Sign*, in which a grateful old lady was taken to vote for the first time in the village squire's car.[86] Understanding the importance of deference, she, like Burneside's vicar, no doubt voted accordingly.

Clergymen were much more fearful of popular religious 'cults' – their term for Spiritualists, Theosophists, the precursors to the Jehovah's Witnesses, Christian Scientists and Christadelphians – all of whom they regarded as heretical 'wolves in the fold'.[87] In contrast, science continued to present few apparent difficulties. Parish-magazine readers were told that the new science of psychology could help their anxieties;[88] articles on natural history were, as formerly, given Christian tone by occasional allusions to the Bible or a moral message tacked onto the end; and archaeological discovery was occasionally employed to prove the accuracy of the Bible.[89] Nevertheless, during the 1920s, parish-magazine references to science began to shift in emphasis by warning that, as the life of the spirit existed quite apart from the material world, it should be approached only through prayer and meditation.[90] In 1925, the Scopes 'monkey trial' at Dayton, Tennessee, led the vicar of Burneside to direct his flock towards inward spiritual enlightenment, instead of searching for the 'truth' elsewhere.[91]

The Prayer Book controversy

Those who have studied the tempestuous Prayer Book controversy of the 1920s might imagine that, despite their post-war lassitude, parish magazines would demonstrate an engagement with arguments for or against the new book.[92] Not so. By then, many parishes had embraced centre-high Anglicanism, their clergy fully accepting the measure, not least out of a sense of loyalty to the bishops, their parishioners, including many women on PCCs and diocesan committees, appearing to support them to the hilt.[93] Often, clergymen sought to make light of the measure's divisive nature by explaining that the new Prayer Book was optional. Parishioners were told that it was possible to use it only as an appendix, and, in any case, as the differences were largely semantic, they would barely notice them.[94] Two theoretically opposed insets – *The Sign* and *The Church Standard* – proffered this same argument, while in October 1928, Sarah Tooley's *Home Words* celebrity interview with the Conservative MP, Sir William Bull – whose parliamentary voting record reveals that he supported the Prayer-Book measure – ignored the subject entirely to concentrate on Bull's beautiful house and successful career.[95]

It was a 'noisy minority' of extremists on both sides, as Burneside's vicar termed them, who joined in the Prayer-Book debate with vigour, not to say venom.[96] The clergy of Saint Cyprian, Clarence Gate, were against the measure because they wanted to go their own ultramontane way, unhampered. The 'Catholic Layman's Protest against the Deposited Book' was inaugurated at Saint Cyprian's in the summer of 1927.[97] Farlam's Thomas Smith slammed the measure with unabated fury. In one of his monthly epistles to parishioners, he regaled them with a dream in which he had vanquished the 'papists' (after which he woke 'much refreshed'), and, in another, he published a letter he had sent to his local MP, threatening him with the loss of his seat if he voted for the measure. Like many conservative evangelicals, Smith disliked the 'Romish' elements of the new Prayer Book, such as reservation of the Sacrament and prayers for the dead, which he thought would 'strike the hour of doom to the Protestant reformed character of our National Church'. He prophesied the adoption of 'purgatory, transubstantiation, Mariolatry and priestly absolutions' if the measure were passed, and urged all parishioners to sign the Protestant Alliance's 'Monster Petition' to Parliament. When most evangelical bishops accepted the measure, he accused them of tasting 'the sweets of popery'.[98]

When the Prayer Book measure failed in its journeys through Parliament, Smith was jubilant.[99] More temperate clergymen suggested to their parishioners that the future of the new Prayer Book was in God's hands, which must have been helpful to the bishops, who eventually went ahead with its introduction.[100] Throughout the Prayer Book storm, the vicar of Saint Paul's, Carlisle, felt a weight of sin falling heavily on the Church. 'Controversy is not religion', he wrote. He was not alone. His retreat to the 'calm and repose in our beloved Saint Paul's on Sundays: how different from the clashing of opinion in the outside world',[101] was echoed in the majority of parishes in the three localities examined in this book. After the Great War, many clergymen felt 'a dead level of dullness' around them: 'worry and anxiety seem to hold all'.[102] Callum Brown has written of the 'mood of depression ... a kind of shambolic aimlessness', in the inter-war period churches.[103] Victorian Anglicanism's endemic anxiety had been a spur to action, seen not only in church-party rivalry and battles with nonconformists, but also in liturgical and parochial innovation; but when post-war parish clergymen and their congregations regrouped, their major aims entailed sober remembrance of their war-dead, the provision of a reverent atmosphere in their parish churches, and much quiet going-about of parish business. If most inter-war parish magazines seem dull, it is because the fight had literally gone out of them.

Coda: into the twenty-first century

Parliamentary debates provide a useful barometer for the reception of Anglican parish magazines into the twenty-first century. In the immediate aftermath of the Great War, if parish magazines were referred to at all, it was usually critically, as evinced in the Prayer-Book debates, when a Scottish MP denounced the ritualism of the parish magazine of Saint Augustine, Haggerston.[104] As the twentieth century progressed, they appear to have been appreciated only by a right-wing minority, the Conservative member for Bournemouth-East in 1974, quoting his local 'vicar's letter' on the media's 'degradation of morals ...the propaganda of disbelief, doubt and dirt', in support of his campaign against obscene publications.[105] The parish magazine could also be seen as a symbol of both dreariness and bad journalism, as when talentless journalists were likened by one MP to 'someone who writes in the parish magazine about the birds and the bees',[106] and another referred to the contents of his long speech as bringing on 'the tedium...which will be very much like my parish magazine'.[107] The rudest parish-magazine insult recorded in Hansard was that made by the Labour MP, Rhys Davies, on Winston Churchill's editorship of the *British Gazette* during the General Strike: 'I would like to know: who is the wonderful editor of this journal? He ought to be appointed editor of a parish magazine.'[108]

From the late 1970s, MPs began to cite parish magazines when providing information and comment from the localities during the course of debates on issues such as abortion,[109] violence in Northern Ireland,[110] and local government transport,[111] the last of which involved an impassioned plea for economic aid to the poor in Liverpool during the Thatcher administration by Labour MP Robert Wareing, utilising information on the local community gleaned from a Liverpool parish magazine. There is little sense of ribaldry or condescension in late-twentieth-century Hansard references to parish magazines: though Bernard Weatherill (Speaker of the House of Commons, 1983–1992) referred amusingly to his local parish magazine when recalling his life at Westminster, his point about the importance of the use of language in written communication was a serious one and his reference to his source was kindly.[112]

Clearly, twentieth-century modernists, some in a profoundly anti-clerical spirit, equated the parish magazine with religion's perceived stranglehold over society during the long nineteenth century. Because religion still held an important place in the nation's psyche, modernists were compelled to confront it, if only to deride it as obstructive to progress. Consequently, the parish magazine was seen by many as a metaphor for backward thinking, the antithesis of cultural progress, while, as part of the weaponry of the Church Establishment, it antagonised both nonconformists and the Celtic nations.[113] The shift in opinion which occurred towards the end of the twentieth century may be linked to the modern sense of the irrelevance of traditional church-going which Callum Brown has dated to the 1960s.[114] No longer seen as a threat to progress in Britain, the activity of the Anglican Church may be regarded nostalgically; hence, Bernard Weatherill's attitude to his parish magazine was amused and quizzical, and *Private Eye*'s satirical 'St. Albion's Parish News' – cited at the beginning of this study – was a commentary on Tony Blair's imputed megalomania, rather than an evaluation of Anglicanism, which was treated with frustrated affection.

Embedded in more recent Hansard references is an admiration for the parish magazine as a reputable organ of local concern. Its community involvement may have helped the parish magazine to survive into the twenty-first century as a useful local means of communication (as intended by many parish clergymen when it began), as its contents again focus on 'the parish pump' as much as on faith and worship, and it extends its readership by publishing ecumenical news and notices. The general standard of its local journalism appears to remain the same, the monthly letters of the parish magazine of St. Stephen, Shepherd's Bush, in 1908, and the parish of Loweswater, Cumbria, in 2010, both being written by the 'vicarage dog'.[115] The only nationally produced inset, *The Sign*, continues to feature Bible-study, sacred poetry and sermons. Though there are now cartoons instead of genre drawings, fiction has been replaced by book reviews, and the magazine is much shorter, a similar proportion is devoted to advertisements. In October 2009 the regular column of a vicar's wife mirrored the nineteenth-century inset by discussing how she reared chickens, but also raised the subject of communicating by tweeting on Twitter, as the Church continues to strive to maintain contemporary relevance while remaining largely conservative at heart.[116]

Conclusion

The Anglican parish magazine, the history of which has until now been largely unexplored, has a cultural significance which extends beyond an examination of its importance to parish life. Its genre, content, production and commercialism tell us much about developments in nineteenth- and early-twentieth-century publishing; changes in its content reveal alterations in the tastes and expectations of readers; its study discloses a great deal about the history of the Church of England and its place in British society, while opening a window on a much wider view of contemporary British cultural and intellectual history at times of intense religious, social and political change.

Like the Sloan family with which this book began, most readers who took parish magazines defined themselves, however loosely, as members of the Church of England. As it became just one denomination amongst many, the Church began to pay attention to parishioners like these, the parish magazine evangelising them through a new kind of propaganda, which built on the religious-tract tradition. Its first readers belonged to a mass market for the newly literate who desired both to be entertained and thought respectable. Many later readers were committed church workers, the parish magazine sustaining them in their connection with Anglicanism. After the Great War, the parish magazine became a greater symbol of 'belonging without (necessarily) believing', facilitating an involvement in Anglican community life which involved minimal church attendance.

The parish magazine always supported clerical status and writing ambition. Parish magazines' efficient method of localisation carried the concerns of the centre to the periphery and vice versa through encouraging parish clergy to become inset-contributors and introducing local news into the insets. Each tiny parish could celebrate its uniqueness through its own magazine, while reports of missionary work and emigration encouraged parishioners to see themselves as integral to both Anglican and imperial success. In allowing all parts of the Church to hear one another, parish magazines may have helped to balance urban–rural and north–south divides, and spread Episcopal Protestantism throughout the world.

The physicality of the text itself was important. The parish magazine was a physical object: a signifier of belonging, but also held; read; borrowed; scribbled in; circulated. For the price of a penny or two, it brought the Church permanently into the home, not just when the vicar or district visitor called. It was potentially for everyone, even for non-churchgoers, as every family member could observe it, read it or look at its illustrations. Discussing who had just been married, or learning the name of the baby born down the road, celebrated and underlined the Anglican basis of the community by bringing the Church right into the kitchen. Moreover, reading the inset as well as local news provided readers with fascinating material. Although Josef Altholz contended that 'Victorians preferred their reading to be safe even if it was stodgy', claiming that the Victorian religious press was 'nearly always dull reading', this book's examination of deaths at sea, socialist standoffs, parochial dissension, congenital madness, love-affairs, bankruptcy, sexual innuendo and much else, proves that parish magazines were anything but dull.

The parish magazine was an objectification of the aims and vision of those individuals who edited it, who made an imaginary world in which parishioners could partake, or which they could contest. As consumers, even the humblest parishioners could make up their own minds on what the Church was offering them, the divisive church-parties debate ensuring that this varied from inset to inset, Church leaders thus demonstrating their inability to control this schism at the heart of Anglicanism. And there were other pressure points: points of tension and rupture which occurred as writers and readers came to grips with social realities. Sometimes political and religious reification was at one, as in imperial propaganda, but at other times it was at odds, as in the response to socialism. Church leaders tolerated the insets rather than embracing them, regarding them as 'leading strings to bring up to better things'; fodder for the working-classes and a means of maintaining harmonious social difference, though, towards the end of the nineteenth century, the parish magazine became a means of encouraging support for an endangered Church.

When readers bought their monthly parish magazines they were not necessarily subscribing only to faith, for study of parish-magazine history reveals constant and multiple tensions between Anglicanism's spiritual purposes and priorities, and worldliness. The Church was devoted to the business of spreading its version of Christianity, but this was a product which had to be marketed in an increasingly pluralistic, secularising and commercial age. To reach out, not only to regular congregations but also to parishioners in Britain and throughout the world, it was thought necessary to espouse many of the practices of the secular press. Insets adopted the format and content of family magazines, incorporated advertisements which demanded sophisticated sales techniques, and employed populist writers who could adjust their secular narratives to the religious market with no loss of appeal. Though he aimed to support Anglicanism, Frederick Sherlock allied himself with secularism by publishing the work of well-known writers like L. T. Meade and Theodore Wood, who appear to have abandoned any pretension to religiosity. Advertising and the popular works of authors such as these ensured that the Church's eternal message was read alongside and often subsumed by the secular and money-making considerations of the age, Church leaders compounding this overriding sense of commercialism by obsessing over the Church's own financial needs.

In a highly commercialised marketplace, the insets were as competitive as any contemporary secular periodical, creating niche-markets which added to, rather than cured, the splintered nature of church-party allegiance, demonstrating the mixed motives of authors, editors and parish clergy. Even the highly regarded SPCK was as businesslike as any of its competitors, exploiting its writers by paying them minimal fees, while, like other inset proprietors, profiting by selling insets at a price readers were expected to afford, and demanding that parish clergy find buyers and make up the difference if buyers could not be found or would not pay. Charles Bullock's entrepreneurialism ensured that his magazines reflected their secular contemporaries, with the result that, though evangelicalism lost its pre-eminence, *Home Words*, by virtue of its populist content, attractive graphics and illustrations, remained the people's long-standing favourite during the period. But while some inset proprietors grew rich, parishes often lost money through buying their product, leading parish clergy to encourage members of the laity with an interest in business to help run their magazine. Local pages were opened up to consumerism through advertisements, which, though sometimes corrupting the Christian message, added much-needed revenue, helped give readers – particularly women – the power of choice and encouraged community solidarity. Advertising, lay assistance and the provision of local news were all methods by which the Anglican parish defended its ancient hegemony, based on the parish church, from the advance of nonconformism and religious doubt.

In common with the sentimental nature of the age, insets always contained genre-pictures of families, children and animals, which were used to encourage a love of home. They suggested the prelapsarian nature of country life to which all readers could return through churchgoing. They supported the old order: pastoral, agrarian, aristocratic, where the Church felt itself to be secure, a vision reified in articles and fiction. At the end of the nineteenth century, local news offered a similar discourse of sweet success: jolly tea-parties given by the village squire offered an Arcadian vision which helped construct Anglicanism for the *fin-de-siècle*. Nonetheless, such sweetness was often undermined by the negativity of both inset contributors and local incumbents, who offered an alternative discourse of criticism and anxiety.

Naturally, parish magazines offered the promise of heaven to all truly Christian readers, though this could only be achieved through a strict regime of temperance, cleanliness and thrift, combined with obedience to authority. While the Christian saints were more central to Anglo-Catholic theology, all parties in the Church revered that icon of chivalrous manhood, St George of England, as parish magazines echoed the era's enormous capacity for hero-worship while encouraging Christian self-sacrifice. Sentimental, martial and patriotic: parish magazines mirrored national sentiment while utilising such emotions to encourage churchgoing and maintain the Church's national position. Yet while parish magazines proffered confident and vigorous opinions, they also disseminated much anxiety about Anglicanism's future, sure that the notion of an endangered national Church would muster lay support. When this assurance was undermined by secularism and the events of the Great War, many clergymen retreated into the quotidian safety of Anglican parish activity, their anxiety intact but their confidence diminished.

Parish magazines reinforced a hierarchical view of the world which many clergy regarded as axiomatic. Their generally negative views on socialism were challenged by Christian Socialists, who regarded such views as unchristian. Until 1914, their contributors' acceptance of science confirmed Anglicanism's ability to negotiate with the world it was in, as a means of survival. After the war, though some clergymen continued to accept new discoveries as part of God's revelation, others began to regard science as materialist and non-transcendent, and thus irrelevant to faith.

To encourage working-class Anglican allegiance, the Church attempted to exploit the family magazine genre, but negotiating with the secular and populist was complex. God's love for man through the Bible's teachings, which was always faithfully taught in parish-magazine sermons, was almost drowned out by a host of other voices, many of which addressed the reader through stories and advertisements which merged God and Mammon. Thus, the format of the parish magazine allowed worldliness, anxiety and fear to creep out of its fractured voice. In the Church's endeavour to ally the agelessness of faith with a commercial, fragmented world, much was achieved, but much was also lost under layers of the temporal and the temporary. After the Great War, a generation brought up on secular periodicals and films found it hard to understand how Mother could have enjoyed reading parish magazines, and fewer insets survived. Nonetheless, this is not a story of inexorable decline, for local parish magazines – now often ecumenical – continue to be published. In celebrating community solidarity, they live on.

Notes

Introduction

1. James Secord (2000) *Victorian Sensation: The Extraordinary Publication, Reception and Secret Authorship of 'Vestiges of the Natural History of Creation'* (Chicago and London), p. 334.
2. Searching the digitised collections of the 'Access to Archives' website (A2A) for 'parish magazine' produced over 2,000 matches in March 2014: www.a2a.org.uk.
3. For the 1851 Religious Census see Hugh McLeod (1996) *Religion and Society in England 1850–1914* (New York), pp. 11–13.
4. For overviews of the secularisation debate see Jeremy Morris (2003) 'The Strange Death of Christian Britain: Another Look at the Secularisation Debate'. *Historical Journal* 46(4): 963–76; David Nash (2013) *Christian Ideals in British Culture: Stories of Belief in the Twentieth Century* (Basingstoke), pp. 2–14.
5. See K. D. M. Snell (2006) *Parish and Belonging: Community, Identity and Welfare in England and Wales 1700–1950* (Cambridge), pp. 499–504.
6. J. S. Leatherbarrow (1954) *Victorian Period Piece: Studies Occasioned by a Lancashire Church* (London), p. 103.
7. Simon Fowler (February 2008) 'Parish Magazines', *Ancestors*, 20: 1.
8. Hugh McLeod (1974) *Class and Religion in the Late-Victorian City* (London); Jeffrey Cox (1982) *The English Churches in a Secular Society: Lambeth, 1870–1930* (Oxford); S. J. D. Green (1996) *Religion in the Age of Decline: Organisation and Experience in Industrial Yorkshire, 1870–1920* (Cambridge); S. C. Williams (1999) *Religious Belief and Popular Culture in Southwark c. 1880–1939* (Oxford); Martin Wellings (2003) *Evangelicals Embattled: Responses of Evangelicals in the Church of England to Ritualism, Darwinism and Theological Liberalism 1890–1930* (Bletchley).
9. Owen Chadwick (1972) *The Victorian Church* (2 vols) II, 2nd edition (London), pp. 426–7.
10. Josef L. Altholz (1989) *The Religious Press in Britain, 1760–1900* (New York), pp. 37, 40, 43. He mentioned *Goodwill* and *Dawn of Day.*
11. Lawrence J. Clipper (1987) (ed.) *The Collected Works of G. K. Chesterton, Vol. 28: The Illustrated London News 1908–1910* (San Francisco), p. 187. Though celebrated as a Roman Catholic, Chesterton remained Anglican until 1922: Bernard Bergonzi, 'Chesterton, Gilbert Keith (1874–1936)', *ODNB*; Graham Greene (1969) *Travels with My Aunt* (London), pp. 173–5; Ian Hislop, Richard Ingrams, Christopher Booker, Barry Fantoni (2002) *Carry On Vicar: St. Albion Parish News, Vol. V* (London). See also Mary Cholmondeley (1899) *Red Pottage* (London).
12. Richard D. Altick (1998) *The English Common Reader: A Social History of the Mass Reading Public, 1800–1900,* 2nd edition (Columbus), p. 364.
13. Kay Boardman (2006) '"Charting the Golden Stream": Recent Work on Victorian Periodicals'. *Victorian Studies* 48(1): 505–17, 506; *The Wellesley Index*

to Victorian Periodicals, http://wellesley.chadwyck.com; *Waterloo Directory of English Newspapers and Periodicals, 1800–1900*; http://www.victorianperiodicals.com, accessed 15 June 2014.

14. Josef Altholz (1994) '"The Wellesley Index" and Religious Periodicals', *Victorian Periodicals Review* (*VPR*) 27(1): 289–93.
15. Margaret Dalziel (1957) *Popular Fiction 100 Years Ago* (London).
16. For early examples see Irene Dancyger (1978) *A World of Women: An illustrated History of Women's Magazines* (Dublin); Wendy Forrester (1980) *Great Grandmother's Weekly: A Celebration of the Girls' Own Paper* (London). Later examples: Patricia J. Anderson (1992) '"Factory Girl, Apprentice and Clerk": the Readership of Mass-Market Magazines, 1830–1860'. *VPR* 25(2): 64–72; Rosemary Scott (1992) 'The Sunday Periodical: Sunday at Home'. *VPR* 25(4): 158–62; Julie Melynk (1996) 'Emma Jane Worboise and the Christian World Magazine: Christian Publishing and Women's Empowerment'. *VPR* 19(2): 131–45. See also Janis Dawson (2013) '"Not for girls alone, but for anyone who can relish really good literature": L. T. Meade, *Atalanta*, and the Family Literary Magazine'. *VPR* 46(4): 475–98.
17. Margaret Beetham (1996) *A Magazine of Her Own? Domesticity and Desire in the Woman's Magazine 1800–1914* (London and New York); Margaret Beetham and Kay Boardman (2001) *Victorian Women's Magazines: An Anthology* (Manchester and New York).
18. Kay Boardman (2006) 'Charting the Golden Stream'. *Victorian Studies* 48(1): 505–17, 515; Jonathan R. Topham (2004) 'The Wesleyan-Methodist Magazine and Religious Monthlies in Early Nineteenth-Century Britain'. In Geoffrey Cantor, Gowan Dawson, Graeme Gooday, Richard Noakes, Sally Shuttleworth, Jonathan R. Topham, *Science in the Nineteenth Century Periodical: Reading the Magazine of Nature* (Cambridge), pp. 67–90.
19. Aileen Fyfe (2004) *Science and Salvation: Evangelical Popular Science Publishing in Victorian Britain* (Chicago and London); Cantor et al.: *Science in the Nineteenth-Century Periodical*.
20. Chris Baggs (2005) '"In the separate Reading Rooms for Ladies are provided those publications specially interesting to them": Ladies' Reading Rooms and British Public Libraries 1850–1914'. *VPR* 38(1): 280–306, 286, 288.
21. K. D. M. Snell (2010) 'Parish Pond to Lake Nyasa: Parish Magazines and Senses of Community'. *Family and Community History* 13(1): 45–69. Rex Walford (2007) *The Growth of 'New London' in Suburban Middlesex (1918–45) and the Response of the Church of England* (Lewiston, Queenston, Lampeter). See also Rosemary and Tony Jewers (2010) *Revelations from Old Parish Magazines* (Dereham).
22. Snell, 'Parish Pond', 45.
23. Mark Connolly (2002) *The Great War, Memory and Ritual: Commemoration in the City and East London 1916–1939* (Woodbridge), pp. 25–35; Michael Austin (1999) *'Almost like a Dream': A Parish at War, 1914–19* (Whitchurch); see also Alan Wilkinson (1978) *The Church of England and the First World War* (London), chapter 3.
24. Michael Snape (2005) *God and the British Soldier: Religion and the British Army in the First and Second World Wars* (London and New York).
25. Robert Lee (2006) *Rural Society and the Anglican Clergy, 1815–1914: Encountering and Managing the Poor* (Cambridge), p. 191.

26. Peter Croft (1993) *The Parish Magazine Inset* (Blandford Forum).
27. Croft, *Inset*, pp. 3, 24.
28. Michael Ledger-Lomas (2009) 'Mass Markets: Religion'. In David McKitterick (ed.) *The Cambridge History of the Book in Britain VI, 1830–1914* (Cambridge), pp. 324–58; Callum G. Brown (2001) *The Death of Christian Britain* (Abingdon and New York), chapter 4.
29. Snell, 'Parish Pond', 48–9.
30. Parish magazines were also common in Ireland, Scotland and Wales: Snell, 'Parish Pond', 45–6. As Scotland's national church is not Anglican, the Churches of Wales and Ireland underwent disestablishment and some Welsh magazines are in the Welsh language, only English parishes were studied; there is an obvious need for further study.
31. LSE Library, Booth Archive: Charles Booth (1902–1903), *Life and Labour of the People in London* (7 vols), Third Series: *Religious Influences* (London): Manuscript Notebooks.
32. *Carlisle Diocese*: CACC, *Carlisle Diocesan Calendar and Clergy List* (1910, Carlisle); the large proportion from Cumbria may be explained by the number of Cumbria's county archive centres (4). *Oxford Diocese*: OHC, MS. Oxf. Dioc. Papers C.365: Diocese of Oxford Clergy Visitation Returns (1899).
33. CACC, DRC Acc H3966: Diocese of Carlisle Clergy Visitation Queries and Returns (1900).
34. Secord, *Victorian Sensation,* p. 40; Jonathan R. Topham (2010) 'Science, Religion, and the History of the Book'. In Thomas Dixon, Geoffrey Cantor and Stephen Pumfrey (eds) *Science and Religion: New Historical Perspectives* (Cambridge), pp. 221–43, 234.
35. Peter Ackroyd (2000) *London, the Biography* (London), pp. 717–24.
36. For example, Jerry White (2007) *London in the 19th Century* (London), p. 3.
37. L. E. Ellsworth (1982) *Charles Lowder and the Ritualist Movement* (London); John Shelton Reed (1996) *Glorious Battle: The Cultural Politics of Victorian Anglo-Catholicism* (Nashville), chapter 3; Edward Norman (1987) *The Victorian Christian Socialists* (Cambridge), pp. 98–120.
38. Congregations' movement between churches is demonstrated in Charles Booth's notebooks: LSE, Booth Archive, *Religious Influences,* Manuscript Notebooks, B243: All Souls Langham Place.
39. D. M. Barratt and D. G. Vaisey (1973) *Oxfordshire* (Oxford); G. V. Cox (1870) *Recollections of Oxford* (Oxford).
40. James Bentley (1978) *Ritualism and Politics in Victorian Britain: The Attempt to Legislate for Belief* (Oxford).
41. William Purcell (1983) *The Mowbray Story* (Oxford). I should like to thank Dominic Vaughan, CEO of *Hymns Ancient and Modern,* for information on the present-day *Sign*, given January 2015.
42. James Obelkevich (1976) *Religion and Rural Society: South Lindsey 1825–1875* (Oxford); S. J. D. Green (1993) 'The Church of England and the Working Classes in Late-Victorian and Edwardian Halifax'. *Transactions of the Halifax Antiquarian Society* NS1: 106–20; Green, *Religion in the Age of Decline*; Richard Sykes (2005) 'Popular Religion in Decline: A Study from the Black Country'. *Journal of Ecclesiastical History* 56(2): 287–307; D. McClatchey (1960) *Oxfordshire Clergy 1777–1869: A Study of the Established Church and of the Role of its Clergy in Local Society* (Oxford); Cox, *English Churches in a Secular*

Society; Williams, *Religious Belief and Popular Culture;* John Burgess (1984) 'The Religious History of Cumbria 1780–1920' (Unpublished PhD thesis, University of Sheffield). Robin Gill (2003) analyses Carlisle Clergy Visitation Returns in *The Empty Church Revisited* (Aldershot).

43. Burgess, 'Religious History of Cumbria', pp. 56–7.
44. 1863: quoted in Chadwick, *Victorian Church,* II, p. 132.
45. Registrar General Records of Marriage Signatures (1839–1845). In D. Marshall and John Walton (1981) *The Lake Counties from 1830 to the Mid-Twentieth Century: A Study in Social Change* (Manchester), p. 15.
46. W. B. Stephens (1987) *Education, Literacy and Society 1830–70: The Geography of Diversity in Provincial England* (Manchester), p. 322; Richard D. Altick (1989) *Writers, Readers and Occasions* (Columbus), p. 143.
47. Annual Reports of the Registrar of Births, Marriages and Deaths: see Stephens, *Education, Literacy and Society,* Appendix D.
48. Snell, 'Parish Pond', 45–6.
49. Croft, *Inset,* pp. 49–50.
50. For a short overview of the debate see John Maiden (2009) *National Religion and the Prayer Book Controversy 1927–1928* (Woodbridge), pp. 4–6.
51. *The Sign, The Church Monthly* and *The Church Standard* were always written with a capitalised 'The' in parish magazines. This policy will be adopted throughout the book, though other periodicals will be awarded the conventional lower-case 'the'.
52. LMA, P94/AND/209: Saint Andrew Stoke Newington PM (February 1918); *Carlisle Journal* (February, May and July 1940); CACK, WPR100/PC/1–2: Grange-over-Sands PCC Minutes (May 1940).
53. J. M. Swift (1939) *The Parish Magazine* (Oxford and London), pp.17–18.
54. Ledger-Lomas, 'Mass Markets: Religion', pp. 327–8, 338.
55. See Beetham, *Magazine of Her Own,* p. 9; Rosemary Scott (1992) also discusses magazine binding in 'The Sunday Periodical: "Sunday at Home"'. *VPR* 25(4): 158–62, 160.
56. Mollie Harris (1986) *From Acre End, Portrait of a Village* (London), p. 85. The parish took *Home Words* (see OHC, SZ/EYN/283).
57. Altholz, *Religious Press,* p. 13.
58. For the Anglican pastoral revival see Gerald Parsons (1988) 'Reform, Revival and Realignment: The Experience of Victorian Anglicanism'. In Gerald Parsons (ed.) *Religion in Victorian Britain I, Traditions* (Manchester), pp. 14–66.
59. Callum G. Brown (2006) *Religion and Society in Twentieth-Century Britain* (Harlow), p. 76.

1 Inventing the Parish Magazine

1. Asa Briggs and Peter Burke (2005) *A Social History of the Media from Gutenberg to the Internet* (Cambridge), pp. 63–5.
2. Aileen Fyfe (2004) *Science and Salvation: Evangelical Popular Science Publishing in Victorian Britain* (Chicago and London), pp. 29–35. For the individual evangelical's religious development through reading see Sujit Sivasundaram (2004) 'The Periodical as Barometer: Spiritual Measurement and the Evangelical Magazine'. In Louise Henson, Geoffrey Cantor, Gowan Dawson,

Richard Noakes, Sally Shuttleworth and Jonathan R. Topham (eds), *Culture and Science in the Nineteenth-Century Media* (Aldershot), pp. 43–55.

3. Richard D. Altick (1998) *The English Common Reader: A Social History of the Mass Reading Public, 1800–1900*, 2nd edition (Columbus), chapter 5, particularly p. 101; Louis James (1974) *Fiction for the Working Man 1830–50* (Oxford), p. 141.
4. Altick, *Common Reader*, p. 103.
5. Anne Stott (2003) *Hannah More, the First Victorian* (Oxford), pp. 169–82; Susan Pedersen (1986) 'Hannah More meets Simple Simon: Tracts, Chapbooks and Popular Culture in Late-Eighteenth-Century England'. *Journal of British Studies* 25(1): 84–113.
6. For reactions to the 'pernicious' literature of the period see Rosemary Scott (1992) 'The Sunday Periodical: Sunday at Home'. *VPR* 25(4): 158–62, 159.
7. *Day of Days* (December 1875).
8. *Home Words* (*HW* forthwith) (1914), 141.
9. CACC, DRC Acc H3966: Carlisle Diocese Clergy Visitation Queries and Returns (1858): Lowick.
10. Sheila Haines (1979) 'Am I My Brother's Keeper? Victorian Tract Societies and Their Work, 1840–1875' (Unpublished PhD thesis, University of Sussex), pp. 2, 7.
11. Revd W. Cadman (1861). In *Church Congress Report* (London), pp. 110–14.
12. J. F. McCaffrey (1981) 'Thomas Chalmers and Social Change'. *Scottish Historical Review* 60(169): 32–60; Callum G. Brown (2001) *The Death of Christian Britain* (Abingdon and New York), pp. 22–5.
13. John Erskine Clarke was known as 'Erskine Clarke': this name has been adopted throughout.
14. *CCR* (1866), p. 248.
15. Brown, *Death of Christian Britain*, p. 47.
16. For the extensive circulation of religious magazines in the first half of the nineteenth century see Jonathan R. Topham (2004) 'The Wesleyan-Methodist Magazine and Religious Monthlies in Early Nineteenth-Century Britain'. In Geoffrey Cantor, Gowan Dawson et al., *Science in the Nineteenth Century Periodical: Reading the Magazine of Nature* (Cambridge), pp. 68–70, 90.
17. Josef L. Altholz (1989) *The Religious Press in Britain, 1760–1900* (New York), pp. 19–22; Josef L. Altholz (1994) '"The Wellesley Index" and Religious Periodicals'. *VPR* 27(1): 292.
18. Terry Barringer (2004) 'What Mrs Jellyby might have read. Missionary Periodicals: A Neglected Source'. *VPR* 37(4): 46–73.
19. Mary F. Thwaite (1972) *From Primer to Pleasure in Reading*, 2nd edition (Boston), pp. 215–16.
20. SPCK (1878) *Annual Report* (London), p. 28.
21. Altholz, *Religious Press in Britain*, pp. 10–13.
22. Michael Twyman (1998) *The British Library Guide to Printing: History and Techniques* (London).
23. David Vincent (1989) *Literacy and Popular Culture: England 1750–1914* (Cambridge), p. 41.
24. Wilkie Collins, 'The Unknown Public', *Household Words* (August 1858), 217–22; Richard D. Altick (1989) *Writers, Readers and Occasions* (Columbus), p. 143.
25. Altick, *Common Reader*, pp. 269–71.

26. Kimberley Reynolds (1990) summarises nineteenth-century anxieties about working-class reading in *Girls Only? Gender and Popular Children's Fiction in Britain, 1880–1910* (Hemel Hempstead), pp. 2–5.
27. Quoted in Scott, 'Sunday Periodical: Sunday at Home', 159.
28. J. Erskine Clarke (1861) 'Cheap Books and how to use them'. In *Church of England Book-Hawking Union Conference Proceedings* (Oxford). Samuel Smiles's philosophy was expressed in *Self Help* (1859), *Character* (1871), *Thrift* (1875) and *Duty* (1880): see H. C. G. Matthew, 'Smiles, Samuel (1812–1904)', *ODNB*.
29. Quoted in Topham, '*Wesleyan-Methodist Magazine*', 70.
30. Gerald Parsons (1988) 'Victorian Roman Catholicism: Emancipation, Expansion and Achievement'. In Gerald Parsons (ed.), *Religion in Victorian Britain 1, Traditions* (Manchester), pp. 147–61.
31. S. J. D. Green (1996) *Religion in the Age of Decline: Organisation and Experience in Industrial Yorkshire, 1870–1920* (Cambridge), chapter 4.
32. 'The Local and Regional Press', *Dictionary of Nineteenth Century Journalism*; http://www.dncj.ugent.be/, accessed 15 June 2014.
33. Peter Croft (1993) *The Parish Magazine Inset* (Blandford Forum), p. 93.
34. LSE Library, Booth Archive: Charles Booth (1902–1903), *Life and Labour of the People in London* (7 vols), Third Series: *Religious Influences* (London): Manuscript Notebooks, B220, B292, B252, B282, B295, B298, B303.
35. Brown, *Death of Christian Britain*, p. 19; Gerald Parsons (1988) 'Liberation and Church Defence: Victorian Church and Victorian Chapel'. In Gerald Parsons (ed.), *Religion in Victorian Britain 2, Controversies* (Manchester), pp. 147–65.
36. Brian Heeney (1972–1973) 'On Being a Mid-Victorian Clergyman'. *Journal of Religious History* 7: 208–24.
37. John Sandford (1845) *Parochialia, or Church, School and Parish* (London); T. C. Whitehead (1861) *Village Sketches* (London).
38. Alan Gilbert (1976) *Religion and Society in Industrial England: Church, Chapel and Social Change, 1740–1914* (London), pp. 165–6; D. W. Bebbington (1989) *Evangelicalism in Modern Britain: A History from the 1730s to the 1980s* (London), p. 136.
39. Edward Royle (1997) *Modern Britain: A Social History, 1770–1997*, 2nd edition (London), p. 311. Gerald Parsons (1988) 'Reform, Revival and Realignment: The Experience of Victorian Anglicanism'. In Gerald Parsons (ed.) *Religion in Victorian Britain 1, Traditions* (Manchester), pp. 14–66.
40. M. A. Crowther (1988) 'Church Problems and Church Parties'. In Gerald Parsons (ed.), *Religion in Victorian Britain 4, Interpretations* (Manchester), pp. 4–27.
41. As Gilbert argues, denominationalism depended upon the support of the laity: *Religion and Society*, p. 167.
42. J. Erskine Clarke, 'The Parish Magazine': *Journal of the Society of Arts* VIII (November 1860), 827–9.
43. David Hempton (2011) *The Church in the Long Eighteenth Century* (London and New York), p. 171.
44. Anthony Russell (1984) *The Clerical Profession* (London), p. 250.
45. BL, MFM, M2707–9: *Hackney Magazine and Parish Reformer* (1833–1838).

46. Owen Chadwick (1972) *The Victorian Church* (2 vols), II, 2nd edition (London), p. 171.
47. LMA, P95/CTC1/21: Christ Church Streatham Hill, Leaflet (February 1864); OHC, PAR76/17/N1: Saint Mary and Saint John, Cowley, Leaflet (1883); LMA, P74/TRI/72–94: Holy Trinity Chelsea, Parish Notes and Sermons (1886–1918); CACC, PR/163/36: Thornthwaite 'Parish Paper' (1901–1918).
48. Frederick Bennett (1909) *The Story of W. J. E. Bennett, Founder of St Barnabas, Pimlico and Vicar of Froome-Selwood* (London), pp. 204–9; see also James C. Whisenant (2003), *A Fragile Unity: Anti-Ritualism and the Division of Anglican Evangelicalism in the Nineteenth Century* (Bletchley), p. 232.
49. LMA, P93/JN1/64: Saint John Limehouse Fields PM (April 1860).
50. Hand-colouring may have occurred in a vestry copy only.
51. James Bentley (1978) *Ritualism and Politics in Victorian Britain: The Attempt to Legislate for Belief* (Oxford). For church attendance see K. D. M. Snell and Paul S. Ell (2000) *Rival Jerusalems: The Geography of Victorian Religion* (Cambridge), p. 72.
52. *Ecclesiastical Gazette or Monthly Register of the Church of England* (July 1870), 280.
53. H. D. Rawnsley (1898) *Henry Whitehead 1825–1896: A Memorial Sketch* (Glasgow), p. 60.
54. LMA, P93/JN1/066: Saint John Limehouse Fields PM (January 1872); Glenn Edward Sadler, 'MacDonald, George (1824–1905)', *ODNB*.
55. S. W. B. Newsom (2006) 'Pioneers in Infection Control: John Snow, Henry Whitehead, and the Broad Street Pump, and the Beginnings of Geographical Epidemiology'. *Journal of Hospital Infection* 64: 210–16.
56. Henry Mayhew (1985) *London Labour and the London Poor: Selections Made and Introduced by Victor Neuburg* (London), pp. 26–7.
57. Rawnsley, *Whitehead*, pp. 8, 175.
58. Saint John Limehouse Fields PM (February 1873).
59. Rex L. Sawyer (1989) *The Bowerchalke Parish Papers: Collett's Village Newspaper 1878–1924* (Gloucester), pp. 12–15. I should like to thank Professor Angus Winchester for drawing my attention to this book. For similar local content see K. D. M. Snell (2010) 'Parish Pond to Lake Nyasa: Parish Magazines and Senses of Community'. *Family and Community History* 13(1): 45–69.
60. CACC, PR/76/77/1–3: *Upperby Quarterly Messenger* (1886–1888).
61. LMA, P91/AUG/25: Saint Augustine Haggerston PM (August 1905).
62. *Carlisle Journal* (29 May 1891).
63. LMA, P73/BAN/452–69: Saint Barnabas Dulwich PM (January 1910); LMA, P84/BAN/46–55: Saint Barnabas Kensington PM (December 1911).
64. CACK, WPR75/Z1–5: Holy Trinity Ulverston PM (January 1902).
65. CACC, PR76/78: Saint John's Upperby PM (January 1915).
66. LMA, P84/LUK/103: Saint Luke Redcliffe Square PM (1910); OHC, PAR247/10/PR/1: Chiselhampton PM (January 1908); CACC, PR/129/12–28: Holme Eden PM (January 1903).
67. LLC: Lanercost and Kirkcambeck PM (1892–1896). I should like to thank Stephen White for drawing my attention to this collection.
68. Jose Harris (1993) *Private Lives, Public Spirit, Britain 1870–1914* (Oxford), pp. 17–23; Charles Booth (1902–1903) *Life and Labour of the People in London* (7 vols), Third Series: *Religious Influences* (London), vol. 2, p. 208.

2 Erskine Clarke and *Parish Magazine*

1. Oxford Alumni Database: Ancestry.co.uk, accessed 15 June 2014.
2. Canon Graham Fuller kindly shared his extensive knowledge of J. Erskine Clarke; subsequent references are to chapters, as at present constituted, of Canon Fuller's forthcoming biography of Clarke, at present entitled *Erskine Clarke, Pioneering Churchman; Writer and Editor; Battersea Patriarch.*
3. J. Erskine Clarke, 'The Parish Magazine': *Journal of the Society of Arts* VIII (November 1860), 827–9, 827.
4. Fuller, *Erskine Clarke,* chapter 12.
5. Josef L. Altholz (1989) *The Religious Press in Britain, 1760–1900* (New York), p. 10.
6. J. Erskine Clarke (1861) *Plain Papers on the Social Economy of the People* (London); Fuller, *Erskine Clarke,* chapter 13.
7. See Edward Norman (1987) *The Victorian Christian Socialists* (Cambridge), pp. 7–9; Kenneth Hylson-Smith (1989) *Evangelicals in the Church of England* (Edinburgh), pp. 208–10; Gerald Parsons (1988) 'Social Control to Social Gospel: Victorian Christian Social Attitudes'. In Gerald Parsons (ed.), *Religion in Victorian Britain 2, Controversies* (Manchester), pp. 39–62.
8. Fuller, *Erskine Clarke,* chapter 13.
9. Fuller, *Erskine Clarke,* chapter 10.
10. A. J. Hobbs (2009) 'When the Provincial Press Was Not the National Press (ca. 1836–1900)'. *International Journal of Regional & Local Studies* 2(5): 16–43; David McKitterick describes the 'shared and independent' nature of such newspapers which allowed readers to read national material alongside their own: David McKitterick (ed.) (2009) *The Cambridge History of the Book in Britain 6, 1830–1914* (Cambridge), p. 66.
11. Fuller, *Erskine Clarke*. 'Dozen of thirteen' refers to the practice of giving thirteen for the price of twelve: a 'baker's dozen'.
12. 'The Parish Magazine'. *Journal of the Society of Arts* VIII (November 1860), 828.
13. *Church Congress Report* (1864) (London), pp. 192–4.
14. Richard D. Altick (1998) *The English Common Reader: A Social History of the Mass Reading Public, 1800–1900,* 2nd edition (Columbus), p. 360. Sally Mitchell (1980) analyses this magazine's content in 'The Forgotten Woman of the Period: Penny Weekly Family Magazines of the 1840s and 1850s'. In Martha Vicinus (ed.), *A Widening Sphere: Changing Roles of Victorian Women* (London), pp. 31–3; see also Sally Mitchell (1981) *The Fallen Angel: Chastity, Class and Women's Reading: 1835–80* (Bowling Green, OH), chapter 1.
15. Flora Thompson (1945, 1973 edition) *Lark Rise to Candleford* (Harmondsworth), pp. 59, 94.
16. Margaret Dalziel (1957) *Popular Fiction 100 Years Ago* (London), pp. 24–5.
17. James, *Fiction for the Working Man,* pp. 44–5; Dalziel, *Popular Fiction,* p. 56.
18. Dalziel, *Popular Fiction,* p. 25.
19. See also Altick, *Common Reader,* p. 361.
20. Callum G. Brown (2001) *The Death of Christian Britain* (Abingdon and New York), p. 52.
21. Dalziel, *Popular Fiction,* p. 64.
22. Reported widely at the time: see the *Quarterly Journal* (7 April 1852).

23. *Chambers' Edinburgh Journal* (5 June 1852).
24. *Parish Magazine* (Jan. 1859), 5–6, 7–12; Robert Mimpriss (1837) *The Acts of the Apostles, and Epistles, historically and geographically delineated according to Greswell's arrangement, etc.* (London).
25. For example, Legh Richmond (1814) *The Dairyman's Daughter* (London); see Driss Knickerbocker (1981) 'The Popular Religious Tract in England 1790–1830' (Unpublished PhD thesis, University of Oxford), pp. 242–7.
26. Dalziel, *Popular Fiction,* pp. 70–1.
27. *Tract Magazine and Christian Miscellany* (1860), 310–11.
28. *Mother's Friend* (1857), 2–3.
29. E.g. 'Little Christel', *Parish Magazine* (May 1865). Callum Brown has commented on the sterility and conservatism of Victorian evangelical poetry: Brown, *Death of Christian Britain,* p. 112.
30. Gerald Parsons (1988) 'Victorian Religion: Paradox and Variety'. In *Religion in Victorian Britain, 1* (Manchester), pp. 1–13.
31. Boyd Hilton (1988) *The Age of Atonement: The Influence of Evangelicalism on Social and Economic Thought, 1795–1865* (Oxford), chapter 8.
32. See Dalziel, *Popular Fiction,* p. 66.
33. Aileen Fyfe (2004) *Science and Salvation: Evangelical Popular Science Publishing in Victorian Britain* (Chicago and London), pp. 269–70.
34. J. M. Swift (1929) *The Parish Magazine* (London and Oxford), pp. 37–8.
35. *Howitt's Journal 2* (1847), 149–52; *Howitt's Journal 3* (1848), 4–7.
36. Quoted in Peter Croft (1993) *The Parish Magazine Inset* (Blandford Forum), pp. 22–3.
37. Elizabeth Lee, 'Mackarness, Matilda Anne (1825–1881)', *ODNB.*
38. See Brown, *Death of Christian Britain,* p. 72.
39. CACC, PR167/4/6/1: Crosthwaite Keswick PM (Jan. 1886); Croft, *Inset,* p. 22.
40. LMA, P95/AND/116–126: St Andrew Earlsfield PM (February 1928).
41. John Maynard (1993) *Victorian Discourses on Sexuality and Religion* (Cambridge), pp. 141–50; Brian Harrison (1967) 'Religion and Recreation in Nineteenth-Century England'. *Past & Present* 38: 98–127.
42. Margaret Beetham and Kay Boardman (2001) (eds) *Victorian Women's Magazines: An Anthology* (Manchester and New York), pp. 221–2.
43. *Parish Magazine* (January 1859).
44. See Michael Twyman (2009) 'The Illustration Revolution'. In David McKitterick (ed.) *The Cambridge History of the Book in Britain VI, 1830–1914* (Cambridge), pp. 117–43, 140–1.
45. J. Erskine Clarke, 'The Parish Magazine'. *Journal of the Society of Arts* VIII (November 1860), 827.
46. Peter Croft (2001) *A Victorian Church Newspaper* (Blandford Forum), pp. 14–15.
47. Fuller, *Erskine Clarke,* chapter 10.
48. For Whitehead, see *Parish Magazine* (December 1885).
49. Goodwin was a known Broad Churchman: P. C. Hammond, 'Goodwin, Harvey (1818–1891)', *ODNB.*
50. Fuller, *Erskine Clarke,* chapter 10.
51. F. J. Harvey Darton (1932) 'The Youth of a Children's Magazine'. In Brian Alderson (1999) (ed.) *Children's Books in England, Five Centuries of Social Life,* 3rd edition (Newcastle, Delaware and London), p. 343.
52. Erskine Clarke (1862) *Church Stories* (London), p. vi.

53. Darton, 'Youth of a Children's Magazine', p. 342.
54. Darton, 'Youth of a Children's Magazine', p. 344.
55. Roger Ingpen, 'Weir, Harrison William (1824–1906), *ODNB*. For an appreciation of Weir's talent see John M. Darton (1879) *Brave Boys who have become illustrious men of our time, forming bright examples for emulation by the youth of Great Britain* (London), pp. 230–5.
56. Fuller, *Erskine Clarke*, chapter 12.
57. John Cordy Jeaffreson (1862) 'Church Stories'. *Athenaeum* (1811): 48.
58. Quoted in Thwaite, *Primer to Pleasure*, p. 217.
59. *Crockford's Clerical Directory* (1908) (London), pp. 275–6.
60. LSE Library, Booth Archive: Charles Booth (1902–1903), *Life and Labour of the People in London* (7 vols), Third Series: *Religious Influences* (London): Manuscript Notebooks, B294; for Battersea PM, see *Birmingham Pictorial and Dart* (January 1898).
61. J. Erskine Clarke, 'The Parish Magazine'. *Journal of the Society of Arts* VIII (November 1860), 827.
62. By 1900 many 'improving' magazines placed their illustrated serial story on the cover: Callum Brown (2001) *The Death of Christian Britain* (Abingdon and New York), p. 71.
63. For 'the church in danger', see David Nash (2013) *Christian Ideals in British Culture: Stories of Belief in the Twentieth Century* (Basingstoke), p. 9.

3 'Cheap as well as Good': The Economics of Publishing

1. Graham Fuller (forthcoming) *Erskine Clarke, Pioneering Churchman; Writer and Editor; Battersea Patriarch*, appendix 3. This is probably a conservative estimate; e.g. in 1859 it appeared in Keswick as an unacknowledged inset in *The Skiddaw Spring*, a local magazine with no obvious church connection. I should like to thank Dr June Barnes for the gift of this bound copy.
2. J. Erskine Clarke, 'The Parish Magazine'. *Journal of the Society of Arts* VIII (November 1860), 827–9, 828. For periodical circulation, see Richard D. Altick (1998) *The English Common Reader: A Social History of the Mass Reading Public, 1800–1900* 2nd edition (Columbus), p. 394; see also Aileen Fyfe (2004) *Science and Salvation: Evangelical Popular Science Publishing in Victorian Britain* (Chicago and London), p. 268.
3. *Parish Magazine* (1862) endpapers.
4. CACC, *Carlisle Diocesan Calendar* (1872): advertisements.
5. Fuller, *Erskine Clarke*, chapter 10.
6. Callum G. Brown (2001) *The Death of Christian Britain* (Abingdon and New York), p. 163.
7. Simon Eliot (1994) *Some Patterns and Trends in British Publishing 1800–1900: Occasional Papers of the Bibliographical Society* (London), pp. 82–3.
8. Eliot, *Patterns*, pp. 86–7.
9. See Peter Croft (1993) *The Parish Magazine Inset* (Blandford Forum), pp. 49–50.
10. Eliot, *Patterns*, p. 87.
11. See Jeremy Morris (2003) 'The Strange Death of Christian Britain: Another Look at the Secularisation Debate'. *Historical Journal* 46(4): 963–76, 966; Brown, *Death of Christian Britain*, pp. 163–5.

12. Michael Ledger-Lomas (2009) 'Mass Markets: Religion'. In David McKitterick (ed.), *The Cambridge History of the Book in Britain VI, 1830–1914* (Cambridge), pp. 341–6.
13. See Frederick Sherlock on the Parochial System (1891) *Church Congress Report* (London), pp. 373–7.
14. SPCK *Annual Reports* (London).
15. PHL, Mowbray Archive, *Sign* Monthly Circulation Chart, n. d.
16. William Purcell (1983) *The Mowbray Story* (Oxford), p. 16.
17. Altick, *Common Reader*, pp. 395–6.
18. Peter Broks (1996) *Media Science before the Great War* (Basingstoke), p. 26.
19. Josef L. Altholz (1989) *The Religious Press in Britain, 1760–1900* (New York), p. 30; Purcell, *Mowbray Story*, p. 16.
20. See *John Bull* (19 December 1874).
21. *Home Words* (*HW*): advertisements (1873, 1877).
22. Croft, *Inset*, p. 63.
23. *HW* (July 1872).
24. In *Home Chat*: see Margaret Beetham (1996) *A Magazine of Her Own? Domesticity and Desire in the Woman's Magazine 1800–1914* (London and New York), p. 193.
25. *Dawn of Day* (May 1900).
26. *HW* Centenary Issue (1971), 5.
27. See *HW* (1888) 233; see also *HW* (1888) 206: engraving of a Walter Goodman drawing, first published in the *Illustrated London News* (20 December 1877).
28. *HW* board covers for binding cost 9d each in 1912: CACC, Caldbeck PM (March 1912).
29. For example 'William Connor Magee, Archbishop of York': *HW* (1891), 58.
30. Beetham, *Magazine of Her Own*, p. 127.
31. *HW*, Souvenir Issue (January 1971).
32. See 'Mrs Randall Davidson': *Church Standard* (February 1910).
33. For example G. W. M. Reynolds, see Anne Humpherys (1990) 'Popular Narrative and Political Discourse in "Reynolds's Weekly Newspaper"'. In Laurel Brake, Aled Jones and Lionel Madden (eds) *Investigating Victorian Journalism* (Basingstoke), pp. 33–47, 35–7.
34. Walter L. Arnstein (1986) 'Queen Victoria and Religion'. In Gail Malmgreen (ed.) *Religion in the Lives of English Women 1760–1930* (Bloomington), pp. 11–40. Bullock's support for Queen Victoria demonstrated evangelical concern for the continuation of a Protestant monarchy: see John Wolffe (1991) 'The End of Victorian Values? Women, Religion and the Death of Queen Victoria'. In W. J. Sheils and Diana Woods (eds) *Studies in Church History 27: Women in the Church* (Oxford), pp. 481–503, 484.
35. John Plunkett (2005) 'Civic Publicness: The Creation of Queen Victoria's Royal Role 1837–61'. In Laurel Brake and Julie F. Codell (eds) *Encounters in the Victorian Press: Editors, Authors, Readers* (Basingstoke), pp. 11–28; David Cannadine (1983) 'The Context, Performance and Meaning of Ritual: The British Monarchy and the "Invention of Tradition" c. 1820–1877'. In Eric Hobsbawm and Terence Ranger (eds) *The Invention of Tradition* (Cambridge), pp. 101–64.
36. *HW* (1887), 36.

37. Charles Bullock (1897) *The Queen's Resolve: I Will Be Good, Hundred and Seventy-Fifth Thousand* (London).
38. Laurel Brake (2001) *Print in Transition, 1850–1900: Studies in Media and Book History* (Basingstoke), pp. 12–15.
39. Flora Thompson (1945, 1973 edition) *Lark Rise to Candleford* (Harmondsworth), p. 240; *HW* (1884), 83.
40. *HW* (1887), 158–61, 186–9; *HW* (1884), 81–5.
41. W. Odom (1917) *Fifty Years of Sheffield Church Life* (London and Sheffield), p. 128; *HW* Centenary Issue (January1971).
42. Croft, *Inset*, p. 46.
43. W. T. Stead (1886) 'The Future of Journalism'. Quoted in Hilary Fraser, Stephanie Green and Judith Johnston (2003) *Gender and the Victorian Periodical* (Cambridge), p. 80. For Bullock and Sherlock at the Church Congress, see *Church Congress Reports*: Bullock (1876), pp. 262–74; (1878), pp. 313–20. Sherlock (1891), pp. 373–7; (1901), pp. 158–65.
44. Sherlock's temperance series, 'Quite a Mistake': *HW* (1885); Croft, *Inset*, p. 48.
45. See *John Bull* (10 October 1891).
46. PHL: Mowbray's Directors' Reports (1907–1914) 2 (4, 11 Apr. 1911).
47. *The Times* (6 July 1911).
48. Croft, *Inset*, p. 47.
49. CACC, PR76/78/1: Upperby PM (1947–1953) incorporating *HW*.
50. Arthur Downer (1938) *A Century of Evangelical Anglican Religion in Oxford* (London), pp. 15–25.
51. Mary Milner (1842) *The Life of Isaac Milner, D.D., F.R.S.* (Cambridge).
52. A. F. Munden, 'Waldegrave, Samuel (1817–1869)', *ODNB*.
53. Owen Chadwick (1972) *The Victorian Church* (2 vols) I, 2nd edition (London), p. 196.
54. A. F. Munden, 'Bardsley, John Wareing (1835–1904)', *ODNB*.
55. *Carlisle Journal* (4 July 1899).
56. *The Times* (9 October 1902).
57. Nigel Yates (1999) *Anglican Ritualism in Victorian Britain 1830–1910* (Oxford), p. 196.
58. Croft, *Inset*, pp. 83–5.
59. Jose Harris (1993) *Private Lives, Public Spirit, Britain 1870–1914* (Oxford), pp. 166–8.
60. CACC, PR167/4/6/2: Saint John Keswick PM (August 1890).
61. C. Mitchell and Co. (1922) *The Newspaper Press Directory and Advertisers' Guide* (London).
62. OHC, SV Stack octavo/283: *Abingdon Ruridecanal Magazine* (1903–1914); *Parochial Magazine* for Penrith, Lowther, Appleby and Kirkby Stephen Deaneries (September 1924) (author's copy).
63. CACC, DX340/17: Raughton Head with Gaitsgill PM (1902–1903). For the amalgamation of country parishes from the 1890s see Chadwick, *Victorian Church*, II, pp. 211–12.
64. K. D. M. Snell (2010) 'Parish Pond to Lake Nyasa: Parish Magazines and Senses of Community'. *Family and Community History* 13(1): 45–69, 47.
65. LMA, P83/MRK/145: Saint Mark Tollington Park PM (January 1900); CACB, BPR27A/7/1–3: Saint Matthew Barrow PM (January 1907). See also J. M. Swift (1939) *The Parish Magazine* (London and Oxford), p. 37.

66. See Simon Eliot (1994) *Some Patterns and Trends in British Publishing 1800–1900: Occasional Papers of the Bibliographical Society* (London), p. 88.
67. Swift, *The Parish Magazine*, pp. 39–48; Charles R. Forder (1959) *The Parish Priest at Work: An Introduction to Systematic Pastoralia* (London), pp. 215–23.
68. CACK, WPR/22: Witherslack PM (November 1907).
69. Snell, 'Parish Pond', 55.
70. CACW, GOS98: Gosforth PM (1897).
71. CACC, *Diocesan Calendar and Clergy List* (1892); CACC, PR/167/4/6/2: Thornthwaite PM (1885); Chadwick, *Victorian Church*, II, p. 209.
72. OHC, PAR127/17/N1/3: Saint Andrew Headington PM (January 1881).
73. E.g. LMA, P92/AGN/40–68: Saint Agnes Kennington PM (1901).
74. Croft, *Inset*, p. 52.
75. *HW* early records were destroyed in 1930: conversation with William Bullock, director of finance from 1969 (3 August 2008). The Mowbray archive does not contain *The Sign*'s early financial records.
76. SPCK *Annual Reports* (London); CUL, SPCK MS, A14/10–13: SPCK Tract Committee Minutes (1872–1893).
77. For reaction to 'red top' *HW*, see CACK, PR75/21–5: St Mark Barrow PM (January 1902).
78. SPCK (1882) *Annual Report*, p. 17; PHL, Mowbray minute books, Vol. 1, 82: the directors adopted *Dawn of Day's* price of 2/9d per 100. In 1894, the vicar of Westward, Cumberland, changed to *DofD* from *The Church Monthly* (*TCM*) 'for it is the best that could be got for the money': CACC, PR56/45, Westward PM (January 1894).
79. OHC, PAR199/17/N6/8–12: Saint Cross Monthly Paper (May 1912).
80. LMA, P95/ANN/308–330: Saint Anne Wandsworth PM (January 1919).
81. *HW* (1883), 252.
82. For these denominations, see CACC, DFCM9/42 andDFCM9/210; see also David M. Butler (1978) *Quaker Meeting Houses of the Lake Counties* (London), p. 73; CACC, PR71/116: Caldbeck PM (January, February 1911, January 1912).
83. *HW* (1914), 141–2.
84. George Kitson Clark, quoted in Dominic Erdozain (2010) *The Problem of Pleasure: Sport, Recreation and the Crisis of Victorian Religion* (Woodbridge), p. 273.
85. SPCK (1888) *Annual Report* (London), p. 50; Brown, *Death of Christian Britain*, p. 67.
86. For advertising agents, see E. S. Turner (1965) *The Shocking History of Advertising*, 2nd edition (Harmondsworth), pp. 85–9.
87. Purcell, *Mowbray Story*, p. 16; PHL: Mowbray Minute Books 1 (10 September 1907); 2 (December 1907).
88. Lori Anne Loeb (1994) *Consuming Angels: Advertising and Victorian Women* (Oxford), p. 105.
89. *DofD* (1896), end-papers.
90. *DofD* (1896), 105–6; see also *TCM* (1907), 42.
91. *Sign* (June 1906).
92. The cycling young lady was a staple of *fin-de-siècle* advertising: Turner, *Shocking History*, pp. 103–4. For the focus on women's bodies in religious journal advertising, see Callum Brown, *Death of Christian Britain*, p. 67.
93. LMA, P83/JNE/699: Saint John Evangelist Upper Holloway PM (March 1903).

94. LMA, P84/MRY1/90: Teddington PM (December 1901).
95. CACC, PR110/1/307: Penrith Deanery Magazine (August 1910).
96. David Nash (2013) *Christian Ideals in British Culture: Stories of Belief in the Twentieth Century* (Basingstoke), pp. 14–15.
97. See Walter E. Houghton (1957) *The Victorian Frame of Mind, 1830–1870* (Newhaven), p. 162.
98. Sarah Flew (2015) *Philanthropy and the Funding of the Church of England, 1856–1914* (London and Vermont), p. 125.
99. Snell, 'Parish Pond', 50.
100. Charles Booth (1902–1903) *Life and Labour of the People in London, Third Series, Religious Influences*, 7 vols (London), 2, p. 89.
101. LMA, P91/AUG/25–6: Saint Augustine Haggerston PM (March 1887).
102. Saint Augustine Haggerston PM (1887–1905); Williams, *Religious Belief*; Cox, *English Churches*, Introduction, n. 5, n. 7.

4 Editors, Writers and Church Parties, 1871–1918

1. See D. W. Bebbington (1989) *Evangelicalism in Modern Britain: A History from the 1730s to the 1980s* (London), p. 3; for Bullock's evangelicalism see Charles Bullock (1861) *'Essays and Reviews': The False Position of the Authors, an Appeal to the Bible and the Prayer Book, a Lecture* (London).
2. See fiction in *HW* (1873).
3. Ronald Bayne, 'Havergal, Frances Ridley (1836–1879)', *ODNB*.
4. Peter Croft (1993) *The Parish Magazine Inset* (Blandford Forum), p. 45; *HW* (1872–1879, 1885, 1893).
5. F. R. Havergal, 'Forgiven Even Until Now': *HW* (1879), 9.
6. 'The Grave of the Dairyman's Daughter': *HW* (1876), 215.
7. For the evangelical model of the 'good' death see Pat Jalland (1996) *Death in the Victorian Family* (Oxford), pp. 39–58.
8. *HW* (1879), pp. 173–5.
9. UK Census (1841, 1851); Croft, *Inset*, p. 44.
10. John Burgess (1984) 'The Religious History of Cumbria 1780–1920' (Unpublished PhD thesis, University of Sheffield), pp. 22, 46; see also Rosemary O'Day (1988) 'The Men from the Ministry'. In Gerald Parsons (ed.) *Religion in Victorian Britain 2, Controversies* (Manchester), pp. 258–79, 265.
11. John Breay (1995) *A Fell-Side Parson: Joseph Brunskill and His Diaries, 1826–1903* (Norwich), chapter 2.
12. Ethel M. Everard (1902) *A Faithful Sower: A Memoir of the Life of the Rev. George Everard M.A.* (London), chapter 11; the chapter was co-written by Bullock.
13. Two hundred seventy-nine titles were listed in the British Library Catalogue in 2014.
14. Ethel Everard, *Faithful Sower*, pp. 7–8.
15. Kenneth Hylson-Smith (1989) *Evangelicals in the Church of England, 1734–1984* (Edinburgh), p. 119.
16. George Everard, Series, 'The Church of our Fathers': *HW* (1879).
17. Everard, 'But Thou Remainest': *HW* (1876), pp. 150–1.
18. UK Census (1861, 1871).

19. William Odom (1931) *Memories and Musings: Personal, Literary, Religious, General, 1846–1931* (Sheffield), pp. 7–10, 12–14, 31.
20. William Odom (1917) *Fifty Years of Sheffield Church Life, 1866–1916* (London and Sheffield), p. 128.
21. *HW* Christmas Supplement (1893), 21.
22. Odom, *Fifty Years*, p. 129.
23. *HW* (1885), 165, 237, 260.
24. John Hume Townsend (1896) *Edward Hoare: A Record of his Life based upon a brief Autobiography* (London), pp. 208–9, 257, 276.
25. Hylson-Smith, *Evangelicals in the Church of England*, p. 227.
26. E. N. Hoare, 'Notes on Immigration', *DofD* (February 1894); E. N. Hoare, 'What about Emigrating?' *TCM* (1893), 100.
27. *HW* (1893), 225–7, 234–5.
28. James C. Whisenant (2001), 'Anti-Ritualism and the Moderation of Anglican Opinion in the Mid-1870s'. *Anglican and Episcopal History* 70(4): 451–77.
29. *Home Words* (*HW*) (December 1871); 'England's Church': *HW* (1874), 136.
30. Whisenant, 'Anti-Ritualism and the Moderation of Evangelical Opinion', 474; Charles Bullock (1883) *Our Bishops and* Clergy (London), p. 57; 'Our Church Portrait Gallery': *HW* (1883) 252; 'Bishop of Liverpool': *HW* (1901), 2
31. Charles Bullock, 'The Story of England's Church': *HW* (1898), 69.
32. For example, E. H. Bickersteth, 'Sowing Time and Family Prayer': *HW* (1892), 75; Adrian Hastings (1991) *A History of English Christianity 1920–1990* (London), p. 75.
33. Bebbington, *Evangelicalism*, p. 148; *HW* (1916), 188; Martin Wellings (2003) *Evangelicals Embattled: Responses of Evangelicals in the Church of England to Ritualism, Darwinism and Theological Liberalism 1890–1930* (Bletchley), pp. 112–21; Hastings, *History of English Christianity*, p. 77.
34. John Shelton Reed (1996) *Glorious Battle: The Cultural Politics of Victorian Anglo-Catholicism* (Nashville), p. 60.
35. Thomas Hardy (1896) *Jude the Obscure* (London), pp. 181–2; *Oxford Mail* (13 September 1983); 'Ecclesiastical Printing: Messrs Mowbray and Co': *The Stationer, Printer and Fancy Trades Register* (November 1896).
36. *Stationer, Printer and Fancy Trades Register* (November 1896); PHL, Mowbray's Minute Books (1903–1938), 2 (20 April 1909).
37. See John Maiden (2009) *National Religion and the Prayer Book Controversy 1927–1928* (Woodbridge), p. 48.
38. Percy Dearmer (1899) *The Parson's Handbook* (London); Percy Dearmer (1903) *Is Ritualism Right?* (Oxford); F. R. Southwell, F. R. Barry, 'Dearmer, Percy (1867–1936)', *ODNB*.
39. UK Census (1901, 1911); William Purcell (1983) *The Mowbray Story* (Oxford), pp. 16–17.
40. See *Sign* (1905), 235.
41. Margaret Beetham (1996) *A Magazine of Her Own? Domesticity and Desire in the Woman's Magazine 1800–1914* (London and New York), p. 165.
42. Rita Stanley (1989) 'Susan Mowbray – A Woman in a Man's World'. In *Oxfordshire Local History* 3, pp. 103–8; Purcell, *Mowbray Story*, p. 16.

43. Nigel Yates (1999) *Anglican Ritualism in Victorian Britain 1830–1910* (Oxford), pp. 321–2; Royal Commission on Ecclesiastical Discipline (1906): http://anglicanhistory.org/ritualism/ (accessed 18 January 2015).
44. *Sign* (June 1906).
45. For correspondence see Margaret Beetham and Kay Boardman (2001) (eds) *Victorian Women's Magazines: An Anthology* (Manchester and New York), p. 166.
46. Royal Commission on Ecclesiastical Discipline (1906): Report, chapter 4, section 2, I.
47. *Sign* (June 1906).
48. *TCM* (January 1888, January 1907).
49. LMA, P70/SAV/141/142: Saint Saviour Wandsworth PM; the parish was pronounced evangelical by Charles Booth: Booth (1902–1903) *Life and Labour of the People in London,* Third Series, *Religious Influences,* 7 vols (London), 5, p. 156.
50. Lanercost PM (December 2008) (author's copy).
51. LMA, P91/COL/102–30: Saint Columba Haggerston PM.
52. *DofD* (January,.March, May and June 1891); Saint John Cowley PM (February 1891).
53. For Anglo-Catholic rivalry see John Maiden (2009) *National Religion and the Prayer Book Controversy 1927–1928* (Woodbridge), pp. 47–51.
54. Morley Lewis Caulfield Headlam M.A. Oxon, 1868–1953, vicar of Saint John's, Keswick, 1906–1918: C. Roy Hudleston and R. S. Boumphrey (1987) *Cumberland Families and Heraldry* (Kendal), p. 152.
55. See Bernarr Rainbow (1970, 2001) *The Choral Revival in the Anglican Church (1839–1872)* (Woodbridge), pp. 5, 223.
56. CACC, PR167/4/6/2: Saint John Keswick PM (February–June 1907).
57. Saint John Keswick PM (April 1907).
58. Saint John Keswick PM (June, July and August 1907).
59. For hymn books see Whisenant, 'Moderation of Evangelical Opinion', 465–8; see also John Wolffe (1988) '"Praise to the Holiest in the Height": Hymns and Church Music'. In John Wolffe (ed.) *Religion in Victorian Britain, 5, Culture and Empire* (Manchester), pp. 59–100, 62–4.
60. Saint John Keswick PM (1885).
61. Saint John Keswick PM (February, April and September 1907, July 1908).
62. Saint John Keswick PM (November 1909).
63. Croft, *Inset,* pp. 63–5.
64. *HW* (1914), 141; Alan Haig (1984) *The Victorian Clergy* (London), p. 18.
65. CACC, PR/71/116: Caldbeck PM (January 1911).
66. LSE, Booth Archive: Charles Booth (1902–1903) *Life and Labour of the People in London* (7 vols), Third Series: *Religious Influences* (London): Manuscript Notebooks, B196: 'Interview with Mr Caudwell'. The inset from 1888 to 1891 was Mowbray's *Gospeller;* see LMA, P94/MTS/114: Saint Matthias Stoke Newington (SN henceforth) PM.
67. Saint Matthias SN PM (July 1893, June 1894).
68. Reed, *Glorious Battle,* pp. 262–3; Saint Matthias SN PM (June 1892).
69. Saint Matthias SN PM (August 1892).
70. Saint Matthias SN PM (July 1893).

71. Saint Matthias SN PM (June 1894).
72. See BL Catalogue.
73. William L. Sachs (2002) *The Transformation of Anglicanism: From State Church to Global Communion* (Cambridge), pp. 214–16.
74. Sachs, *Transformation*, p. 212; Saint Matthias SN PM (April 1895).
75. For the significance of *Merrie England*, see Deborah Mutch (2005) 'The Merrie England Triptych: Robert Blatchford, Edward Fay and the Didactic Use of *Clarion* Fiction'. *VPR* 38(1): 83–103; Robert Blatchford (1895) *Merrie England*, 2nd edition (London).
76. Thomas Dixon (2008) *The Invention of Altruism: Making Moral Meanings in Victorian Britain* (Oxford), p. 241.
77. McLeod, *Class and Religion*, pp. 118–20.
78. Sachs, *Transformation*, p. 216.
79. Saint Matthias SN PM (May 1895).
80. Quoted in Hugh McLeod (1999) '"These Fellows in Black Coats": Anti-Clericalism in Later Victorian and Edwardian England'. *University of Helsinki Theological Publication Society* 104: 1, 85–93, 86.

5 Manly Men and Chivalrous Heroes

1. PHL: Mowbray's Minute Books, 1 (5 August 1904, 26 June 1906).
2. Richard D. Altick (1977) *Writers, Readers and Occasions: Selected Essays on Victorian Literature and Life* (Columbus), p. 97.
3. *The Church Monthly* (*TCM*) (1909).
4. See Owen Chadwick (1972) *The Victorian Church* (2 vols), II, 2nd edition (London), pp. 359–65.
5. CACK, WDX/762: Preston Patrick PM (July 1897).
6. John Tosh (2005) *Manliness and Masculinities in Nineteenth-Century Britain: Essays on Gender, Family and Empire* (Harlow), pp. 8–9, 31.
7. Mark Girouard (1981) *The Return to Camelot: Chivalry and the English Gentleman* (New Haven).
8. For an overview of 'the problem of male religiosity' see Callum G. Brown (2001) *The Death of Christian Britain* (Abingdon and New York), pp. 41–2, 156–61.
9. Charles Booth (1902–1903) *Life and Labour of the People in London*, Third Series, *Religious Influences*, 7 vols, 1 (London), p. 104.
10. Brown, *Death of Christian Britain*, p. 159; John Wolffe (1991) 'The End of Victorian Values? Women, Religion and the Death of Queen Victoria'. In W. J. Sheils and Diana Woods (eds) *Studies in Church History 27: Women in the Church* (Oxford), pp. 481–503, 497.
11. See CACC, PR167/4/6/1: Crosthwaite Keswick PM (January 1887); on Christmas Eve, 1886, the ringers rang 1,440 changes.
12. Jeffrey Cox (1982) *The English Churches in a Secular Society: Lambeth, 1870–1930* (Oxford), pp. 82–3; LMA, P91/COL/119–25: Saint Columba Haggerston PM (December 1903); LMA, P95/CTC2/051: Christ Church Union Grove PM (February 1907)
13. Saint John Keswick PM (February 1907); Brown, *Death of Christian Britain*, p. 137.
14. LUL, 8MWR: Elizabeth Roberts (1981) *Social and Family Life in Barrow and Lancaster 1870–1925*, Manuscripts: Transcripts of Recorded Interviews, Lancaster and Barrow, Mrs J1L.

15. An observation supported by K. D. M. Snell (2010) 'Parish Pond to Lake Nyasa: Parish Magazines and Senses of Community'. *Family and Community History* 13(1): 52.
16. LMA, P94/MTS/114/039: Saint Matthias Stoke Newington PM (May 1893).
17. OHC, PAR 127/17/N1/4: Headington Quarry Advent Pamphlet (1868); Raphael Samuel (1975) 'Quarry Roughs'. In *Village Life and Labour* (London), pp. 141–263, 146–9; LMA, P70/SAV/141: Saint Saviour Battersea Park PM (September 1872).
18. Nigel Yates (1999) *Anglican Ritualism in Victorian Britain 1830–1910* (Oxford), pp. 321–2.
19. LMA, P91/AUG/25: Saint Augustine Highbury PM (March 1897).
20. Saint Columba Haggerston PM (May 1901).
21. OHC, PAR216/10/C1/4: Letters on ritualism (1910) Saints Philip and James, Oxford.
22. Chadwick, *Victorian Church*, II, p. 222.
23. See Saint Columba Haggerston PM (January 1873); see also CACB, BPR/11/1: Saint George Barrow PM (March 1902).
24. CACK, WPR22/15/1/3: Witherslack PM (November 1903).
25. The Anglican harvest festival was inaugurated by R. S. Hawker, vicar of Morwenstow, Cornwall, in 1843: Piers Brendon, 'Hawker, Robert Stephen (1803–1875)', *ODNB*.
26. Open University, 'Charles Booth and Social Investigation' (A427 SG) Archive CD Rom: Booth's Digest, Duckworth's London Walks, District 13.
27. Witherslack PM (January 1903).
28. Witherslack PM (October 1907).
29. Brown, *Death of Christian Britain*, p. 88.
30. Brown, *Death of Christian Britain*, pp. 58–9, 88–9.
31. See Margaret Maison (1961) *"Search Your Soul, Eustace": A Survey of the Religious Novel in the Victorian Age* (London), chapter 4.
32. See *Parish Magazine* (1884), 13; *HW* (1898), 194.
33. In 1835: see Michaela Giebelhausen (2006) *Painting the Bible: Representation and Belief in Mid-Victorian Britain* (Aldershot), chapter 4. See also Sean Gill (2000) 'Ecce Homo: Representations of Christ as the Model of Masculinity in Victorian Art and Lives of Jesus'. In Andrew Bradstock et al. (eds) *Masculinity and Spirituality in Victorian Culture* (Basingstoke), pp. 164–78.
34. Gillian Beer (1970) *The Romance* (London), p. 67.
35. Nina Auerbach (1982) *Woman and the Demon: The Life of a Victorian Myth* (Cambridge, MA), p. 77.
36. Giebelhausen, *Painting the Bible*, chapter 4; Sean Gill (1998) 'How Muscular Was Victorian Christianity? Thomas Hughes and the Cult of Christian Manliness Reconsidered'. In R. N. Swanson (ed.) *Studies in Church History 34, Gender and Christian Religion* (Woodbridge), pp. 421–30, 427.
37. David Morgan (2005) *The Sacred Gaze: Religious Visual Culture in Theory and Practice* (Berkeley), pp. 201–16.
38. CROK, WDX/995: Saint Lawrence Appleby PM (December 1906); Brown, *Death of Christian Britain*, p. 93.
39. Gill, 'Ecce Homo', p. 167.
40. For early periodicals, see Dalziel, *Popular Fiction*, p. 102; for Charlotte Yonge, see Louis James (2006) *The Victorian Novel* (Oxford), p. 211.

41. Walter E. Houghton (1957) *The Victorian Frame of Mind* (New Haven), pp. 305–15.
42. H. C. Adams, 'Leslie Rice's First Curacy': *TCM* (1889), 273; H. C. Adams (1895) *Fighting His Way or Leslie Rice's First Curacy* (London).
43. Guy Arnold, 'Adams, Henry Cadwallader (1817–1899)', *ODNB*.
44. David Newsome (1961) *Godliness and Good Learning: Four Studies on a Victorian Ideal* (London), pp. 235–6.
45. David Rosen (1994) 'The Volcano and the Cathedral'. In Donald E. Hall (ed.) *Muscular Christianity: Embodying the Victorian Age* (Cambridge), pp. 17–44, 21–2.
46. *ODNB*, Adams.
47. Girouard, *Return to Camelot,* p. 166.
48. Argued by Hilary Fraser et al. (2003) *Gender and the Victorian Periodical* (Cambridge), p. 7; John Shelton Reed (1996) *Glorious Battle: The Cultural Politics of Victorian Anglo-Catholicism* (Nashville), p. 231; Maison, *Save your Soul, Eustace,* p. 74.
49. Kimberley Reynolds (1990) *Girls Only? Gender and Popular Children's Fiction in Britain, 1880–1910* (Hemel Hempstead), pp. 82–90; see also Patrick A. Dunae (1980) 'Boys' Literature and the Idea of Empire, 1870–1914'. *Victorian Studies* 24: 105–21. Other *TCM* schoolboy stories included Revd J. Hasloch-Potter's, 'Playing for His Colours: A Tale of School Life' (1893).
50. J. S. Bratton (1981) *The Impact of Victorian Children's Fiction* (London), p. 34; Ballantyne: *HW* (1884, 1888, 1894).
51. T. S. Millington: *HW* (1890, 1891, 1893, 1895).
52. Edward G. Salmon, 'What Boys Read': *Fortnightly Review* (February 1886), 248–59.
53. John Sutherland (1988) *The Longman Companion to Victorian Fiction* (Harlow), pp. 39–40; see also Brown, *Death of Christian Britain,* pp. 92–3, 107.
54. R. M. Ballantyne, 'Jeff Benson or the Young Coastguard': *HW* (1888).
55. G. M. Fell, 'A Life's Eclipse': *DofD* (1894). See Sandra Kemp, Charlotte Mitchell, and David Trotter (1997) *The Oxford Companion to Edwardian Fiction* (Oxford), p. 128.
56. LMA, P75/CAT/40–3: Saint Catherine Hatcham PM (January 1893).
57. Jose Harris (1993) *Private Lives, Public Spirit: Britain 1870–1914* (Oxford), pp. 251–6.
58. See John Kucich (2001) 'Intellectual Debate in the Victorian Novel: Religion, Science, and the Professional'. In Deirdre David (ed.) *The Cambridge Companion to the Victorian Novel* (Cambridge), pp. 212–33.
59. See Helen Kanitkar (1994) '"Real True Boys": Moulding the Cadets of Imperialism'. In Andrea Cornwell and Nancy Lindisfarne (eds) *Dislocating Masculinity: Comparative Ethnographies* (New York), pp. 184–96, 185.
60. Adams, *Fighting His Way*, chapter 23.
61. S. J. Stone (1872) *The Knight of Intercession* (London).
62. *TCM* (1888–1905); *HW* (1872–1879); Valerie Bonham, 'Stone, Samuel John (1839–1900)', *ODNB*.
63. *Sunday at Home* (1872), 810–12.
64. R. J. B. Golding-Bird, 'Return to Town': *TCM* (September 1895). The poem resembles Matthew Arnold's *East London.*
65. See Brown, *Death of Christian Britain,* pp. 98–9; Snell, 'Parish Pond', 56–8.

66. *HW* (1907), 48, 120.
67. For example, CACK, WPR103, 'Free with the Magazine'; photograph of the curate of Saint John's: Saint John's Windermere PM (October 1905).
68. The curate in the English novel could be weak, but was much courted, as described by Barbara Pym (1950) *Some Tame Gazelle* (London).
69. CACC, PR167/4/6/2: Saint John Keswick PM (July 1896).
70. See Brown, *Death of Christian Britain*, p. 99.
71. A vicar's daughter recalled her father wearing a special suit while visiting in Poplar in 1904. It was never allowed near his children for fear of disease: Eileen Baillie (1958) *The Shabby Paradise* (London), p. 38.
72. LMA, P91/TRI/73/74: Holy Trinity Hoxton PM (1891–1892).
73. OHC, PAR167/17/N1/1–17: Bicester, Ambrosden and Merton PM (February 1892).
74. CACK, WPR/75/Z1–5: Grasmere PM (November 1902).
75. Robert Tressell (1955) *The Ragged Trousered Philanthropists* (London), p. 186.
76. Hugh McLeod (1999) '"These Fellows in Black Coats" Anti-Clericalism in Later Victorian and Edwardian England': *University of Helsinki Theological Publication Society* 104: 85–93, 86.
77. 'Changing their Jobs': *Parish Magazine* (August 1884).
78. Girouard, *Return to Camelot*, p. 144; Richard Jefferies (1880) 'A Modern Country Curate'. In *Hodge and His Masters* (London), pp. 162–72; Mrs Humphry Ward (1888) *Robert Elsmere* (London).
79. See Anthony Russell (1984) *The Clerical Profession* (London), pp. 226–7; Brian Heeney (1983) 'Women's Struggle for Professional Work and Status in the Church of England, 1900–1930'. *Historical Journal* 26(2): 334–6.
80. Chadwick, *Victorian Church*, II, pp. 169–70.
81. CACC, PR163/36: Thornthwaite PM (February 1890, December 1893–January 1897).
82. For superstition in country places see Pamela Horn (1984) *The Changing Countryside in Victorian and Edwardian England and Wales* (London), p. 181.
83. John Burgess (1984) 'The Religious History of Cumbria 1780–1920' (Unpublished PhD thesis, University of Sheffield), p. 43.
84. Russell, *Clerical Profession*, chapter 16.
85. Stuart Marriott, 'Shaw (George William) Hudson (1859–1944)', *ODNB*.
86. Adrian Hastings (1991) *A History of English Christianity 1920–1990* (London), pp. 91–2.
87. Dominic Erdozain (2010) *The Problem of Pleasure: Sport, Recreation and the Crisis of Victorian Religion* (Woodbridge), pp. 272–3. See also John Lowerson (2006) 'Sport and the Victorian Sunday: The Beginnings of Middle-Class Apostasy'. In J. A. Mangan (ed.) *A Sport-Loving Society: Victorian and Edwardian Middle-Class England at Play* (Abingdon), pp. 179–97; Snell, 'Parish Pond', 58.
88. Open University CD: Booth, Digest, Duckworth's Report, District 13.
89. Peter Bailey (1978) *Leisure and Class in Victorian England: Rational Recreation and the Contest for Control 1830–1885* (London), pp. 138, 145.
90. Open University CD: Booth, Digest, Duckworth's Report, District 13; Charles Poulsen (1976) *Victoria Park: A Study in the History of East London* (London), p. 52.
91. 'The National Game': *HW* (1893), 162–3; 'Fifty Not Out': *HW* (1898), 160–1.
92. W. G. Grace: *TCM* (1896), 18–19.

93. Open University CD: Booth Digest, Parish Notes, 10, 11, 12: Bethnal Green, Bow, Poplar. LSE: Booth Religious Interviews: B169, Revd Cowan, Saint John, Isle of Dogs.
94. See Jenifer Hart (1977) 'Religion and Social Control in the Mid-Nineteenth Century'. In A. P. Donajgrodzki (ed.) *Social Control in Nineteenth-Century Britain* (London), p. 129.
95. CROK, WPR/75/Z1–5: Grange-over-Sands PM (May 1902); CROK, WPR/76/21–5: Saint James Barrow PM (Jan.1902); OSL, SV/AB/283: Abingdon PM (March 1902).
96. Saint Matthias SN PM (July 1892, May 1893, December 1894).
97. Saint Matthias SN PM (January 1893).
98. *Wigton Advertiser* (26 December 1914); LMA, P74/TRI/073–094: Holy Trinity Chelsea PM (October 1914).
99. *Church Standard* (February 1910, October 1910).
100. Girouard, *Return to Camelot,* pp. 222–3; Eleanor F. Rawnsley (1923) *Canon Rawnsley: An Account of His Life* (Glasgow), pp. 1–28; Newsome, *Godliness and Good Learning,* pp. 220–2.
101. National Trust (n.d.) *The Most Active Volcano in Europe: A Short Life of Canon Hardwicke Drummond Rawnsley, Vicar of Crosthwaite 1883–1917, Originator of the National Trust* (Keswick); *TCM* contributions (1888, 1893, 1894, 1896, 1902, 1906).
102. Crosthwaite Keswick PM (May 1893–December 1904).
103. A. Kennerley, 'Bullen, Frank (1857–1915)', *ODNB*; Sandra Kemp et al. (1997) *The Oxford Companion to Edwardian Fiction* (Oxford), pp. 48–9.
104. Frank Bullen, 'The Taming of a Tiger: *HW* (1906); 'Boys I Have Met': *HW* (1906); 'An Author's Testimony': *TCM* (1900). For the patriotism, militarism and racism which permeated such literature see John M. Mackenzie (1986) *Propaganda and Empire* (Manchester), chapter 8.
105. Dunae, 'Boys' Literature and the Idea of Empire', p. 105.
106. *Punch* (1 October 1898, 13 June 1900).
107. Crosthwaite PM (October 1889, December 1890, February 1892), in which Rawnsley listed the periodicals where his poems had first appeared.
108. Crosthwaite PM (April 1902).
109. Snell, 'Parish Pond', 62.
110. OHC, PAR216/17/N1/2: Saint Philip and Saint James PM (1880–1882).
111. Saint Philip and Saint James PM (March 1883).
112. Crosthwaite PM (January 1898).
113. Quoted in Cynthia F. Behrman (1971) 'The Creation of Social Myth; Journalism and the Empire'. *Victorian Periodicals Newsletter* 11, 1: 9–13, 12.
114. Charles Bullock, 'General Gordon': *HW* (1884), 243, 278.
115. 'General Gordon': *Parish Magazine* (May 1884).
116. For coats of arms covers see CACC, PR/123/27: Saint John Carlisle PM (October 1915).
117. CROK, WDX/402/3/9: H. D. Rawnsley (1900) *St. George and the Dragon: A Sermon for St. George's Day* (Keswick); Sara Atwood (2011) *Ruskin's Educational Ideals* (Farnham), pp. 151–64.
118. Crosthwaite PM (February 1900).
119. Mark S. Looker (1998) '"God save the Queen": Victoria's Jubilees and the Religious Press'. *VPR* 21(3): 115–19, 115; Elizabeth Hammerton and David

Cannadine (1981) 'Conflict and Consensus on a Ceremonial Occasion: The Diamond Jubilee in Cambridge in 1897'. *Historical Journal* 24(1): 111–46.
120. H. D. Rawnsley, 'Coronation Bonfires': *HW* (1902), 132–3.
121. For late-Victorian historical awareness, see Mary R. Anderson (1993) 'Cultural Dissonance and the Ideology of Transition in Late-Victorian England'. *VPR* 26(2): 108–13; Robert Baden-Powell (1908, 2004) *Scouting for Boys* (Oxford), p. 230.
122. Girouard, *Return to Camelot,* 253–8; John Springhall (1987) 'Baden-Powell and the Scout Movement before 1920: Citizen Training or Soldiers of the Future?' *English Historical Review* 102(405): 934–42.
123. Saint Augustine Highbury PM (January 1915).
124. H. D. Rawnsley (1916) *The European War 1914–1915: Poems* (London), p. 117.

6 'Scribbling Women': Female Authorship of Inset Fiction

1. Callum G. Brown (2001) *The Death of Christian Britain* (Abingdon and New York), pp. 69–80, 195.
2. This view accords with that of J. S. Bratton (1981) *The Impact of Victorian Children's Fiction* (London).
3. 'The Cords of Sin': *HW* (1872).
4. Kimberley Reynolds, 'Tucker, Charlotte Maria (1821–1893)', *ODNB*; Bratton, *Impact,* 70–9; Agnes Giberne (1895) *A Lady of England: The Life and Letters of Charlotte Maria Tucker* (London); John Sutherland (1988) *The Longman Companion to Victorian Fiction* (Harlow), pp. 641–2.
5. Charles Bullock, 'The Late Harriet Beecher Stowe': *HW* (1896), 203–4.
6. Quoted in Margaret Dalziel (1957) *Popular Fiction 100 Years Ago* (London), p. 67.
7. Cordiality between female writers and editors is examined by Bernard Lightman (2007) *Victorian Popularizers of Science: Designing Nature for New Audiences* (Chicago), pp. 116–24, and exemplified in L. B. Walford (1910) *Recollections of a Scottish Novelist* (London), p. 150. For Marshall, see Margaret Nancy Cutt (1979) *Ministering Angels: A Study of Nineteenth-Century Evangelical Writing for Children* (Wormley), p. 174.
8. 'Christmas Book Notices': *Monthly Packet* (1 December 1892), 701; D. M. Entwhistle (1990) 'Children's Reward Books in Nonconformist Sunday Schools, 1870–1914, Occurrence, Nature and Purpose' (Unpublished PhD thesis, University of Lancaster), appendix 6.
9. See Sally Mitchell (1981) *The Fallen Angel: Chastity, Class and Women's Reading, 1835–1880* (Bowling Green, OH), pp. 142–7.
10. For the purifying power of suffering, see Mitchell, *Fallen Angel,* p. 130.
11. George Eliot (1856) 'Silly Novels by Lady Novelists': *Westminster Review* 66, 243–54.
12. Agnes Giberne, 'A Bicyclist's Purse': *HW* (1898).
13. *HW* (1885), 82; Agnes Giberne (n.d.) *Tim Teddington's Dream or Liberty Equality and Fraternity* (London).
14. 'Matthew Hart's Dream': *Parish Magazine* (April, May, 1864).
15. See David Cannadine (2000) *Class in Britain* (London), pp. 108–13; see also Richard Price (1999) *British Society, 1680–1880* (Cambridge), pp. 289, 300.

16. Entwhistle, 'Reward Books', pp. 329–35.
17. 'Books and Authors': *Hearth and Home* (9 June 1892).
18. Anna Clark (1995) *The Struggle for the Breeches: Gender and the Making of the British Working Class* (Berkeley and Los Angeles), p. 269.
19. Andrea Ebel Brozyna (1999) *Labour, Love and Prayer: Female Piety in Ulster Religious Literature, 1850–1914* (Montreal), pp. 24–5.
20. Isaac J. Reeve (1865) *The Wild Garland or Curiosities of Poetry* (London), p. 191.
21. *HW* (May 1871).
22. E. J. Hardy (1889) *The Five Talents of Women: A Book for Girls and Women* (London), p. 19.
23. Margaret Beetham (1996) *A Magazine of Her Own? Domesticity and Desire in the Woman's Magazine 1800–1914* (London and New York), p. 135; *HW* (May 1871); Penrith Rural Deanery Magazine (January 1907) (author's copy).
24. J. A. James (1852) *Female Piety or the Young Woman's Friend and Guide through Life to Immortality* (London), pp. 72–115; Charlotte Elizabeth Tonna (1843) *The Wrongs of Women* (London), chapter 1.
25. See *Parish Magazine*: illustrations (1865–1868).
26. F. K. Prochaska (1980) *Women and Philanthropy in Nineteenth-Century England* (Oxford), pp. 1–17.
27. LMA, P95/ANN/308–330: Saint Anne Wandsworth PM (February 1918).
28. Morice Gerard, 'The Secret of the Moor': *HW* (1907).
29. Agnes Giberne, 'Her Brother's Keeper': *Home Words* (1906), 197, 199, 223, 247.
30. Quoted in Entwhistle, 'Children's Reward Books', pp. 134–5.
31. SPCK (1882) *Annual Report* (London), p. 16.
32. Justin Corfield (1993) *The Corfields: A History of the Corfields from 1180 to the Present Day* (Rosanna, VIC); R. C. Alston (1990) *A Checklist of Women Writers 1801–1900* (London), pp. 94–5.
33. See Gillian Avery (1975) *Childhood's Pattern: A Study of the Heroes and Heroines of Children's Fiction 1770–1950* (London), pp. 117–18.
34. Christina Rossetti, 'True in the Main': *Dawn of Day* (*DofD* forthwith) (May, June, 1882).
35. Lindsay Duguid, 'Rossetti, Christina Georgina (1830–1894)', *ODNB*.
36. W. K. Lowther-Clarke (1959) *A History of the S.P.C.K.* (London), p. 185.
37. SPCK Tract Committee Minutes (1876–80), pp. 133, 138, 151.
38. Bratton, *Impact,* pp. 191–2, 200.
39. Edward Salmon, 'Literature for the Little Ones': *Nineteenth Century* (1887), 563–80, 574.
40. SPCK (1878) *Annual Report* (London), p. 22.
41. Quoted in Lowther-Clarke, *S.P.C.K.,* p. 187; Peter Keating (1989) *The Haunted Study, A Social History of the English Novel 1875–1914* (London), pp. 48–51.
42. Lowther-Clarke, *S.P.C.K.,* p. 186. For author remuneration see Simon Eliot (2001) 'The Business of Victorian Publishing'. In Deirdre David (ed.) *The Cambridge Companion to the Victorian Novel* (Cambridge), pp. 37–60, 55–7; *The Times* (9 October 1890, 26 May 1891).
43. Lowther-Clark, *S.P.C.K.,* pp. 186–7.
44. Written in 1855; quoted in Milton R. Stern (1991) *Contexts for Hawthorne: The Marble Faun and the Politics of Openness and Closure in American Literature* (Chicago), p. 39.

45. George Eliot, 'Silly Novels by Lady Novelists': *Westminster Review* 66 (1856), 244.
46. Rosemary Mitchell, 'Marshall, Emma (1828–1899), *ODNB*; Lightman, *Victorian Popularizers of Science*, p. 428.
47. Beetham, *Magazine of Her Own*, p. 131.
48. Laurie Langbauer (1999) *Novels of Everyday Life: The Series in English Fiction, 1850–1930* (Ithaca and London), pp. 47–8.
49. CACC, DX1954: Diaries of Helen James of Clarghyll Hall Alston (1858–1911). I should like to thank Mr and Mrs Robert Huggard for allowing me access to the James Family papers.
50. Diaries of Helen James of Clarghyll Hall, 1 (5 October 1874).
51. 'Conversation on Books': *Monthly Packet* (January 1881), 35.
52. *The Great Round World, and what is going on in it* (April 1897).
53. *DofD* (August 1878); Bratton, *Impact*, p. 192.
54. SPCK Tract Committee Minutes (11 November 1884, 12 May 1885); *DofD* (May 1886).
55. See Jennifer Phegley (2004) *Educating the Proper Woman Reader: Victorian Family Literary Magazines and the Cultural Health of the Nation* (Columbus), Introduction.
56. Edward Salmon, 'What Girls Read': *The Nineteenth Century* (1886), 515–29, 522.
57. Charlotte Mitchell, 'Doudney, Sarah (1841–1926)', *ODNB*; Doudney was the author of *HW* serial stories (1899, 1901, 1902).
58. Austin Clare, 'The Red Geranium': *DofD* (1896).
59. Austin Clare, 'The Shadow of a Cloud': *DofD* (1905).
60. SPCK (1878) *Annual Report* (London), p. 27.
61. David Trotter (1993) *The English Novel in History 1895–1920* (London), p. 170; *The Times* (17 Feb. 1894), 5; Joseph Conrad (1907) *The Secret Agent* (London).
62. G. M. Robins (Mrs Baillie Reynolds) (1895) *To Set Her Free* (London); CACC, DX1954: Diaries of Helen James of Clarghyll Hall, Alston (1858–1911).
63. Trotter, *English Novel*, pp. 170–2.
64. For the countryside in inset fiction see Chapter 8.
65. Sandra Kemp et al. (1997) *The Oxford Companion to Edwardian Fiction* (Oxford): p. 81 (crime fiction), p. 207 (invasion and scare stories), p. 317 (political fiction).
66. Richard D. Altick (1989) *Writers, Readers and Occasions: Selected Essays on Victorian Literature and Life* (Columbus), p. 98.
67. George Eliot, 'Silly Novels by Lady Novelists': *Westminster Review* 66 (1856), 243–54.
68. *The Church Monthly* (1906: 99, 1905: 126).
69. Helen Bittel (2006) 'Required Reading for "Revolting Daughters"? The New Girl Fiction of L.T. Meade'. *Nineteenth-Century Gender Studies* 2(2): 1–36.
70. Bittel, 'Required Reading', 6; *New York Times* (18 July 1908).
71. Sally Mitchell, 'Meade, Elizabeth Thomasina (1844–1914)', *ODNB*; Bittel, 'Required Reading', 25–8.
72. L. T. Meade (1908) *Betty of the Rectory* (London); *TCM* (1906), 260; *TCM* (1907).
73. For Paul Hardy see http://myweb.tiscali.co.uk/speel/paint/hardy.htm, accessed 8 Sept. 2014; George Manville Fenn (1904) *To Win or to Die*

(London); Thomas Babbington Macaulay (1907) *The Lays of Ancient Rome* (London).

74. Quoted in Kate Flint (1993) *The Woman Reader, 1837–1914* (Oxford), p. 165. Bosanquet was writing in 1901.
75. Mary Elizabeth Braddon (1862) *Lady Audley's Secret* (London).
76. John Kucich (2001) 'Intellectual Debate in the Victorian Novel: Religion, Science and the Professional'. In Deirdre David (ed.) *The Cambridge Companion to the Victorian Novel* (Cambridge), pp. 212–33, 217–18; Trotter, *The English Novel,* p. 117. For drug addiction see Timothy Alton Hickman (2007) *The Secret Leprosy of Modern Days: Narcotic Addiction and Modern Crisis in the United States, 1870–1920* (Massachusetts), pp. 33–6.
77. Meade's earliest article was an exposé of outpatient departments at London teaching hospitals: Kemp et al., *Oxford Companion to Edwardian Fiction,* p. 276.
78. Bratton, *Impact,* p. 207.
79. Callum Brown (2001) *The Death of Christian Britain* (Abingdon and New York), pp. 71–2.
80. Flint, *Woman Reader,* p. 166.
81. For a discussion of the omission of male weakness in heroism rhetoric, see Walter E. Houghton (1957) *The Victorian Frame of Mind 1830–1870* (New Haven and London), p. 417.
82. Michael Wheeler (2013) *English Fiction of the Victorian Period* (Abingdon), p. 4.
83. *TCM* (1907), p. 260.
84. SPCK (1895) *Annual Report* (London), p. 43.
85. Patrick Braybrooke (1928) *Some Goddesses of the Pen* (New York).
86. Braybrooke, *Goddesses,* pp. 143, 155–6. *Punch* (31 October 1917); Film Database Search, http://www.citwf.com/person30168.htm, accessed 17 May 2014.
87. See Barbara Onslow (2000) *Women of the Press in Nineteenth Century Britain* (Basingstoke), p. 109.
88. PHL, Mowbray's Minute Book 1 (20 Mar. 1906, 10 Apr. 1906); *The Times* (31 May 1912, 4 December 1919).
89. Frank Tyrer (2003) *A Short History of St Mary's, Little Crosby* (Little Crosby).
90. M. E. Francis (1893) *In a North Country Village* (London).
91. Joan Rees (2006) *Matilda Betham-Edwards, Novelist, Travel-Writer and Francophile* (Hastings), pp. 30–7, 83–4; *HW* (1898), 23.
92. LLC, Prevost Bequest, 64K-69K, K116–K119: Austin Clare.
93. Austin Clare (1908) *The Conscience of Dr. Holt* (London).
94. 'In Duty Bound': *Quiver* (1870); Ann B. Shteir (1997) 'Gender and "Modern" Botany in Victorian England'. *Osiris* 2(12): 29–38; Lightman, *Victorian Popularizers of Science,* p. 109.
95. Agnes Giberne (1889) *Among the Stars or Wonderful Things in the Sky* (London); see also Lightman, *Victorian Popularizers of Science,* pp. 426–8.
96. Nicola D. Thompson (1999) 'Responding to the Woman Questions: Re-reading non-canonical Victorian Woman Novelists'. In N. D. Thompson (ed.) *Victorian Woman Writers and the Woman's Question* (Cambridge), pp. 1–23, 3–4.

97. See Barbara Kanner (1977) 'The Women of England in a Century of Social Change 1815–1914: A Select Bibliography'. In Martha Vicinus (ed.) *A Widening Sphere: Changing Roles of Victorian Women* (London), pp. 199–270, 264.
98. May Wynne, 'Amber Brooke': *TCM* (1910); Lucy Delap (2005) '"Thus does man prove his fitness to be master of things": Shipwrecks, Chivalry and Masculinities in Nineteenth- and Twentieth-Century Britain'. *Cultural and Social History* 2: 1–30.
99. Avery, *Childhood's Pattern*, p. 203; Langbauer, *Novels of Everyday Life*, p. 78.
100. Bratton, *Impact,* pp. 194–5.
101. Quoted in Flint, *Woman Reader,* p. 169.
102. Quoted in Brown, *Death of Christian Britain,* p. 141.
103. LMA, P83/AUG1/119–137: St Augustine Highbury PM (January 1915).
104. Born Olive Mabel Hopper: UK Census (1881).
105. Louis James (2006) *The Victorian Novel* (Oxford), p. 57.
106. See *Sign* (1905), 171–2; see also Avery, *Childhood's Pattern,* pp. 150–3.
107. L. D. O. Walters (1920) (ed.) *The Year's at the Spring: An Anthology of Recent Poetry* (New York).
108. I should like to thank Dan Fishman for allowing me access to his private collection of Queenie Scott-Hopper papers. For Scott-Hopper's publications, see the British Library Catalogue online: http://explore.bl.uk/ (accessed 14 January 2015); see also Google Books (accessed 13 January 2015).
109. Wells, Gardner, Darton (1913) *Sunday Reading for the Young,* 412. W. T. Stead's *Books for the Bairns* series contains two books by Scott-Hopper: (1904) *In the Christmas Firelight* (London); (1906) *The Story of Hiawatha* (London).
110. See *Blackie's Children's Annual* (1924); Walters (ed.) *The Year's at the Spring.* For Scott-Hopper publications by Harrap, Nelson, Boosey and Novello, see The British Library Catalogue.
111. The address book is part of the Fishman collection of Scott-Hopper papers. Ella King-Hall is discussed in Barry Phelps (1992) *P.G. Wodehouse: Man and Myth* (London), p. 77. For literary agents' engagement with female writers see Mary Ann Gillies (2007) *The Professional Literary Agent in Britain, 1880–1920* (Toronto, Buffalo, London), chapter 4.
112. Letter written by Walter Besant, *The Times* (26 May 1891); see also Keating, *Haunted Study,* p. 69.
113. Writers' Year Books of 1902 and 1916 concur with this figure: see Sally Mitchell (1992) 'Careers for Girls: Writing Trash'. *Victorian Periodicals Review* 25(3): 109–13, 110.
114. *London Gazette* (14 July 1893, 6 January 1905).
115. Queenie Scott-Hopper (1920) *Rock Bottom* (London).
116. *Newcastle Daily Journal* (7 February 1924, 7; 8 February 1924, 5).
117. *DofD* (1911), 7–8.
118. Quoted in Mitchell, 'Careers for Girls', 109.
119. Flint, *Woman Reader,* pp. 128–32.
120. The growth of the Anglican women's movement is discussed in Brian Heeney (1983) 'Women's Struggle for Professional Work and Status in the Church of England, 1900–1930'. *Historical Journal* 26(2): 329–47.

7 Parish Magazine Readers

1. Patricia J. Anderson (1992) '"Factory Girl, Apprentice and Clerk": the Readership of Mass-Market Magazines, 1830–1860'. *Victorian Periodicals Review* (*VPR*) 25(2): 64–72; Margaret Beetham (1996) *A Magazine of Her Own? Domesticity and Desire in the Woman's Magazine 1800–1914* (London and New York); Kate Flint (1993) *The Woman Reader, 1837–1914* (Oxford); Patrick Brantlinger (1998) *The Reading Lesson: The Threat of Mass Literacy in Nineteenth-Century British Fiction* (Bloomington); Louis James (1974) *Fiction for the Working Man 1830–1850,* 2nd edition (Harmondsworth); David Vincent (1981) *Bread, Knowledge and Freedom: A Study of Nineteenth-Century Working Class Autobiography* (London); David Vincent (1983) 'Reading in the Working-Class Home'. In *Leisure in Britain 1780–1939,* John K. Walton and James Walvin (eds) (Manchester), pp. 207–26; Jonathan Rose (2001) *The Intellectual Life of the British Working Classes* (New Haven and London).
2. Fraser et al. (2003) *Gender and the Victorian Periodical* (Cambridge), pp.15–16.
3. Archdeacon of Southwark: *HW* (1896), 177.
4. Beetham, *Magazine of Her Own,* p. 3.
5. See LMA, P73/CAM/105–128: Camden Church Camberwell PM (November 1895).
6. *Home Words* (*HW* henceforth) (1873): inside-front cover. There were more readers than purchasers, as magazines were passed around family and servants, see Altick, *Common Reader,* pp. 322–3.
7. Beetham, *Magazine of Her Own,* discusses the purchase of cheap family magazines by middle- and working-class women: pp. 46–50.
8. Callum G. Brown (2001) *The Death of Christian Britain* (Abingdon and New York), p. 113.
9. Quoted in Flint, *Woman Reader,* p. 192.
10. Florence Bell (1907, 1969) *At the Works: A Study of a Manufacturing Town* (Newton Abbot), pp. 156–67.
11. See Beetham, *Magazine of Her Own,* pp. 46–7.
12. K. D. M. Snell (2010) 'Parish Pond to Lake Nyasa: Parish Magazines and Senses of Community'. *Family and Community History* 13(1): 45–69, 55. For middle-class women and embroidery, see Beetham, *Magazine of Her Own,* p. 67.
13. LMA, P85/ALL1/61/1–386: All Saints South Lambeth PM.
14. CACC, PR 123/52: Saint John Carlisle Bazaar Programme (1900).
15. F. K. Prochaska (1980) *Women and Philanthropy in Nineteenth-Century England* (Oxford), p. 65.
16. CACC, PR167/4/6/1: Crosthwaite PM (September 1888).
17. For clerical opposition to church bazaars see Sarah Flew (2015) *Philanthropy and the Funding of the Church of England, 1856–1914* (London and Vermont), pp. 105, 117–19, 130. See also S. J. D. Green (1996) *Religion in the Age of Decline: Organisation and Experience in Industrial Yorkshire, 1870–1920* (Cambridge), pp. 165–76.
18. Flew, *Philanthropy*, p. 130.
19. Beetham, *Magazine of Her Own*, pp. 48, 51.
20. Ruth Lamb, 'Poor Lil's Baby': *The Church Monthly* (*TCM* forthwith) (1900), 33, 56.
21. Fraser et al., *Gender and the Victorian Periodical*, p. 63.

22. Holy Trinity Carlisle PM (June & August 1910).
23. Lori Anne Loeb (1994) *Consuming Angels: Advertising and Victorian Women* (Oxford), pp. viii, 158.
24. *HW* (1907), 7, 124, 161; Norfolk Record Office, MC 2678: Diaries of Revd W. Pelham Burn (1859–1901). Competition success was often the first step in achieving a professional writing career: see Sally Mitchell (1992) 'Careers for Girls: Writing Trash'. *VPR* 25(3): 109–13, 110; see also Jonathan Rose (2001) *The Intellectual Life of the British Working Classes* (Newhaven and London), p. 419.
25. *Church Standard* (1910).
26. Lina Orman Cooper, 'A Home of their Own': *HW* (1907).
27. Sally Mitchell (1981) *The Fallen Angel: Chastity, Class and Women's Reading, 1835–1880* (Bowling Green, Ohio), p. 2; see also Callum G. Brown (2001) *The Death of Christian Britain* (London and New York), pp. 149–56; Gregory Anderson (1976) *Victorian Clerks* (Manchester), pp. 1–2.
28. See CACC, DX340/19: Wetheral PM (August 1905); for examples of hymn music see *TCM* (1896); see also Jonathan Rose, '*Intellectual Life of the British Working Classes*, pp. 197–99.
29. E. J. Hardy (1885) *How to be Happy Though Married* (London), p. 102.
30. *HW* (1914), 15, 92, 188.
31. 'Consider the Lilies': *Parish Magazine* (July 1874); LMA, P93/JN1/065–066: Saint John Limehouse PM (October 1872).
32. *HW* (1914), 228.
33. F. K. Prochaska (2006) *Christianity and Social Service in Modern Britain: The Disinherited Spirit* (Oxford), pp. 61–5; see also Brian Heeney (1988) *The Women's Movement in the Church of England 1850–1930* (Oxford), pp. 28–33.
34. CACC, PR120/51: Crosthwaite Memoranda Book (1879–1882).
35. OHC, PAR126/18/1/A/1: Headington District Visitor Notes (1876–1885).
36. 'Dear Chelsea China': *Monthly Packet* (1 October 1895); James Covert (2000) *A Victorian Marriage: Mandell and Louise Creighton* (London and New York), p. 91.
37. 'District Visiting': *TCM* (1897), 3–4. Attempting to address different social classes within the same wrapper also occurred in the *Girl's Own Paper*: M. Cadogan and P. Craig (1976) *You're a brick Angela! A new look at girls' fiction from 1839–1975* (London), pp. 74–5.
38. 'A plea for more District Visitors': *Dawn of Day* (*DofD* forthwith) (November 1886).
39. Felicia Hemans, 'The Stately Homes of England': *DofD* (April 1882).
40. Susan Bone was the author's grandmother.
41. Agnes Giberne, 'Miles Murchison': *HW* (1892).
42. David Cannadine (2000) *Class in Britain* (London), pp. 48, 117, 160.
43. F. W. Farrar, 'The Working-Man's Bookshelf': *TCM* (1900), 68; Rose, *Intellectual Life of the British Working Classes,* chapter 4.
44. P. H. Ditchfield (1907) *The Parish Clerk* (London); P. H. Ditchfield, 'The Parish Clerk': *TCM* (1909), 350–2.
45. 'Taking a Look Round': *TCM* (February 1902).
46. *TCM* (1896), 18–19.
47. 'The Ministry of the Laity': *TCM* (1896), 135.

48. 'How to Restore a Church': *HW* (1907), 230; 'Disestablishment': *TCM* (1905), 230, 253; Frederick Sherlock, 'An Appeal to the Laity': *TCM* (1905), 4.
49. *Church Standard* (November & December 1910).
50. Margaret Stacey (1960) *Tradition and Change: A Study of Banbury* (Oxford), pp. 65–6.
51. Quoted in Albert Fried and Richard M. Elman (1969) (eds) *Charles Booth's London: A Portrait of the Poor at the Turn of the Century Drawn from His 'Life and Labour of the People in London'* (London), pp. 239–40.
52. Snell, 'Parish Pond', 53.
53. 'A Church Service in a Railway Station': *HW* (1907), 276–7.
54. *DofD* (1900), 67.
55. Holy Trinity Carlisle PM (January 1910); Saint Cross Holywell PM (March 1875) (author's copy).
56. Miles Taylor and Michael Wolff (2004) *The Victorians since 1901: Histories, Representations and Revisions* (Manchester), p. 3.
57. *TCM* (1896), 279.
58. LMA, P73/CAM/105–28: Camden Church Camberwell PM (October 1922).
59. CACC, PR/56/45, Westward PM (January 1893).
60. LMA, P85/ALL1/061/001: All Saints South Lambeth PM (January 1884). For railwaymen's respectability see P. W. Kingsford (1970) *Victorian Railwaymen: The Emergence and Growth of Railway Labour, 1830–1870* (London), p. xiii.
61. Brown, *Death of Christian Britain*, p. 166.
62. Grace Davie (1994) *Religion in Britain since 1945: Believing without Belonging* (Oxford).
63. CACC, PR167/4/6/2: Saint John Keswick PM (January 1895). This spelling was customarily used when referring to the religious form of the 'almanack'.
64. Margaret Dalziel (1957) *Popular Fiction 100 Years Ago* (London), pp. 6–7; Katharine Anderson (2004) 'Almanacks and the Profits of Natural Knowledge'. In Louise Henson et al. (eds) *Culture and Science in the Nineteenth-Century Media* (Aldershot), pp. 97–112.
65. Peter Croft (1993) *The Parish Magazine Inset* (Blandford Forum), p. 34.
66. *Church Congress Report* (1885, London), p. 364.
67. 'Straight Tips for Working-Men': *DofD* (February 1886).
68. 'Roseen Astore': *TCM* (1905), p. 35.
69. As did Fraser et al.: *Gender and the Victorian Periodical*, pp. 70–1.
70. For example, *HW* (1876), 23; *DofD* (January 1889).
71. *HW* (1907), 7, 124, 160–1.
72. *HW* (1907), 70.
73. Margaret Pelham Burn became an agony aunt. Over 40 of Lettice Bell's novels for the young, dating from 1908, are listed in the British Library Catalogue.
74. 'Asked and Answered': *TCM* (1888, 1907).
75. *TCM* (February 1907).
76. For clerical advice to save with the Post Office Savings Bank as a form of social control, see Paul Johnson (1993) 'Class Law in Victorian England'. *Past & Present* 141: 147–69, 151–4.
77. *TCM* (June 1888).
78. CCL, Saint Paul Carlisle PM (1896); LMA, P91/COL/126: Saint Columba Haggerston PM: 'All Things Considered': *Goodwill* (March 1909).

79. Michael Ledger-Lomas (2009) 'Mass Markets: Religion'. In David McKitterick (ed.) *The Cambridge History of the Book in Britain 6, 1830–1914* (Cambridge), pp. 324–58, 327.
80. Douglas M. Peers (2004) 'Britain and Empire'. In Chris Williams (ed.) *A Companion to Nineteenth-Century Britain* (Oxford), pp. 53–78, 59.
81. Snell, 'Parish Pond',. 63–4.
82. *TCM* (December 1905), 267.
83. Edward Royle (1997) *Modern Britain: A Social History 1750–1997*, 2nd edition (London), p. 65.
84. Snell, 'Parish Pond', 63.
85. National Library of Australia (http://www.nla.gov.au/); National Library of Canada (http://www.collectionscanada.gc.ca/index-e.html), accessed 14 June 2014.
86. *TCM* (1900), 89, 243.
87. K. D. M. Snell (2006) *Parish and Belonging: Community, Identity and Welfare in England and Wales 1700–1950* (Cambridge), p. 503.
88. Rose, *Intellectual Life of the British Working Classes*, p. 353.
89. LMA, P73/CAM/105–28: Camden Church Camberwell PM (January 1892).
90. Saint John Keswick PM (March 1890).
91. Saint John Keswick PM and Crosthwaite PM (August 1890).
92. CACC, PR/110/1/229: Saint Andrew Penrith PM (July 1886). Note use of 'ladies' and 'mothers'.
93. Peers, 'Britain and Empire', pp. 66–7.
94. Snell, 'Parish Pond', 64.
95. With the spread of literacy, obituaries had first become commonplace among evangelicals, see Brown, *Death of Christian Britain*, pp. 60–5; Penrith Ruridecanal Magazine (January 1907); Snell, 'Parish Pond', 52.
96. Crosthwaite PM (October 1897).
97. Crosthwaite PM (December 1901).
98. For the vicar's daughter as magazine distributor see OHC, PAR/163/10/PR2/1–2: Littlemore PM (December 1903).
99. CACC, DRC Acc H3966: Diocese of Carlisle Clergy Visitation Queries and Returns (1900).
100. CACC, DX340/2: Aspatria PM (January–May 1903).
101. *Church Standard* (Dec. 1909); Michelle O'Callaghan, 'Wither, George (1588–1667)': *ODNB*.
102. Snell, 'Parish Pond', 49.
103. Dalston PM (January 1896) (parish copy).
104. Chris Baggs (2005) '"In the separate Reading Rooms for Ladies are provided those publications specially interesting to them": Ladies' Reading Rooms and British Public Libraries 1850–1914'. *VPR*, 38(1): 280–306, 290–1.
105. OHC, PAR214/17/N1: Saint Peter-Le-Bailey PM (January 1880); LMA, P83/JNE/699: Saint John Evangelist Upper Holloway PM (February 1903).
106. LMA, P73/CAM/105–128: Camden Church Camberwell PM (November 1891); LMA, P91/TRI/74: Holy Trinity, Hoxton PM (February 1896).
107. Christine Bloxham and Susanne Shatford (1996) *The Changing Faces of Headington, Book 1* (Witney), p. 83.
108. OHC, PAR127/17/N1/4: Headington Quarry PM (1893).
109. OHC, PAR126/18/1/A/1: Headington District Visitors' Notebook, 1876–1885 (6 September, 6 December 1880).

110. *Monthly Packet* (October 1895).
111. Edward G. Salmon, 'What the Working Classes Read'. *The Nineteenth Century* (1886), 108–17, 116.
112. Barringer, 'What Mrs Jellyby might have read', 52; 'Weekday Work for Churchmen': *HW* (1902), 12–13.
113. LUL, Elizabeth Roberts, *Social and Family Life in Barrow and Lancaster 1870–1925*: MS Transcripts of Recorded Interviews (1981).
114. Richard Hoggart (1998) *The Uses of Literacy* (New Brunswick and London), pp. 121–31.
115. See Altick, *Common Reader*, pp. 363–4.
116. Hoggart, *Uses of Literacy*, p. 120.
117. See *Thompson's Weekly News* (November 1908).
118. Norman Nicholson (1975) *Wednesday Early Closing* (London), p. 23.
119. For *Home Notes* (1894–1957), see Margaret Beetham and Kay Boardman (2001) (eds) *Victorian Women's Magazines: An Anthology* (Manchester and New York), p. 222.
120. CACK, WPR/75: Holy Trinity Millom PM (1893–1902).
121. Distington PM with *HW* (1901) (author's copy).
122. Margaret Forster (1995) *Hidden Lives: A Family Memoir* (London).
123. Saint Mary Carlisle PM (January 1895, February 1895, October 1895).
124. CCL, St Mary's PM (June 1895).
125. Beetham, *Magazine of Her Own*, p. 106.
126. For example, LMA, P84/MRY1/86–107: Saint Mary Boltons PM (December 1896); LMA, P77/AND/123/14: Saint Andrew Fulham PM (January 1902).
127. For example, LMA, P73/CAM/131: Camden Church, Camberwell PM (March 1921).
128. Forster, *Hidden Lives*, p. 129.
129. For female dominance of congregations during the fin-de-siècle, see Flew, *Philanthropy*, p. 80.

8 Stormy Waters: 'How Can the Waves the Bark O'erwhelm, With Christ the Pilot at the Helm?'

1. Walter F. Houghton (1957) *The Victorian Frame of Mind* (New Haven), pp. 341–8.
2. Houghton, *Victorian Frame of Mind*, chapter 3.
3. Callum G. Brown (2001) *The Death of Christian Britain* (Abingdon and New York), p. 16.
4. David Nash (2013) *Christian Ideals in British Culture: Stories of Belief in the Twentieth Century* (Basingstoke), pp. 161–2; Sarah Flew (2015) *Philanthropy and the Funding of the Church of England, 1856–1914* (London and Williston, VT), chapter 4.
5. Nash, *Christian Ideals*, pp. 19, 187.
6. For example, 'Reflections at the Sea-side': *TCM* (1906), 179; see also Mrs Sitwell, 'Saved by the Sea': *DofD* (1890), 185.
7. For example, Mary A. Conley (2009) *From Jack Tar to Union Jack: Representing Naval Manhood in the British Empire, 1870–1918* (Manchester), pp. 144–7; Lucy Delap (2005) '"Thus does man prove his fitness to be master of things": Shipwrecks, Chivalry and Masculinities in Nineteenth- and Twentieth-Century Britain'. *Cultural and Social History* 2: 1–30.

8. Cynthia F. Behrman (1977) *Victorian Myths of the Sea* (Athens, OH).
9. George P. Landow (1982) *Images of Crisis: Literary Iconology, 1750 to the Present* (Boston), pp. 4–22, 56–7.
10. Behrman, *Victorian Myths,* chapter 5, p. 28; 'The Princess of Wales': *HW* (1879), 124.
11. Frank Bullen, 'The Taming of a Tiger': *Home Words* (*HW* henceforth) (1906).
12. *HW* (1876), 83; *HW* (1879), 74; E. N. Hoare, 'The Jessops, an Emigration Story': *The Church Monthly* (*TCM* henceforth) (1894).
13. Quoted in Brian Heeney (1972–1973) 'On Being a Mid-Victorian Clergyman'. *Journal of Religious History* 7: 208–24, 216. Noted by K. D. M. Snell (2010), quoting Bream PM (Dec. 1868): 'Parish Pond to Lake Nyasa: Parish Magazines and Senses of Community'. *Family and Community History* 13(1): 45–69, n. 40.
14. 'The Sexton's Hero': *Parish Magazine* (October 1859).
15. OHC, PAR214/17/N1/1–4: Saint Peter-Le-Bailey PM (February 1872).
16. Agnes Giberne, 'Everybody's Business': *HW* (1896), 29.
17. For example, Mrs Charles Garnett, 'Business First' (philanthropy and romance), *HW* (1899); Revd John Isabell, 'Silver Spoons or the Fishers of Nangizel' (jealousy and forgiveness), *HW* (1902); C. Lockhart-Gordon, 'Homeward Bound' (drunkenness), *TCM* (1899); Morice Gerard (Revd J. J. Teague), 'The Secret of the Moor' (detective story), *HW* (1906).
18. Landow, *Images of Crisis,* p. 110; Houghton, *Victorian Frame of Mind,* pp. 54–89.
19. Richard D. Altick (1991) *The Presence of the Present: Topics of the Day in the Victorian Novel* (Columbus), p. 638.
20. Barbara Weiss (1986) *The Hell of the English: Bankruptcy and the Victorian Novel* (London and New Jersey).
21. Weiss, *Hell of the English,* p. 157.
22. C. E. M., 'The Great Goldmine': *Dawn of Day* (*DofD* henceforth) (1896).
23. George Robb (1992) *White-Collar Crime in Modern England: Financial Fraud and Business Morality 1845–1929* (Cambridge), pp. 103, 108–10.
24. This was typical procedure: see Robb, *White-Collar Crime,* p. 103.
25. Oldham workingmen invested heavily in cotton companies during the 1850s and 1860s; see Rob McQueen (2009) *A Social History of Company Law: Great Britain and the Australian Colonies, 1854–1920* (Farnham), p. 160.
26. James Taylor (2006) *Creating Capitalism: Joint-Stock Enterprise in British Politics and Culture, 1800–1870* (Woodbridge), p. 56. A novelist cited by Taylor, Mrs Riddell, was an inset story contributor: 'The Rusty Sword', *DofD* (1893).
27. Taylor, *Creating Capitalism*, p. 22.
28. Andy Croll (2004) 'Popular Leisure and Sport'. In Chris Williams (ed.) *A Companion to Nineteenth-Century Britain* (Oxford), pp. 396–411, 401.
29. Landow, *Images of Crisis*, 60–9.
30. See Peter Keating (1989) *The Haunted Study, A Social History of the English Novel 1875–1914* (London), chapter 2.
31. Owen Chadwick (1972) *The Victorian Church* (2 vols) II, 2nd edition (London), pp. 112–13.
32. Chadwick, *Victorian Church*, II, pp. 427–39.
33. Jose Harris (1993) *Private Lives, Public Spirit: Britain 1870–1914* (Oxford), p. 252.
34. Lori Anne Loeb (1994) *Consuming Angels: Advertising and Victorian Women* (Oxford), p. 69.

35. Grace Carter-Smith, 'The Good Old Times, or the Effect of Disestablishment on Christmas 1935': *Parish Magazine* (December 1886). Grace Carter-Smith was a daughter of the vicar of Saint Andrew's, Haverstock Hill: UK Census (1871).
36. W. Blake Atkinson (rector of Bradley, Redditch), 'The Good Old Church of England': *HW* (1896), 218–9.
37. 'Church Defence': *TCM* (1900), 209.
38. For disestablishment see Chadwick, *Victorian Church*, II, pp. 301–7, 427–39.
39. CACC, PR167/4/6/1: Crosthwaite PM (December 1885).
40. Crosthwaite PM (January 1886).
41. Flew, *Philanthropy*, pp. 2, 5, 104–19, 123–7, 130, 137, 140.
42. 'What Every Churchman Ought to Know': *TCM* (1899), 58–9.
43. 'Duty and Privilege': *DofD* (June 1900).
44. 'The Religious Inheritance in Our Parish Church': *TCM* (1900), 65–6.
45. LMA, P73/CAM/105–128: Camden Church Camberwell PM (December 1896). Churchgoers celebrated after being officially declared free of debt.
46. See OHC, PAR127/17/N1/2–3: Headington PM (March 1877).
47. See Chadwick, *Victorian Church*, II, p. 169.
48. 'A Hint to Churchwardens': *TCM* (1894), 52.
49. 'A Neglected Opportunity': *TCM* (1894), 242.
50. 'Thrift': *Parish Magazine* (February 1885).
51. Charles Bullock, 'Thy Word is Truth: The Wonderful Book': *HW* (January 1898).
52. Frank Langbridge, 'I Know a Bank': *HW* (1898), 203.
53. Pamela Horn (1984) *The Changing Countryside in Victorian and Edwardian England and Wales* (London), pp. 182–5.
54. E. A. Campbell, 'John Harker's Bond': *TCM* (1893). For the connection between speculation and gambling see Taylor, *Creating Capitalism*, chapter 2; see also David C. Itzkowitz (2009) 'Fair Enterprise or Extravagant Speculation: Investment, Speculation and Gambling in Victorian England'. In Nancy Henry, Cannon Schmitt (eds) *Victorian Investments: New Perspectives on Finance and Culture* (Bloomington), pp. 98–119.
55. Taylor, *Creating Capitalism*, p. 177; Charles W. Munn (1994) 'Review: White-Collar Crime in Modern England: Financial Fraud and Business Morality, 1845–1929'. *Economic History Review* 47(1): 199–200; Matthew Rubery (2009) *The Novelty of Newspapers: Victorian Fiction after the Invention of the News* (Oxford), p. 72.
56. 'The Forge of Life': *Parish Magazine* (1865).
57. 'The Home Philosopher: Advertising Swindles': *Girl's Own Paper* (1886), 325–6; see also Matthew Sweet (2001) *Inventing the Victorians* (London), pp. 50–1.
58. A. R. Buckland, 'The Patience of Two': *TCM* (1893) anticipates H. G. Wells' *Tono Bungay* by 16 years.
59. For commercial exploitation in literature, see Keating, *Haunted Study*, pp. 102–3.
60. Mrs C. Will Hawksley, 'Out of Darkness': *TCM* (1894).
61. Landow, *Images of Crisis*, p. 109; Houghton, *Victorian Frame of Mind*, pp. 54–89.
62. *Church Congress Report* (1906) (London), pp. 198–205.
63. For social surveys see Harold J. Perkin (2002) *The Rise of Professional Society: England since 1880*, 3rd edition (London), p. 103.

64. 'Religion and the Working Man': *TCM* (1893), 154–5; Sarah Tooley, 'Bishop of Chelmsford': *Home Words* (*HW* henceforth) (1914), 195.
65. G. S. Reaney, 'Why do they not come to Church': *TCM* (1900), 167.
66. 'Bread and Coals': Saint John Limehouse Fields PM (1861).
67. CACC, PR167/4/6/2: Saint John Keswick PM (April 1912).
68. CACC, PR167/4/6/1: Crosthwaite PM (May, June 1888).
69. Sarah Wise (2008) *The Blackest Streets: The Life and Death of a Victorian Slum* (London), pp. 87, 143–6.
70. LMA, P87/JS/127/128: Saint James Paddington PM (Febuary, March 1887) and SDF Campaign Poster (January 1887).
71. LMA, P94/MTS/038–45: Saint Matthias SN PM (March 1895). Jack Cade led a peasant revolt against Henry VI in 1450: Alexander L. Kaufman (2009) *The Historical Literature of the Jack Cade Rebellion* (Farnham), Introduction.
72. LMA, P91/COL/119–25: Saint Columba Haggerston PM (January 1890).
73. St John Keswick PM (July, August 1888).
74. Acton PM (May 1896) (author's copy).
75. *HW* (1896), 109, 162.
76. Ronald Bayne, 'Lambert, Brooke (1834–1901)', *ODNB*; G. A. Patrick, 'Westcott, Brooke Foss (1825–1901)', *ODNB*.
77. 'Work in the Vineyard': *TCM*, November 1889.
78. E. N. Hoare, 'A Living Wage': *TCM* (1903).
79. Callum G. Brown (2006) *Religion and Society in Twentieth-Century Britain* (Harlow), p. 79 (quoting the Scottish Christian socialist, Robert Flint).
80. Jan Marsh (1982) *Back to the Land: The Pastoral Impulse in England, from 1880 to 1914* (London), pp. 222–7; for Christian-Socialist inset interest in the garden-city movement, see *Goodwill* (June 1907).
81. Quoted in John R. Short (1991) *Imagined Country: Environment, Culture and Society* (Syracuse NY), pp. 28–39, 167; Houghton, *Victorian Frame of Mind*, pp. 79–80. For rural nostalgia in Victorian advertising see Loeb, *Consuming Angels*, p. 23.
82. For agriculture, see Michael Winstanley (2004) 'Agriculture and Rural Society'. In Chris Williams (ed.) *A Companion to Nineteenth-Century Britain* (Oxford), pp. 205–22, 209–11.
83. Snell, 'Parish Pond', 55.
84. OHC, SV/AB/283: Abingdon PM (July 1902, January 1904).
85. Saint John Limehouse Fields PM is an exception: see Chapter 1.
86. Snell, 'Parish Pond', 54; OHC, PAR127/17/N1/2–3: Headington PM (February 1877). For parish schools see Edward Royle (2009) 'The Parish Community through the Vicarage Window: Nineteenth-Century Clergy Visitation Returns'. *Family & Community History*, 12(1): 14–15; Michael J. G. Gray-Fow (1990) 'Squire, Parson and Village School: Wragby, 1830–1886'. In Patrick Scott and Pauline Fletcher (eds) *Culture and Education in Victorian England* (Lewisburg), pp. 162–73.
87. Morice Gerard, 'The Silent Conquest': *HW* (1907); David Powell (1996) *The Edwardian Crisis, 1901–1914* (Basingstoke), p. 140.
88. Houghton, *Victorian Frame of Mind*, pp. 346–7; Colleen McDannell (1986) *The Christian Home in Victorian America 1840–1900* (Bloomington), pp. 128–33.
89. 'Waiting for "a Footstep that We Know"': *HW* (1877) 35.

90. See E. S. Turner (1965) *The Shocking History of Advertising,* 2nd edition (Harmondsworth), p. 88.
91. John Wolffe (2000) *Great Deaths: Grieving, Religion and Nationhood in Victorian and Edwardian Britain* (Oxford), p. 219.
92. James Walvin (1987) *Victorian Values* (London), p. 108; Eric Hobsbawm (1983) 'Introduction', and David Cannadine (1983) 'Context, Performance and Meaning of Ritual', pp. 101–38. Both in *The Invention of Tradition* (eds) Eric Hobsbawm and Terence Ranger (Cambridge), pp. 1–14, 101–38.
93. Snell, 'Parish Pond', 61.
94. See 'The Home Life of the King and Queen', and 'The King with his Grandchildren': *HW* (1902), 20–1.
95. For example, CACK, WPR79: Flookburgh PM (February 1917); LMA, P94/MTS/038/039–045: Saint Matthias Stoke Newington PM (February 1894); Revd J. Isabell, 'Silver Spoons': *HW* (1902), 206.
96. *Parish Magazine* (September 1864).
97. John Flint, 'Crowther, Samuel Ajayi (*c.*1807–1891)': *ODNB*; *HW* (1890), 86–7. In 2014, Archbishop Welby of Canterbury led a service of repentance: Crowther had been 'betrayed and let down and undermined' (Sermon: Canterbury Cathedral, June 2014).
98. 'Crowther', *ODNB*.
99. Martin Wellings (1991) 'Anglo-Catholicism, the "Crisis in the Church" and the Cavalier Case of 1899'. *Journal of Ecclesiastical History* 2(2): 238–57.
100. 'Clerical Lawlessness': *DofD* (November 1900), 246.
101. Houghton, *Victorian Frame of Mind,* pp. 413–14.
102. *HW* (1889), 206.
103. Frederick Sherlock, 'Lay Hinderers': *TCM* (1900), 259–60.
104. 'Vagrancy in Religion': *TCM* (1900), 162.
105. For example, 'Lay Hinderers' beside 'Thy Sins Be Forgiven Thee': *TCM* (1900), 48.
106. 'Children's Church on the Sands': *TCM* (August 1910).

9 The Challenges of Modernity

1. 'Between Old and New': *The Church Monthly* (*TCM* henceforth) (1900).
2. Callum G. Brown (2006) *Religion and Society in the Twentieth Century* (Harlow), p. 74.
3. Revd McClure (1884) 'Popular Literature': *Church Congress Report* (London), p. 90.
4. Michael Ledger-Lomas (2009) 'Mass Markets: Religion'. In David McKitterick (ed.) *The Cambridge History of the Book in Britain VI, 1830–1914* (Cambridge), pp. 324–58, 353.
5. See Peter Broks (1996) *Media Science before the Great War* (Basingstoke), chapter 5.
6. Broks, *Media Science,* p. 27.
7. For example, CACC, PR32/6//1/1–8: Holy Trinity PM (April 1910).
8. OHC, PAR127/17/MS4/1: Headington Quarry Library Catalogue (1889).
9. CACC, DSO/56/1: Alston Literary Institute Library Catalogue (1924).

10. 'Science Gossip': *Dawn of Day* (*DofD* henceforth) (October 1895). Articles in 'Science Gossip' were much shorter and shallower than those in the Victorian magazine of the same name: see Broks, *Media Science*, p. 33.
11. Suzanne Le-May Sheffield (2004) 'The "Empty-Headed Beauty" and the "Sweet Girl Graduate": Women's Science Education in *Punch*, 1860–90'. In Louise Henson et al. (eds) *Culture and Science in the Nineteenth-Century Media* (Aldershot), pp. 15–28.
12. Broks, *Media Science*, pp. 24, 31–2.
13. 'Spinning Jenny', *Home Words* (*HW* henceforth) (January 1871); Edison: *HW* (1888), 255
14. *HW* (1902), 105; *HW* (1914), 67.
15. *DofD* (August 1878).
16. CACC, PR167/4/6/1–2: Crosthwaite PM (July 1891, February 1899).
17. Keir Waddington (2008) 'Health and Medicine'. In Chris Williams (ed.) *A Companion to Nineteenth-Century Britain* (Oxford), pp. 412–29. For fictional narratives which include doctors, see chapter 6.
18. 'Messengers of Mercy': *TCM* (1906), 14.
19. For example, Revd G. S. Reaney: *TCM* (1900), 167.
20. For example 'I believe only what I can see': *Parish Magazine* (June 1864); 'The Bible and Our Faith': *HW* (January 1871).
21. Charles Bullock (1861) *"Essays and Reviews": The False Position of the Authors, an Appeal to the Bible and the Prayer Book, a Lecture* (London).
22. Bullock, *"Essays and Reviews"*.
23. Broks, *Media Science*, pp. 63–4.
24. John Polkinghorn, 'Tears and Laughter': *DofD* (September 1900); for Darwin's funeral, see Thomas Dixon (2008) *Science and Religion: A Very Short Introduction* (Oxford), pp. 58–9.
25. Owen Chadwick (1972) *The Victorian Church* (2 vols) II (London), pp. 27–8.
26. *TCM* (1894), 244.
27. Chadwick, *Victorian Church*, II, p. 23; 'Distant Cousins': *HW* (1896), 16–17; 'God and Missions': *HW* (1898), 21.
28. 'Science Gossip': *DofD* (December 1898).
29. For the popular appeal of the science of inherited characteristics see Harriet Ritvo (2004) 'Understanding Audiences and Misunderstanding Audiences: Some Publics for Science'. In Geoffrey Cantor and Sally Shuttleworth (eds) *Science Serialized: Representations of the Sciences in Nineteenth-Century Periodicals* (Cambridge, MA), pp. 331–49.
30. Morice Gerard, 'The Silent Conquest': *HW* (1907); Mrs G. S. Reaney, 'Better than Rubies': *TCM* (1901).
31. See Charles H. Smith, 'Wallace, Alfred Russel (1823–1913)', *ODNB*; F. W. Farrar, 'The Working-Man's Bookshelf': *TCM* (1900), 20, 28, 68; T. P. Garnier: *DofD* (October, November 1900).
32. Charles Darwin (1928) *The Origin of Species by Means of Natural Selection, or the Preservation of Favoured Races in the Struggle for Life*, 6th edition (London), p. 667.
33. Dixon, *Science and Religion*, p. 72.
34. See Broks, *Media Science*, p. 83.
35. LMA, P73/CAM/105–128: Camden Church Camberwell PM (March 1915).

36. Charlotte Elizabeth Woods (1917) *Archdeacon Wilberforce, His Ideals and Teaching* (London), pp. 96–101.
37. Chadwick, *Victorian Church*, II, pp. 9–12.
38. Aileen Fyfe (2004) *Science and Salvation: Evangelical Popular Science Publishing in Victorian Britain* (Chicago and London), pp. 105–6, 276.
39. Broks, *Media Science*, pp. 56–8.
40. 'Limnias or The Wonders of the Pond': *Parish Magazine* (September 1859); Bernard Lightman (2007) *Victorian Popularizers of Science: Designing Nature for New Audiences* (Chicago), pp. 82–7.
41. *Good Words* and other monthly magazines included a similar proportion: Broks, *Media Science*, p. 27.
42. Broks, *Media Science*, chapter 6.
43. 'God's Wonderful Works': *DofD* (January 1878).
44. See Lightman, *Victorian Popularizers of Science*, pp. 426–38.
45. Agnes Giberne, 'Away in Space': *TCM* (February 1893).
46. Jonathan R. Topham (2004) 'Science, Natural Theology and the Practice of Christian Piety in Early-Nineteenth-Century Religious Magazines'. In Geoffrey Cantor and Sally Shuttleworth (eds) *Science Serialized: Representations of the Sciences in Nineteenth-Century Periodicals* (Cambridge, MA), pp. 37–66, 42–9; Jonathan R. Topham (2004) 'The Wesleyan-Methodist Magazine and Religious Monthlies in Early Nineteenth-Century Britain'. In Geoffrey Cantor, Gowan Dawson, Graeme Gooday, Richard Noakes, Sally Shuttleworth, Jonathan R. Topham, *Science in the Nineteenth Century Periodical: Reading the Magazine of Nature* (Cambridge), pp. 67–90, 77–8.
47. Frank Buckland; William Houghton; F. O. Morris; J. G. Wood: see Lightman, *Victorian Popularizers of Science*.
48. Lightman, *Victorian Popularizers of Science*, p. 180.
49. Lightman, *Victorian Popularizers of Science*, pp. 45–8; series: *HW* (1877).
50. H. C. G. Moule, 'The Fossil Trees on the Lulworth Coast': *HW* (1902), 179.
51. Jonathan R. Topham (2010) 'Science, Religion, and the History of the Book'. In Thomas Dixon, Geoffrey Cantor and Stephen Pumfrey (eds) *Science and Religion: New Historical Perspectives* (Cambridge), pp. 221–43, 224–8.
52. 'A Sermon from Nature': *Church Standard* (May, 1928).
53. Richard Noakes, 'The *Boy's Own Paper*', p. 159. See Theodore Wood in *TCM* (1893–1896, 1899–1903, 1905–1906).
54. For example, Thomas Dixon (2008) *The Invention of Altruism: Making Moral Meanings in Victorian Britain* (Oxford), pp. 160–1.
55. Wood, 'What I Found on a Rose Bush': *TCM* (1893), 205–6.
56. Dixon, *Altruism*, p. 161.
57. Edward Step, 'Ferns', 'Grasses': *TCM* (1894, 1896).
58. Michael Tracy (2008) *The World of the Edwardian Child as seen in Arthur Mee's Children's Encyclopædia, 1908–1910* (York), pp. 58–9, 225.
59. OHC, SV/ADOE/283: Dorchester Abbey PM (December 1905).
60. For a flourishing local scientific society, see CACC, PR167/4/6/2: Saint John Keswick PM (October 1888; October 1892).
61. OHC, Headington Quarry Library Catalogue (1889); T. S. Ackland (1873) *The Story of Creation as told by Theology and by Science* (London).
62. CACC, PR167/4/6/2: Saint John Keswick PM (February 1893). For a more nuanced view of Kidd, see Dixon, *Altruism*, pp. 302–20. See also Thomas Seccombe, 'Laing,

Samuel (1812–1897)', *ODNB*; D. P. Crook, 'Kidd, Benjamin (1858–1916)', *ODNB*; W. B. Selbie, 'Fairbairn, Andrew Martin (1838–1912)', *ODNB*.

63. LMA, P93/JN1/065–066: Saint John Limehouse Fields PM (Oct. 1871).
64. Saint John Limehouse Fields PM (October 1872).
65. For phrenology and its popularity through cheap editions, see James A. Secord (2000) *Victorian Sensation: The Extraordinary Publication, Reception and Secret Authorship of 'Vestiges of the Natural History of Creation'* (Chicago and London), pp. 69–76.
66. 'That Troubles Our Monkey Again' – Female descendant of Marine Ascidian: "Darwin, say what you like about *man*, but I wish you would leave my *emotions* alone"': *Fun* (November 1872).
67. For the indifferent majority, see Chadwick, *Victorian Church*, II, pp. 23–4.
68. George P. Landow (1982) *Images of Crisis: Literary Iconology, 1750 to the Present* (Boston), pp. 23–4.
69. Dixon, Cantor et al., *Science and Religion: New Historical Perspectives*, pp. 14–15.
70. Saint John Keswick PM (September 1914). It was common opinion that Germany had sold its soul to the devil: Albert Marrin (1974) *The Last Crusade: The Church of England in the First World War* (Durham, NC), p. 252.
71. Hilda D. Oakeley (1915) 'German Thought: The Real Conflict'. *Church Quarterly Review* 79, 96–7; quoted in Shannon Ty Bontrager (2002) 'The Imagined Crusade: The Church of England and the Mythology of Nationalism and Christianity during the Great War'. *Church History* 71(4): 774–98, 778.
72. Bontrager, 'Imagined Crusade', 775.
73. Saint John Keswick PM (September 1914); Michael Snape (2005) *God and the British Soldier: Religion and the British Army in the First and Second World Wars* (London and New York), p. 115. Clerical opinion of the 'just war' is analysed in David Nash (2013) *Christian Ideals in British Culture: Stories of Belief in the Twentieth Century* (Basingstoke), pp. 81–8.
74. Alan Wilkinson (1978) *The Church of England and the First World War* (London), chapter 3.
75. OHC, SV/AB/283: Abingdon PM (October, November, 1914).
76. CACC, PR129/12–28: Holme Eden PM (September 1915).
77. See Michael Austin (1999) *'Almost like a Dream': A Parish at War 1914–19* (Whitchurch).
78. H. D. Rawnsley (1916) *The European War 1914–1915* (London), p. 117.
79. CACC, PR71/116–118: Caldbeck PM (September 1914).
80. Brown, *Religion and Society*, p. 89; Caldbeck PM (November 1914).
81. Caldbeck PM (February 1915).
82. *Carlisle Journal* (19 January 1915), 7–8; *Carlisle Journal* (2 July 1915), 2. Soldiers' letters were printed in PMs during the Second Boer War: see CACK, WPR/75/21–5: Burneside PM (April 1900); see also Austin, *'Almost like a Dream'*, pp. 1–109.
83. CACC, PR121/290–95: Lanercost PM (July, September 1915).
84. Caldbeck PM (September 1915).
85. Camden Church Camberwell PM (October 1914–July 1917); John Oxenham (1915) 'To You who have Lost'. In *'All's Well!' Some Helpful Verse for These Dark Days of War* (London). Terraneau's letters are reminiscent of Julian Grenfell's: see Wilkinson, *Church of England and the First World War*, p. 20.

86. Michael Finn (2010) 'Local Heroes: War News and the Construction of "Community" in Britain, 1914–18'. *Historical Research* 83(221): 520–38, 538.
87. LMA, P72/JSG/118/1: St James-the-Great Bethnal Green Parish Scrapbook (1916)
88. Mark Connolly (2002) *The Great War, Memory and Ritual: Commemoration in the City and East London 1916–1939* (Woodbridge), pp. 25–35.
89. Finn, 'Local Heroes', 525–6; H. G. Cocks (2009) *Classified: The Secret History of the Personal Column* (London), chapter 2; Caldbeck PM (February 1916).
90. Caldbeck PM (May 1916).
91. Caldbeck PM (July 1916).
92. Caldbeck PM (November 1917).
93. LMA, P83/PHE/27–9: Saint Philip Arlington Square PM (January 1916).
94. Camden Church Camberwell PM (October–December 1914).
95. Simon Fowler (1999) 'War Charity Begins at Home'. *History Today* 49(9): 17–23.
96. Snape, *God and the British Soldier,* pp. 89–90.
97. Snape, *God and the British Soldier,* pp. 83–4, 90–2, 103.
98. Saint James-the-Great Scrapbook (November 1917, October 1922).
99. Saint James-the-Great Scrapbook: PM Extract (1917).
100. CACK, WPR/79: Flookburgh PM (May, October 1917). Flookburgh was in Carlisle diocese.
101. Flookburgh PM (June 1918; March 1919).
102. David Raw (1989) *'It's Only Me', A Life of the Rev. Theodore Bayley Hardy V.C., D.S.O., M.C., 1863–1918, Vicar of Hutton Roof, Westmorland* (Kendal). See also John Bickersteth (1995) (ed.) *The Bickersteth Diaries 1914–1918* (London), for the war-time experiences of members of a famous clerical family.
103. Caldbeck PM (November 1918).
104. Noted also by Brown, *Religion and Society,* pp. 91–2.
105. Bontrager, 'Imagined Crusade', 775–6.
106. Saint John Keswick PM (January, July 1916).
107. *Sign* (1916), 171.
108. 'War and Our Duty': *DofD* (October 1914); Brown, *Religion and Society,* p. 92.
109. Saint John Keswick PM (April, November 1916).
110. Brown, *Religion and Society,* p. 92.
111. LMA, P97/MRK/030–033: Saint Mark Plumstead PM (May 1918). See also Spencer Wade (2013) *Both Hands before the Fire* (Bloomington), pp. 81–2.
112. William L. Sachs (2002) *The Transformation of Anglicanism: From State Church to Global Communion* (Cambridge), p. 260.
113. Bontrager, 'Imagined Crusade', 786.
114. Eric James (1991) (ed.) *A Last Eccentric: A Symposium concerning the Reverend Canon F. A. Simpson* (London), pp. 22–7.
115. Quoted in Alan Wilkinson (1978) *The Church of England and the First World War* (London), p. 78; Hensley Henson is quoted in Sachs, *Transformation of Anglicanism,* p. 260.
116. Saint John Keswick PM (July, December 1916).
117. See Peter Croft (1993) *The Parish Magazine Inset* (Blandford Forum), pp. 49–50.

118. PHL, Mowbray's Directors' Reports 3 (14 March 1916, 16 January 1917, 31 May 1917, 19 March 1918, 1 June 1920); SPCK (1916) *Annual Report* (London), p. 23; SPCK (1918) *Annual Report* (London), p. 20; LMA, P95/ANN/308–330: Saint Anne Wandsworth PM (January 1919).
119. Saint John Keswick 'War Magazine' (April 1917); Holme Eden PM (August 1918).
120. For example, 'The Call': *TCM* (November 1914).
121. May Wynne (1916) 'Granesty Farm'; May Wynne (1918) 'Lest We Forget, the Love Story of a British Nurse in Serbia': both *HW.*
122. *HW* (1916, 1917).
123. 'The National Mission': *HW* (1916), 242–3.
124. 'Presents for the church': Saint James-the-Great Scrapbook (1918); Stefan Goebel (2007) *The Great War and Medieval Memory: War, Remembrance and Medievalism in Britain and Germany, 1914–1940* (Cambridge), pp. 88–90. For newspaper battle reports see Finn, 'Local Heroes', 522.
125. Phrase used by Harry Rolfe, vicar of Saint Michael's Derby, in his PM (September 1917): Austin, *'Almost like a Dream'*, p. xxi. For different forms of spirituality see Nash, *Stories of Belief*, p. 9.
126. See Brown, *Religion and Society*, pp. 103–4.
127. Mark Girouard (1981) *The Return to Camelot: Chivalry and the English Gentleman* (New Haven and London), pp. 278–9.
128. David Clarke (1981) *The Angel of Mons: Phantom Soldiers and Ghostly Guardians* (Chichester); see also Girouard, *Return to Camelot*, pp. 284–5.
129. *Sign* (September 1915), cover.
130. OHC, SV/EASTb/283: Blewbury and Aston Turold PM (September 1929).
131. Agnes Giberne, 'Visions which our soldiers saw': *HW* (February 1920).
132. Isaiah 6:2–3 (New Revised Standard Version); LMA, P87/MAA/33–7/38: Saint Michael and All Angels Paddington PM (October 1920).
133. Quoted in Wilkinson, *Church of England and the First World War*, p. 63.
134. Saint John Keswick PM (January–June 1918).

10 Anglican Parish Magazines 1919–1929 and Beyond

1. For Revd Theodore Hardy see Chapter 9.
2. CACC, PR167/4/6/2: Saint John Keswick PM (January–June 1918).
3. Arthur Conan Doyle, 'The Parish Magazine': *Strand* (August 1930); 'Whose Fault': *Punch* (January 1897).
4. Mary Cholmondeley (1899) *Red Pottage* (London), pp. 254–69.
5. George Orwell (1935) *The Clergyman's Daughter* (London), p. 7; Barbara Pym (1950) *Some Tame Gazelle* (London), pp. 8, 20, 79, 91.
6. Alan Wilkinson, 'Sheppard, Hugh Richard Lawrie (1880–1937)': *ODNB.*
7. Dick Sheppard (1924) *The Human Parson* (London), p. 93.
8. Sheppard, *Human Parson*, pp. 55, 94–5.
9. LMA, P82/JNE/022: Saint John Evangelist Red Lion Sq. PM (January 1924); CACC, PR34/83: Mungrisdale PM (November 1924); J. M. Swift (1939) *The Parish Magazine* (London and Oxford), p. 11.
10. J. B. Goodliffe (1933) *The Parson and His Problems* (London), pp. 115–16.

11. Swift, *The Parish Magazine*, pp. 11–12, 26. 'A Conversation between a Clergyman and One of His Parishioners': *Parish Magazine* (1874), 14–20.
12. For the ultimate fruitfulness of such an undertaking see Dave Russell (2006) 'The *Heaton Review*, 1927–1934: Culture, Class and a Sense of Place in Inter-war Yorkshire'. *20th Century British History* 17(3): 323–49.
13. CACC, PR34/24: Mungrisdale PCC Minutes (December 1926).
14. Adrian Hastings (1991) *A History of English Christianity* (London), p. 194.
15. William Purcell (1983) *The Mowbray Story* (Oxford), p. 16; PHL, Mowbray Archive: *Sign* monthly circulation figure, n.d.; *Sign* (November 1925).
16. *Home Words* (*HW* forthwith) (January 1971).
17. Correspondence with Dominic Vaughan, CEO of *Hymns Ancient and Modern*, January 2015.
18. *Sign* website: http://www.the-sign.co.uk/, accessed 10 September 2014.
19. Callum G. Brown (2001) *The Death of Christian Britain* (Abingdon and New York), p. 165.
20. SPCK (1920) *Annual Report*, p. 142; see Hastings, *History of English Christianity*, p. 195.
21. The Oxford parish evidence for this period is too small for accurate comparison.
22. CUL, SPCK A22/1: Minutes of the Religious Literature Committee 1916–1925 (11 February 1919). In the 1920s most parish magazines retailed at 2d: LMA, P73/CAM/131: Camden Church Camberwell (January 1922).
23. SPCK (1929) *Annual Report* (London), p. 243.
24. *HW* (1971) Centenary Issue, 6.
25. 'Talks on Labour': *Church Standard* (1925), 68; 'Mining Parishioners': *Church Standard* (January 1926).
26. *HW* (December 1920, November 1925); John Maiden (2009) *National Religion and the Prayer Book Controversy 1927–1928* (Woodbridge), pp. 69–70.
27. LMA, DRO/071/035–6: Saint Gabriel Bounds Green PM (January–December 1920).
28. For Wade, see *London Evening News* (8 December 1920); for Tooley, see Terri Doughty (2012) 'Representing the Professional Woman: The Celebrity Interviewing of Sarah Tooley'. In F. E. Gray (ed.) *Women in Journalism at the Fin de Siècle: Making a Name for Herself* (Basingstoke) pp. 165–81. For May Wynne, see Chapter 6.
29. For example, 'What I Remember, by an Old Lay Reader' and 'Forty Years at Oxford': *Sign* (1924), part of a series. See also, 'The Anglo-Catholic Movement': *Sign* (January 1926); Maiden, *National Religion*, p. 47; Callum G. Brown (2006) *Religion and Society in Twentieth Century Britain* (Harlow), p. 139.
30. *Sign* (November 1925).
31. *Sign* (1924), 92, 135; *Sign* (1927), 98; see also, Maiden, *National Religion*, p. 48.
32. *Sign* (November 1925); Hastings, *English Christianity*, p. 36. See also Nigel Yates (1991) *Buildings, Faith and Worship: The Liturgical Arrangement of Anglican Churches 1600–1900* (Oxford), pp. 173–4.
33. *Sign* (July 1925); LMA, P91/ANN/075–080, 1–12: Saint Anne Shoreditch PM (June 1926).

34. LMA, P74/TRI/095–105: Holy Trinity Sloane Street Chelsea PM (November 1925).
35. Holy Trinity Sloane Street PM (December 1925).
36. LMA, P89/CYP/J/01/005: Saint Cyprian Clarence Gate PM (1922, 1923).
37. Anthony Symondson, 'Comper, Sir (John) Ninian (1864–1960)': *ODNB*.
38. Saint Cyprian Clarence Gate PM (March 1924).
39. CACC, DX173/29: Farlam and Midgeholme PM (January–October 1925). For evangelical factions as a response to ritualism see Martin Wellings (2003) *Evangelicals Embattled: Responses of Evangelicals in the Church of England to Ritualism, Darwinism and Theological Liberalism 1890–1930* (Bletchley), pp. 110–21.
40. Farlam and Midgeholme PM (March 1924).
41. Farlam and Midgeholme PM (April 1924). For further description of evangelical factions during the 1920s, see Maiden, *National Religion*, pp. 58–60. For the CMS split see Wellings, *Evangelicals Embattled*, pp. 281–9.
42. Farlam and Midgeholme PM (November 1925).
43. Maiden, *National Religion*, pp. 8–10.
44. Saint John Evangelist Red Lion Sq. PM (October 1912).
45. CACK, WPR54/15/1: Burneside PM (1912–1927).
46. Burneside PM (November 1921, January 1924)
47. LMA, P87/MAA/033–038: Saint Michael and all Angels Paddington PM (October 1920).
48. Brian Heeney (1988) *The Women's Movement in the Church of England 1850–1930* (Oxford), p. 63.
49. Burneside PM (May 1922).
50. For the Mothers' Union see Heeney, *Women's Movement*, pp. 17, 43–5; see also *HW* (1926), 130–1.
51. Susan Mumm (2004) 'Women, Priesthood and the Ordained Ministry in the Christian Tradition'. In John Wolffe (ed.) *Religion in History: Conflict, Conversion and Coexistence* (Manchester), pp. 190–216, 196.
52. LMA, DRO/004/I/01/001: Saint Andrew and Saint Michael Enfield PM (May 1927); CACC, PR167/4/6/5: Saint John Keswick PM (November 1928).
53. 'Our Query Corner': *Sign* (February 1925); 'Mrs Baxter: A Willing Tool': *Sign* (1925), 143–4; 'The Joy of Service': *Sign* (January 1926); 'The Work of a Deaconess': *Sign* (August 1926); See also Heeney, *Women's Movement*, p. 87.
54. See CACC, PR/32/94: Holy Trinity Carlisle PM (June–August 1910), for the work of 'Sister Arnold' of the Church Army. For health care, see *Dawn of Day* (*DofD*) (1921), 136–7; Frank Prochaska (2006) *Christianity and Social Service in Modern Britain: The Disinherited Spirit* (Oxford), p. 88.
55. See Rex Walford (2007) *The Growth of 'New London' in Suburban Middlesex (1918–1945) and the Response of the Church of England* (Lewiston, Queenston, Lampeter), pp. 154–5.
56. 'Meg and her Milkman': *DofD* (1921); Mrs E. M. Field, 'Long Long Thoughts': *Sign* (June 1927).
57. Heeney, *Women's Movement*, pp. 89–90.
58. See also, S. J. D. Green (2011) *The Passing of Protestant England: Secularisation and Social Change c. 1920–1960* (Cambridge), p. 61.

59. Camden Church Camberwell PM (March–June 1922); OHC, SV/EASTb/283: Hagbourne and Northbourne PM (October–December 1923). See also Clive Aslet (2012) *War Memorial: The Story of One Village's Sacrifice from 1914 to 2011* (London), pp.170–4. For an example of delay, see CACC, PR71/116–118: Caldbeck PM (June, September and October 1922).
60. Hagbourne and Northbourne PM (December 1923); Holy Trinity Chelsea PM (December 1925); Brown *Religion and Society,* p. 126.
61. Green, *Passing of Protestant England,* pp. 61–2.
62. Saint Cyprian Clarence Gate PM (November 1923); Camden Church Camberwell PM (October 1922).
63. OHC, SV/Eastb/283: Blewbury and Aston Tirrold PM (January 1929).
64. Burneside PM (November 1925, December 1928); CACC, PR121/ 296–45: Lanercost PM (March 1926).
65. Jeremy Morris: writing in Walford, *Growth of 'New London',* p. vii.
66. Farlam and Midgeholme PM (July 1924); Brown, *Death of Christian Britain,* pp. 165–6. Rex Walford gives a more nuanced view of interwar church attendance: Walford, *Growth of 'New London',* p. 353.
67. CACC, PR116/69: Great Salkeld Rector's Memoranda Book (1861–1925); Mungrisdale PM (November 1925).
68. Walford, *Growth of 'New London',* p. 151.
69. Camden Church Camberwell PM (October 1923, September 1925); Mungrisdale PM (May 1925).
70. Saint Andrew and Saint Michael Enfield PM (August 1927).
71. 'A Glorious Adventure': *HW* (1921), 122.
72. Wellings, *Evangelicals Embattled,* p. 281.
73. For example, 'Home for the Holidays in India': *DofD* (September 1921). See also Heeney, *Women's Movement,* pp. 59–63.
74. See also LMA, P89/ALL1/078: All Saints St John's Wood PM (August–September 1926).
75. Saint Andrew and Saint Michael Enfield PM (September 1926).
76. For example, Camden Church Camberwell PM (1927); Burneside PM (July 1924); Blewbury and Aston Tirrold PM (1927–1929); Hagbourne and Northbourne PM (1924–1926). See also Callum G. Brown (2006) *Religion and Society in Twentieth-Century Britain* (Harlow), p. 141.
77. CACC, PR167/4/6/5: Saint John Keswick PM (November 1928); Camden Church Camberwell PM (April, July 1923); Saint Andrew and Saint Michael Enfield PM (February 1927).
78. LMA, P91/ANN/075–080, 1–12: Saint Anne Shoreditch PM (1921).
79. CACK, WPR9/15/1/1: Lunesdale District Magazine (December 1925); for shortage of candidates for the ministry see Green, *Passing of Protestant England,* pp. 62–3.
80. Saint Andrew and Saint Michael Enfield PM (February 1929); Camden Church Camberwell PM (June 1922).
81. Camden Church Camberwell (June 1926; February 1929); Burneside PM (January 1923).
82. Inevitably, given the choice of locations, this study omits the parish of Thaxted, Essex, where Conrad Noel carried out his socialist ministry: see Hastings, *History of English Christianity,* p. 174.

83. CACB, BPR23/M4: Saint James Barrow PM (February 1924, October 1926); *Torch* (September 1926).
84. *National Review* 81 (1923), 136.
85. Burneside PM (May–July 1926). For the General Strike see Hastings, *History of English Christianity*, chapter 10.
86. 'Granny's Vote': *Sign* (1924), 24–5.
87. *HW* (1922), 66–7; *Sign* (1925), 154; *Sign* (1926), 14; Farlam PM (July–August 1926).
88. 'Overwork': *HW* (1928), 111.
89. 'Catkin Time': *Sign* (March 1927); 'Stars in Winter': *Sign* (December 1926); 'Bumble Bees': *Sign* (July 1926).
90. 'The Garden Tomb': *HW* (1925), 156.
91. Burneside PM (August 1925); see also Brown, *Religion and Society*, pp. 117–19.
92. See John Maiden (2009) *National Religion and the Prayer Book Controversy 1927–1928* (Woodbridge).
93. For example, Saint John Keswick PM (March 1927–December 1928).
94. Lunesdale District Magazine (November 1925); Camden Church Camberwell PM (May 1923); LMA, P97/MRY/201–202: Saint Mary Magdalene Woolwich PM (June 1927); Burneside PM (November 1928); Mungrisdale PCC Minutes (August 1927); Saint Paul Carlisle PM (December 1927); CACC, PR32/98–100: Holy Trinity Carlisle PM (February 1927).
95. *Church Standard* (February 1927); *Sign* (series, 1925); 'Sir William Bull MP (a distinguished layman)': *HW* (October 1928). Hansard: http://hansard.millbanksystems.com/commons/1928/jun/14/prayer-book-measure-1928, accessed 11 September 2014.
96. Burneside PM (July 1928).
97. Saint Cyprian Clarence Gate PM (January–July 1927).
98. Farlam and Midgholme PM (June 1926–December 1928); for the evangelical and anti-Catholic background to the controversy, see Maiden, *National Religion*, pp. 90–101, 169–76.
99. Farlam and Midgholme PM (January 1928).
100. Hastings, *History of English Christianity*, p. 207.
101. CACC, PR47/105–06: Saint Paul Carlisle PM (July 1928).
102. Camden Church Camberwell PM (June 1922).
103. Brown, *Religion and Society*, p. 151.
104. Hansard, http://hansard.millbanksystems.com/sittings: HC Deb. 13 June 1928, vol. 218, cc 1003–1039, accessed 7 January 2015.
105. Hansard, HC Deb. 3 December 1974, vol. 882, cc 1371–484.
106. Hansard, HC Deb. 8 May 1963, vol. 249, cc 705–806.
107. Hansard, HC Deb. 11 December 1963, vol. 686, cc 467–516.
108. Hansard, HC Deb. 10 May 1926, vol. 195, cc 699–786.
109. Hansard, HC Deb. 19 April 1978, vol. 948, cc 628–42.
110. Hansard, HC Deb. 14 March 1983, vol. 440, cc 562–89.
111. Hansard, HC Deb. 7 November 1984, vol. 67, cc 125–207.
112. Hansard, HL Deb. 18 July 2001, vol. 626, cc 1480–553.
113. For Irish, Scottish and Welsh opposition to Anglican changes to the Prayer Book in 1928 see Iain McLean and Alistair McMillan (2005) *State of the Union:*

Unionism and the Alternatives in the United Kingdom since 1707 (Oxford), p. 218.
114. Callum G. Brown (2006) *Religion and Society in Twentieth-Century Britain* (Harlow), chapter 7.
115. LMA, P80/STE/188–201, Saint Stephen Shepherd's Bush PM, January 1908; Loweswater PM, as described in the Inglewood Churches, Cumbria, PM, June 2010 (author's copy).
116. *The Sign*, October 2009.

Bibliography

PRIMARY SOURCES

Archive Sources other than Parish Magazines

Booth, Charles (1902–1903), *Life and Labour of the People in London* (7 vols), Third Series: *Religious Influences* (London): Manuscript notebooks
Cambridge University Library
Carlisle Diocesan Calendar and Clergy Lists
'Charles Booth and Social Investigation' (A427 SG), Archive CD ROM: Booth's Digest, Duckworth's London Walks: District 13
Christ Church, Carlisle, Vestry Minute Book (1896–1903)
Crosthwaite District Visitors' Memoranda Book (1879--1882)
Cumbria Archives Centre, Carlisle
Diaries of Helen James of Clarghyll Hall, Alston (1858–1911)
Diaries of Revd William Pelham Burn (1893–1901)
Diocese of Carlisle, Clergy Visitation Queries and Returns (1858, 1900)
Diocese of Oxford Clergy Visitation Queries and Returns (1899)
Fishman Collection of Queenie Scott-Hopper Papers
Great Salkeld Rector's Memoranda Book (1861–1925)
Headington Quarry Library Catalogue (1889)
James Family Papers of Susan (James) Huggard, Toronto
Kirkby Stephen Ritualism Controversy Notebook (1915)
Lancaster University Library
London Metropolitan Archives
London School of Economics
Minutes of the Meetings of the Headington District Visitors (1876–1885)
Mowbray Papers
Norfolk Record Office
Open University
Oxfordshire History Centre
Private Collections
Pusey House Library, Oxford
Roberts, Elizabeth, *Social and Family Life in Barrow and Lancaster 1870–1925*, MS transcripts of recorded interviews, Lancaster and Barrow (1981)
Saint James-the-Great, Bethnal Green, Parish Scrap-Book (1887–1922)
Saint Philip and Saint James, Oxford, Letters (1881, 1910)
SPCK Tract Committee Minutes (1872–1893)

Parish Magazines (1833–1929)

(Found in the following archive collections unless stated otherwise: see endnotes for references)
British Library

Cambridge University Library
Carlisle Cathedral Library
Cumbria Archives Centre, Barrow
Cumbria Archives Centre, Carlisle
Cumbria Archives Centre, Kendal
Cumbria Archives Centre, Whitehaven
Lancaster University Library
Lanes Library, Carlisle
London Metropolitan Archives
National Library of Australia
National Library of Canada
Oxfordshire History Centre

Other Periodicals and Newspapers

Athenaeum (1862)
Birmingham Pictorial and Dart (1898)
Carlisle Journal (1891, 1899, 1915, 1940)
Chambers' Edinburgh Journal (1852)
Christian Herald
Daily Graphic
Daily Mail
Day of Days (1875)
Ecclesiastical Gazette or Monthly Register of the Church of England (1870)
Fortnightly Review (1886)
Fun (1872)
Girl's Own Paper (1886)
Great Round World (1897)
Hearth and Home (1892)
Home Chat (1895)
Household Words (1858)
Howitt's Journal (1847, 1848)
John Bull (1874)
John O'London's Weekly
Journal of the Society of Arts (1860)
Little Folks
London Evening News (1920)
London Gazette (1893, 1905)
London Magazine
Monthly Packet of Evening Readings for Members of the English Church (1881, 1892, 1895)
Mother's Friend (1857–1858)
Newcastle Daily Journal (1924)
New York Times (1908)
Nineteenth Century: a Monthly Review (1886, 1887)
Punch or the London Charivari (1897, 1898, 1900)
Quarterly Journal (1852)
Queensland Times (1915)
Quiver (1870)
St George's Magazine Stationer, Printer and Fancy Trades Register (1896)

Strand (1930)
Sunday at Home (1872)
Sunday Reading for the Young (1913)
The Times (1890, 1891, 1902)
Thompson's Weekly News (1908)
Tract Magazine and Christian Miscellany (1860)
Westminster Review (1856)
Wigton Advertiser (1914)

Books and articles

(The place of publication is London unless specified otherwise)
Ackland, T. S. (1873) *The Story of Creation as told by Theology and by Science.*
Adams, H. C. (1895) *Fighting His Way or Leslie Rice's First Curacy.*
Baden-Powell, Robert (1908, 2004) *Scouting for Boys* (Oxford).
Bell, Florence (1907, 1969) *At the Works: a Study of a Manufacturing Town* (Newton Abbot).
Bennett, Frederick (1909) *The Story of W. J. E. Bennett, founder of St Barnabas, Pimlico and Vicar of Froome-Selwood.*
Blackie's Children's Annual (1924).
Blatchford, Robert (1895) *Merrie England,* 2nd edition.
Booth, Charles (1902–1903) *Life and Labour of the People in London* (7 vols), Third Series: *Religious Influences.*
Braddon, Mary Elizabeth (1862) *Lady Audley's Secret.*
Braybrooke, Patrick (1928) *Some Goddesses of the Pen* (New York).
Bullock, Charles (1861) *'Essays and Reviews': The False Position of the Authors, an Appeal to the Bible and the Prayer Book, a Lecture.*
—— (1883) *Our Bishops and Clergy.*
—— (1887) *The Royal Year.*
—— (1897) *The Queen's Resolve: I will be Good. Hundred and Seventy-Fifth Thousand.*
Cholmondeley, Mary (1899) *Red Pottage.*
Clare, Austin (1908) *The Conscience of Dr. Holt.*
Clarke, J. Erskine (1861) 'Cheap Books and how to use them'. In *Church of England Book-Hawking Union Conference Proceedings* (Oxford).
—— (1861) *Plain Papers on the Social Economy of the People.*
—— (1862) *Church Stories.*
Conrad, Joseph (1907) *The Secret Agent.*
Cox, G. V. (1870) *Recollections of Oxford* (Oxford).
Crockford's Clerical Directory (1908).
Darton, F. J. Harvey (1932) 'The Youth of a Children's Magazine'. In Brian Alderson (ed.) (1999) *Children's Books in England: Five Centuries of Social Life,* 3rd edition (Newcastle, Delaware and London).
Darton, John M. (1879) *Brave boys who have become Illustrious Men of our Time, forming Bright Examples for Emulation by the Youth of Great Britain.*
Darwin, Charles (1928) *The Origin of Species by Means of Natural Selection, or the Preservation of Favoured Races in the Struggle for Life,* 6th edition.
Dearmer, Percy (1899) *The Parson's Handbook.*
—— (1903) *Is Ritualism Right?* (Oxford).
Ditchfield, P. H. (1907) *The Parish Clerk.*

Downer, Arthur (1938) *A Century of Evangelical Anglican Religion in Oxford.*
Everard, Ethel M. (1902) *A Faithful Sower: A Memoir of the Life of the Rev. George Everard M.A.*
Fenn, George Manville (1904) *To Win or to Die.*
Francis, M. E. (1893) *In a North Country Village.*
Giberne, Agnes (1889) *Among the Stars or Wonderful Things in the Sky.*
—— (1895) *A Lady of England: The Life and Letters of Charlotte Maria Tucker.*
—— (n. d.) *Tim Teddington's Dream or Liberty Equality and Fraternity.*
Goodliffe, J. B. (1933) *The Parson and His Problems.*
Hardy, E. J. (1885) *How to Be Happy Though Married.*
—— (1889) *The Five Talents of Women: A Book for Girls and Women.*
Hardy, Thomas (1896) *Jude the Obscure.*
James, J. A. (1852) *Female Piety or the Young Woman's Friend and Guide through Life to Immortality.*
Jefferies, Richard (1880) *Hodge and His Masters.*
Macaulay, Thomas Babbington (1907) *The Lays of Ancient Rome.*
Meade, L. T. (1908) *Betty of the Rectory.*
Milner, Mary (1842) *The Life of Isaac Milner, D.D., F.R.S.* (Cambridge).
Mimpriss, Robert (1837) *The Acts of the Apostles, and Epistles, historically and geographically delineated according to Greswell's arrangement, etc.*
Mitchell, C. and Co (1922) *The Newspaper Press Directory and Advertisers' Guide.*
Odom, William (1917) *Fifty Years of Sheffield Church Life, 1866–1916* (Sheffield).
—— (1931) *Memories and Musings: Personal, Literary, Religious, General, 1846–1931* (Sheffield).
Orwell, George (1935) *The Clergyman's Daughter.*
Oxenham, John (1915) *'All's Well!' Some Helpful Verse for These Dark Days of War.*
Rawnsley, Eleanor F. (1923) *Canon Rawnsley: An Account of His Life* (Glasgow).
Rawnsley, H. D. (1898) *Henry Whitehead 1825–1896: A Memorial Sketch* (Glasgow).
—— (1900) *St. George and the Dragon: A Sermon for St. George's Day* (Keswick).
—— (1916) *The European War 1914–1915.*
Reeve, Isaac J. (1865) *The Wild Garland or Curiosities of Poetry.*
Richmond, Legh (1814) *The Dairyman's Daughter.*
Robins, G. M. (Mrs Baillie Reynolds) (1895) *To Set Her Free.*
Sandford, John (1845) *Parochialia, or Church, School and Parish.*
Scott-Hopper, Queenie (1904) *In the Christmas Firelight.*
—— (1906) *The Story of Hiawatha.*
—— (1920) *Rock Bottom.*
Sheppard, Dick (1924) *The Human Parson.*
SPCK, *Annual Reports.*
Stead, W. T. (1896–1920) (ed.), *Books for the Bairns.*
Stone, S. J. (1872) *The Knight of Intercession.*
Swift, J. M. (1939) *The Parish Magazine* (London and Oxford).
Tonna, Charlotte Elizabeth (1843) *The Wrongs of Women.*
Townsend, John Hume (1896) *Edward Hoare: A Record of His Life Based upon a Brief Autobiography.*
Tuck and Sons (n.d.) (eds), *My Favourite Stories in Prose and Verse.*
Walford, L. B. (1910) *Recollections of a Scottish Novelist.*

Walters, D. O. (1920) (ed.) *The Year's at the Spring: An Anthology of Recent Poetry* (New York).
Ward, Mrs Humphrey (1888) *Robert Elsmere*.
Whitehead, T. C. (1861) *Village Sketches*.
Woods, Charlotte Elizabeth (1917) *Archdeacon Wilberforce, His Ideals and Teaching*.

SECONDARY SOURCES

Periodicals and Newspapers

Ancestors (2008)
Oxford Mail (1983)

Books and Articles

Ackroyd, Peter (2000) *London, the Biography* (London).
Alston, R. C. (1990) *A Checklist of Women Writers 1801–1900* (London).
Altholz, Josef L. (1994) '*The Wellesley Index* and Religious Periodicals'. *Victorian Periodicals Review* 27(1): 289–93.
—— (1989) *The Religious Press in Britain, 1760–1900* (New York).
Altick, Richard D. (1989) *Writers, Readers and Occasions* (Columbus).
—— (1991) *The Presence of the Present: Topics of the Day in the Victorian Novel* (Columbus).
—— (1998) *The English Common Reader: A Social History of the Mass Reading Public, 1800–1900*, 2nd edition (Columbus).
Anderson, Gregory (1976) *Victorian Clerks* (Manchester).
Anderson, Katharine (2004) 'Almanacs and the Profits of Natural Knowledge'. In Louise Henson, Geoffrey Cantor, Gowan Dawson, Richard Noakes, Sally Shuttleworth and Jonathan R. Topham (eds) *Culture and Science in the Nineteenth-Century Media* (Aldershot), pp. 97–112.
Anderson, Mary R. (1993) 'Cultural Dissonance and the Ideology of Transition in Late-Victorian England'. *Victorian Periodicals Review* 26(2): 108–13.
Anderson, Patricia J. (1992) '"Factory Girl, Apprentice and Clerk": the Readership of Mass-Market Magazines, 1830–1860'. *VPR* 25(2): 64–72.
Arnstein, Walter L. (1986) 'Queen Victoria and Religion'. In Gail Malmgreen (ed.) *Religion in the Lives of English Women, 1760–1930* (Bloomington), pp. 11–40.
Aslet, Clive (2012) *War Memorial: The Story of One Village's Sacrifice from 1914 to 2011* (London).
Atwood, Sara (2011) *Ruskin's Educational Ideals* (Farnham).
Auerbach, Nina (1982) *Woman and the Demon: The Life of a Victorian Myth* (Cambridge, MA).
Austin, Michael (1999) *'Almost like a Dream': A Parish at War 1914–19* (Whitchurch).
Avery, Gillian (1975) *Childhood's Pattern: A Study of the Heroes and Heroines of Children's Fiction 1770–1950* (London).
Baggs, Chris (2005) '"In the separate Reading Rooms for Ladies are provided those publications specially interesting to them": Ladies' Reading Rooms and British Public Libraries 1850–1914'. *Victorian Periodicals Review* 38(1): 280–306.

Bailey, Peter (1978) *Leisure and Class in Victorian England: Rational Recreation and the Contest for Control 1830–1885* (London).
Baillie, Eileen (1958) *The Shabby Paradise* (London).
Barratt, D. M., and D. G. Vaisey (1973) *Oxfordshire* (Oxford).
Barringer, Terry (2004) 'What Mrs Jellyby might have read. Missionary Periodicals: A Neglected Source'. *Victorian Periodicals Review* 37(4): 46–73.
Bebbington, D. W. (1989) *Evangelicalism in Modern Britain: A History from the 1730s to the 1980s* (London).
Beer, Gillian (1970) *The Romance* (London).
Beetham, Margaret (1996) *A Magazine of Her Own? Domesticity and Desire in the Woman's Magazine 1800–1914* (London and New York).
Beetham, Margaret, and Kay Boardman (2001) (eds) *Victorian Women's Magazines: An Anthology* (Manchester and New York).
Behrman, Cynthia F. (1971) 'The Creation of Social Myth: Journalism and the Empire'. *Victorian Periodicals Review* 11(1): 9–13.
—— (1977) *Victorian Myths of the Sea* (Athens, OH).
Bentley, James (1978) *Ritualism and Politics in Victorian Britain: The Attempt to Legislate for Belief* (Oxford).
Bickersteth, John (1995) (ed.) *The Bickersteth Diaries 1914–1918* (London).
Bittel, Helen (2006) 'Required Reading for "Revolting Daughters"? The New Girl Fiction of L. T. Meade'. *Nineteenth-Century Gender Studies* 2(2): 1–36.
Bloxham, Christine, and Susanne Shatford (1996) *The Changing Faces of Headington, Book 1* (Witney).
Boardman, Kay (2006) 'Charting the Golden Stream'. *Victorian Studies* 48(1): 505–17.
Bontrager, Shannon Ty (2002) 'The Imagined Crusade: The Church of England and the Mythology of Nationalism and Christianity during the Great War'. *Church History* 71(4): 774–98.
Boyd, Kelly (2003) *Manliness and the Boy's Story Paper in Britain: A Cultural History 1855–1940* (Basingstoke and New York).
Brake, Laurel (2001) *Print in Transition, 1850–1900: Studies in Media and Book History* (Basingstoke).
Brantlinger, Patrick (1998) *The Reading Lesson: The Threat of Mass Literacy in Nineteenth-Century British Fiction* (Bloomington).
Bratton, J. S. (1981) *The Impact of Victorian Children's Fiction* (London).
Breay, John (1995) *A Fell-Side Parson: Joseph Brunskill and His Diaries, 1826–1903* (Norwich).
Briggs, Asa, and Peter Burke (2005) *A Social History of the Media from Gutenberg to the Internet* (Cambridge).
Broks, Peter (1996) *Media Science before the Great War* (Basingstoke).
Brown, Callum G. (2001) *The Death of Christian Britain* (Abingdon and New York).
—— (2006) *Religion and Society in Twentieth-Century Britain* (Harlow).
Brozyna, Andrea Ebel (1999) *Labour, Love and Prayer: Female Piety in Ulster Religious Literature, 1850–1914* (Montreal).
Butler, David M. (1978) *Quaker Meeting Houses of the Lake Counties* (London).
Cadogan, M., and P. Craig (1976) *You're a Brick, Angela! A New Look at Girls' Fiction from 1839–1975* (London).
Cannadine, David (1983) 'The Context, Performance and Meaning of Ritual: The British Monarchy and the "Invention of Tradition" *c.* 1820–1877'. In Eric

Hobsbawm and Terence Ranger (eds) *The Invention of Tradition* (Cambridge), pp. 101–64.
—— (2000) *Class in Britain* (London).
Chadwick, Owen (1972) *The Victorian Church* (2 vols), 2nd edition (London).
Clark, Anna (1995) *The Struggle for the Breeches: Gender and the Making of the British Working Class* (Berkeley and Los Angeles).
Clarke, David (1981) *The Angel of Mons: Phantom Soldiers and Ghostly Guardians* (Chichester).
Clipper, Lawrence J. (1987) (ed.) *The Collected Works of G. K. Chesterton, vol. 28: The Illustrated London News 1908–1910* (San Francisco).
Cocks, H. G. (2009) *Classified: The Secret History of the Personal Column* (London).
Conley, Mary A. (2009) *From Jack Tar to Union Jack: Representing Naval Manhood in the British Empire, 1870–1918* (Manchester).
Connolly, Mark (2002) *The Great War, Memory and Ritual: Commemoration in the City and East London* 1916–1939 (Woodbridge).
Corfield, Justin (1993) *The Corfields: A lHistory of the Corfields from 1180 to the Present Day* (Rosanna, VIC).
Covert, James (2000) *A Victorian Marriage: Mandell and Louise Creighton* (London and New York).
Cox, Jeffrey (1982) *The English Churches in a Secular Society: Lambeth, 1870–1930* (Oxford).
Croft, Peter (1993) *The Parish Magazine Inset* (Blandford Forum).
Croll, Andy (2004) 'Popular Leisure and Sport'. In Chris Williams (ed.) *A Companion to Nineteenth-Century Britain* (Oxford), pp. 396–411.
Crowther, M. A. (1988) 'Church Problems and Church Parties'. In Gerald Parsons (ed.) *Religion in Victorian Britain, 4, Interpretations* (Manchester), pp. 4–27.
Cutt, Margaret Nancy (1979) *Ministering Angels: A Study of Nineteenth-Century Evangelical Writing for Children* (Wormley).
Dalziel, Margaret (1957) *Popular Fiction 100 Years Ago* (London).
Dancyger, Irene (1978) *A World of Women: An Illustrated History of Women's Magazines* (Dublin).
Davie, Grace (1994) *Religion in Britain since 1945: Believing without Belonging* (Oxford).
Dawson, Janis (2013) '"Not for girls alone, but for anyone who can relish really good literature": L. T. Meade, *Atalanta*, and the Family Literary Magazine'. *Victorian Periodicals Review* 46(4): 475–98.
Delap, Lucy (2005) '"Thus does man prove his fitness to be master of things": Shipwrecks, Chivalry and Masculinities in Nineteenth- and Twentieth-Century Britain'. *Cultural and Social History* 2: 1–30.
Dixon, Thomas (2008) *Science and Religion, a Very Short Introduction* (Oxford).
—— (2008) *The Invention of Altruism: Making Moral Meanings in Victorian Britain* (Oxford).
Doughty, Terri (2012) 'Representing the Professional Woman: The Celebrity Interviewing of Sarah Tooley'. In F. E. Gray (ed.) *Women in Journalism at the Fin de Siècle: Making a Name for Herself* (Basingstoke).
Dunae, Patrick A. (1980) 'Boys' Literature and the Idea of Empire, 1870–1914'. *Victorian Studies* 24: 105–21.
Eliot, Simon (1994) *Some Patterns and Trends in British Publishing 1800–1900: Occasional Papers of the Bibliographical Society* (London).

—— (2001) 'The Business of Victorian Publishing'. In Deirdre David (ed.) *The Cambridge Companion to the Victorian Novel* (Cambridge), pp. 37–60.

Ellsworth, L. E. (1982) *Charles Lowder and the Ritualist Movement* (London).

Erdozain, Dominic (2010) *The Problem of Pleasure: Sport, Recreation and the Crisis of Victorian Religion* (Woodbridge).

Finn, Michael (2010) 'Local Heroes: War News and the Construction of "Community" in Britain, 1914–18'. *Historical Research* 83(221): 520–38.

Flew, Sarah (2015) *Philanthropy and the Funding of the Church of England, 1856–1914* (London and Vermont).

Flint, Kate (1993) *The Woman Reader, 1837–1914* (Oxford).

Forder, Charles R. (1959) *The Parish Priest at Work: An Introduction to Systematic Pastoralia* (London).

Forrester, Wendy (1980) *Great Grandmother's Weekly: A Celebration of the Girls' Own Paper* (London).

Forster, Margaret (1995) *Hidden Lives: A Family Memoir* (London).

Fowler, Simon (1999) 'War Charity begins at Home'. *History Today* 49(9): 17–23.

Fraser, Hilary, Stephanie Green and Judith Johnston (2003) *Gender and the Victorian Periodical* (Cambridge).

Fried, Albert, and Richard M. Elman (1969) (eds) *Charles Booth's London: A Portrait of the Poor at the Turn of the Century Drawn from His 'Life and Labour of the People in London'* (London).

Fuller, Graham (forthcoming) *Erskine Clarke, Pioneering Churchman; Writer and Editor; Battersea Patriarch*.

Fyfe, Aileen (2004) *Science and Salvation: Evangelical Popular Science Publishing in Victorian Britain* (Chicago and London).

Giebelhausen, Michaela (2006) *Painting the Bible: Representation and Belief in Mid-Victorian Britain* (Aldershot).

Gilbert, Alan (1976) *Religion and Society in Industrial England: Church, Chapel and Social Change, 1740–1914* (London).

Gill, Robin (2003) *The Empty Church Revisited* (Aldershot).

Gill, Sean (1998) 'How Muscular Was Victorian Christianity? Thomas Hughes and the Cult of Christian Manliness Reconsidered'. In R. N. Swanson (ed.) *Studies in Church History 34, Gender and Christian Religion* (Woodbridge), pp. 421–30.

—— (2000) 'Ecce Homo: Representations of Christ as the Model of Masculinity in Victorian Art and Lives of Jesus'. In Andrew Bradstock, Sean Gill, Anne Hogan and Sue Morgan (eds) *Masculinity and Spirituality in Victorian Culture* (Basingstoke), pp. 164–78.

Girouard, Mark (1981) *The Return to Camelot: Chivalry and the English Gentleman* (New Haven).

Goebel, Stefan (2007) *The Great War and Medieval Memory: War, Remembrance and Medievalism in Britain and Germany, 1914–1940* (Cambridge).

Gray-Fow, Michael J. G. (1990) 'Squire, Parson and Village School: Wragby, 1830–1886'. In Patrick Scott, and Pauline Fletcher (eds) *Culture and Education in Victorian England* (Lewisburg), pp. 162–73.

Green, S. J. D. (1993) 'The Church of England and the Working Classes in Late-Victorian and Edwardian Halifax'. *Transactions of the Halifax Antiquarian Society* NS1: 106–20.

—— (1996) *Religion in the Age of Decline: Organisation and Experience in Industrial Yorkshire, 1870–1920* (Cambridge).

—— (2011) *The Passing of Protestant England: Secularisation and Social Change c. 1920–1960* (Cambridge).
Greene, Graham (1969) *Travels with My Aunt* (London).
Haig, Alan (1984) *The Victorian Clergy* (London).
Hammerton, Elizabeth, and David Cannadine (1981) 'Conflict and Consensus on a Ceremonial Occasion: The Diamond Jubilee in Cambridge in 1897'. *Historical Journal* 24(1): 111–46.
Harris, Jose (1993) *Private Lives, Public Spirit, Britain 1870–1914* (Oxford).
Harris, Mollie (1986) *From Acre End, Portrait of a Village* (London).
Harrison, Brian (1967) 'Religion and Recreation in Nineteenth-Century England'. *Past & Present* 38: 98–127.
Hart, Jenifer (1977) 'Religion and Social Control in the Mid-Nineteenth Century'. In A. P. Donajgrodzki (ed.) *Social Control in Nineteenth-Century Britain* (London), pp. 108–37.
Hastings, Adrian (1991) *A History of English Christianity 1920–1990* (London).
Heeney, Brian (1972–3) 'On Being a Mid-Victorian Clergyman'. *Journal of Religious History* 7: 208–24.
—— (1983) 'Women's Struggle for Professional Work and Status in the Church of England, 1900–1930'. *Historical Journal* 26(2): 329–47.
—— (1988) *The Women's Movement in the Church of England 1850–1930* (Oxford).
Hempton, David (2011) *The Church in the Long Eighteenth Century* (London and New York).
Hickman, Timothy Alton (2007) *The Secret Leprosy of Modern Days: Narcotic Addiction and Modern Crisis in the United States, 1870–1920* (Massachusetts).
Hilton, Boyd (1988) *The Age of Atonement: The Influence of Evangelicalism on Social and Economic Thought, 1795–1865* (Oxford).
Hislop, Ian, Richard Ingrams, Christopher Booker and Barry Fantoni (2002) *Carry On Vicar: St. Albion Parish News, vol. V* (London).
Hobbs, A. J. (2009) 'When the Provincial Press Was Not the National Press (*c.*1836–1900)'. *International Journal of Regional & Local Studies* 2(5.1): 16–43.
Hobsbawm, Eric (1983) 'Introduction'. In Eric Hobsbawm and Terence Ranger (eds) *The Invention of Tradition* (Cambridge), pp. 1–14.
Hoggart, Richard (1998) *The Uses of Literacy* (New Brunswick and London).
Horn, Pamela (1984) *The Changing Countryside in Victorian and Edwardian England and Wales* (London).
Houghton, Walter E. (1957) *The Victorian Frame of Mind 1830–1870* (New Haven and London).
Hudleston, C. Roy, and R. S. Boumphrey (1987) *Cumberland Families and Heraldry* (Kendal).
Humpherys, Anne (1990) 'Popular Narrative and Political Discourse in "Reynolds's Weekly Newspaper"'. In Laurel Brake, Aled Jones and Lionel Madden (eds) *Investigating Victorian Journalism* (Basingstoke), pp. 33–47.
Hylson-Smith, Kenneth (1989) *Evangelicals in the Church of England* (Edinburgh).
Itzkowitz, David C. (2009) 'Fair Enterprise or Extravagant Speculation: Investment, Speculation and Gambling in Victorian England'. In Nancy Henry, Cannon Schmitt (eds) *Victorian Investments: New Perspectives on Finance and Culture* (Bloomington), pp. 98–119.
Jalland, Pat (1996) *Death in the Victorian Family* (Oxford).

James, Eric (1991) (ed.) *A Last Eccentric: A Symposium concerning the Reverend Canon F. A. Simpson* (London).
James, Louis (1974) *Fiction for the Working Man 1830–1850*, 2nd edition (Harmondsworth).
—— (2006) *The Victorian Novel* (Oxford).
Jewers, Rosemary, and Tony Jewers (2010) *Rev.elations from Old Parish Magazines* (Dereham).
Johnson, Paul (1993) 'Class Law in Victorian England'. *Past & Present* 141: 147–69.
Kanitkar, Helen (1994) '"Real True Boys": Moulding the Cadets of Imperialism'. In Andrea Cornwell and Nancy Lindisfarne (eds) *Dislocating Masculinity: Comparative Ethnographies* (New York), pp. 184–96.
Kanner, Barbara (1977) 'The Women of England in a Century of Social Change 1815–1914: A Select Bibliography'. In Martha Vicinus (ed.) *A Widening Sphere: Changing Roles of Victorian Women* (London), pp. 199–270.
Kaufman, Alexander L. (2009) *The Historical Literature of the Jack Cade Rebellion* (Farnham).
Keating, Peter (1989) *The Haunted Study, A Social History of the English Novel 1875–1914* (London).
Kemp, Sandra, Charlotte Mitchell and David Trotter (1997) *The Oxford Companion to Edwardian Fiction* (Oxford).
Kingsford, P. W. (1970) *Victorian Railwaymen: The Emergence and Growth of Railway Labour, 1830–1870* (London).
Kucich, John (2001) 'Intellectual Debate in the Victorian Novel: Religion, Science, and the Professional'. In Deirdre David (ed.) *The Cambridge Companion to the Victorian Novel* (Cambridge), pp. 212–33.
Landow, George P. (1982) *Images of Crisis: Literary Iconology, 1750 to the Present* (Boston).
Langbauer, Laurie (1999) *Novels of Everyday Life: The Series in English Fiction, 1850–1930* (Ithaca and London).
Leatherbarrow, J. S. (1954) *Victorian Period Piece: Studies Occasioned by a Lancashire Church* (London).
Ledger-Lomas, Michael (2009) 'Mass Markets: Religion'. In David McKitterick (ed.) *The Cambridge History of the Book in Britain, VI, 1830–1914* (Cambridge), pp. 324–58.
Lee, Robert (2006) *Rural Society and the Anglican Clergy, 1815–1914: Encountering and Managing the Poor* (Cambridge).
Lightman, Bernard (2007) *Victorian Popularizers of Science: Designing Nature for New Audiences* (Chicago).
Loeb, Lori Anne (1994) *Consuming Angels: Advertising and Victorian Women* (Oxford).
Looker, Mark S. (1998) '"God Save the Queen": Victoria's Jubilees and the Religious Press'. *Victorian Periodicals Review* 21(3): 115–19.
Lowerson, John (2006) 'Sport and the Victorian Sunday: The Beginnings of Middle-Class Apostasy'. In J. A. Mangan (ed.) *A Sport-Loving Society: Victorian and Edwardian Middle-Class England at Play* (Abingdon).
Lowther-Clarke, W. K. (1959) *A History of the S.P.C.K.* (London).
McCaffrey, J. F. (1981) 'Thomas Chalmers and Social Change'. *Scottish Historical Review* 60(169): 32–60.

McClatchey, D. (1960) *Oxfordshire Clergy 1777–1869: A Study of the Established Church and of the Role of Its Clergy in Local Society* (Oxford).

McDannell, Colleen (1986) *The Christian Home in Victorian America 1840–1900* (Bloomington).

Mackenzie, John M. (1986) *Propaganda and Empire* (Manchester).

McKitterick, David (2009) (ed.) *The Cambridge History of the Book in Britain 6, 1830–1914* (Cambridge).

McLeod, Hugh (1974) *Class and Religion in the Late-Victorian City* (London).

—— (1996) *Religion and Society in England 1850–1914* (New York).

—— (1999) '"These Fellows in Black Coats": Anti-Clericalism in Later Victorian and Edwardian England'. *University of Helsinki Theological Publication Society* 104: 1, 85–93.

McQueen, Rob (2009) *A Social History of Company Law: Great Britain and the Australian Colonies, 1854–1920* (Farnham).

Maiden, John (2009) *National Religion and the Prayer Book Controversy 1927–1928* (Woodbridge).

Maison, Margaret (1961) *'Search Your Soul, Eustace': A Survey of the Religious Novel in the Victorian Age* (London).

Marrin, Albert (1974) *The Last Crusade: The Church of England in the First World War* (Durham, NC).

Marsh, Jan (1982) *Back to the Land: The Pastoral Impulse in England, from 1880 to 1914* (London).

Marshall, D., and J. Walton (1981) *The Lake Counties from 1830 to the Mid-Twentieth Century: A Study in Social Change* (Manchester).

Mayhew, Henry (1985) *London Labour and the London Poor: Selections Made and Introduced by Victor Neuburg* (London).

Maynard, John (1993) *Victorian Discourses on Sexuality and Religion* (Cambridge).

Melynk, Julie (1996) 'Emma Jane Worboise and the Christian World Magazine: Christian Publishing and Women's Empowerment'. *Victorian Periodicals Review* 19(2): 131–45.

Mitchell, Sally (1980) 'The Forgotten Woman of the Period: Penny Weekly Family Magazines of the 1840s and 1850s'. In Martha Vicinus (ed.) *A Widening Sphere: Changing Roles of Victorian Women* (London), pp. 31–33.

—— (1981) *The Fallen Angel: Chastity, Class and Women's Reading: 1835–80* (Bowling Green, OH).

—— (1992) 'Careers for Girls: Writing Trash'. *Victorian Periodicals Review* 25(3): 109–113.

Morgan, David (2005) *The Sacred Gaze: Religious Visual Culture in Theory and Practice* (Berkeley).

Morris, Jeremy (2003) 'The Strange Death of Christian Britain: Another Look at the Secularisation Debate'. *Historical Journal* 46(4): 963–76.

Mumm, Susan (2004) 'Women, Priesthood and the Ordained Ministry in the Christian Tradition'. In John Wolffe (ed.) *Religion in History: Conflict, Conversion and Coexistence* (Manchester), pp. 190–216.

Munn, Charles W. (1994) 'Review: White-Collar Crime in Modern England: Financial Fraud and Business Morality, 1845–1929'. *Economic History Review* 47(1): 199–200.

Mutch, Deborah (2005) 'The Merrie England Triptych: Robert Blatchford, Edward Fay and the Didactic Use of *Clarion* Fiction'. *Victorian Periodicals Review* 38(1): 83–103.

Nash, David (2013) *Christian Ideals in British Culture: Stories of Belief in the Twentieth Century* (Basingstoke).

National Trust (n.d.) *The Most Active Volcano in Europe: A Short Life of Canon Hardwicke Drummond Rawnsley, Vicar of Crosthwaite 1883–1917, Originator of the National Trust* (Keswick).

Newsom, S. W. B. (2006) 'Pioneers in Infection Control: John Snow, Henry Whitehead, and the Broad Street Pump, and the Beginnings of Geographical Epidemiology'. *Journal of Hospital Infection* 64: 210–16.

Newsome, David (1961) *Godliness and Good Learning: Four Studies on a Victorian Ideal* (London).

Nicholson, Norman (1975) *Wednesday Early Closing* (London).

Norman, Edward (1987) *The Victorian Christian Socialists* (Cambridge).

Obelkevich, James (1976) *Religion and Rural Society: South Lindsey 1825–1875* (Oxford).

O'Day, Rosemary (1988) 'The Men from the Ministry'. In Gerald Parsons (ed.) *Religion in Victorian Britain 2, Controversies* (Manchester), pp. 258–79.

Onslow, Barbara (2000) *Women of the Press in Nineteenth Century Britain* (Basingstoke).

Parsons, Gerald (1988) 'Introduction', 'Reform, Revival and Realignment: The Experience of Victorian Anglicanism'; 'Victorian Roman Catholicism: Emancipation, Expansion and Achievement'. In Gerald Parsons (ed.) *Religion in Victorian Britain I, Traditions* (Manchester), pp. 1–66, 147–61.

—— (1988) 'Social Control to Social Gospel: Victorian Christian Social Attitudes'; 'Liberation and Church Defence: Victorian Church and Victorian Chapel'. In Gerald Parsons (ed.) *Religion in Victorian Britain 2, Controversies* (Manchester), pp. 39–62, 147–65.

Pedersen, Susan (1986) 'Hannah More Meets Simple Simon: Tracts, Chapbooks and Popular Culture in Late-Eighteenth-Century England'. *Journal of British Studies* 25(1): 84–113.

Peers, Douglas M. (2004) 'Britain and Empire'. In Chris Williams (ed.) *A Companion to Nineteenth-Century Britain* (Oxford), pp. 53–78.

Perkin, Harold J. (2002) *The Rise of Professional Society: England since 1880*, 3rd edition (London).

Phegley, Jennifer (2004) *Educating the Proper Woman Reader: Victorian Family Literary Magazines and the Cultural Health of the Nation* (Columbus).

Phelps, Barry (1992) *P. G. Wodehouse: Man and Myth* (London).

Plunkett, John (2005) 'Civic Publicness: The Creation of Queen Victoria's Royal Role 1837–61'. In Laurel Brake and Julie F. Codell (eds) *Encounters in the Victorian Press: Editors, Authors, Readers* (Basingstoke), pp. 11–28.

Poulsen, Charles (1976) *Victoria Park: A Study in the History of East London* (London).

Powell, David (1996) *The Edwardian Crisis, 1901–1914* (Basingstoke).

Price, Richard (1999) *British Society, 1680–1880* (Cambridge).

Prochaska, F. K. (1980) *Women and Philanthropy in Nineteenth-Century England* (Oxford).

—— (2006) *Christianity and Social Service in Modern Britain: The Disinherited Spirit* (Oxford).

Purcell, William (1983) *The Mowbray Story* (Oxford).

Pym, Barbara (1950) *Some Tame Gazelle* (London).

Rainbow, Bernarr (1970, 2001), *The Choral Revival in the Anglican Church (1839–1872)* (Woodbridge).
Raw, David (1989) *'It's Only Me', A Life of the Rev. Theodore Bayley Hardy V.C., D.S.O., M.C., 1863–1918, Vicar of Hutton Roof, Westmorland* (Kendal).
Reed, John Shelton (1996) *Glorious Battle: The Cultural Politics of Victorian Anglo-Catholicism* (Nashville).
Reynolds, Kimberley (1990) *Girls Only? Gender and Popular Children's Fiction in Britain, 1880–1910* (Hemel Hempstead).
Ritvo, Harriet (2004) 'Understanding Audiences and Misunderstanding Audiences: Some Publics for Science'. In Geoffrey Cantor and Sally Shuttleworth (eds) *Science Serialized: Representations of the Sciences in Nineteenth-Century Periodicals* (Cambridge, MA), pp. 331–49.
Robb, George (1992) *White-Collar Crime in Modern England: Financial Fraud and Business Morality 1845–1929* (Cambridge).
Rose, Jonathan (2001) *The Intellectual Life of the British Working Classes* (New Haven and London).
Rosen, David (1994) 'The Volcano and the Cathedral'. In Donald E. Hall (ed.) *Muscular Christianity: Embodying the Victorian Age* (Cambridge), pp. 17–44.
Royle, Edward (1997) *Modern Britain: A Social History, 1770–1997*, 2nd edition (London).
Rubery, Matthew (2009) *The Novelty of Newspapers: Victorian Fiction after the Invention of the News* (Oxford).
Russell, Anthony (1984) *The Clerical Profession* (London).
Russell, Dave (2006) 'The *Heaton Review*, 1927–1934: Culture, Class and a Sense of Place in Inter-war Yorkshire'. *20th Century British History* 17(3): 323–49.
Sachs, William L. (2002) *The Transformation of Anglicanism: From State Church to Global Communion* (Cambridge).
Samuel, Raphael (1975) *Village Life and Labour* (London).
Sawyer, Rex L. (1989) *The Bowerchalke Parish Papers: Collett's Village Newspaper 1878–1924* (Gloucester).
Scott, Rosemary (1992) 'The Sunday Periodical: "Sunday at Home"'. *Victorian Periodicals Review* 25(4): 158–62.
Secord, James (2000) *Victorian Sensation: The Extraordinary Publication, Reception and Secret Authorship of 'Vestiges of the Natural History of Creation'* (Chicago and London).
Sheffield, Suzanne Le-May (2004) 'The "Empty-Headed Beauty" and the "Sweet Girl Graduate": Women's Science Education in *Punch*, 1860–90'. In Louise Henson, Geoffrey Cantor, Gowan Dawson, Richard Noakes, Sally Shuttleworth and Jonathan R. Topham (eds) *Culture and Science in the Nineteenth-Century Media* (Aldershot), pp. 15–28.
Short, John R. (1991) *Imagined Country: Environment, Culture and Society* (Syracuse, NY).
Shteir, Ann B. (1997) 'Gender and "Modern" Botany in Victorian England'. *Osiris* 2(12): 29–38.
Sivasundaram, Sujit (2004) 'The Periodical as Barometer: Spiritual Measurement and the Evangelical Magazine'. In Louise Henson, Geoffrey Cantor, Gowan Dawson, Richard Noakes, Sally Shuttleworth and Jonathan R. Topham (eds) *Culture and Science in the Nineteenth-Century Media* (Aldershot), pp. 43–55.
Snape, Michael (2005) *God and the British Soldier: Religion and the British Army in the First and Second World Wars* (London and New York).

Snell, K. D. M. (2006) *Parish and Belonging: Community, Identity and Welfare in England and Wales 1700–1950* (Cambridge).

—— (2010) 'Parish Pond to Lake Nyasa: Parish Magazines and Senses of Community'. *Family and Community History* 13(1): 45–69.

Snell, K. D. M., and Paul S. Ell (2000) *Rival Jerusalems: The Geography of Victorian Religion* (Cambridge).

Springhall, John (1987) 'Baden-Powell and the Scout Movement before 1920: Citizen Training or Soldiers of the Future'. *English Historical Review* 102(405): 934–42.

Stacey, Margaret (1960) *Tradition and Change: A Study of Banbury* (Oxford).

Stanley, Rita (1989) 'Susan Mowbray – A Woman in a Man's World'. *Oxfordshire Local History 3* (Oxford), pp. 103–8.

Stephens, W. B. (1987) *Education, Literacy and Society 1830–70: The Geography of Diversity in Provincial England* (Manchester).

Stern, Milton R. (1991) *Contexts for Hawthorne: The Marble Faun and the Politics of Openness and Closure in American Literature* (Chicago).

Stott, Anne (2003) *Hannah More, The First Victorian* (Oxford).

Sutherland, John (1988) *The Longman Companion to Victorian Fiction* (Harlow).

Sweet, Matthew (2001), *Inventing the Victorians* (London).

Sykes, Richard (2005) 'Popular Religion in Decline: A Study from the Black Country'. *Journal of Ecclesiastical History* 56(2): 287–307.

Taylor, James (2006) *Creating Capitalism: Joint-Stock Enterprise in British Politics and Culture, 1800–1870* (Woodbridge).

Taylor, Miles, and Michael Wolff (2004) *The Victorians since 1901: Histories, Representations and Revisions* (Manchester).

Thompson, Flora (1945, 1973) *Lark Rise to Candleford* (Harmondsworth).

Thompson, Nicola D. (1999) 'Responding to the Woman Questions: Re-reading Non-Canonical Victorian Woman Novelists'. In N. D. Thompson (ed.) *Victorian Woman Writers and the Woman's Question* (Cambridge), pp. 1–23.

Thwaite, Mary F. (1972) *From Primer to Pleasure in Reading,* 2nd edition (Boston).

Topham, Jonathan R. (2004) 'The Wesleyan-Methodist Magazine and Religious Monthlies in Early Nineteenth-Century Britain'. In Geoffrey Cantor, Gowan Dawson, Graeme Gooday, Richard Noakes, Sally Shuttleworth, Jonathan R. Topham, *Science in the Nineteenth Century Periodical: Reading the Magazine of Nature* (Cambridge), pp. 67–90.

—— (2004) 'Science, Natural Theology and the Practice of Christian Piety in Early-Nineteenth-Century Religious Magazines'. In Geoffrey Cantor and Sally Shuttleworth (eds) *Science Serialized: Representations of the Sciences in Nineteenth-Century Periodicals* (Cambridge, MA), pp. 37–66.

—— (2010) 'Science, Religion, and the History of the Book'. In Thomas Dixon, Geoffrey Cantor and Stephen Pumfrey (eds) *Science and Religion: New Historical Perspectives* (Cambridge), pp. 221–43.

Tosh, John (2005) *Manliness and Masculinities in Nineteenth-Century Britain: Essays on Gender, Family and Empire* (Harlow).

Tracy, Michael (2008) *The World of the Edwardian Child as seen in Arthur Mee's Children's Encyclopædia, 1908–1910* (York).

Tressell, Robert (1955) *The Ragged Trousered Philanthropists* (London).

Trotter, David (1993) *The English Novel in History 1895–1920* (London).

Turner, E. S. (1965) *The Shocking History of Advertising*, 2nd edition (Harmondsworth).
Twyman, Michael (1998) *The British Library Guide to Printing: History and Techniques* (London).
—— (2009) 'The Illustration Revolution'. In David McKitterick (ed.) *The Cambridge History of the Book in Britain, Vol. VI, 1830–1914* (Cambridge), pp. 117–43.
Tyrer, Frank (2003) *A Short History of St Mary's, Little Crosby* (Little Crosby).
Vincent, David (1981) *Bread, Knowledge and Freedom: A Study of Nineteenth-Century Working Class Autobiography* (London).
—— (1983) 'Reading in the Working-Class Home'. In John K. Walton and James Walvin (eds) *Leisure in Britain 1780–1939* (Manchester), pp. 207–26.
—— (1989) *Literacy and Popular Culture: England 1750–1914* (Cambridge).
Waddington, Keir (2008) 'Health and Medicine'. In Chris Williams (ed.) *A Companion to Nineteenth-Century Britain* (Oxford), pp. 412–29.
Wade, Spencer (2013) *Both Hands before the Fire* (Bloomington).
Walford, Rex (2007) *The Growth of 'New London' in Suburban Middlesex (1918–1945) and the Response of the Church of England* (Lewiston, Queenston, Lampeter).
Walton, J. K., and James Walvin (1983) (eds.) *Leisure in Britain 1780–1939* (Manchester).
Walvin, James (1987) *Victorian Values* (London).
Weiss, Barbara (1986) *The Hell of the English: Bankruptcy and the Victorian Novel* (London and New Jersey).
Wellings, Martin (1991) 'Anglo-Catholicism, the "Crisis in the Church" and the Cavalier Case of 1899'. *Journal of Ecclesiastical History* 2(2): 238–57.
—— (2003) *Evangelicals Embattled: Responses of Evangelicals in the Church of England to Ritualism, Darwinism and Theological Liberalism 1890–1930* (Bletchley).
Wheeler, Michael (2013) *English Fiction of the Victorian Period* (Abingdon).
Whisenant, James C. (2001) 'Anti-Ritualism and the Moderation of Anglican Opinion in the Mid-1870s'. *Anglican and Episcopal History* 70(4): 451–77.
—— (2003) *A Fragile Unity: Anti-Ritualism and the Division of Anglican Evangelicalism in the Nineteenth Century* (Bletchley).
White, Jerry (2007) *London in the 19th Century* (London).
Wilkinson, Alan (1978) *The Church of England and the First World War* (London).
Williams, S. C. (1999) *Religious Belief and Popular Culture in Southwark c. 1880–1939* (Oxford).
Winstanley, Michael (2004) 'Agriculture and Rural Society'. In Chris Williams (ed.) *A Companion to Nineteenth-Century Britain* (Oxford), pp. 205–22.
Wise, Sarah (2008) *The Blackest Streets: The Life and Death of a Victorian Slum* (London).
Wolffe, John (1988) '"Praise to the Holiest in the Height": Hymns and Church Music'. In John Wolffe (ed.) *Religion in Victorian Britain 5, Culture and Empire* (Manchester), pp. 59–100.
—— (1991) 'The End of Victorian Values? Women, Religion and the Death of Queen Victoria'. In W. J. Sheils and Diana Woods (eds) *Studies in Church History 27: Women in the Church* (Oxford), pp. 481–503.
—— (2000) *Great Deaths: Grieving, Religion and Nationhood in Victorian and Edwardian Britain* (Oxford).
Yates, Nigel (1991) *Buildings, Faith and Worship: The Liturgical Arrangement of Anglican Churches 1600–1900* (Oxford).
—— (1999) *Anglican Ritualism in Victorian Britain 1830–1910* (Oxford).

Theses

Burgess, John (1984) 'The Religious History of Cumbria 1780–1920' (Unpublished PhD thesis, University of Sheffield).

Entwhistle, D. M. (1990) 'Children's Reward Books in Nonconformist Sunday Schools, 1870–1914, Occurrence, Nature and Purpose' (Unpublished PhD thesis, University of Lancaster).

Haines, Sheila (1979) 'Am I My Brother's Keeper? Victorian Tract Societies and Their Work, 1840–1875' (Unpublished PhD thesis, University of Sussex).

Knickerbocker, Driss (1981) 'The Popular Religious Tract in England 1790–1830' (Unpublished PhD thesis, University of Oxford).

Websites

Access to Archives (A2A): http://apps.nationalarchives.gov.uk/a2a/

Ancestry: http://home.ancestry.co.uk/

Booth, Charles, Online Archive, Religious Influences Series: http://booth.lse.ac.uk/static/a/5_3.html

British Library Catalogue: http://explore.bl.uk/

Clergy of the Church of England Database: www.theclergydatabase.org.uk

Dictionary of Nineteenth-Century Journalism online: http://www.dncj.ugent.be/

Film Database Search: http://www.citwf.com/indexx.asp

Google books: https://www.google.co.uk/search?q=queenie+scott-hooper

Hansard: http://hansard.millbanksystems.com/sittings http://hansard.millbanksystems.com/commons/1928/jun/14/prayer-book-measure-1928

Hardy, Paul (Illustrator): Speel 19th Century Art: http://myweb.tiscali.co.uk/speel/paint/hardy.htm

Royal Commission on Ecclesiastical Discipline (1906): http://anglicanhistory.org/ritualism/

Sign: http://www.the-sign.co.uk/

Waterloo Directory of English Newspapers and Periodicals: http://www.victorianperiodicals.com/

Wellesley Index to Victorian Periodicals: http://wellesley.chadwyck.com/

Index

Parish magazines referenced are Anglican parish magazines

Printed and bound in the United States of America